Contemporary African Art and Shifting Landscapes

Contemporary African Art and Shifting Landscapes

Edited by
Gilane Tawadros and
Sarah Campbell

Institute of International Visual Arts, London,
in collaboration with the Forum for African Arts
and the Prince Claud Fund

Published in the United Kingdom by the Institute of International Visual Arts (inIVA) in collaboration with the Forum for African Arts and the Prince Claus Fund

Institute of International Visual Arts
6-8 Standard Place
Rivington Street
London EC2A 3BE
www.iniva.org

Designed by Untitled
Production co-ordinated by Uwe Kraus
Printed in Italy

Prince Claus
Fund Library

Published on the occasion of the exhibition *Fault Lines: Contemporary African Art and Shifting Landscapes*
15 June – 2 November 2003
Fault Lines is presented as part of the 50th International Art Exhibition, La Biennale di Venezia, *Dreams and Conflicts: The Dictatorship of the Viewer*.

la Biennale di Venezia

The exhibition and publication have been produced by the Forum for African Arts and made possible by the generous support of the Ford Foundation.

FORD FOUNDATION

Additional financial support has been provided by AFAA (Association Française d'Action Artistique), Arts Council England and the British Council.

programmeafriqueencréations

ISBN 1-899846-38-7

A catalogue record of this book is available from the British Library.

Contents

Essays

Artists

Reference

Preface

Salah Hassan

This volume, *Fault Lines: Contemporary African Art and Shifting Landscapes*, brings together contemporary artists and writers from Africa and the African diaspora whose works explore as well as theorise the idea of modernity and modernism in the African and the African diasporic public sphere, thereby enriching the ongoing debate about modernity and its manifestations inside and outside the West. Its companion exhibition, conceived and led by Gilane Tawadros, the prominent London-based Egyptian art historian, art critic, and founding Director of inIVA (Institute of International Visual Arts), brings together fifteen artists from Africa and the African diaspora whose works – across a range of media – trace the fault lines that are shaping our contemporary experience, locally and globally. 'Resisting any notion of an authentic or one-dimensional African experience', this exhibition and its companion book have, as envisioned by Tawadros in the exhibition proposal, effectively explored, 'the ambivalent space where tradition and modernity, past histories and future possibilities are mapped out in the work of contemporary African and African diaspora artists, writers and thinkers'. Hence, Tawadros reminds us that 'we have become accustomed to thinking about modernism and modernity in Western terms as a decisive break or rupture with the past and yet it is almost always experienced as an uneven negotiation between past and future that can remain unresolved.'

Despite profound inequalities and the absolute hegemonic and centralising primacy of Western modernity and capitalism, artistic practice is not being homogenised. In the keynote address, 'Museums of Modern Art and the End of History', that he gave at the Tate Gallery in 1999 (subsequently published in 2001 by inIVA in *Modernity and Difference*), Stuart Hall convincingly reminds us:

> In terms of the condition of consciousness within which these people start to make artistic practices, they inhabit a world which is torn, on the one hand, by the centralising force of Western modernity, with all the goodies it entails, and, on the other, by the dissemination and proliferation of notions of what it would be like to be vernacular and modern. We are embarking on a hundred different ideas of 'the modern', not one, and therefore, of a thousand practising modern artists, who require recognition within the terms of the criteria that we have stitched into our museum space.

The exclusionary mechanisms built into modernism, as defined in the West, have attracted a number of important critiques, from within Europe itself, and from non-Western perspectives. Postcolonial theory offers powerful critiques of modernity and modernism, by showing how the very terms of the debate are necessarily Eurocentric. While modernities are seen as irreducibly plural and fully global, the standard theorisation of modernity and modernism, emphasising Western social transformations and artistic experiments, relegates the social developments and artistic expressions of other regions as necessarily belated, derivative and secondary to the Western modern. Suggesting that parallel, or separate, modernities have been enacted in other sites outside the West, e.g., an African modernity, does not necessarily alleviate the problem. As Naoki Sakai has forcefully argued in his essay in *Unpacking Europe* (Rotterdam: NAi Publishers and Museum Boijmans van Beuningen, 2001), emphasising the spatiality of a particular geographic space for modernity leads to a suspension of its temporal character, which will effectively negate its temporality, and consequently relegate it as non-modern. However, the problem remains as to how do we articulate modernity outside the West, and more specifically, African modernities or postmodernities?

As I have repeatedly argued, elusive as it may be, Africa is a complex intellectual construct as well as a highly differentiated historical entity and global presence. In that context, whatever it is that we mean by 'African', including of course, African modernism, is the product of this historically complex entity and global presence. By European standards, the period we designate as modern in Africa may be short, and modernism in African terms is certainly much more recent. However, modernism is also uneven as a phenomenon within the continent. In places like Egypt and other parts of North Africa one could trace instances of modernism in all aspects of art and society as early as the turn of the twentieth century. African modernism is also specifically marked by certain experiences that affected Africa, and other parts of the developing world, such as colonialism and the violent rupture it created with tradition. In that sense, the conscious claim to modernity implies a sense of resistance, for modernity in Africa was born out of the struggle for decolonisation, hence, the significance of decolonisation and liberation movements as the defining moment of the modernist project in Africa. Western intervention or patronage may have been a determinant factor in shaping the discourse on modernity and modernism in Africa, but so too was the nationalistic cultural resurgence that swept many newly independent African countries, where government patronage and interest in the arts was deployed in nation-building and the refashioning of the self in modern terms. These are the ingredients of the fault lines, which Tawadros eloquently articulates as having 'been etched into the physical fabric of our world through the effects of colonialism and postcolonialism, of migration and globalisation'.

Most importantly, as *Fault Lines* amply documents, the modernist project in Africa has existed at the intersections of pan-Africanism and pan-Arabism, the struggle for liberation and decolonisation, and the intellectual dialectics of this struggle have come to symbolise the relationships among Africa, the West and the world. The works included in this exhibition stands as the greatest witness to those intersections of intellectual and political movements such as Nasserism, pan-Arabism, pan-Africanism and negritude. As the synchronicity of practising artists from Egypt, South Africa, Algeria, Ethiopia, the United States or the Caribbean in this exhibition testifies, Africa or African diasporic modernity can no longer be looked at through Orientalist prisms and essentialising approaches. The works included in the exhibition range from those that highlight the challenges faced by the early generations in mastering the idiom and language of modernism, and others that transcend dependence on European modernism by creating a new visual language that has come to define African modernism. The latter may be seen in the works of Hassan Fathy and Frank Bowling. Moreover, younger artists clearly display the influences of new discourses and imperatives, such as gender, feminism, and postmodernism; we see this in the works of Zarina Bhimji, Moshekwa Langa and Salem Mekuria, who represent the new generation of African and African diaspora artists living and working in the Western metropolis.

Presented as part of the 50th Venice Biennale, *Fault Lines* is the second in a series of exhibitions organised under the auspices of Africa in Venice, a major initiative by the Forum for African Arts that was inaugurated at the 49th Venice Biennale in June 2001. The Forum's major goal is to promote contemporary African visual arts and culture and to strengthen and sustain the African and African diaspora artists in international art biennales and other exhibitions. As amply documented in published reviews, the first phase of the Africa in Venice project, represented by the critically acclaimed exhibition *Authentic/Ex-Centric* at the 49th Venice Biennale, has been by all measures, a profound success. It has fully achieved its goals and much more. Its remarkable success has been demonstrated further by the gains and rewards cultivated by the participating artists in terms of exhibitions, residencies and other forums to which they have been invited as a direct result of their inclusion in the exhibition. Such positive developments help to advance the careers of the participating artists in the international arena, which is important in establishing the presence of African modernism in the art world, art history and the museum.

With *Fault Lines* we move several steps forward. This second reincarnation would not have been possible without the continued enthusiasm and encouragement of friends and institutions from across the globe. It is due to their tireless support that *Fault Lines* and its companion book are now made into a reality. Due to the limitation of space and vagaries of memory it is impossible to mention them all and I, therefore, apologise in advance. Damien Pwono, of the Ford Foundation, has been the driving force and the visionary who nurtured this initiative since its inception and has guided it through all the steps and obstacles to Venice. The progressive vision and unconditional support of Els van der Plas, of the Prince Claus Fund, have helped shape the exhibition and its publication in the best way possible. Olivier d'Arvor and Florence Alexis, of AFAA (Association Française d'Action Artistique) with their Afrique en Creations Programme, have been consistent and unwavering in their support of this project. Our colleague Okwui Enwezor has been an enthusiastic advocate for this project in the international arena. In designing and building the exhibition we could not have found a better team than the architect Tom Postma and colleagues, Alexander Schabracq, Job Goedhart, and Haco de Redder, whose excellence, dedication and immaculate work ethics are unmatched. Working with the editor Sarah Campbell and the staff of inIVA has been a delightful experience and a lesson in excellence and quality of production.

In Venice many people have helped us implement this project. The enthusiasm and patience of the art critic and scholar Eriberto Eulisse, whose hard work and dedication to this project is stark proof that contemporary African artists have a great friend in Italy. We are very grateful to Francesco Bonami, the Artistic Director of the 50th Venice Biennale, for his cooperation and for including *Fault Lines* in his main roster of exhibitions. We are honoured to work with a curator whose track record and curatorial vision have consistently been reflective of the global and complex realities of the art world today.

Above all, our utmost appreciation goes to Gilane Tawadros for her brilliant curatorial vision, and to the participating artists for their creative energy that made the exhibition possible.

The Revolution Stripped Bare

Gilane Tawadros

In geological terms, fault lines reveal themselves as fractures in the earth's surface but they also mark a break in the continuity of the strata. Fault lines may be a sign of significant shifts, or even of impending disaster, but they also create new landscapes. *Fault Lines: Contemporary African Art and Shifting Landscapes* brings together contemporary artists from Africa and the African diaspora whose works trace the outlines of fault lines that are shaping contemporary experience locally and globally. These fault lines have been etched into the physical fabric of our world through the effects of colonialism and postcolonialism, of migration and globalisation. Their reverberations echo through contemporary lived experience and in the work of these fifteen artists working across a range of media from painting and sculpture through to architecture, photography and installation. Their works span five decades, four continents and three generations, resisting any notion of an authentic or one-dimensional African experience.

The nationalist struggles of the first decades of the twentieth century gave rise in the second half of the century to postcolonial independence and a new self-determination in Africa and beyond that articulated themselves in a heightened political consciousness but also in new forms of visual and architectural practices. These new practices sought to negotiate the difficult and, as yet, unexplored terrain between tradition and modernity, between formal concerns and political contingencies. Modernism and modernity is too often defined in Western terms as a decisive break or rupture with the past and yet it is almost always experienced as an uneven negotiation between past and future that can remain unresolved. This exhibition explores the ambivalent space where tradition and modernity, past histories and future possibilities are mapped out in the work of contemporary artists.

Globalisation and its impact are a theme that underpins this assemblage of art works but globalisation here is understood not purely in terms of the exchange of global commodities and the erosion of nation states in favour of corporate multinationals. Rather, the patterns of globalisation are traced through the experiences of political exiles, disenfranchised citizens, immigrants and refugees, amongst others. Ultimately, the fault lines of our contemporary world manifest themselves in the contradictions of everyday life which daily present us with both the closure of opportunity and the possibility of change, at one and the same time. This exhibition proposes a space where we can engage with these complexities of lived experience through the work of artists who have embraced the ambiguities and inconsistencies of the contemporary world through artworks that are by turns witty and serious, monumental and understated.

I A Common Struggle

On a hot July night in 1952, at the stroke of midnight, three thousand troops and some two hundred officers took control of the key army headquarters barracks in Abbasiyya, Cairo, precipitating a military coup by the Free Officers Movement. Troops commanded by Free Officers and their supporters occupied the headquarters of the Frontier Force, all airports, the broadcasting station headquarters and its relaying facilities at Abu Za'bal, the Cairo telecommunications centre and all major roads and bridges in the city.
At 7am on 23 July, the first announcement was made to the public over Cairo radio by Anwar al-Sadat. The military coup would swiftly lead to the forced abdication and exile of King Farouk and the eventual overthrow of the monarchy in 1953, and the appointment of Gamal Abdel-Nasser as the first indigenous leader of Egypt for centuries. This was the final chapter in the colonial

struggle against the British that culminated in the Suez crisis. Together with the Algerian War of Independence of 1954–62, the Suez crisis of 1956 marked the last attempts of Britain and France to reassert their position in North Africa and gave rise to powerful articulations of a new postcolonial, pan-African and non-aligned world order that would arise phoenix-like from the ashes of colonial struggles throughout the continent.

> Since the region is one and the same with the same conditions, the same problems, the same future and the same enemy, no matter how different the masks he might wear in an endeavour to conceal his identity, why should our efforts be dissipated? The experiences we have gone through after July 23 have manifestly demonstrated the pressing need for a common struggle.[1]

President Nasser's rallying cry for a new nationalism and independence not only in the Arab world but throughout the African continent and the developing world galvanised a postcolonial movement that aspired towards independence from the Super Powers, and social reforms in the direction of greater equality and greater union between Arab, African and Islamic countries. Nasser characterised them as three circles – the Arab Circle, the African Continent Circle and the Circle of 'our Bretheren-in-Islam' – as though they were concentric circles, radiating from the hub of a shared battle for independence. The call for unity and the invocation to a common struggle, expressed so compellingly by leaders such as Nasser and Kwame Nkrumah, emerged directly from the shared experience of shedding the mantle of colonialism. It propelled the idea of Africa as a unified geographical and political entity that eventually took institutional form as the Organisation for African Unity, founded in 1963.

> The movement for independence in Africa which gained momentum after the Second World War has spread like a prairie fire throughout the length and breadth of Africa.... The 'wind of change' has become a raging hurricane, sweeping away the old colonialist Africa. The year 1960 was Africa's year. In that year alone, seventeen African States emerged as proud and independent sovereign nations. Now the ultimate freedom of the whole of Africa can no more be in doubt.[2]

But what role was culture to play in this new world order? Could one speak of a single African cultural identity in the same way as a unified political identity? Would a spectrum of new national cultures emerge in the wake of these new nations throughout the African continent? How could the native intellectual and artist free themselves of the intellectual and cultural lens of colonialism that had consistently distorted and misrepresented indigenous experiences. Speaking of Morocco's experience in the postcolonial aftermath and the struggle to write the Maghreb's history in its own terms, Abdullah Laroui asks, 'What each one of us wants to know today is how to get out of ourselves, how to escape from our mountains and sand-dunes, how to define ourselves in terms of ourselves and not of someone else, how to stop being exiles in spirit.'[3]

First published in France in 1961, *The Wretched of the Earth* was a thorough and prescient study of the national liberation struggle as witnessed in the Algerian War of Independence. The work of Martiniquan psychiatrist and writer Frantz Fanon who had been assigned to a hospital in Algeria during the rising against the French, *The Wretched of the Earth* became a manifesto of decolonisation and the liberation struggles taking place throughout the continent. For Fanon, there could be no separation between the struggle for liberation from colonial rule and the formation of a national culture. The two were inextricably linked, creating the essential conditions not only for national cultural expression but for the cultural expression of the whole continent.

> To fight for national culture means in the first place to fight for the liberation of the nation, that material keystone which makes the building of a culture possible. There is no other fight for culture which can develop apart from the popular struggle. To take an example: all those men and women who are fighting with their bare hands against French colonialism in Algeria are not by any means strangers to the national culture of Algeria. The national Algerian culture is taking on form and content as the battles are being fought out, in prison, under the guillotine and in every French outpost which is captured or destroyed.... It is around the peoples' struggles that African-Negro culture takes on substance, and not around songs, poems or folklore. Adherence to African-Negro culture and to the cultural unity of Africa is arrived at in the first place by upholding unconditionally the peoples' struggle for freedom. No one can truly wish for the spread of African culture if he does not give practical support to the creation of the conditions necessary to the existence of that culture; in other words, to the liberation of the whole continent.[4]

Fanon was not calling for a Soviet-style agitprop or social realist art that would uncritically celebrate and eulogise the triumphs of the revolution. Nor was he making the case for a romantic return to traditional artistic practices. 'A national culture is not a folklore', wrote Fanon, 'nor an abstract populism that believes it can discover the people's true nature'. On the contrary, Fanon emphasises the futility of looking back to outmoded customs for artistic inspiration. More often than not, these traditions, he argues, are taken up as 'mummified fragments', static and out-of-date traces of a dynamic culture which has in fact moved on as a result of the struggle for independence from colonial rule. Most importantly, perhaps, Fanon makes it clear that he is not advocating nationalism or nationalist culture but rather 'national consciousness' which, he concludes, is the most elaborate form of culture. The responsibility of the artist or intellectual, according to Fanon, 'is not a responsibility vis-à-vis his national culture', but rather, 'a global responsibility with regard to the totality of the nation', of which culture is only one aspect. While Fanon rejected the notion of an essentialist African culture or cultural identity, he recognised that it was colonialism and the struggle for liberation from colonial rule that connected different African nations. This struggle was, by its very nature, internationalist in its form and it was this interplay between the national and the international or, the local and the global as we might say now, that created the pre-conditions for the making of culture.

> National consciousness, which is not nationalism, is the only thing that will give us an international dimension. The problem of national consciousness and of national culture takes on in Africa a special dimension. The birth of national consciousness in Africa has a strictly contemporaneous connexion with the African consciousness.... Far from keeping aloof from other nations, therefore, it is national liberation which leads the nation to play its part on the stage of history. It is at the heart of national consciousness that international consciousness lives and grows. And this two-fold emerging is ultimately the source of all culture.[5]

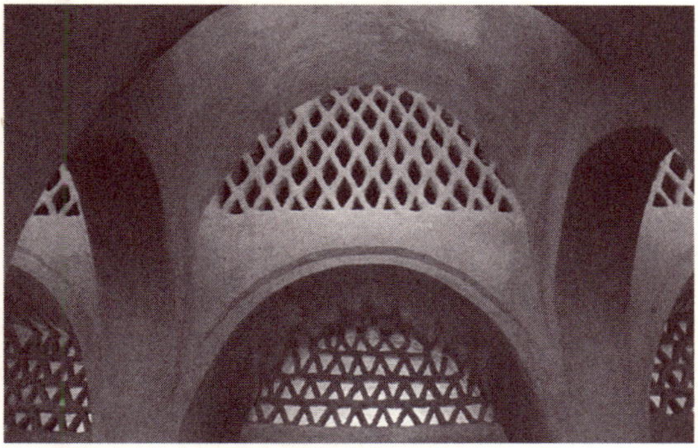

Hassan Fathy, New Baris Village, Kharga, Egypt, 1967. © Aga Khan Trust for Culture.

II A Vernacular Modernity

It is precisely this negotiation between a national and an international consciousness that emerges from the life and work of the Egyptian architect Hassan Fathy. As Nasser Rabbat points out, Fathy's career 'more or less mirrored what was happening in Egypt, a country undertaking the long and torturous journey from colonialism to independence to development and its aftermath entangled with grand dreams of regional supremacy during the same period'.[6] The son of wealthy landowners from Upper Egypt, Fathy was well-schooled in European ideas and, as a young architect, he had learnt the language of contemporary European architecture, experimenting with various different architectural styles before defining, what I would term, the vernacular modernity for which he subsequently became famous with his New Gourna project (1948–61). An ambitious scheme to rebuild an entire rural village in Upper Egypt, New Gourna provided Fathy with the opportunity to establish a cost-effective and modern solution to the problem of mass housing for the rural poor in Egypt while also staying true to indigenous materials and methods of construction. Working with highly skilled Nubian master builders from Aswan, Fathy built a village of domed and vaulted adobe courtyard houses that were, as Rabbat points out, 'a mixture of rural traditional and modern, utopian principles'. Fathy's brand of vernacular modernity which he defined in his treatise *Architecture for the Poor* was indeed utopian and idealistic but it was also a radical rebuttal of the universalising tendencies of Western modernism. Rejecting the claims of Europe's modernists to have discovered universal solutions to contemporary living, Fathy's architectural response was an attempt to forge local, indigenous traditions of architecture with contemporary ideas and technologies. He refracted the lessons learnt from modern architecture through the lens of national consciousness, traditional building methods and the particular context of the Egyptian *fellaheen* or rural poor. Fathy believed passionately in the importance of articulating a distinctive 'Egyptian accent' to national architecture through a 'living' – as opposed to stagnant – tradition of indigenous architecture. Tradition and modernity could coexist, insisted Fathy, each modulating the other but neither should be adopted as a stylistic device or architectural orthodoxy.[7]

If, in the first decades of the twentieth century, modernism professed to speak universally from the privileged bastion of Western metropolises, then the vernacular modernity that emerged so vociferously in Egypt and throughout Africa in the middle of the twentieth century responded with an equally emphatic insistence on national and local specificities that were nonetheless in constant dialogue with an 'international consciousness'. Rather than replacing one brand of universalism with another, the artists, architects and intellectuals constructed these vernacular modernities as responses to the popular, national fight for liberation from colonialism and they emerged as an integral part of the struggle for national and continental self-determination. Fathy's subsequent career saw him departing from his version of vernacular modernity and his architectural ideas evolved in parallel to the changing ideology of Egypt, 'from 1920s and 1930s Egyptianism, to Nasserist pan-Arabism in the 1960s, to Islamism in the 1980s', as Nasser Rabbat points out. These political and ideological shifts would be mirrored in different ways throughout the continent in the latter half of the twentieth century and were brought about, to a great extent, by the failure to realise fully the aspirations and dreams of the liberation struggles in Africa.

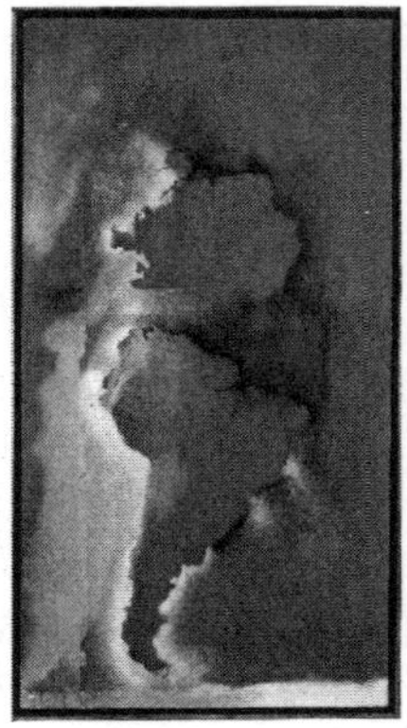

Frank Bowling, *South America Squared*, 1967.
Mixed media (silkscreen, acrylic on canvas),
221 x 114cm.

III Mapping Space

Just as Hassan Fathy sought to negotiate the intellectual and technical concerns of architectural modernism and Egypt's shifting political and cultural contingencies, other artists and intellectuals in Africa and the African diaspora in the second half of the twentieth century were also seeking to depart from modernism's universalising agenda in order to re-articulate contemporary art and literature through their own ideas and experiences. One of the most important artists of his generation, Frank Bowling created map paintings in the late 1960s and early 1970s that combine his investigations into the formal properties of picture making with his political preoccupations. Bowling not only put the political into Pop Art but also put postcolonial concerns into contemporary art, thereby creating a sublime tension between form and content and laying the ground for subsequent generations of artists for whom aesthetic and political concerns are never mutually exclusive.

Bowling began making map paintings in 1967, at a time when maps were not uncommon in the work of cutting-edge artists of the 1960s and, as Kobena Mercer identifies, the motif of the globe attracted artists who were responding to the social and political turmoil of the time.

In the same way that Fathy found a way to reconcile the demands of tradition and modernity, Bowling did not distinguish a hierarchy of form over content or content over form. The edges of Bowling's canvases frequently spill over across the frame that fails to rein in or constrain the rich, accumulated brush strokes, creating visual spaces that extend, like a horizon line, beyond our immediate field of vision. It is as though Bowling's brush is probing beyond the surface of the visible world to elicit a hidden reality that threatens to slip out of reach. In the sumptuous deep reds, pinks and purples of Bowling's epic work *Marcia H. Travels* (1970), the artist constructs out of pure colour a vast, three-dimensional oceanic space in which the outlines of the continental land masses recede and protrude like the ebb and flow of waves on the surface of the sea. The distinctive colourings of imperial possession that characterised the maps of colonial textbooks throughout Africa and the Caribbean become submerged beneath the thick, layered strokes of the artist's brush. The clearly delineated outlines of *South America Squared* (1967) had yielded by the end of the decade to a richly textured abstraction in which a radically new cartography could be glimpsed enlarging and receding into the depths of the paint. As Mercer puts it, these canvases represent nothing less than 'a painterly act of postcolonial re-vision':

> In the darkening vertical stains that threaten to engulf the outlines of Europe and the Americas in *Marcia H. Travels*, it is possible to suggest that the world picture imprinted by the Empire project was being placed 'under erasure'. By virtue of the ways in which they tackle the subject of postcolonial history, the map paintings were critically rewriting the Eurocentric projection of the globe.[8]

The ink drawings of Clifford Charles represent a very different kind of postcolonial re-visioning and yet they share with Bowling's canvases the search through painterly abstraction for a new visual and physical space that reflects a profoundly altered social and political reality. They are, in Bheki Peterson's words, 'a provocatively ingenious response to South Africa's "altered states"... of governance and consciousness'.[9] Charles's works are preoccupied with the same double consciousness of 'blackness and abstraction' that Mercer locates in Bowling's paintings, evoked through

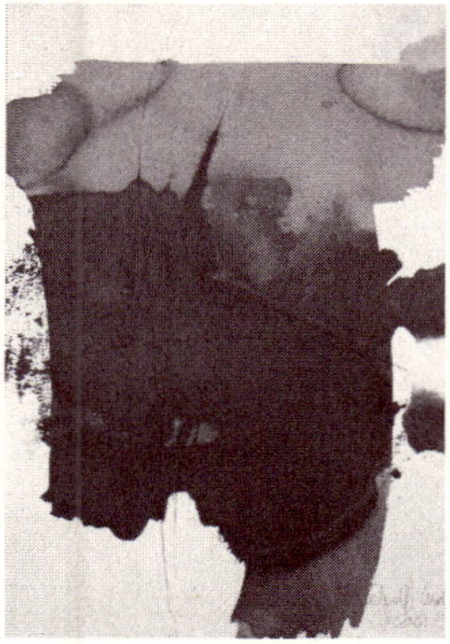

Clifford Charles, *Interaction*, *Haiku* series, 2001. Ink on paper, 30 x 42cm.

the motif of an endlessly repeated journey, moving from the past to the present and back again. Sitting tangentially to Clifford Charles's series of ink drawings is a documentary journey 'We've Also Been to Soweto', a fictional text by Prince Massingham that recounts a sightseeing tour of Soweto. Written in a kind of South African esperanto that interweaves English, Sotho, slang, Afrikaans, Zulu, Tswana and Tsonga, Massingham's text effects a parallel movement to the ink drawings, moving backwards and forwards between the city's apartheid past and its post-apartheid present.

Charting the passage of both space and time, Charles's drawings and Massingham's text unmask the illusion of arbitrary dividing lines that demarcate one distinct historical moment from another, from slavery to freedom, from colonialism to postcolonialism, from apartheid to post-apartheid. The reality of lived experience is somewhat different, bearing witness to incompleteness, slippage, multiple layers, forgetfulness and erasure. Charles's series of drawings that has the generic title *Painting on Water* (2002–3) evokes the uneven and slippery ground that the present occupies, balancing precariously on the past. The black ink flows unevenly across the surface of the white paper, dense and impenetrable in some areas, in other areas staining the paper only lightly, at times almost transparent. In *Interaction* (2001), an inky mass spreads across the centre of the paper; while in *Looking Glass* (2001), the ink is contained in a tight oval, rocklike shape. In other drawings, the ink spills in fluid, unconstrained movements across the paper. As Peterson points out, this new series of works recalls an earlier body of work, a series of oil paintings under the composite title of *Metamorphosis* where Charles made physical incisions on the canvas that were then layered with ink upon ink resonating with the 'incisions upon the body as it was literally scarred, tortured and reconfigured under the violence of apartheid'. But here Peterson discerns a witty displacement that is contained in the very materiality of Charles's drawings, 'a displacement of whiteness with the intricacies of blackness':

> They recall the black marks (usually blocks) that apartheid censors used to hide faces and material that was considered subversive.... Let us not forget the sardonic humour of apartheid that euphemistically called areas populated by black people outside of the homeland reserves, as 'black spots' that needed to be removed from South Africa.[10]

Through their investigations of the material qualities of paint on canvas and ink on paper, Bowling and Charles make tangible particular political and social spaces in transition. In the case of Bowling, this is the postcolonial reconfiguration of political and cultural geographies in the aftermath of the independence movements of formerly colonised nations. In the case of Charles, it is the articulation of a more recently won post-apartheid space that is resolutely unsentimental or romantic. In both instances, these spaces do not constitute a neat and uncomplicated break with the past, but rather are continual, forced reminders. In Charles's case, they are engagements with what has historically taken place, 'another necessary archival project', whereas in Bowling's works it is more a question of the unenunciated difference which hardens on the surface of his canvases, 'intervening in the codes of culture to delay and postpone the closure of the signifying chain'. As Mercer writes, 'Frank Bowling's map paintings activate an awareness of the agency of something that is not there anymore.'[11]

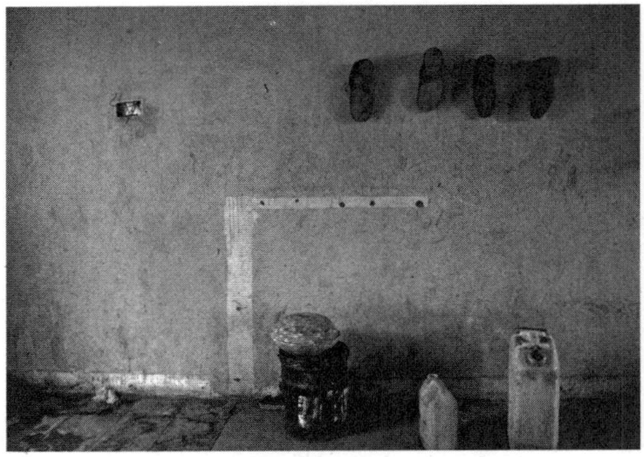

Zarina Bhimji, *Memories Were Trapped Inside the Asphalt*, 1998–2003. Transparency in light box, 130 x 170 x 12.5cm.

IV The Algebra of Difference

The echoes of 'something that is not there anymore' haunt the works of Zarina Bhimji. Her triptych of large-scale light boxes is like an altarpiece, appropriate to a secular, postmodern age. Whereas the main protagonists and narratives of the traditional Christian altarpiece would have been familiar to their audience of worshippers, the narrative of Bhimji's irreligious triptych is enigmatic and difficult to pin down. The works provoke an overwhelming sense of absence and loss, an immediate emotional response in the first instance and, only after an interval, an intellectual response. Epic in scale, Bhimji's works reflect on the minutiae of people's lives, abandoned in the haste of sudden, enforced exile. A collection of fans have been felled from the ceiling and lie abandoned on the floor of a large empty space. Another evacuated room is occupied only by a shaft of light that spills through an open door. A pair of shoes, hanging forlornly on the wall, is the last remaining evidence of human presence in an uninhabited room. Enlarged and illuminated, these minute residues are the only clues to what has taken place and they evoke a disturbing sense of cataclysmic events that have shaken the everyday patterns of human activity, giving, 'a sense of unspeakable horrors... but also a sense of long-term decay'.[12]

Bhimji has described the works as being concerned with 'learning to listen to "difference", the difference in shadows, microcosms and sensitivity to difference in its various forms. Listening with the eyes, listening to changes in tone, difference of colour... it is about making sense through the medium of aesthetics.' Far removed from the realm of factual history or documentary photography, Bhimji's approach proposes a new way of mapping the tragic and seismic events that have characterised a period of history riven by ethnic and racial conflicts not only in Africa but throughout the globe. How does one begin to picture the devastating effects of elimination, extermination and erasure on a vast scale? If, as Stalin allegedly once chillingly observed, the death of one man is a tragedy and the death of millions a statistic, how is it possible for us to engage with the scale of mass trauma on an intimate, and even poetic, level? Bhimji extrapolates from the historically and geographically specific situation, distancing it and thereby transcending it; from the particular and personal residues of human activity, her work extracts a deafeningly quiet question: Whether in Paris or Rwanda, London or Kosovo, why does it seem impossible for us to live creatively with difference?

It is the indexing of difference from the 'multicultural managerialism' of art circuits and the cultural industry in the 1990s through to the rigid, compartmentalising logic of apartheid that Sarat Maharaj exposes in 'Fatal Natalities'.[13] The fields of representation and cultural authority, according to Maharaj, are not so far removed from the exigencies of political power and conflict in their expression of incommensurate difference. Presented in opposition to this process of differentiation – of measuring, scanning and classifying difference – but ultimately bound up with it are the 'natalising' tendencies that Maharaj discerns in the articulation of post-apartheid South Africa's Rainbow Nation but which have emerged at various junctures in different parts of the continent. Maharaj identifies the search for the 'authentically native place' as a reaction to apartheid's 'fraudulent natalities' and its 'map of homelands, racial areas, Bantustans'. Ultimately, the search for authentic, fixed identities is born from the negative space cast by the dismantling of apartheid, or by the failure of liberation movements to realise the aspirations of their peoples, or by the disempowering effects of globalisation. Caught in that sphere of

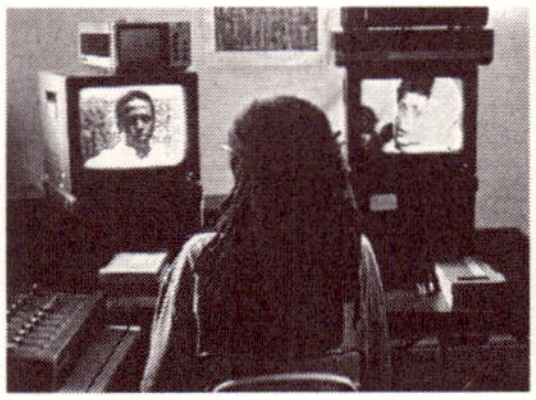

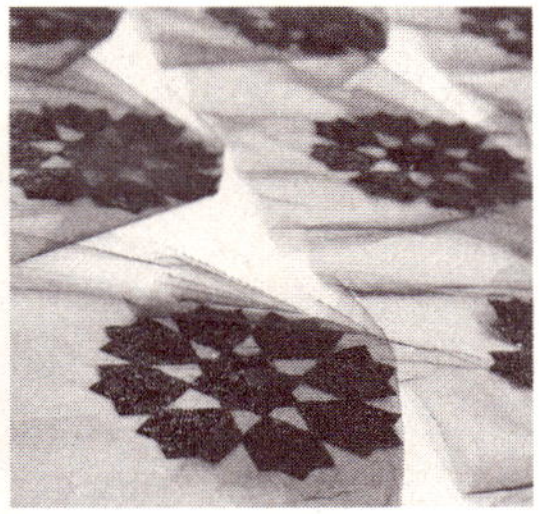

Far left: Salem Mekuria, *DELUGE*, 1997. Video still.
Left: Samta Benyahia, *La Vie en Paillettes*, 2003. Installation using material, sequins, beads and wood. Musée d'Art Roger Quilliot, Clermont-Ferrand. Photograph: Régis Nardoux.

negativity, of reaction to something outside of itself, a space is opened up for ideological polarities, intransigent orthodoxies and fundamental opposites that brings in its wake religious and ethnic conflict, political uncertainty and civil war.

Salem Mekuria's *RUPTURES: A Many Sided Story* (2003) is explicitly rooted in the recent political and social history of Ethiopia. Mirroring the tripartite structure of traditional Ethiopian Orthodox religious art, Mekuria's triptych video installation examines the turbulent events, from within and without, that have erupted periodically in the lives of Ethiopian people in recent decades. Visually referencing the Trinity – Father, Son and the Holy Spirit – in Ethiopian Orthodox faith, Mekuria's installation explores the chronological synchronicity which characterises contemporary Ethiopian life, namely the coexistence of past, present and future experienced simultaneously in the present. 'Time is circular', observes Mekuria, 'one is never too far from encounters with the pre-historic, the pre-modern, the modern and the post-modern in the course of a few moments.' As new images emerge on the three-screen video projection, the old presences linger, never far from the surface. The coexistence of more than one temporal space and multiple perspectives lies at the heart of Mekuria's intervention that contests the dominance of a single, unifying narrative of Ethiopian experience. As Elsabet Giorgis writes, 'her work acknowledges the varieties and complexities of Ethiopian culture and questions the ability of any single philosophical rationalisation to be the primal context of conventional value'.[14]

Whether within the religious context of Ethiopian Orthodoxy or the ideological framework of Marxism, Mekuria's fractured narrative of Ethiopian contemporary experience resists yielding to a single authoritative voice, replacing this instead with a palimpsest of images and voices that constitute the complex layers of Ethiopian lived experience. Her work speaks, more generally, to the contradictions and tensions that lie beneath the surface of contemporary societies in the so-called developed as well as 'developing' world; contradictions expressed through the push and pull of the totalising narratives of ideological or religious unity on the one hand and the centrifugal forces of migration, exile and diaspora on the other.

Defying the political violence that has marked Algeria from the colonial struggle to present-day conflicts, Samta Benyahia's architectural installation (a tribute to the great Algerian writer Kateb Yacine) creates a utopian space in which the past and present are no longer in conflict with one another; here a multiplicity of viewpoints becomes possible at one and the same time. Benyahia's wooden structure is a circular construction in three dimensions, built with sharp exterior angles in the form of a star-shaped polygon. As Benyahia describes it, the interior of the polygon is 'a space one enters like a cocoon, made up of seven recesses through which the spectator or the visitor discovers seven different stained glass windows… and on which the key motif is the blue rosace, a form carrying the name of a woman, Fatima, in the Arab-Andalucian repertoire.' Yacine's poetic concept of the 'starry polygon' (*le polygone étoilé*) stands as a metaphor for a utopian political and social space in which ideological and cultural polarities are negated. In direct dialogue with the rosace motif, the starry polygon is a structure without a defined beginning or end but is experienced as a kind of vortex that eradicates everything in its orbit, thereby holding out the possibility of a fresh beginning, a new start.

Rotimi Fani-Kayode, *Untitled*, *Communion* series, 1995. R-type colour print, 137 x 137cm. © the artist's estate. Courtesy of Autograph: Association of Black Photographers, London.

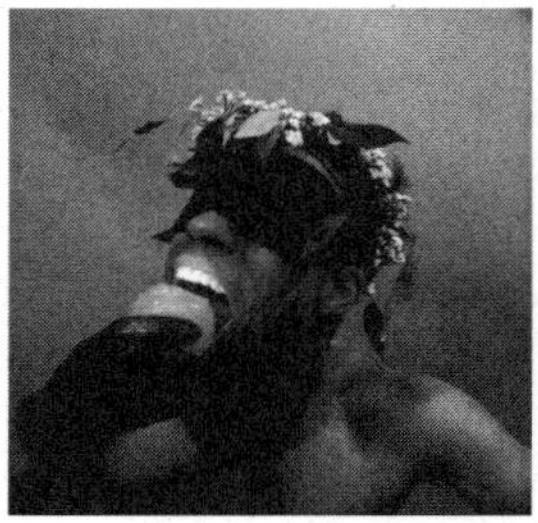

> Ali La Pointe and all those condemned to death are children of the polygon. They live a violent death, just as I write in an impasse. And the obsessive star that haunts prisons is a night star. For the condemned man walking to his death, this sleepless, sputtering night wipes out everything, begins everything afresh, to infinity. This is the inextricable completeness of the polygon, the empty interior which is extinguished like a campfire, all forms abolished.... Peace to its ashes. But we may also inhabit the scaffold, holding our heads under our arms. This is the lot of the poet. Then we sing of the 'black sun of melancholy' and wander the Orient like Gérard de Nerval! We may also haunt a castle, like [Franz] Kafka, or pace the paths of a labyrinth. Or again, like [Henri] Michaux, we may send this 'inside space' for which we have lost the keys flying into pieces. Then there is no more East, no more West. The polygon reasserts its rights. And if the streets of Dublin find echoes in Algiers, it is because the creative artist does not inhabit, but is inhabited by a sort of starry vertigo, which is even starrier for those of us whose starting point is the darkest point in the darkest corner of an alleyway.[15]

The circular movement that takes us (the viewers) around Benyahia's starry polygon evokes the movement of Muslim pilgrims around the Ka'ba, the rectangular building which Muhammad had purged of idols and made the centre of Muslim devotion. But the circle also assumes a particular structural and symbolic significance in the literature of Kateb Yacine as a symbol of freedom that straddles both the spatial and the temporal. According to Yacine, the image of the circle is 'the reality of the revolutionary world, the freedom of men who are always on the move, freedom in both space and time'. Benyahia has created an ideal space, tinged with a deep, azure blue that underscores the notion of an ideal existence in complete contrast to the context of conflict and chaos that has scarred Algeria' s recent history. Entering Benyahia's utopian structure provides a space for reflection and memory, respite, if only for a short time, from the conflict and chaos that exists beyond its idyllic confines.

V Signs and Meanings

The possibility of reconciling different world views underpins the work of Rotimi Fani-Kayode who creates a photographic world in which 'the body is the focal point for an exploration of the relationship between erotic fantasy and ancestral spiritual values'.[16] Situated at the vanguard of work that explored the politics of identity, Fani-Kayode's images insist upon the sensuality of the photographic image and its ability to elicit both an emotional and an intellectual response. Politics and aesthetics were not mutually exclusive terms in Fani-Kayode's visual vocabulary, nor were the different facets of his identity and artistic practice.

> In my case, my identity has been constructed from my own sense of otherness, whether cultural, racial or sexual. The three aspects are not separate within me. Photography is the tool by which I feel most confident in expressing myself. It is photography, therefore – Black, African, homosexual photography – which I must use not just as an instrument, but as a weapon if I am to resist attacks on my integrity and indeed, my existence on my own terms.[17]

Far from being a self-indulgent practice that meditated on personal experience and identity as the self-contained subject and object of his artworks, Fani-Kayode located his images within wider political, historical and cultural contexts. A committed activist on issues of race and sexuality, Fani-Kayode saw his

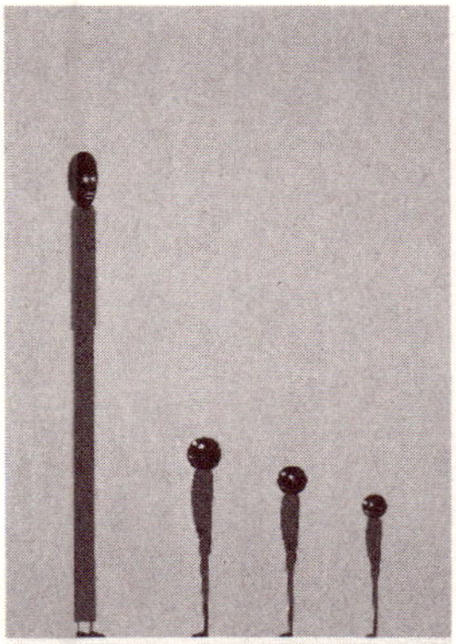

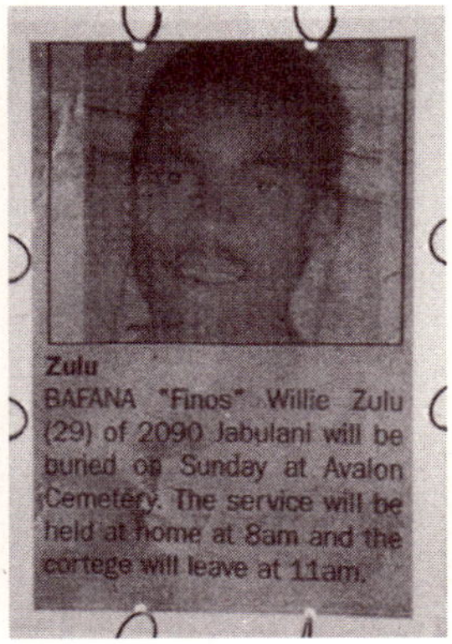

Far left: Laylah Ali, *Untitled*, 2001.
Gouache on paper, 69 x 46cm.
Courtesy of 303 Gallery, New York.
Left: Pitso Chinzima, *Archive* (detail), 2003.
Installation.

political engagement as bound up with his own creative practice and that of others. He saw parallels between his own work and that of the Osogbo artists in Yorubaland who 'themselves have resisted the cultural subversions of neo-colonialism and who celebrate the rich, secret world of our ancestors'.[18] The rich saturated colours of Fani-Kayode's photographs, his use of chiaroscuro and mise-en-scène contribute to the construction of what Mark Sealy describes as a 'twilight cross-cultural zone' where Fani-Kayode erodes the lines 'between black and white, gay and straight, acceptance and taboo'.[19] Ultimately, Fani-Kayode's images contest the idea of a settled world view dominated by an established canon of ideas and iconography; he disturbs fixed notions of African-ness, blackness and homosexuality that rely too heavily on an essentialist and uncomplicated view of the world and human experience.

While Fani-Kayode and Benyahia offer up alternative constructions of the world which insist on the coexistence of different world views and the possibility of multiple interpretations, Laylah Ali paints an altogether darker, dystopian realm. Evoked through her ongoing series of brightly coloured gouache paintings, Ali's cartoon-like images are deeply disturbing and ambiguous narratives that suggest repeated episodes of violence and conflict underpinned by the dynamics of race and power. Inspired by the graphic style of comic strips, Ali constructs a world in which the identities of her varied Greenhead characters are difficult to pin down and their behaviour both ambivalent and contradictory. The apparent simplicity of Ali's work masks a sophisticated aesthetic strategy that, as Lisa Fischman points out, implicates the viewer in the process of de-coding and interpreting the works, making the viewer responsible for the meaning they elicit from the images.[20] At first glance, the hard-edged contours of Ali's characters suggest that the content of the paintings might be as unequivocal and clear-cut as traditional comic strips in which the dividing lines between 'goodie' and 'baddie' are clearly drawn and the narrative conclusion foregone. But Ali's world is unsettlingly equivocal. Her strange wide-eyed creatures – part human, part alien – with gigantic heads play their parts in a series of narrative fragments without a clear beginning or end and, as Fischman notes, explode 'simplistic binary categorisations – human/alien, male/female, good/evil, black/white – forcing their re-examination… allowing them, as [Laylah Ali] puts it, to "act like a question mark"'.[21] The moral ambiguity of Ali's characters and their actions makes the viewer's active role as interpreter and participant in these bizarre tales all the more uncomfortable. It is as though Ali is making us aware of our own position as both spectator and protagonist in the 'real' world and the ethical choices that we make on a daily basis to watch or participate, or maybe even our mute culpability as spectators whose very inaction allows unspeakable things to happen.

Underpinning Ali's work is an acknowledgement of the social and political violence that consistently subverts human relations and erodes the will to effect political change. Ali's work signals a disillusion with the redemptive narratives of radical politics and liberation struggles but also a desire to re-engage without the benefit of rose-tinted spectacles.

Pitso Chinzima and Veliswa Gwintsa's installation *At Least One Person Was Killed* addresses the cumulative effects of relentless social violence as a global phenomenon that militates against the efforts of ordinary people to realise a full and meaningful existence. Rejecting the notion that social violence is a peculiarly South African experience, Chinzima and Gwintsa suggest that violence is one of the more

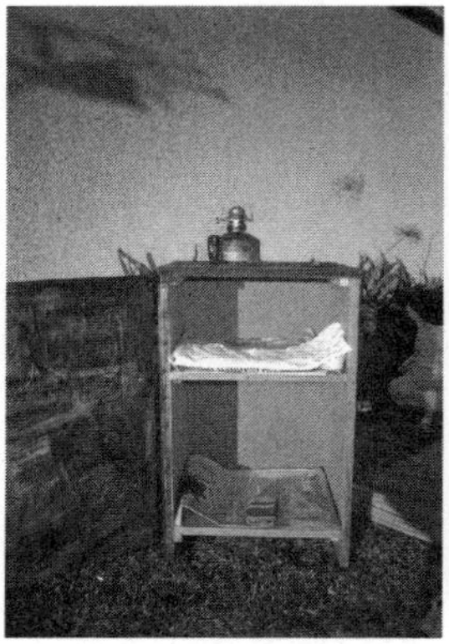

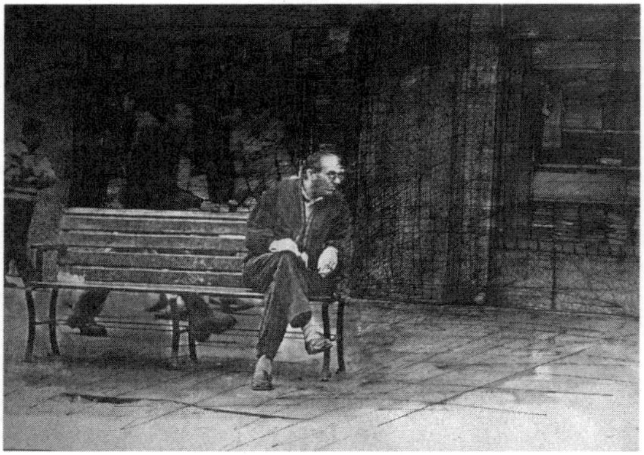

Right: Veliswa Gwintsa, *1913 The Inception*, 1997. Mixed media installation.
Far right: Sabah Naim, *Untitled*, 2003. Mixed media. Photograph: Muhammad Saif.

troubling effects of globalisation and its discontents. Chinzima and Gwintsa describe their installation of children's furniture and toys covered with newspaper clippings of the dead as a 'visual monument for the dead'. Critical of the media representation of death as a daily spectacle, their work appears particularly resonant in the context of the recently waged war against Iraq and the saturation of media coverage. Does the media's representation of death bring us any closer to its reality, ask Chinzima and Gwintsa? Or does the incessant repetition and proliferation of the iconography of death simply distance us from its devastating impact on people's lives? By picturing death, do we take steps to avert it or do we simply fuel a dehumanising abstraction of individual lives? This questioning assumes even greater significance in the context of South Africa's recent history where the murder of ordinary black people, whether in the townships of South Africa or in the camps of exiled South Africans in the countries bordering South Africa, were a daily occurrence under the former apartheid regime. But, as Prince Mbusi Dube underlines in his essay, while Chinzima and Gwintsa's work emerges from their lived experience as black South Africans, it is not a reflection on death within a South African context; rather, it demands a recognition of the common threads that bind us in a shared humanity that transcends specific geographical context or unique individual experience.

It is the increasingly widening gap between two incommensurate worlds that informs the work of Sabah Naim: namely, that of the international arena of the media and global politics on the one hand and the everyday world of Egyptians and their daily effort to survive on the other. Naim's images are frequently populated by ordinary Cairenes going about their daily business: two policemen sit on a bench; a group of people waiting for a bus or a crowd of people crossing a busy street. Naim's works represent an artistic intervention into the arena of media representation, offering alternative images which are characterised by their ordinariness, documents of the banality of everyday life that stand in stark contrast to the exaggerated depictions of Middle Eastern life that proliferate in the global media. But Naim's images are also a comment upon the process of mediation itself. The surfaces of her photographic images have been physically disturbed. Drawn upon, painted, scratched, inked, decorated, the images are irrevocably altered by the artist's hand. The act of marking and revising the photographs draws attention to the ways in which our experiences have become subject to greater and greater mediation. Paired with Naim's photographs are three-dimensional sculptures, moulded from newspapers and magazines (selected by the artist from both Egyptian and foreign print media), which are meticulously rolled and shaped by the artist. In their form, these bifurcated installations – half-photograph, half-sculpture – physically reflect a divided public realm in which the words and images of the global media are rendered as abstractions and the 'real' documentary evidence of Cairene street life is 'tampered with', assuming a peculiarly heightened realism.

As Yasmeen Siddiqui points out, together with other Cairo-based artists, Naim is concerned with 'how the city is organised and how public space is occupied and territorialised'.[22] Perhaps, this is not surprising given the history of Cairo, whose Arabic name 'the victorious' evokes what was once a global metropolis at the centre of an Islamic empire that has since waned and given way to new empires and global formations. But Naim is less concerned with Cairo's glorious past as with its dynamic present. With her adoption of the moving image and sound, Naim's video work takes not one

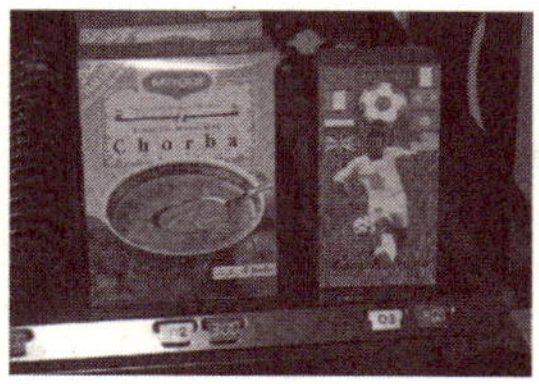

Kader Attia, *La Machine à Rêves* (Dream Machine), 2002–3. Detail of installation.

image but hundreds of individual frames that are manipulated and worked upon like her photographs. It is the city that assumes the role of chief protagonist in Naim's urban tale and 'the street', notes Naim, 'becomes the stage. All those who walk through it actors, a microcosmic glance at the larger Egyptian society. Each of the players walks through the scene [enclosed/isolated] in their own world, carrying a mixed bag of emotions and concerns, unaware of that which surrounds them.'[23] Her technique of manipulating the photographic image which, by turns, obscures or highlights particular details of the scene, removes individual characters out of their environment, isolating them and alienating them from their everyday surroundings. It is difficult not to read Naim's work as a poetic critique of the alienation of thousands of people from the new political and economic global order and the re-inscription of other experiences and ways of living on to the international stage.

VI Cities under Construction

> The culture from which I am descended (my Algerian roots) has nothing in common with the culture from which I come.… In contrast to the ancient culture of the *bled*, the culture of these [housing] estates is still under construction (through grafitti, street gear, rap, break dancing etc.)[24]

Contradicting claims that a settled political, economic and cultural regime has been established worldwide as a result of a 'new world order' that materialised after the crumbling of the Communist regimes in Eastern Europe, the work of Kader Attia paints a picture of an assymetrical globalisation and of cities (and cultures) in the heart of Europe that are still under construction. Continuously monitoring the world for signs of shifts and changes (while also longing romantically for the developing world to remain frozen in an idealised past), the European metropolises, that were once the centres of empires, recoil from the cultural transformations that are taking place in their midst. Globalisation, in this sense, has come home to roost in the figure of migrants, refugees and asylum seekers who, together with the second- and third-generation children of earlier migrants, are transfiguring indigenous European cultures irrevocably. It is these signs of cultural difference and dissonant experience that Attia marks in his photographs and installations.

In his slide installation piece *La Piste d'Atterrissage* (The Landing Strip, 1998–2000), Attia depicts the lives of Algerian transvestites and transsexuals in Paris. Intimate and domestic, Attia's portraits evoke the lives of people who are on the margins of both Algerian and French society. Exiled from Algeria and living illegally (*sans papiers*) in Paris, Attia likens the protagonists of *La Piste d'Atterrissage* to medieval saints, describing them as 'people who take everything upon themselves, who are persecuted, abused, ridiculed and finally adulated'.[25] Excluded from both Algeria and France, the figures who populate Attia's work represent the lived experience of globalisation and its disaffected and disenfranchised 'non-citizens'. But, for Attia, they also paradoxically represent the triumph of personal freedom over conformity and of difference over assimilation. In this sense, Attia's protagonists might be seen as the vanguard of an alternative world order that is still 'under construction'.

Like Chaucer's *Canterbury Tales* (*c*. 1387) that evokes the daily lives and experiences of a group of medieval pilgrims, Attia's work also carries a warning. In *La Machine à Rêves* (Dream Machine, 2002–3), Attia critiques the hegemonising effects of consumer society whose brands, labels and logos recall the rigid laws of medieval heraldry. A designer-clad young *beurre*

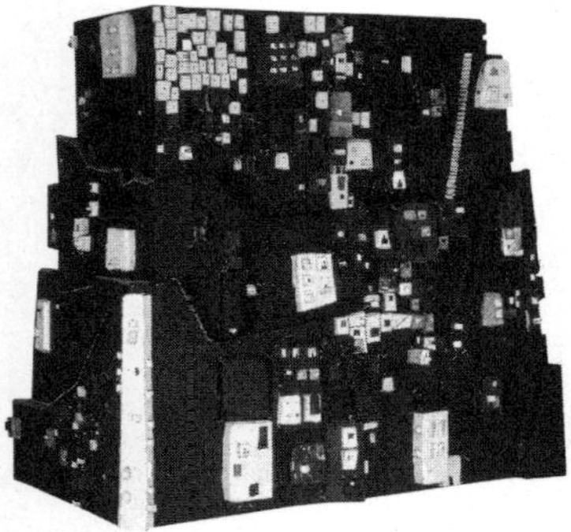

Wael Shawky, *Untitled*, 2001. Installation (detail), tarmac, galvanised wire, liquid tar, silver paint and wood, approx 2.95 x 4 x 1.75m.

Moataz Nasr, *Water*, 2002. Video still.

(French-born Algerian youth) stands in front of an automatic vending machine that distributes an assortment of desirable objects that reflect sardonically on life in France's cross-cultural housing estates. Dispensing syringes, kosher salami, Mecca Cola, condoms and *hijabs* (veils), Attia's vending machine stands as a metaphor for the widening net of globalisation and consumer society which absorbs and appropriates difference, transforming it into yet another consumable object with only the outer wrapping of difference.

Like Attia, Wael Shawky interrogates the uneven, discontinuous effects of globalisation and mass migration. Constructing his own massive cityscape in the centre of the exhibition space, Shawky's city is a hybrid metropolis, part-rural, part-urban. Encircled by perimeter walls, Shawky's *Asphalt Quarter* (2003) evokes the popular, urban districts of downtown Cairo and, yet, it lacks any distinguishing features that fix it as any city *in particular*. Drenched in asphalt and liquid tar, the buildings rise up, some separated by narrow alleyways, some topped on their rooftops by plasma screens, reminiscent of the billboards that litter today's cityscapes. A series of images alternate randomly on these screens, each the length of a standard television commercial: a group of Arab Bedouins build cement houses and cover them with liquid tar against the backdrop of a desertscape close to the sea; Bedouin children create a runway from liquid tar; a nomad leaves his mud shelter, pulling a water buffalo behind him.

The convergence of incongruous elements is a frequent motif in Shawky's work. In an earlier video and installation piece entitled *Sidi El Asphalt's Mulid* (2001), Shawky set the rhythmic, hypnotic movements of a Sufi religious trance to the sounds of Cypress Hill.[26] The unlikely melding of the two results in a disquieting convergence between American hip-hop and a traditional Egyptian religious festival that points to the wider contradictions and incongruities of contemporary life effected by the dual processes of migration and globalisation. As Niru Ratnam comments: 'Can you get perfect fits between constituencies that know little and care to know little about the other?… Or is the act of fitting them together the site of productivity and questioning?'[27]

Sidi El Asphalt's Mulid reflects upon the effects of modernisation on contemporary Egyptian culture and the dramatic shifts that have taken place in the country in recent decades, from the economic transformations of the 1970s, through the waves of immigration to the Gulf in the 1980s, leading up to the impact of globalisation from the 1990s to the present. In this context, the *mulid* is, according to Shawky, 'a stereotypical image of Egyptian society that encompasses all its coexisting contradictions without allowing any of its poles to affect the other negatively or positively'. In the same way that Attia points to the surprising convergence between the conformity demanded by consumer society and that defined by new forms of religious orthodoxy, Shawky suggests that these opposite poles of cultural experience coexist and come together to create a hybrid social and cultural reality which has many equivalences:

> Via its nomadic nature, the Bedouin community becomes a metaphor for globalisation: borders and space are broken, and the tribal tendencies of nomads find an equivalent in the notion of shared interests raised by the owners of capital – the driving force behind globalisation. The mutated water buffalo represents an amalgamation of the agricultural with the nomadic; its artificial hump comes to epitomise the nomadic. At issue here are the Poetics of Modernisation, where the primitive

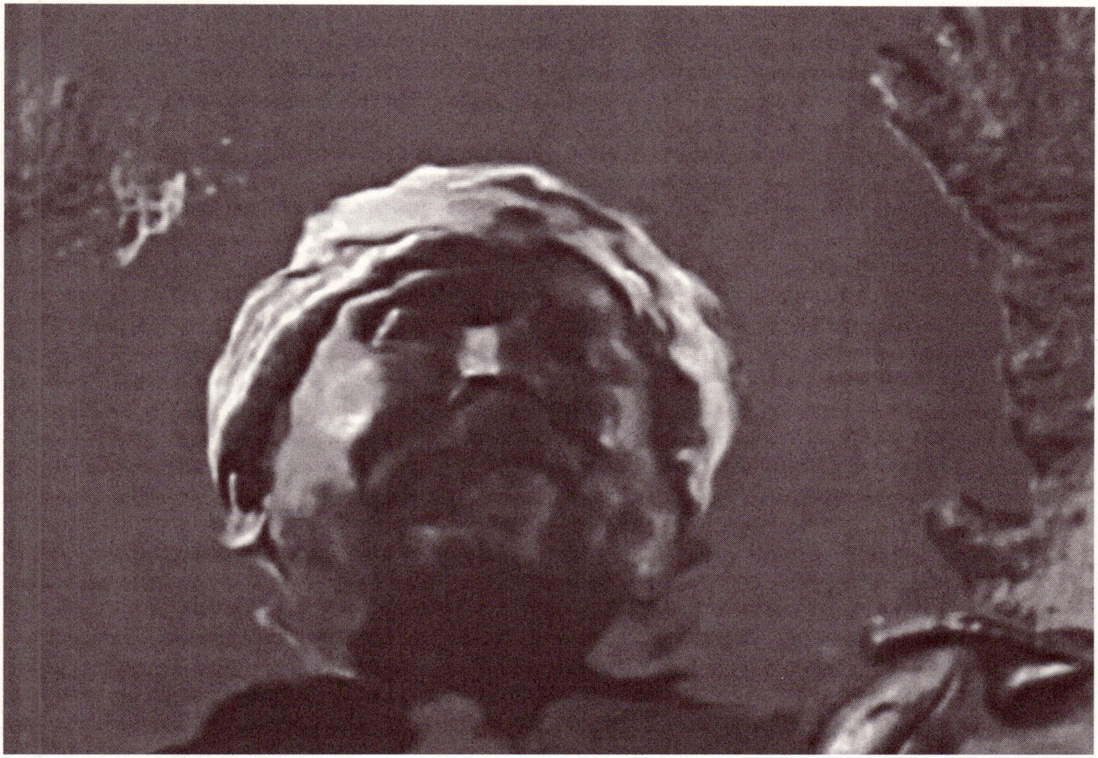

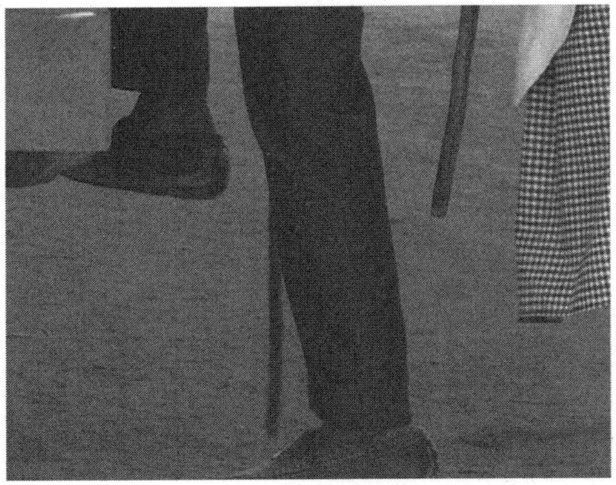

Moshekwa Langa, *Where do I Begin?*, 2001.
Video still, 4 mins 20 secs.

becomes urban, the nomadic agricultural, the bourgeois aristocratic, the popular bourgeois, and the sacred consumer.[28]

VII Notes on the Postcolony

The notion 'postcolony' identifies specifically a given historical trajectory – that of societies recently emerging from the experience of colonisation and the violence which the colonial relationship, *par excellence*, involves.... The postcolony is characterised by a distinctive style of political improvisation, by a tendency to excess and a lack of proportion as well as by distinctive ways in which identities are multiplied, transformed and put into circulation.[29]

Fifty years after the revolution that dispensed with colonial rule, Moataz Nasr's mesmerising video installation presents a powerful critique of the cynicism of politicians and the indifference of their electorate in post-revolutionary, postcolonial Egypt. But while Nasr's work emerges from a specific historical and cultural context, it transcends that context. As Bheki Peterson writes of Charles's work, Nasr's artistic practice is 'deeply inscribed with historical specificity', yet 'stubbornly refuses to be reduced to, solely defined by, or more correctly, confined to the exigencies of time and place'.[30] Simon Njami accurately locates Nasr's work in the context of a generation of postcolonial artists who are raising questions about the nature of the postcolony and its regimes of power. Born of historical upheavals, as Njami points out, these artists are 'more or less the same age as the independent states of Africa' and they expose the 'illusion of pan-Africanism which never came to pass or the illusion of independence movements which happened to become nothing but failures and disappointments'. At a historical juncture where the autonomy of the nation state has yielded power to corporate multinationals whose GDP (gross domestic product) often exceeds that of smaller nations, these questions assume a universal poignancy that extends beyond Egypt, Africa, or the so-called developing world, to encompass the entire globe.

We are all in the postcolony now.

At the far end of an enclosed space, a man is playing a *tabla* (drum). His legs are wrapped around the curves of its finely crafted clay base, inlaid with mother of pearl and ivory. Remaining out of sight, the man's face and body extend beyond the edge of the large video screen. He plays out a repertoire of traditional Arab compositions, invoking a spectrum of emotions by his music that ranges from nationalistic cries of war to melancholic love ballads. Extending across the floor of the space, Nasr creates a river of four hundred hollow clay drums of various sizes. Raw and unpolished, these drums map the demographic structure of the Nile Delta, densely concentrated at the centre and gradually dispersing across the space. Nasr's work resists what Achille Mbembe calls the 'binary categories used in standard interpretations of power – resistance *v.* passivity, autonomy *v.* subjection, state *v.* civil society'. Nasr articulates instead the contingency of rulers and ruled and the intricate web into which both are locked together. Describing the condition of the postcolony, Nasr's work raises questions equally about the conditions that exist in the urban metropolises of Europe and elsewhere, where political and economic configurations are increasingly converging to those of the postcolony.

We are all in the postcolony now.

If everyday struggles have taken the place of nationalist struggles in this new postcolonial world order, then waiting has displaced action. Moshekwa Langa's collages and installations reflect upon the continuous displacements and shifts not only in linguistic and visual representation but equally in the physical landscape of contemporary Africa. In this installation of large-scale drawings and video works, he presents a story in several parts, a 'non story' in three acts in which people are waiting to get on a bus, waiting in doorways passing the time or just smoking and waiting, waiting, waiting.... As Langa writes, 'The whole presentation really is like a drama without actors.... It is a fluid essay-like thing with footnotes and so on so that the main text and the subtext and the offpaths are never quite differentiated.... I have always enjoyed and preferred the interwoven structure of spoken language and actual physicality or physical presentation over cleanliness and demarcation when it comes to art making.'[31] Made up of a series of collages and drawings that relate tangentially to a series of video pieces mounted on rough-hewn crates and dispersed across the exhibition space, Langa's work avoids any clear beginning, middle or end, but rather constructs a number of sequences or acts which have no linear narrative structure but yet are inter-related. The separate elements of Langa's work could be read as the stories of nation states dispersed across the map of Africa or of individuals connected and yet disconnected from each other in spite of their experiences in common.

The title of Langa's installation *Waiting* (2003) evokes Samuel Beckett's *Waiting for Godot*, in which two homeless tramps wander from place to place, always returning to the same location. They are of no fixed abode and no fixed identity. Their names – Vladimir and Estragon – are indeterminate and they could almost be refugees from another place. Like recent migrants grappling with a second language, they frequently muddle colloquial expressions. The existential question for Vladimir and Estragon, 'Why are we here?', has been answered. They are waiting for Godot. But Vladimir and Estragon have been asking the wrong question. Continually returning to the same place and repeating the same task, Beckett's tramps have neither a history nor a memory. But for Langa, as for so many of us from the postcolony, we cannot escape from the exigencies of history and memory. Emerging from what Okwui Enwezor defines as the 'postcolonial constellation' are a host of artists and artistic practices who are 'expanding the definition of what constitutes contemporary culture and its affilations in other domains of practice; the intersection of historical forces aligned against the hegemonic imperatives of imperial discourse'.[32] In this context, the artist like the poet, has a critical role to play; a role which is radical and revolutionary but which nonetheless should never be in the service of politicians or regimes of power. Reflecting divergent views, the artist, according to Kateb Yacine, should 'create their own revolution within the political revolution', operating at the heart of trouble as 'perpetual troublemakers'. For the artist, like the poet, 'is the revolution stripped bare, the very movement of life in an unending explosion'.[33]

Maps of Emergency: Fault Lines and Tectonic Plates

Stuart Hall

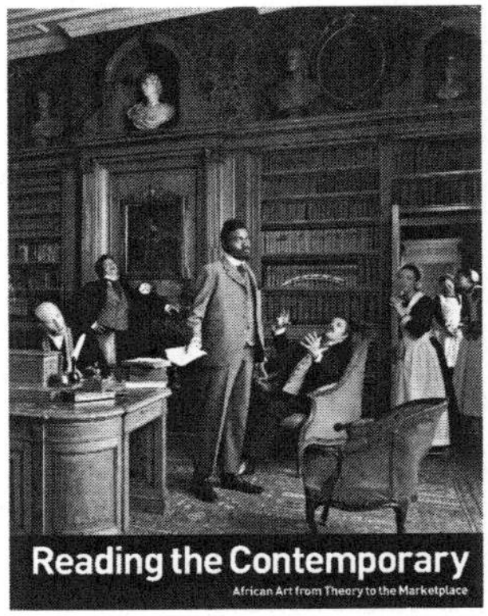

Published by inIVA and MIT Press. Courtesy of Yinka Shonibare.

The fifteen African artists presented in *Fault Lines* at the 2003 Venice Biennale follow the global traffic along pathways increasingly tracked by artistic production and the work of art in the age of trans-national globalisation. Not long ago, this relationship was most conveniently expressed in terms of centre and periphery. Differences persist. But they are no longer adequately convened within these fixed spatial poles. Still, one cannot resist the impression that this work has crossed, or migrated even, across a series of invisible frontiers, to one 'world' – the space of international exhibitions – from another 'world', that of the troubled, unsettled, non-spatialised places of the 'South'. As such, the *Fault Lines* artists have something quite unique and challenging to contribute to the discourses that define the so-called international art world that is the Biennale's traditional stamping ground.

The internationalism of that first 'world' remains a peculiarly skewed affair. Nevertheless, whatever its structure of inclusions and exclusions, this work from the edge now belongs irrevocably to global circuits. Okwui Enwezor and Olu Oguibe in *Reading The Contemporary* date this 'entry [of contemporary African art] into greater circulation in the global network of international exhibitions, museums, galleries, residencies etc'[1] from 1989. Not only because of the key critical responses generated that year in reaction to the (in)famous *Magiciens de la Terre* exhibition in Paris, but also because of the end of the Cold War (which had so constrained Africa in the strait-jacket of global polarisation) and because of the collapse of apartheid in South Africa, the date has truly global significance. However, Enwezor and Oguibe also remind us of the deep ambiguities which attach to the incorporation of the margins, and the danger when the very specific differences which continue to separate margin from centre are absorbed into the *indifference* of the postmodern celebration of difference.

This work, then, continues to sit awkwardly in the contemporary pantheon. It reminds us of the diversity of visions, artistic practices and forms of life – still largely unknown outside the continent – which are shaping the contemporary African imaginary today. Of course, the forces which are producing these novel effects of similarity and difference are no longer easily distributed between 'North' and 'South'. Given the scale of migration and the trans-national character of flows in the globalising, postcolonial moment, they belong to a shared, deeply intertwined, but highly uneven and unfinished global world, from whose impact none is excluded. Considered in their concrete artistic particularity, of course, each work demands to be seen in its own right. Each is the outcome of a conjuncture between a particular artistic vision and an individual practice. Each is in the process of freeing itself from 'the burden of representation'. There is no one 'Africa' here to be positively affirmed. The exhibition radically disrupts that lazy but necessary signifier; disturbing the sight lines on Africa from within and without, it gives, on this specific occasion, a greater continental centrality in the field of vision to Africa's northern, Islamic and Arab zones and a particularly diasporic inflexion to Africa's unfinished self-definition.

The idea of 'an essential African aesthetic' – a totality of works 'immersed in a sort of mythological retrospection which seems to issue from the collective unconscious'[2] – has metamorphosed out of existence. Clifford Charles, reflecting on his own practice, argues that his refusal to be frustrated 'by the shifting grounds that inform our life… the trauma and horror of our incomplete/unresolved past… the hoarding and social "bravado" of the displaced and recently empowered' has drawn his art into 'an introspective gaze.… This talking to

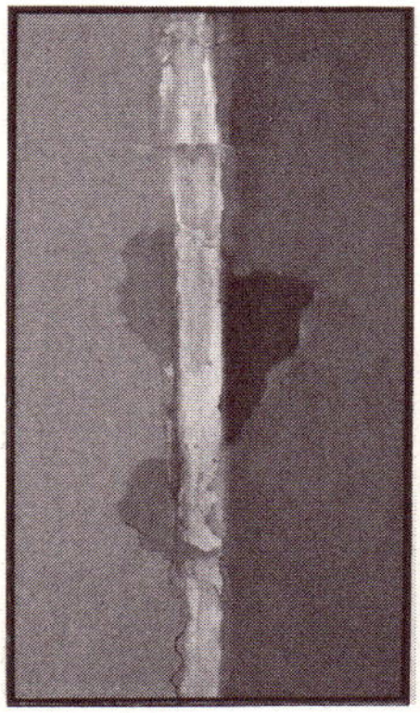

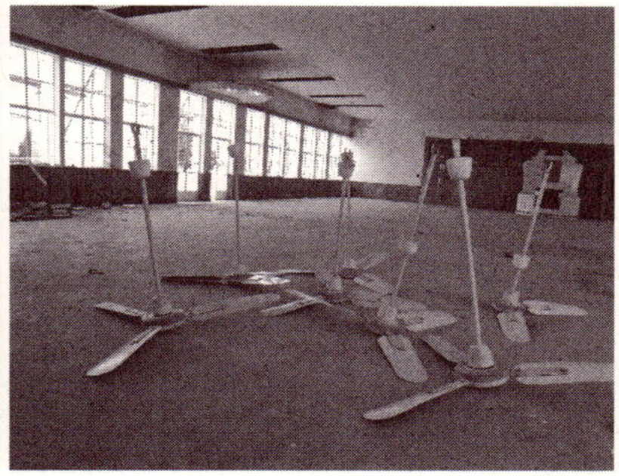

Far left: Frank Bowling, *Who's Afraid of Barney Newman?*, 1968. Acrylic on canvas, 234 x 123cm. Left: Zarina Bhimji, *Howling Like Dogs, I Swallowed Solid Air*, 1998–2003. Transparency in light box, 130 x 170 x 12.5cm.

myself becomes a silent self-reflection.'[3] However, a few minutes spent with the large, bold, unnervingly black, fluid shapes of his ink-on-paper paintings – clearly still struggling, long after the end of apartheid, with what Frantz Fanon once called 'the fact of blackness' – show that this self-reflection has not diverted his work into a false, solipsistic individualism. What we are looking at is more a decisive shift of register, an enhanced freedom of eye, hand and medium in relation to form and project, but not a disconnection. His work remains immersed in what he calls 'critically assessing… the existing patterns of our thinking'.[4]

The work of the *Fault Lines* artists implies a confidence in the individual's subjective aesthetic sensibility and practice – an indulgence long considered the privilege of the Western eye/subject alone. (Individuation, after all, was understood as the gift of the Enlightenment to Western modernity; African art, being 'less evolved', was supposed to be, by definition, more anonymously collective.) Each of the artists fully inhabits the range of languages and materials available to contemporary art practice – painting and multimedia, video and film installation, abstraction and neo-figurative, conceptual and collage – though often from within a distinctly non-European, postcolonial paradigm. Each work has its own way of negotiating the tension between tradition and modernity, so critical to Africa's troubled, ongoing dialogue with its Others. Each speaks out of a specific historical conjuncture. Each is engaged in a labour of remapping. Each finds its own way, not so much to address, as to take a new sighting on Africa's present 'state(s) of emergency'.

We find this, for example, in the earliest work in *Fault Lines* – the remapping that is clearly evident in Frank Bowling's astonishing, postcolonial or diasporic, planetary cartographies. Only here and there do their oceanic swathes of translucent colour echo a Mercator projection;[5] only here and there do they reveal, faintly, a replaced outline, a reimagined coastal indentation, the hint of a new continental shelf; and only *very* occasionally do they allow the shape of something more tangible and familiar – a house? a dwelling place? – to half-surface through the thick integument of the paint. Or we see it in Rotimi Fani-Kayode's sensuously erotic remappings of desire around the transgressive black body, with its triple diasporic displacements, familial, geographic/cultural and sexual.

We find it also in certain effects of *disturbance* in the work: surfaces fractured by a sudden upsurge of violence, rupture or dis-location. Look, for example, at Pitso Chinzima and Veliswa Gwintsa's meditations, out of the heart of the South African experience, on death and the contagion of violence, as it spreads indiscriminately from one location to another, becoming a general global phenomenon. Or look at Zarina Bhimji's light boxes, which, like the eerily evacuated Ugandan landscapes of her recent film *Out of Blue* (2002), speak volumes through absence, summoning up the profound sense of emptiness and loss which forced exile produces, and the silent devastation left behind by those who wreak a brutal revenge on difference. Or, in quite a different register, Laylah Ali's disturbingly aggressive and ambiguous cartoon shapes zoom around with their beady, alien eyes fixed on random targets or line up, as victims, waiting passively for the devastating impact.

We see it, in a different measure, in the way the formal arrangement – the 'logic of assembly' – of various works mysteriously echoes the way events shatter and disrupt the daily struggle for existence. Wael Shawky's work – reflecting the ambivalent effects of migration and global (so-called) modernisation on the life and culture of the Cairo street – requires us to make this connection. As does Salem Mekuria's triptych video installation, in which the regimes of Ethiopian Orthodoxy and Marxism are

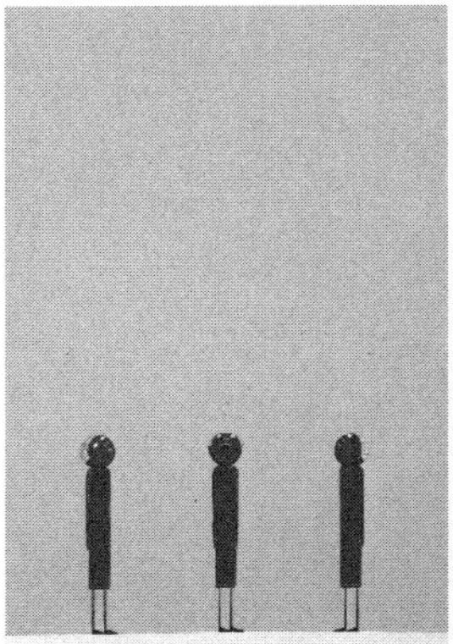

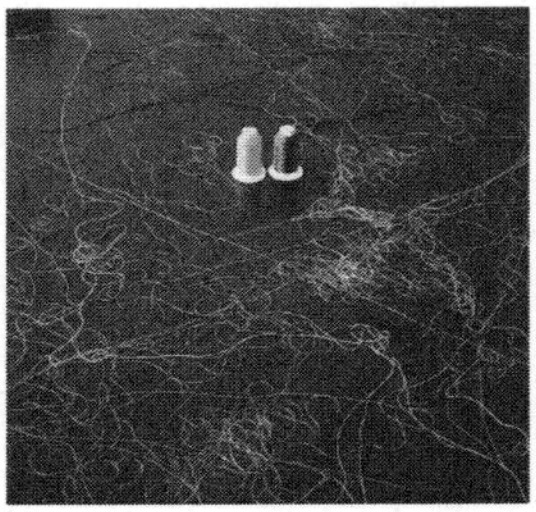

Right: Laylah Ali, *Untitled*, 2001. Gouache on paper, 69 x 46cm. Courtesy of 303 Gallery, New York.
Far right: Moshekwa Langa, *Fieldwork*, 2001. Installation with thread, text and red linoleum, Museum Fridericianum, Kassel. Photograph © Werner Maschmann.

caught in a repeating circle: systems obliged to echo and confront one another across time and space, made to answer to the breakdown of the 'grand narratives' of past and present in that troubled country and to the chaotic lives which they have left behind. In their broken sequences, these works seem to refract the violent displacements which have visited the continent – the fragmentation of time and continuity, the dispersal of innocent and frightened civilians, the forced migrations, the ethnic cleansing, the privatisation of war, the rebel gangs, the conscription of children, the 'global' trade in arms and gems, the break-up or breakdown of known or settled communities and relationships – of family, group, home, tribe, nation, language, religion, cognitive and epistemological worlds.

In her book *Terra Infirma*, Irit Rogoff interrogates geography as a settled signifying system, placing people and identities in relation to place and territory. This 'knowledge map', she argues, is now challenged by the 'unhomed geographies' offered by many contemporary artists. Rogoff insists on the links between the experiential and the epistemological effects of this crisis between the 'subjects' experience of disruption and… [the] prevailing conditions of disrupted knowledge orders… [a] crisis of the ability to represent any form of stable geographic knowledge as a set of guidelines regarding identity, belonging and rights'.[6] The work of the *Fault Lines* artists is participating in such a 'crisis' of representation.

The work is no longer produced out of a settled 'geography' of postcolonial Africa any more than it is the product of the optimistic vision of a decolonising Africa, fired by the dream of cultural revival and national reconstruction. This is the 'new world order', the post-Cold War, post-apartheid, postcolonial world of globalisation and debt, mass migration and civil war, famine and malnutrition. These landscapes are either shadowed by the threat of impending disaster or already scarred by its aftermath. We glimpse this crisis of representation almost joyously 'at play' in the scratched surfaces, montaged interiors and broken compositional planes of Moshekwa Langa's work, with its overwritten, cryptic, often playful, disseminated effects, distributed according to some enigmatic logic of dispersal we cannot exactly fathom. As Gilane Tawadros puts it, the artists seem to be 'tracing the fault lines that are shaping contemporary experience locally and globally', whose reverberations 'echo through contemporary lived experience'.[7]

'In geographical terms', Tawadros argues, 'fault lines reveal themselves as fractures in the earth's surface but they also mark a break in the continuity of the strata. Fault lines may be a sign of significant shifts or even of impending disaster, but they also create new landscapes.'[8] The metaphor provides a novel and challenging frame through which to interrogate the postcolonial and geopolitical situation of the work of contemporary African artists. When fault lines open up, they disrupt, break up, fragment. They *dis*place and *re*place. Villages become a war zone. The homed become *un*homed, and then simply the homeless – the *sans papiers,* the ones on the move, without documents, the multitudes: dispersal without the promise of return, unending exodus.

Of course, fault lines, like other relations of power (as Michel Foucault would remind us) are also *productive*. Those escaping the vertical lines of force forge new lateral connections. New formations appear where older ones disappear beneath the sand. Borders, which divide, become sites of surreptitious crossing. Separate and inviolable worlds meet and collide. Where only the pure, the orthodox, were valorised, a new universe of vernaculars and creole forms comes into existence. Multiple logics of identification and translation operate.

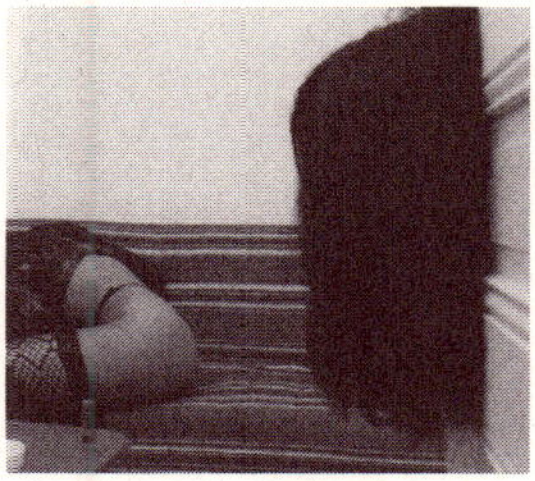

Kader Attia, *La Piste d'Atterrissage* (The Landing Strip), 1998–2000. Slide show.

Everything becomes what Edward Said calls 'contrapuntal' – 'this plurality of vision gives rise to an awareness of simultaneous dimensions… habits of life, expression, or activity in the new environment inevitably occur against the memory of these things in another environment'.[9] Obliged to travel these trans-cultural circuits, Spinoza's new multitudes of the displaced – economic migrants, refugees, illegal aliens and asylum seekers, the fall-out from extreme situations of displacement and exclusion everywhere – are also, paradoxically, its advance party, its *avant garde*. Marginality is both unliveable *and* a productive space. The dispossessed disappear from view into the black holes of the migrant metropolis, only to reappear, permanently at risk, but also contingently hybridised, like the trans-gendered and transsexual migrants from Algeria in Kader Attia's work, who have found an illegal refuge in Paris. More and more, we depend on writers, artists, film-makers, musicians and video-makers to map this emergent cartography, to report on its shifting outlines, and to bring us accounts from its dangerous interior depths: contrapuntal figures 'whose writing travels across temporal, cultural and ideological boundaries in unforeseen ways to emerge as part of a new ensemble *along with* later history and subsequent art'.[10]

We need to think further about the deeply contradictory effects of the postcolonial maelstrom in Africa, and its global and geoeconomic entanglements, which form the context for this body of work – the shifting tectonic plates, if you like, *below* the surface, which are producing these fracturing effects. Fault lines, Tawadros observes, 'have been etched into the physical fabric of our world' – and, we can add, into its mental landscapes, its social and material relationships, its frame of seeing – 'through the effects of colonialism and postcolonialism, of migration and globalisation'.[11] Can we move from this surface topography of implosion, emergence and emergency to the deeper structures of tectonic upheaval without imposing on the work of art some simple, message, some 'deeper causation', some arbitrary or reductively referential logic?

Colonialism is, in many ways, an old story in Africa, its aftermath long and protracted. The direct colonisation of Africa is largely a nineteenth-century affair. Its brutal impact culminates with the 'high noon' of European imperialism between the 1870s and the First World War when, in a 'scramble for Africa', the imperial powers participated in the massive carve-up of the continent. The pattern laid down then – the opening up and exploitation of the vast, productive land and its natural resources, raw materials, precious minerals, cheap labour and open markets to the advantage of the industrially developed imperial powers – provided the basic template which has shaped much of Africa ever since. Between 1880 and 1914, 'about a quarter of the world's land surface was distributed or redistributed as colonies among a half-dozen states. This represented the climax of the creation of a single global economy, progressively reaching into the most remote corners of the world, an increasingly dense web of economic transactions, communications and movements of goods, money and people linking the developed countries with each other and with the undeveloped world.'[12]

In this period, the empires continued to expand, even if more often under the banner of indirect rule, protectorates, 'spheres of influence', white settlement and the dreaded mandate than by overt colonisation.[13] One historian described these intermediary forms of empire as 'the crudity of conquest draped in the veil of morality'.[14] Many conflict situations which have returned to trouble the world today arise from these later imperial conquests, accretions and settlements – now, of course,

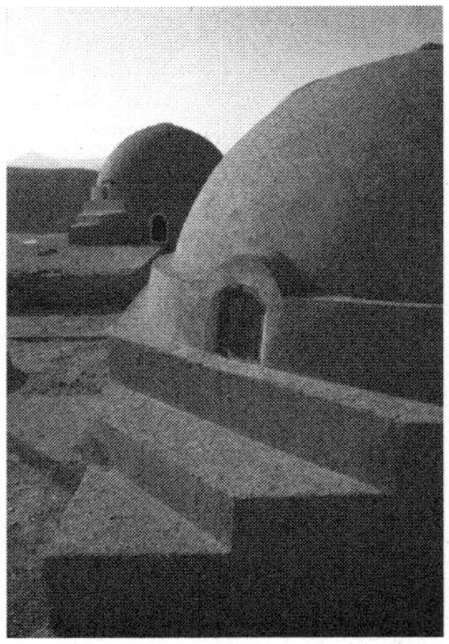

Hassan Fathy, Stoppelaere House, Luxor, Egypt, 1950. © Aga Khan Trust for Culture.

largely forgotten. Many recent conflicts in North and sub-Saharan Africa had their origins here.

Africa, then, was shaped from the beginning by a certain kind of globalisation. That contemporary catchword needs to be contextualised as a historical process, *à longue durée.* In fact, if the age of European exploration and conquest at the end of the fifteenth century was the first, tentative, movement towards globalisation (i.e., what Marx identified as Europe's first steps in the creation of a world market), then naval and trade supremacy was the second, and colonisation, in which trading enclaves were consolidated into colonial possessions and a system of colonial governance, was the third such phase. The late nineteenth-century imperial carve-up constitutes the fourth phase; the inter-war (1918–45) period the fifth; and the collapse of empires, decolonisation and the new postcolonial nations after the Second World War constitutes the sixth phase of the process. The Cold War, when conflicts indigenous to Africa were subordinated to the wider geopolitical and military polarisation between the two rival models of development, was the seventh. The period we are now in, from the mid-1970s onwards – with its global interdependencies, massive financial investment, technological flows and trans-national production, climaxing with the era of neo-liberal globalisation and American Super Power hegemony – is at least the eighth phase of globalisation, understood as a historical process. A careful periodisation could unearth more, although this does not undermine the specific features and distinctions of each phase. The basic point, however, is that, in Africa, and for a very long time, everything has depended on the different ways in which its complex internal histories and regional ecologies have been articulated (one might say, *dis*-articulated) with the changing forms of global capital and imperial rule.

Colonisation, then, was driven by the imperatives and conveniences of imperial interests and colonial governance. Effectively, it erased layer after layer of earlier African historical evolution and its complex cultural formations. It superimposed imperial frontiers, territorial boundaries and Western political institutions on countries arbitrarily defined as colonies, with little reference to their mosaic of tribes, groups, languages and religions, to their intricate histories of conflict and alliances, to their ethnic traditions, ecological regions and land tenures. The anti-imperialist movements which came together after the First World War constitute a unifying cause that fed directly off the growing opposition to this process and drew inspiration from the dream of national restitution, often including the nativist revival of precolonial traditions. However, it was *nationalism* which underpinned the different kinds of independence struggle and provided the basis of the postcolonial nations which emerged.

In recent years, many commentators have come to regard nationalism as a negative force. However, as Edward Said has argued, nationalism, 'as a mobilized political force, instigated and then advanced the struggle against Western domination everywhere in the non-European world. It is no more useful to oppose than to oppose Newton's discovery of gravity.'[15] In a similar vein, Partha Chatterjee observes that 'nationalism challenged colonial rule… administered a check on a specific form of metropolitan capital dominance. In the process, it dealt a death blow to such blatantly ethnic slogans of dominance as the colonizing mission of the West, the white man's burden, etc.'[16]

Nationalism was also a powerfully creative force. It inspired artists, writers, scholars, architects, scientists and critics as well as mobilising the masses. One thinks here of the work of Hassan Fathy, and his project of 'an architecture for the people', revived in the context of the

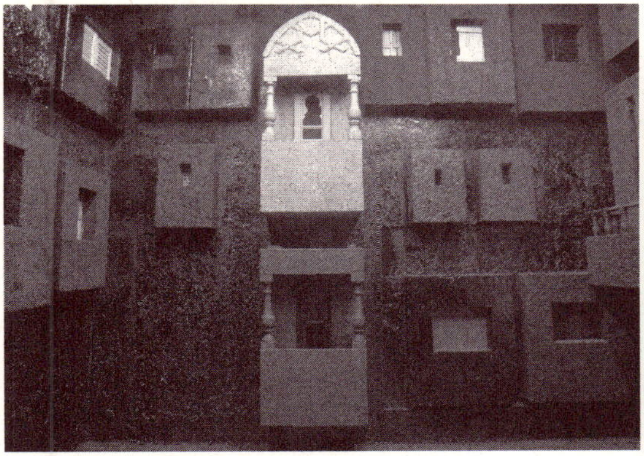

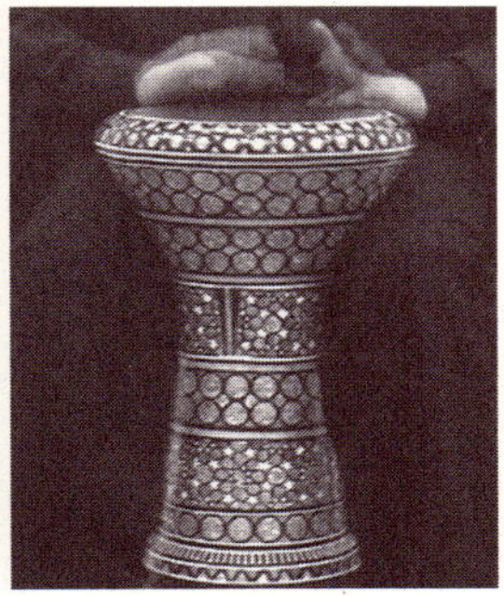

Far left: Wael Shawky, *Sidi El Asphalt's Mulid*, 2001. Installation, asphalt, liquid tar, *gazairya* (traditional Egyptian sweets), silver paint, speakers, projector and mixed media, three rooms, each approx. 440 x 550 x 650cm. Left: Moataz Nasr, *Tabla*, 2003. Video still.

Fault Lines exhibition. Fathy was clearly inspired by the search for some creative synthesis between traditional (especially domestic) Islamic architecture and archiectural modernism. His practice and ideas were deeply grounded in Egyptian secular nationalist aspirations and the break with colonial dependency; and, as Nasser Rabbat points out, the evolution of his work 'mirrors the trajectory of modern Egypt' from 'colonisation to independence to development and its aftermath entangled in grand dreams of regional pre-eminence'.[17] It is difficult to overestimate the surge of national feeling, for example, which accompanied the emergence of Abdel-Nasser in Egypt.

For the latest instalment of this story, however, we have to progress from the utopia of Fathy's urban vision to the shadowing of the stalled project of contemporary Egypt in the dystopian viscosity of Wael Shawky's asphalt and petroleum metropolis. The nationalist project had serious limitations. There was always a tension between its modernising and nativist impulses which remains unresolved. Chatterjee highlights nationalism's failure to resolve the conflict between the idea of the 'people-nation' and metropolitan capital: 'by absorbing the political life of the nation into the body of the state… the state proceeds to find for "the nation" a place in the global order of capital, while striving to keep the contradictions between capital and the people in perpetual suspension'.[18]

The problem, as Frantz Fanon clearly foresaw, was not nationalism as such; he believed the Algerian liberation struggle demanded a moment of 'national consciousness'. The danger was that the project would get stuck there and fail to 'go beyond nationalism' to the deeper social, cultural and political transformations which were its essential tasks. In such circumstances, Fanon predicted, nationalism could undergo 'a process of regression', in which 'the nation is passed over for the race, and the tribe is preferred to the state'.[19] Early anti-imperial and independence leaderships, like those of Nkrumah, Nyerere, Cabral, Mandela, the ANC (African National Congress) and the FLN (Front de Liberation Nationale), had projected a powerful vision for the postcolonial era. However, in 'The Pitfalls of National Consciousness', Fanon foresaw post-independence leaderships 'colonising' the nationalist struggle for their own interests. This elite, he suggested, could become 'the transmission belt between the nation and… capitalism' and the main beneficiaries would be the rising middle classes – the new postcolonial native elites – whom Fanon regarded as a 'national bourgeoisie'. The result, he prophesied, would be the neglect of the countryside, a yawning gap between leaders and people, 'the greatest wealth surrounded by the greatest poverty', where 'scandals are numerous, members of parliament feather their own nests', and everyone is invited to join 'the great procession of corruption'.[20] Moataz Nasr's video installation in *Fault Lines* directly addresses this issue of the gap between politicians and the people in post-nationalist Egypt.

In the degeneration which Fanon predicted, the people would increasingly be regarded 'as a blind force… held in check either by mystification or by the fear inspired by the police force'. The principal agent of this process would be the single political party or 'one-party state' or a populist figure, dictator or military man, providing 'the direction of affairs by a strong authority', which underdeveloped countries were increasingly said to require. Leader, nation, party and people would be absorbed into a single political will, allowing no space for new social forces, real opposition or genuine democratic contestation. Oppositions would be intimidated, critics imprisoned on trumped-up charges, 'brought to heel… by dint of baton charges… condemned first to silence and then to clandestine existence'.[21]

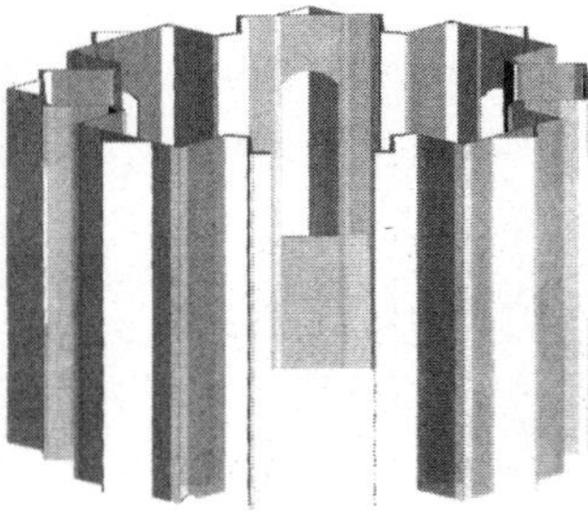

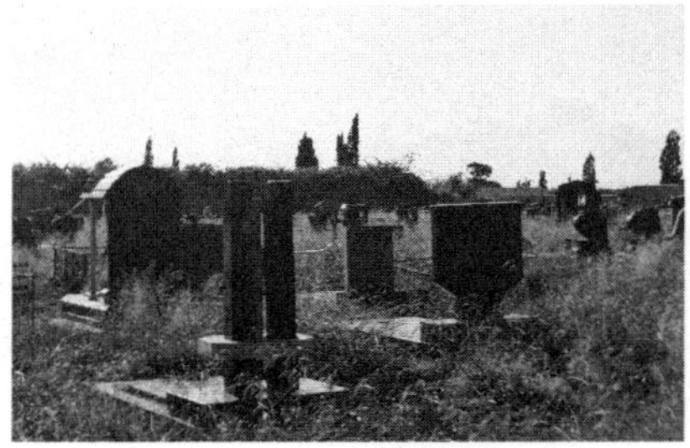

Right: Samta Benyahia, *Le Polygone et le Dédale* (The Polygon and the Maze), work in progress, 2003.
Far right: Pitso Chinzima, *Exitzone*, 2003. Installation.

This was a grim forecast, which may now seem over-drawn and too pessimistic. It was also not a comprehensive picture; it omitted religion, the radicalisation of Islam and religious fundamentalism which were decisive in derailing the nationalist project in Algeria. Samta Benyahia's architectural installation in *Fault Lines,* which looks beyond the political violence that has torn Algeria apart, to a utopian space in which past and present do not always destroy one another, was conceived in response to this trauma. However, in other respects, Fanon's dystopic vision has proved disturbingly prescient about many aspects of the 'crisis of the postcolonial state' or 'postcolony' which has overtaken one African society after another since decolonisation. Without significant social or economic reform, many African postcolonial states have failed to redistribute national resources, improve living standards or raise the prospects of the mass of ordinary people. They have been unable to improve subsistence levels, develop sustainable agriculture, or stabilise the price of raw materials on world markets and their populations are regularly exposed to endemic poverty, malnutrition, ill-health and disease. Millions are without food, education or clean water. Their people have little medical protection against the pandemics – malaria, TB, HIV/AIDS, etc. – that rampage through the continent. A nationalism which cannot deliver to the mass of ordinary people, or project social aspirations and cultural self-images which connect with an indigenous imaginary, has proved incapable of holding the nation together and has increasingly lost its grip on popular hopes and aspirations.

Consequently, in many parts of Africa, internal tensions and conflicts have surfaced, unleashing powerfully fissiparous and disintegrative tendencies in the form of rural/urban, regional, ethnic, tribal, racial and religious conflict. In state after state, the army has become the 'unifying' agent of last resort. Dictators have flourished, elections been rigged, conflict 'ethnicised' and social fragmentation 'militarised'. Torture and imprisonment have become recognised instruments of governance. Weak governments are challenged by military coups, armed rivals for state power, insurgent regional breakaways, lawless militias, invading foreign armies. Increasingly, this crisis of the postcolonial state in Africa has assumed the form of civil unrest, tribal warfare, ethnic cleansing and the killing fields of civil war. The work of Pitso Chinzima and Veliswa Gwintsa, of Salem Mekuria and of Laylah Ali all speak eloquently if obliquely to these developments.

The inevitable effect has been the mass displacement of peoples – the homeless multitudes on the move, the burgeoning temporary 'geography' of refugee and transit camps, the flight from impending violence and lawlessness, abandoning homes, families, cattle and land. A host of outside forces have a hand in this crisis – the old colonising powers, foreign investors and banks, the international arms trade, 'development' agencies, NGOs (non-governmental organisations), aid and humanitarian programmes.

This is the profoundly contradictory ground of *the postcolonial,* to which the work of the *Fault Lines* artists manifestly belongs. The term 'postcolonial' signals, at one and the same time, the continuing hope that real freedom, popular democracy and economic change may one day come to Africa despite its present travail *and* the recognition of the 'states of emergency' into which many parts of the continent have been propelled. Certainly it references a temporal process: postcolonial = what followed after colonialism. But, as I have tried to suggest, this cannot mean that colonialism and its effects are *finished*, in the wider sense of 'completed and settled'. 'After' also means 'in the aftermath' of colonialism – caught in its wake, exposed to its after-effects, which

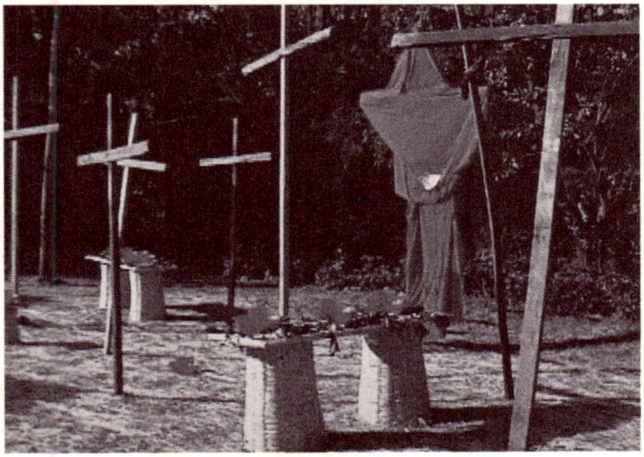

Salem Mekuria, *RUPTURES: A Many Sided Story*, 2003. Video still of 2003 installation by Bekele Mekonnen.

continue in significantly transformed ways. We must think of the emergence of the postcolonial as a *passage of forms*, rather than the mere passing of time.

The postcolonial therefore marks out, not the successful conclusion of the colonial order, but the opening of a new stage in the relationships of postcolonial dependency. We find 'the persistence of many of the effects associated with colonization, but at the same time their *displacement* from the colonizer/colonized axis and their [projection inwards or] *internalization* within de-colonized society itself'.[22] External problems of colonial domination are now reworked and lived as internal crises of the postcolonial state. At the same time, the relations of dependency become more global. Conflicts which at an earlier point could be staged as a struggle between the emergent 'people-nation' and the external coloniser are replaced by a more complex set of struggles between weak 'independent' states, the different forces struggling for ascendancy *within* postcolonial society, and the connections of this whole complex to the neo-liberal global capitalist system and the geopolitical, US-dominated 'new world order'. An example here is the war of liberation led by the Algerian FLN against the French. After independence, this became a more complex struggle between social, national, secular and Islamist forces within Algeria, further complicated by a shift in Algeria's continuing postcolonial relationships with France (e.g., the problem of North African migrants, the 'differential racism' experienced by this diaspora and the rise of an anti-immigrant racist politics). Now, also, the political crisis of the Algerian state and of the French Algerian metropolitan diaspora is reworked through the new geopolitics dominated by a post-11 September, US-led 'global war on terror'. In this scenario, 'the colonial' is not yet dead, since it lives on in its neo-imperial, postcolonial and globalised forms and after-effects.

This rightly shifts the focus in the crisis of the postcolonial from the shortcomings of the independence movements and the contradictions of nationalism to the larger question of the continuing relations of *dependency* which link postcolonial Africa to the developed world. We can identify at least three stages. First, neo-colonialism, locking dependency to underdevelopment in ways identified by the dependency theorists. Second, the Cold War, when Africa's complex internal crises became subordinated to the East-West struggle, its governments became 'clients' of the Super Powers and inter-continental rivalries were fought out by proxy on African terrain. Third, in more recent times, the era of neo-liberalism and globalisation, which has redefined the relations of subordination between African societies and the global capitalist and geopolitical system as a whole. These articulations set the framework for the so-called failure of the postcolony in Africa.

This most recent phase of globalisation is the free market, neo-liberal system of worldwide interdependencies and global flows which began to emerge in the mid-1970s. At its heart are the new multinational corporations, set free from national boundaries and constraints, with their trans-national systems of production, directly linking the capital interests of the 'North' to the cheap labour reserves and favourable investment regimes of the 'South'.[23] This is underpinned by the massively enhanced financial and investment flows, powered by the information technology revolution and the spreading net of global consumption sponsored by global media and the cultural industries, promoting the gospel of Western lifestyles among poor and hungry communities. These linkages and space-time condensations rework the profound gaps between rich/developed and poor/developing countries into a highly uneven and unequal but more globally integrated and interdependent 'world system'.

Some developing societies – the 'Tigers' of South-East Asia, for example – have managed to ride the globalisation tide with some success. But they had a larger manufacturing and trade base to start from and greater reserves of indigenous capital to partner foreign investment. Besides, their development has depended upon a massive state intervention, often without replicating much of the political infrastructure of democratic elections, rule of law, free speech and human rights conditions which successful free markets are supposed to require. Africa, with its overwhelmingly rural background, has not been so lucky.

The new system does not follow the old lines of colonial connection. The globe has become an open, borderless market. The trans-national corporations and their financial supporters can influence the shape of development simply by their power in world markets, their capacity to switch funds globally to wherever the most favourable terms-of-trade conditions prevail, as well as by buying directly into productive enterprises or setting up branches of productive activity locally and integrating them globally. In Africa, their principal effect has been to stimulate large-scale agricultural and cash-crop production, at the expense of subsistence agriculture which feeds people and sustains incomes and local employment. Also, the large-scale extraction of raw materials for export is at the mercy of world commodity prices, which have been systematically falling as the foreign extraction companies are able to scour world markets for the lowest prices. Western agri-businesses are free to push open aggressively foreign markets at the expense of indigenous production and to dump surpluses which – counter to free trade gospel – are massively subsidised and sold below cost.[24] The trans-nationals manage rural economies at a distance by supplying high-cost fertilisers and by patenting plant and seed varieties and other genetic sequences which give them effective control over what and when local farmers can plant. They promote free market criteria, at the expense of ecological sustainability. Famine in East Africa was used to introduce genetically modified food, against local demand. But the pharmaceutical companies continue to keep prices of 'priceless' drugs high and tobacco companies dump the most carcinogenic cigarettes cheap on unsuspecting young smokers in urban Africa. The mining and raw material resources are extracted within fortified, high-wage enclaves and integrated into global markets, in whose profitability local elites may participate but from which governments derive little (and much of what they receive leaks away into private bank accounts or to the international illegal traders and arms merchants).

The central feature of this globalised system, however, is the way it has been coupled with or harnessed to the emerging structure of global governance and international 'regulation' (sic). The stage was set by the 'structural adjustment' programmes imposed by the International Monetary Fund (IMF) and the World Bank on one African government after another. The underlying purpose was to 'shrink the role of the state and soften markets for private investors'.[25] This strategy effectively ruled Africa, a continent in desperate need, out of the whole idea of a 'social wage' (the funding of public health-care, education, food and other welfare and development programmes out of taxation). It mercilessly promoted market fundamentalism at the expense of the notion of public goods.

Once restructured in this way, postcolonial states were deemed eligible for huge international bank loans, the effect of which, as we know, was to cripple them in massive debt. They were required to open their borders, to encourage foreign investment, to deregulate markets and labour conditions, to let market forces operate freely and to participate in free trade as if on a level playing field

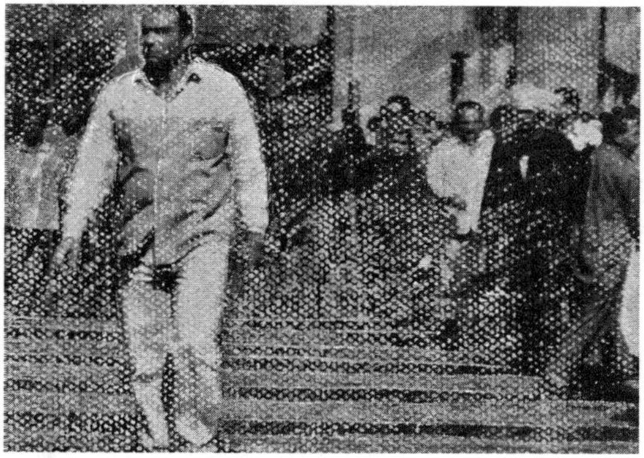

Sabah Naim, *Untitled*, 2003. Mixed media. Photograph: Muhammad Saif.

with their much wealthier, more powerful and already developed international competitors. Wealth, they were assured, would eventually trickle down. This was the full neo-liberal, free market, fundamentalist programme. The World Trade Organisation (WTO), the IMF and the World Bank have been driving the latest phase of deregulation – the privatisation of public utilities and services – which has vigorously promoted the sell-off of water, power and electricity, educational and health-care public services to private interests, especially foreign utility corporations, of which the infamous ENRON was only one example. They then restrict supplies, raise charges and oblige local authorities to purchase these goods privately.

This is the heart of the new global capitalist system as its bears down on Africa. Its powerful driving centres continue to lie primarily in the developed Western societies. But it is no longer a simple North/South affair, since it includes new kinds of profitable arrangement or 'contract' between private foreign capital and the growing business elites of the developing world. In this sense, it is a less 'territorialised', more trans-national affair, a world without fixed centres in the old spatialised sense because its sites of power and wealth are multiple and ultimately globally disseminated: what Hardt and Negri called a new kind of 'empire'.[26]

As the Cold War recedes and the US emerges as the single military and economic Super Power, its dominant role, though of course globally based, becomes more manifest. A borderless world, in which the conditions of a free market, free trade, corporate-inclined system must be permanently secured, and its fruits unequally delivered, is increasingly a dangerous, restless, envious and fissiparous one, potentially fracturing violently along several fault lines at once. Its frontiers now lie on the banks of the Tigris, in the Bearing Straits, on the Red Sea, in the Horn of Africa, at the tourist resorts of the Pacific and along the oil pipelines from Uzbekistan.

Although the system ideally works without direct intervention – at a distance, through the hidden hand of the free market – since 11 September, a new interventionism has emerged. Founded on the absolute sanctity of Western interests and values, it is guided by the new doctrine of pre-emptive strikes and organised ideologically along the Manichean lines of 'with us – or with the terrorists'. Intervention is judged legitimate, not only to deal with terrorist threats, to police the peripheries and destroy any opposition 'by overwhelming force', but also but to stabilise, long-term, whole regions of the globe: to precipitate regime-change where necessary; to reconstruct so-called 'traditional' societies into Western-style 'liberal democracies'; to secure key markets and raw material supplies; and, above all, to ensure the general conditions favourable to 'peaceful' investment by international capital and the universal hegemony of Western values. The dream of a multi-polar world, which the word 'globalisation' ambiguously carried, has disappeared. This is 'the new world order', neo-liberal globalisation's new *civilisational mission.*

What all this means for Africa – and for African art – we have still to see. But the anticipatory shockwaves of the crisis are already registering at some seismic levels in global culture. In Sabah Naim's film installations, for example, she intervenes directly in the image, scratching and scarring it to bring out the violent contemporary disjuncture between the global media and the minutiae of daily existence in the postcolony. In this and other ways, *Fault Lines* invites us not only to read the fractured lines and what they mean, but to read *between them*, for the intimations they offer of our uncertain futures.

Need for Unity

Gamal Abdel-Nasser

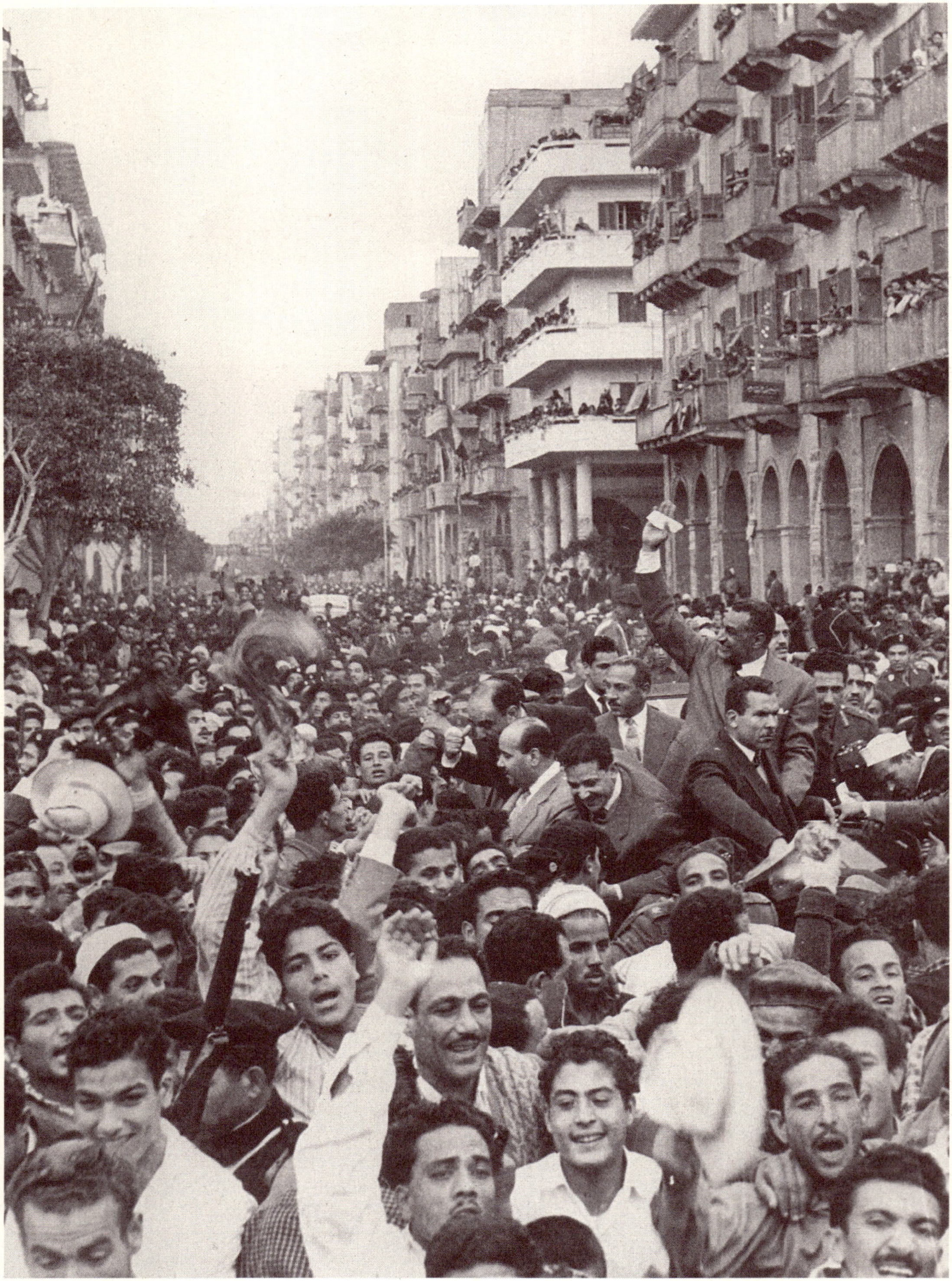

Anonymous, *Gamal Abdel-Nasser Carried by the Crowd, Port Said, Egypt*, Collection Amr Sherif/FAI. © Fondation Arabe pour l'Image.

Now I revert to what I was saying, that Imperialism is the great power laying round the whole of this region a siege incomparably more vigorous and more rigorous than the siege that had surrounded our trenches in Faluja and all our armies and governments in the capitals from which we received our orders.

I began to believe, after all these facts had become firmly established in my mind, in one common struggle.

I said to myself that since the region is one and the same with the same conditions, the same problems, the same future and the same enemy, no matter how different the masks he might wear in an endeavour to conceal his identity, why should our efforts be dissipated?

The experiences we have gone through after July 23 have manifestly demonstrated the pressing need for a common struggle and considerably corroborated this theory.

The hidden features of the picture have begun to be revealed – the darkness enshrouding them has begun to be dissipated.

But I must admit I also began to see the great obstacles that barred the way to a common struggle. But I began at the same time to believe, however, that these same obstacles should disappear for the simple reason that they were the work of that very same enemy.

I actually began political contacts to ensure the unification of the struggle, whatever the means to be adopted, and came out of these contacts with one important result. I found that the main obstacle that lay in our way was doubt, and it was manifest that the needs of this doubt had been implanted in our souls by that one and same enemy to stand between us and that common struggle.

I remember I recently sat talking to a friend – an Arab politician. A colleague of his was also present. I began to talk, and he began to reply to my statement.

Every time he spoke he turned to his colleague to see the effect of his words on him, instead of trying to find out their effect on me.

I remember I counselled him to cast away his doubts and open his heart to me, looking me straight in the eye, and not looking the other way.

I am not trying to lessen the gravity of the obstacles that bar the way to the unification of the struggle. There is no doubt some of them are of a complicated nature extending in their origin to the geographical position and historical circumstances of the countries themselves and the external conditions and influences affecting the life of their peoples. But I am sure with [a] little flexibility, based on far-sightedness – not on carelessness – a front could be formed in which all would, without any equivocation or bias, stand in readiness to carry out the common struggle.

Sources of Strength

I do not doubt for a moment that our united struggle will realise for us and for our peoples all we desire and hope for them.

I shall always continue to emphasise that we are strong. But the great tragedy is that we do not realise the extent of our strength.

We, however, make a mistake in defining strength. To shout at the top of one's voice is not strength. Real strength lies in acting positively with all the determination and power you possess.

When I come to analyse the elements of our strength, I cannot help being struck by three sources standing in bold relief, which should be taken into account before everything else.

The first of these sources lies in the fact that we are a group of neighbouring nations welded into a homogeneous whole by every possible material and moral tie that would unite any such a group of nations.

Moreover, our peoples possess peculiarities, potentialities and a civilisation inspired by the spiritual principles of the three divine religions which can never be overlooked in any attempt to build a new stable and peaceful world.

Thus much for the first source.

The second source is our land itself, and the position it occupies on the map of the world – that important strategic position which rightly makes of it the world's crossroads – the main route of its trade and the highway of its armies.

There remains the third source. This is oil – oil which is considered the back-bone of material civilisation, and without which all the world's largest factories, all means of land, sea and air communication, all war weapons, be they the fighters and bombers flying high above the clouds or the submarines diving deep into the unfathomable depths of the ocean, would become mere iron blocks, devoid of motive power and rusty.

I should like to dwell on the subject of oil. Perhaps its existence as a concrete fact, established by statistics and figures may serve as an ideal basis for [a] discussion on the importance of our sources of strength.

I have recently read a report published by the Chicago University on oil. I wish every Arab would have the occasion of reading that report, grasping its meaning and meditating upon the great moral that lies behind its figures and statistics.

That report states, for instance, that prospecting for oil in Arab countries does not entail much expense.

Oil companies had spent sixty million dollars in Colombia since 1916 to strike oil only in 1938.

These companies had spent forty-four million dollars in Venezuela to strike oil only after fifteen years.

These companies had also spent thirty-nine million dollars in the Dutch East Indies before they finally succeeded in striking oil.

The final results recorded in that report were:

- The capital required for the extraction of one barrel of oil in the United States is 78 cents.
- The capital required for the extraction of one barrel of oil in South America is 48 cents.
- The capital required for the extraction of one barrel of oil in the Arab countries is only 10 cents.

The centre of world oil production has shifted from the United States, where oil wells have been exhausted, land prices have risen and wages have increased, to the Arab regions where oil wells are still untapped, vast tracts of land can be had for next to nothing, and labour is incredibly cheap.

It has been established that half of the world's known oil reserves lie buried in the Arab zone. The other half is distributed among the United States, Russia, the Caribbean zone and other world areas.

It has also been established that the average daily output of an oil well is 11 barrels in the United States, 230 barrels in Venezuela and 4,000 barrels in the Arab zone.

If I have succeeded in explaining the extent of the importance of this vital element of strength, as I sincerely hope I have, it would thus follow that we are strong – strong not through wailing, shouting or appealing for help at the top of our voices, but strong through our composure, or our correct estimation, supported by figures, of our capacity for work, and our true understanding of the strength of the ties that bind our peoples together, those ties which make of our homeland an integral and indivisible whole, which should be defended as such and not as an isolated unit.

Thus much for the First Circle – the Arab Circle within the framework of which we should endeavour to turn, move and act with all our force.

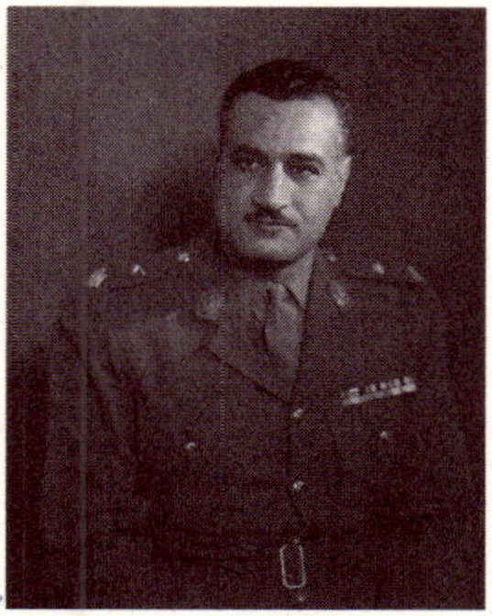

Armand, *Gamal Abdel-Nasser*, Cairo, Egypt 1950-52. Collection Armand/FAI. © Fondation Arabe pour l'Image.

As for the Second Circle – the African Continent Circle – I should say, without the necessity of going into details, that we cannot under any condition even if we wanted to, stand aloof from the terrible and terrifying battle now raging in the heart of that Continent between five million whites and two hundred million Africans.

We cannot stand aloof for one important and obvious reason – we ourselves are in Africa.

Surely the people of Africa will continue to look at us – we who are the guardians of the Continent's northern gate, we who constitute the connecting link between the Continent and the outer world.

We certainly cannot, under any condition, relinquish our responsibility to help to our utmost in spreading the light of knowledge and civilisation up to the very depth of the virgin jungles of the Continent.

There remains another equally important reason – the Nile, the life artery of our country, springs from the heart of the Continent.

There still remains one more reason – the beloved Sudan, whose boundaries extend to the heart of the Continent and which is bound by neighbourly relations with the sensitive spots in its centre.

There is no denying the fact that Africa is now the scene of a strange and stirring commotion. The white man, who represents several European nations, is again trying to change the map of the Continent. We surely cannot under any condition stand as mere onlookers, deluding ourselves into the belief that we are in no way concerned with these machinations.

Indeed, I shall continue to dream of the day on which I shall see in Cairo a great Africa Institute, seeking to reveal to us the various aspects of the Continent, to create in our minds an enlightened African consciousness, and to associate itself with all those working in all parts of the world for the progress, prosperity and welfare of the peoples of Africa.

There remains the Third Circle – the circle encompassing continents and oceans which, as I have said, is the circle of our Brethren-in-Islam who, wherever their place under the sun, turn with us towards the same Qibla, their lips solemnly saying the same prayers.

My faith in the magnitude of the positive effectiveness that could result from strengthening the Islamic tie that binds all Moslems grew stronger when I accompanied the Egyptian mission to Saudi Arabia to offer condolences on the death of its great King.

As I stood before the Qaaba, with my thoughts wandering round every part of the world which Islam has reached, I fully realised the need for a radical change of our conception of the Pilgrimage.

I said to myself: 'The journey to the Qaaba should no longer be construed as an admission card to Paradise, or as a crude attempt to buy forgiveness of sins after leading a dissipated life.'

The Pilgrimage should have a potential political power. The world Press should hasten to follow and feature its news not by drawing attractive pen pictures of its rites and rituals for the delectation of readers, but by its representation as a periodical political conference at which the heads of all the Islamic States, leaders of opinion, scientists, eminent industrialists and prominent business men assemble to draw up at this world Islamic Parliament the broad lines of the policies to be adopted by their respective countries and lay down the principles ensuring their close co-operation until they have gathered together in the following session.

They assemble demure and devout, but mighty, strong; unambitious of power, but active and full of energy; submissive to Divine Will, but immutable in difficulties and implacable with their enemies.

They assemble confirmed believers in the Life to Come, but are equally convinced that they have a place under the sun which they should occupy.

I remember I expressed some of these views to His Majesty King Saud.

His Majesty assented saying, 'Truly this is the real purpose of the Pilgrimage'.

To tell the truth I personally cannot think of any other conception.

As I contemplate the eighty million Moslems in Indonesia, the fifty million in China, the few millions in Malaya, Thailand and Burma, the hundred million in Pakistan, the well nigh over hundred million in the Middle East, the forty million in the Soviet Union, and the millions of others in other remote and far-flung corners of the earth – as I ponder over these hundreds of millions of Moslems, all welded into a homogenous whole by the same Faith, I come out increasingly conscious of the potential achievements co-operation among all these millions can accomplish – co-operation naturally not going beyond their loyalty to their original countries, but which will ensure for them and their Brethren-in-Islam unlimited power.

I then once more revert to the role which is still wandering in search of an exponent. That is our role, and those are its features, and that is its stage. And it is we, and we alone, in virtue of our position, who can play the part.

I Speak of Freedom: A Statement of African Ideology

Kwame Nkrumah

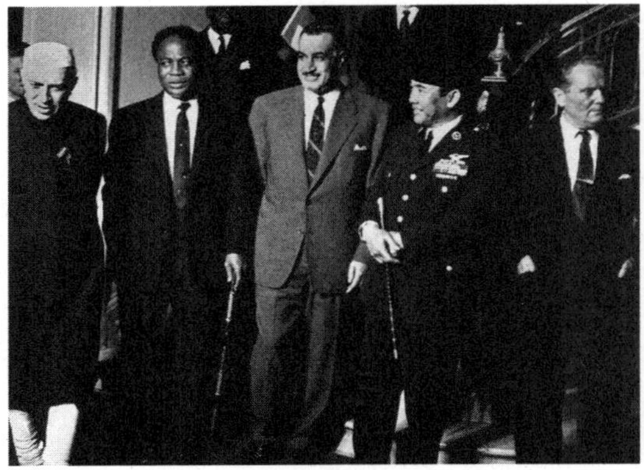

Five Top Neutralist Countries Meet, Yugoslavia, 29 September 1960. From left to right: Prime Minister Pandit Jawaharlal Nehru of India, President Kwame Nkrumah of Ghana, President Gamal Abdel-Nasser of the United Arab Republic of Egypt, President Sukarno of Indonesia and President Tito of Yugoslavia. © Bettmann/CORBIS.

The movement for independence in Africa which gained momentum after the Second World War has spread like a prairie fire throughout the length and breadth of Africa. The clear, ringing call for freedom which the eight independent states of Africa sounded in Accra in April 1958, followed by the All-African People's Conference in December of that year, stirred up the demand for independence from Conakry to Mogadishu, from Fort Lamy to Leopoldville. The 'wind of change' has become a raging hurricane, sweeping away the old colonialist Africa. The year 1960 was Africa's year. In that year alone, seventeen African States emerged as proud and independent sovereign nations. Now the ultimate freedom of the whole of Africa can no more be in doubt.

For centuries, Europeans dominated the African continent. The white man arrogated to himself the right to rule and to be obeyed by the non-white; his mission, he claimed, was to 'civilise' Africa. Under this cloak, the Europeans robbed the continent of vast riches and inflicted unimaginable suffering on the African people.

All this makes a sad story, but now we must be prepared to bury the past with its unpleasant memories and look to the future. All we ask of the former colonial powers is their goodwill and co-operation to remedy past mistakes and injustices and to grant independence to the colonies in Africa.

The new African nations from the very nature of things cannot but be economically weak at the early stages of their nationhood as compared with the older and long established nations of the world. The long dependence on European and American financial and technical enterprise has prevented the growth of local capital and the requisite technical knowledge to develop their resources. They need economic help, but in seeking outside aid they lay themselves open to a grave new danger which not merely threatens but could even destroy their hard-won freedom.

It is unreasonable to suppose that any foreign power, affluent enough to give aid to an African state, would not expect some measure of consideration or favour from the state receiving the aid. History has shown how one colonial empire in liquidation can easily be replaced by another, more insidious, because it is a disguised form of colonialism. The fate of those territories in Europe and North Africa which once formed the Turkish Empire is a warning to Africa today. It would be a tragedy if the initial weakness of the emergent African nations should lead to a new foreign domination of Africa brought about by economic forces.

It may be argued that the existence of the United Nations Organisation offers a guarantee for the independence and the territorial integrity of all states, whether big or small. In actual fact, however, the U.N. is just as reliable an instrument for world order and peace as the Great Powers are prepared to allow it to be. The present division of the world into rival blocs, and the dictates of power politics, offer little hope that this international body will ever become an effective instrument for world peace. Recent events in the Congo have not helped to foster confidence in the U.N. in the face of Great Power interests. Patrice Lumumba, democratically elected Prime Minister of the Congo Republic, who himself invited the U.N. to the Congo, was murdered along with two of his Ministers because the U.N. failed in its mission to maintain law and order.

It is clear that we must find an African solution to our problems; and that this can only be found in African unity. Divided we are weak; united, Africa could become one of the greatest forces for good in the world.

Although most Africans are poor, our continent is potentially extremely rich. Our mineral resources, which are being exploited with foreign capital only to enrich foreign investors, range from gold and diamonds to uranium and petroleum. Our forests contain some of

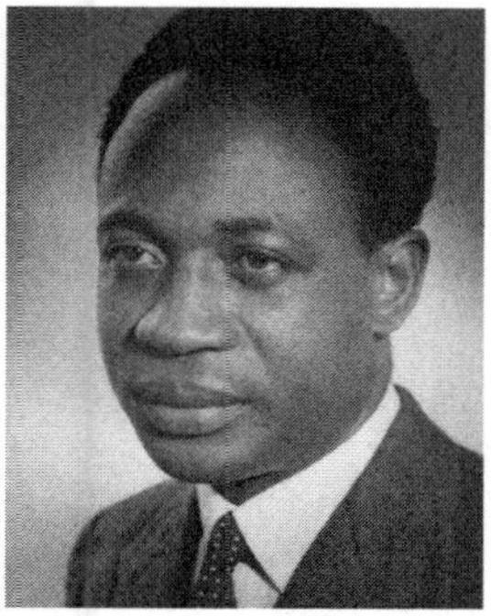

President Kwame Nkrumah of Ghana. Foreign and Commonwealth Library Collection (Ghana/23) © Crown copyright material reproduced with the permission of the Controller of Her Majesty's Stationery Office and Queen's Printer for Scotland.

the finest woods to be grown anywhere. Our cash crops include cocoa, coffee, rubber, tobacco and cotton. As for power, which is an important factor in any economic development, Africa contains over 40% of the total potential water power of the world, as compared with about 10% in Europe and 13% in North America. Yet so far, less than 1% has been developed. This is one of the reasons why we have in Africa the paradox of poverty in the midst of plenty, and scarcity in the midst of abundance.

Never before have a people had within their grasp so great an opportunity for developing a continent endowed with so much wealth. Individually, the independent states of Africa, some of them potentially rich, others poor, can do little for their people. Together, by mutual help, they can achieve much. But the economic development of the continent must be planned and pursued as a whole. A loose confederation designed only for economic co-operation would not provide the necessary unity of purpose. Only a strong political union can bring about full and effective development of our natural resources for the benefit of our people.

The political situation in Africa today is heartening and at the same time disturbing. It is heartening to see so many new flags hoisted in place of the old; it is disturbing to see so many countries of varying sizes and at different levels of development, weak and, in some cases, almost helpless. If this terrible state of fragmentation is allowed to continue it may well be disastrous for us all.

There are at present some 28 states in Africa, excluding the Union of South Africa, and those countries not yet free. No less than nine of these states have a population of less than three million. Can we seriously believe that the colonial powers meant these countries to be independent, viable states? The example of South America, which has as much wealth, if not more than North America, and yet remains weak and dependent on outside interests, is one which every African would do well to study.

Critics of African unity often refer to the wide differences in culture, language and ideas in various parts of Africa. This is true, but the essential fact remains that we are all Africans, and have a common interest in the independence of Africa. The difficulties presented by questions of language, culture and different political systems are not insuperable. If the need for political union is agreed by us all, then the will to create it is born; and where there's a will there's a way.

The present leaders of Africa have already shown a remarkable willingness to consult and seek advice among themselves. Africans have, indeed, begun to think continentally. They realise that they have much in common, both in their past history, in their present problems and in their future hopes. To suggest that the time is not yet ripe for considering a political union of Africa is to evade the facts and ignore realities in Africa today.

The greatest contribution that Africa can make to the peace of the world is to avoid all the dangers inherent in disunity, by creating a political union which will also, by its success, stand as an example to a divided world. A union of African states will project more effectively the African personality. It will command respect from a world that has regard only for size and influence. The scant attention paid to African opposition to the French atomic tests in the Sahara, and the ignominious spectacle of the U.N. in the Congo quibbling about constitutional niceties while the Republic was tottering into anarchy, are evidence of the callous disregard of African Independence by the Great Powers.

We have to prove that greatness is not to be measured in stock piles of atom bombs. I believe strongly and sincerely that with the deep-rooted wisdom and dignity, the innate respect for human lives, the intense humanity that is our heritage, the African race, united under one federal government, will emerge not as just another world bloc to flaunt its wealth and strength, but as a Great Power whose greatness is indestructible because it is built not on fear, envy and suspicion, nor won at the expense of others, but founded on hope, trust, friendship and directed to the good of all mankind.

The emergence of such a mighty stabilising force in this strife-worn world should be regarded not as the shadowy dream of a visionary, but as a practical proposition, which the peoples of Africa can, and should, translate into reality. There is a tide in the affairs of every people when the moment strikes for political action. Such was the moment in the history of the United States of America when the Founding Fathers saw beyond the petty wranglings of the separate states and created a Union. This is our chance. We must act now. Tomorrow may be too late and the opportunity will have passed, and with it the hope of free Africa's survival.

Provisional Notes on the Postcolony

Achille Mbembe

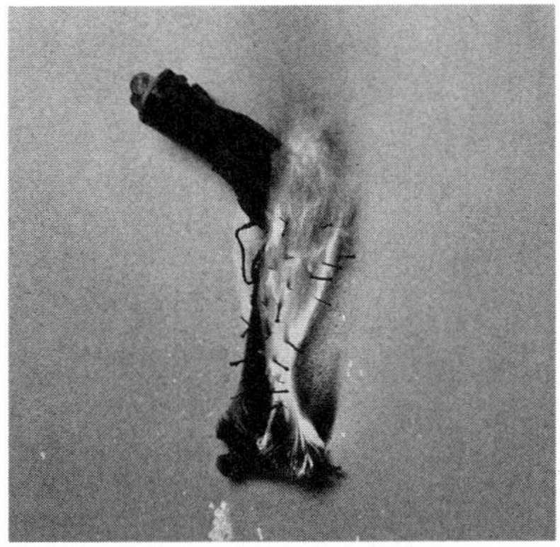

Fernando Alvim, *Xingula*, 1994. Mixed media, 100 x 100 x 100cm.

In this article I will examine the banality of power in the 'postcolony'. By banality of power I am not simply referring to the way bureaucratic formalities or arbitrary rules, implicit or explicit, have been multiplied, nor am I simply concerned with what has become routine, though certainly 'banality' implies the predictability of routine if only because it is made up of repeated daily actions and gestures. Instead I am referring here to those elements of the obscene and grotesque that Mikhail Bakhtin claims to have located in 'non-official' cultures but which in fact are intrinsic to all systems of domination and to the means by which those systems are confirmed or deconstructed.[1]

The notion 'postcolony' identifies specifically a given historical trajectory – that of societies recently emerging from the experience of colonisation and the violence which the colonial relationship, *par excellence*, involves. To be sure, the postcolony is chaotically pluralistic, yet it has nonetheless an internal coherence. It is a specific system of signs, a particular way of fabricating simulacra or re-forming stereotypes. It is not, however, just an economy of signs in which power is mirrored and *imagined* self-reflectively. The postcolony is characterised by a distinctive style of political improvisation, by a tendency to excess and a lack of proportion as well as by distinctive ways in which identities are multiplied, transformed and put into circulation.[2] But the postcolony is also made up of a series of corporate institutions and a political machinery which, once they are in place, constitute a distinctive regime of violence. In this sense, the postcolony is a particularly revealing (and rather dramatic) stage on which are played out the wider problems of subjection and its corollary, discipline.

In a postcolony of this kind, then, I am concerned with the ways in which state power (1) *creates*, through its administrative and bureaucratic practices, a world of meanings all its own, a master code which, in the process of becoming the society's primary central code, ends by governing – perhaps paradoxically – the various logics that underlie all other meanings within that society; (2) attempts to institutionalise its world of meanings as a 'socio-historical world'[3] and to make that world fully real, turning it into a part of people's common sense not only by instilling it in the minds of the *cibles*, or 'target population',[4] but also by integrating it into the consciousness of the period.

The basic argument of this article is that, in order to account for both the mind-set and the effectiveness of postcolonial relations of power, we need to go beyond the binary categories used in standard interpretations of domination, such as resistance *v.* passivity, autonomy *v.* subjection, state *v.* civil society, hegemony *v.* counter-hegemony, totalisation *v.* detotalisation. These oppositions are not helpful;[5] rather, they cloud our understanding of postcolonial relations.[6] In the postcolony the *commandement*[7] seeks to institutionalise itself, in order to achieve legitimation and hegemony (*recherche hégémonique*), in the form of a *fetish*.[8] The signs, vocabulary and narratives that it produces are not meant merely to be symbols; they are officially invested with a surplus of meanings which are not negotiable and which one is officially forbidden to depart from or challenge. So as to ensure that no such challenge takes place, the champions of state power invent entire constellations of ideas; they adopt a distinct set of cultural repertoires and powerfully evocative concepts;[9] but they also have resort, if necessary, to the systematic application of pain.[10] The basic goal is not just to bring a specific political consciousness into being but to make it effective. We therefore need to examine the way the world of meanings thus produced is ordered, the types of institutions, the knowledges, norms and practices that structure this new 'common sense' as well as the light that the use of visual imagery and discourse throws on the nature of domination and subordination....

It is only through such a shift in perspective that we can come to understand that the postcolonial relationship is not primarily a relationship of resistance or of collaboration but can best be characterised as illicit cohabitation, a relationship made fraught by the very fact of the *commandement* and its 'subjects' having to share the same living space. It is precisely this logic – the necessary familiarity and domesticity in the relationship – that explains why there has not been (as might otherwise have been expected from those so dominated) the resistance or the accommodation, the disengagement or the 'refusal to be captured', the contradiction between overt acts and gestures in public and the covert responses made 'underground' (*sous maquis*). Instead, it has resulted in the mutual zombification of both the dominant and those whom they apparently dominate. This zombification meant that each robbed the other of their vitality and has left them both impotent (*impouvoir*).

The examples to be offered in this article indeed suggest that the postcolony is made up not of one single 'public space' but of several, each having its own separate logic yet nonetheless liable to be entangled with other logics when operating in certain specific contexts: hence the postcolonial 'subject' has had to learn to bargain in this conceptual market place. Furthermore, subjects in the postcolony have also had to have a marked ability to manage not just a single identity for themselves but several, which are flexible enough for them to negotiate as and when required....[11]

Excess, and the Creativity of Abuse[12]

A few additional explanatory remarks are necessary. First, there is the question of the grotesque and the obscene being used as means of erecting, ratifying or demonstrating particular regimes of violence and domination. In a study devoted to what has been termed 'political derision' in Togo, C. Toulabour shows how, under one-party rule, people developed ways of separating words or phrases off from their conventional meanings and using them in quite another sense. He illustrates how they thus built up a whole vocabulary, equivocal and ambiguous, that ran parallel to the official discourse. Togo was until recently the perfect example of postcolonial construction....

Thus there were avenues of escape from the *commandement*, and whole areas of social discourse eluded control, for longer or shorter periods of time. Verbal acts of this kind offer some good examples – and are excellent indices of what can be considered commonplace (and hence banal). For instance, when Togolese were called upon to shout the party slogans, many would travesty the metaphors meant to glory state power. With a simple tonal shift, one metaphor could take on many meanings. Under cover, therefore, of official slogans, people sang about the sudden erection of the 'enormous' and 'rigid' presidential phallus, of how it remained in this position and of its contact with 'vaginal fluids'. 'The powerful key of Eyadéma penetrates the keyhole. People, applaud!' 'Eat your portion, Paul Biya,' echoed the Cameroonians, making allusion to the intensified prebendalisation[13] of their state since 1982, when Ahidjo resigned and was replaced constitutionally by his former Prime Minister....

The obsession with orifices, odours and genital organs came to dominate Togolese popular laughter. But the same is also to be found in writings and speech in other sub-Saharan countries.... The emphasis on orifices and protuberances has to be understood in relation to two factors especially. The first derives from the fact that the *commandement* in the postcolony has a marked taste for lecherous living. Festivities and celebrations, in this regard, are the two key vehicles for indulging the taste.

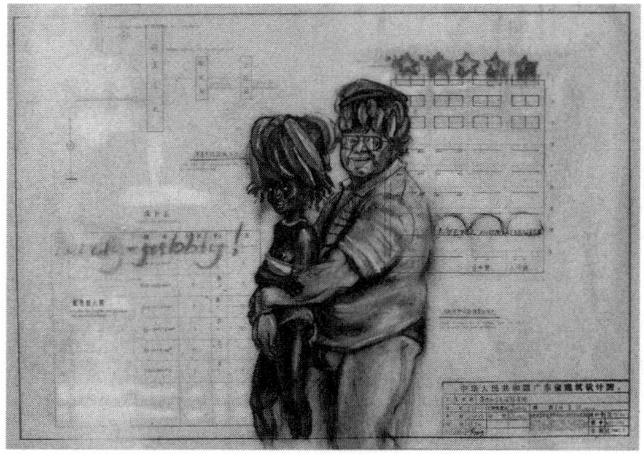

Johannes Phokela, *Lovely Jubbly*, 2002. Oil on tracing paper, 84 x 60cm.

But the idiom of its organisation and its symbolism focus, above all, on the mouth, the belly and the phallus....[14] 'Mouth', 'belly', 'phallus', when used in popular speech and jokes, have above all to be located in the real world, located in real time, as play, as fun. In short, they are active statements about the human condition, and as such contribute integrally to the making of political culture in the postcolony. Every reference, then, to mouth, belly or phallus is consequently a discourse on the world and on death, a means of auto-interpretation, and of negotiating that interpretation and the forces which may shape it....

Is it enough to say that the postcolonial subject, as a *homo ludens*, is simply making fun of the *commandement*, making it an object of derision, as would seem to be the case if we were to apply Bakhtin's categories? To a large extent, the outbursts of ribaldry and derision are actually taking the official world seriously, at face value or at least at the value officialdom itself gives it.[15] In the end, whether the encounter of state and people is 'masked' or not does not matter. The key point is that in this very specific historical context of domination and subjection the postcolony neither minces nor spares its words. Indeed, the purest expression of *commandement* is conveyed by a total lack of restraint, by a great delight too in getting really dirty. Debauchery and buffoonery readily go hand in hand. The body of the despot, his frowns and smiles, his decrees and commands, the public notices and communiqués repeated over and over again: these are the primary signifiers, it is these that have force, that get interpreted and reinterpreted, and feed back further significance into the system....

Confrontation occurs the moment the *commandement*, with vacuous indifference to any sense of truth, seeks to compel submission and force people into dissimulation. The problem here is not that they do not obey nor even pretend to obey. Conflict arises from the fact that the postcolony is chaotically pluralistic and that it is in practice impossible to create a single, permanently stable system out of all the signs, images and markers current in the postcolony; and that is why they are constantly being shaped and reshaped, as much by the rulers as by the ruled, in attempts to rewrite the mythologies of power.[16] This is why, too, the postcolony is, *par excellence*, a hollow pretence, a regime of unreality (*régime du simulacre*). By making it possible to play and have fun outside the limits set by officialdom, the very fact that the regime is a sham allows ordinary people (1) to simulate adherence to the innumerable official rituals that life in the postcolony requires – such as the wearing of uniforms and the carrying of the party card, making public gestures of support and sticking up portraits of the autocrat in one's home; (2) to say the unsayable and to recognise the otherwise unrecognisable. In other words, the fetish, seen for the sham it is, is made to lose its might, and becomes merely an idol....

It is with the conscious aim of avoiding... trouble that ordinary people locate the fetish of state power in the realm of ridicule; there they can tame it or shut it up and render it powerless. This done, the fetish takes on the status of an idol, an idol that in this instance is a familiar friend, a member of the family as much for the rulers as for the ruled.[17] This double act of both distancing and domesticating is not necessarily the expression of a fundamental conflict between worlds of meaning which are in principle antagonistic. In fact officialdom and the people have many references in common, not the least of which is a certain conception of the aesthetics and stylistics of power, the way it operates and expands....

It seems, then, that we can reasonably conclude from these preliminary remarks that the postcolony is a world of anxious virility, a world hostile to continence, frugality,

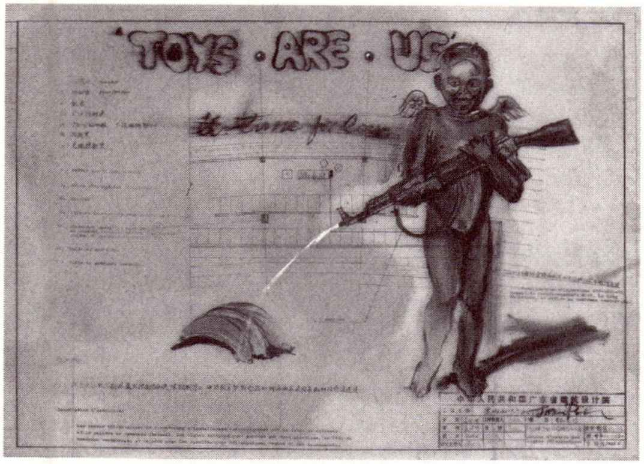

Johannes Phokela, *Toys Are Us*, 2002. Oil on tracing paper, 84 x 60cm.

sobriety. Furthermore, the set of images and idioms evoked above is used as much by those we designate as dominant as by the dominated. Those who laugh, whether they do so in the public arena or in the private domain, are not necessarily bringing about the collapse of power or even resisting it. Confronted with the state's eagerness to cover up its actual origins, people are simply bearing witness, often unconsciously, to the fact that the grotesque is no more foreign to officialdom than the common man is impervious to the charms of majesty….

Peculiar also to the postcolony is the way the relationship between rulers and ruled is forged by means of a specific practice: simulacrum (*le simulacre*). This explains why dictators can go to sleep at night lulled by the roars of adulation and support only to wake up the next morning to find their golden calves smashed and their tablets of law overturned. The applauding crowds of yesterday have become today a cursing, abusive mob. That is to say, people whose identities have been partly confiscated have been able, precisely because there was this pretence, to glue back together the bits and pieces of their fragmented identities. By taking over the signs and language of officialdom, people have been able to remythologise their own conceptual universe while in the process turning the *commandement* into a sort of zombie. Strictly speaking, this process does not increase either the depth of people's subordination or their levels of resistance; it simply produces a situation of disempowerment (*impouvoir*) for both the ruled and the rulers.[18] The process is fundamentally magical: though it may demystify the *commandement* or even erode its supposed legitimacy, it does not do violence to the *commandement*'s material base. At best it creates pockets of indiscipline on which the *commandement* may stub its toe, though otherwise it glides unperturbed over them….

Forced labour (*les forçats*) in the postcolony, then, is of a different kind. Authorities can requisition people's bodies and make them join in the displays and ceremonies of the *commandement*, requiring them to sing or dance or wriggle their bodies about in the sun…. We can watch these dancers, 'these hung-over rounds of meat reeking of wine and tobacco, the heavy mouths, dead eyes, the smiles and the faces', carried away by the staccato rhythm of the drums as a presidential procession goes by, on a day set aside to celebrate the party or the 'Shining Guide of the Nation'.

These bodies could just as easily be in a state of abandon, caught, as the novelist says, 'by the beer, the wine, the dancing, the tobacco, the love pumped out like spit, the strange drinks, the sects, the palaver – everything that might stop them being the bad conscience of their Excellencies'. These same bodies can be neutered whenever they are thought to be 'disfiguring' a public place, or are considered a threat to public order (just as demonstrations are crushed in bloodshed)[19] – or whenever the *commandement*, wishing to leave imprinted on the minds of its subjects a mark of its enjoyment, sacrifices them to the firing squad….

In this way a public execution not only reveals the total power of the state but it becomes a social transaction. The public face of domination can make use of the execution's threatening implications…. The ranking that operates at such ceremonies (first the governor, then the prefect, the representatives of justice, the police, the gendarmerie, the clergy, the medical profession…) is evidence that power is not an empty space. It has its hierarchies and its institutions, it has its techniques. But, above all, in the postcolony it is *an economy of death* – or, more precisely, it opens up a space for enjoyment at the moment it is making room for death; hence the wild applause which, like the bullets, stifled the cries of the condemned.

This accounts for the baroque character of the postcolony: its unusual and grotesque art of representation, its taste for the theatrical and its violent pursuit of wrongdoing to the point of shamelessness. Obscenity here resides in a mode of expression that might seem macabre were it not that it is an integral part of the stylistics of power. The notion of obscenity has no moral connotation here; it harks back to the 'radiation' things can emit, to the headiness of social forms—including the suppression of life (since through such an important act of authority as an execution a whole hermeneutic is laid out for madness, pleasure, intoxication)....[20]

The Domain of Drunkards

On 5 October 1988, the head of state, Mr Paul Biya, returned from a trip to the United Nations, where, like most heads of state, he had addressed the General Assembly. His speech was very short. It offered not one idea or proposition which spoke to the contemporary preoccupations of international opinion. It was an altogether ordinary speech given by one of those leaders of one of those small, obscure African states where nothing happens of any consequence for the general stability of the world. But, as always, the speech was televised in Cameroon. The trip itself was described as a 'long, complex yet triumphant tour' (*périple*).[21]

This is perhaps why, on his return, the mayor of the capital, Yaoundé, published a 'communiqué' calling upon 'all the people' of the town 'to gather as one to show the support of the whole Cameroonian people for His Excellency, Mr Paul Biya, champion of the Third World and architect of co-operation without discrimination'.[22] To facilitate the 'spontaneous' participation of the masses in an 'exceptional welcome', shops were to be closed from one o'clock on. All traders and stallholders from the market and the Chamber of Agriculture, as well as all merchants downtown, were 'invited to fill Avenue du 20 mai from the post office roundabout to the Carrefour Warda'.[23] It is common practice, so common that it has become banal. It is part of the permanent public demonstration of grandeur that Cameroon shares with the other postcolonies of sub-Saharan Africa.[24] In this sense the return of Paul Biya was in no way unusual. The staging that accompanied it marked simply one instance of the dramatisation of a specific mode of domination which dates back to the 1960s. It has had the time to routinise itself and to invent its own rules – the aim being, on each occasion, to make use of an event which is in itself banal (in this case, addressing the General Assembly of the United Nations) and quite anodyne, given the way such events are seen by the rest of the world, and turn it into a source of prestige, illusion, magic....

The dramatisation of the postcolonial *commandement* takes place especially during those ceremonies which make up the state's liturgical calendar. Indeed, after decolonisation Cameroon consciously developed a ceremonial system which, in many respects, recalls ones that operated in communist regimes. The system of festivals institutionalised during the Ahidjo regime (1958–82) was very like communist ceremonials in the way it took on para-religious and dogmatic features both of which were to be most easily found in the general economy of public life. The ceremonies organised during the last ten years of Ahidjo's reign always produced an intense degree of emotional and symbolic expression. They had a repetitive character typical of myth and of cyclical time. In the end, their very regularity invested them with the power of custom. 'Massive, spontaneous and enthusiastic' participation was expected of the masses. The official calendar marked the different sequences of social time. The regime ultimately created its own rhythms of time, work and leisure, and from them acquired a degree of predictability. For example, it was well known that every important victory achieved in pan-African sporting competitions (especially soccer) was almost automatically the occasion for a 'national holiday on full pay'.

At the same time the regime tried to invent for itself a genealogy that served to compensate for the lack of legitimacy which marked the early years of decolonisation. In 1958 the French colonial administration had decided it was in its long-term interest to distance itself from the nationalist movement and to ensure that instead its own local clients got the resources of power that would become available at independence. This attempt to legitimate a political order born amidst contempt gave rise to a certain amount of violence being done to the facts and the historical figures of the nationalist period. The state's obsession with remaking the past in its own image remains one of the most conspicuous characteristics of the regimes that have come to power in Cameroon since the colonial era.

It was during Ahidjo's presidency that the practice was started of putting up portraits of the head of state in public places. Admittedly no statues have been erected in Ahidjo's honour, but the largest stadium in the capital and some of the main boulevards and public spaces were named after him while he was alive. Formerly an employee of the colonial postal service, he was nevertheless awarded a doctorate *honoris causa* by the local university. 'Votes of confidence' (*motions de soutien*) are also products of this period. They added to a personality cult which also found expression in the various titles that Ahidjo's courtiers gave him: 'Father of the Nation', 'Great Comrade', 'Apostle of Peace', 'Providential Guide', 'Indefatigable Builder of the Nation', 'The Man of February 1958', 'The Great Peasant', 'The Great Sportsman', 'Far-sighted Guide', 'The Great Helmsman'....

It is therefore not unusual to find the effigy of the head of state in or around people's houses. It is part of the furniture as well as a decorative object. It is found in offices, along avenues, in airport terminals, in police stations and in places of torture. It is always near by. You wear it. It is on people's bodies, as in the case of women who wear the party's clothes. In this way, and with great attention to detail, the apparatus of state finds ways of getting into its subjects' most intimate spaces....

Consider instead the visits by foreign heads of state, for example. In October 1987 when a reception for Abdou Diouf, the President of Senegal, was to be organised, forty-two dance troupes were brought to the airport several hours before his arrival. Most of the dancers as usual had oblong cowbells attached to their ankles and above their knees. They were accompanied by drums, tambourines, guitars, xylophones and flutes made from bamboo or from gazelle or antelope horn in different sizes. There were bullroarers and other wind instruments of various shapes and material, some of iron, others made from gourds with necks slotted together – these made a specially deep, hoarse sound. There were percussion instruments, iron gongs and bells made out of metal shells, and tubes whose speciality was a metallic sound to set the rhythm of the dance. Once synchronised together these instruments could bring on possession, 'enchant' the dancers or, failing that, deafen the crowd – a necessary magnifier of power....

In the world of self-adoration that is the postcolony, the troupes summoned to perform their dances bear witness to the central place accorded the body in the processes of *commandement* and submission. Under colonial rule it was the bodies of convicts and labourers that were requisitioned for public works or for porterage. In the postcolony bodies have been used to entertain the powerful in ceremonies and official parades. On such

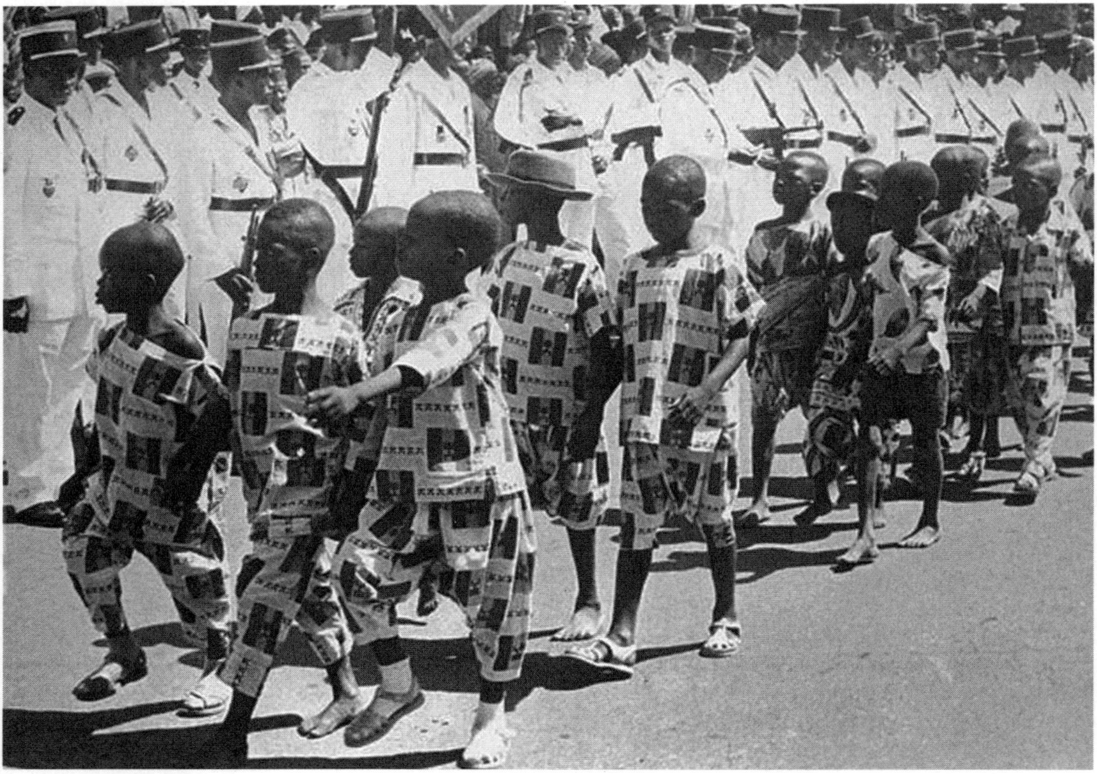

Children Marching in Bamako, Mali, 22 June 1960. © Bettmann/CORBIS.

occasions some of the bodies have had the marks of famine upon them: flaky scalps, scabies, skin sores. Other bodies have attracted small crowds of flies. But that has not stopped them from breaking into laughter or peals of joy when the presidential limousines approached....

Power had thus colonised – at least for the moment of official ceremonial – the dances which previously were linked to particular rituals and followed specific rules. Amidst the cacophony accompanying such a show of strength there can be found scattered here and there the debris of ritual actions from the past – here, elements from rites before the hunt to enlist the help of spirits; there, bits of former ceremonies for funerals or initiations, for women's fertility or of preparation for war. All the elements, juxtaposed and intertwined in a single web, form the edifice of postcolonial dramaturgy....

Finally, let us end with one last practice. I suggested earlier that the mouth, the belly and the penis constitute the classic ingredients of *commandement* in the postcolony. Yet the process by which pleasure is transformed into a site of death was not adequately examined. I will limit my remarks here to suggesting how, in this context, the very act of exercising command cannot be separated from the way licentiousness is produced. For example, having come to install in their posts the headmaster of the high school and the director of the training college for assistant instructors at Abong-Mbang in January 1988, the prefect of the department of Haut Nyong, Ename Ename Samson, urged the teachers to 'have only pedagogic and healthy, not intimate and culpable, relationships with their students'. The prefect was well aware of the excessive rights to take women that bureaucrats arrogate to themselves.... One can add to them the Ministers who explore virgins on hotel beds and the priests who turn somersaults over the 'deep behinds' of young girls and, while digging a 'delicious void in their bellies, make them cry out the final ho-hi-hi-hi'. Not to mention the real 'kings of the bush' – the sub-prefects and prefects, the police officers and gendarmes – who have practically unlimited rights over those under them (*droits de cuissage*)....

Such practices no longer refer back to customs which in some past societies made it discourteous to leave guests to sleep alone without offering a girl to 'warm their feet' during the night – a practice from which the colonial settlers and their successors greatly profited. And it has even less connection with the large-scale polygamy of the years of transition to colonial rule, the function of which was more economic and social – creating alliances with those in power, cementing relationships, producing and reproducing. The problem instead is how, in the postcolony, these baroque practices have become an integral part of the bureaucrat's life style, how the economy of pleasure has become inseparable from vice.

The Intimacy of Tyranny[25]

In the postcolony an intimate tyranny links the rulers with the ruled, just as obscenity is only another aspect of munificence and vulgarity a normal condition of state power. If subjection appears more intense than it might be, it is because the subjects of the *commandement* have internalised the authoritarian epistemology to the point where they reproduce it themselves in all the minor circumstances of daily life, such as social networks, cults and secret societies, culinary practices, leisure activities, modes of consumption, dress styles, rhetorical devices, and the whole political economy of the body. It is also because, were they to detach themselves from these ludic resources, they would, as subjects, lose the possibility of multiplying their identities.

Yet it is precisely this possibility of assuming multiple identities which accounts for the fact that the body which dances, dresses in the party uniform, fills the roads,

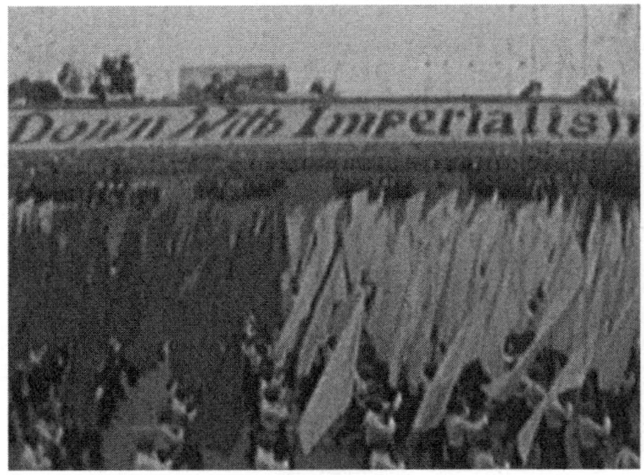

Salem Mekuria, *DELUGE*, 1997. Video still of footage from Ethiopian television showing a Menigistu parade.

'assembles *en masse*' along the main avenues to applaud the passing of the presidential procession in a ritual of confirmation, is nonetheless willing to dramatise its subordination through these small tokens of fealty. At the same time, instead of keeping silent in the face of obvious official lies and the effrontery of elites, this body breaks into laughter. And by laughing it drains officialdom of meaning and sometimes obliges it to function empty and powerless. This is what allows us to assert that, by dancing publicly for the benefit of power, the 'postcolonised subject' is providing his or her loyalty and by compromising with the corrupting control that state power tends to exercise at all levels of everyday life (over benefits, services, pleasures...) the subject is reaffirming that it is incontestable – precisely in order the better to play with it and modify it whenever possible.

Thus the public affirmation of the 'postcolonised subject' is not necessarily found in acts of 'opposition' or 'resistance' to the *commandement*. What defines the postcolonised subject is the ability to engage in baroque practices which are fundamentally ambiguous, fluid and modifiable even in instances where there are clear, written and precise rules. These simultaneous yet apparently contradictory practices ratify, *de facto*, the status of fetish that state power so forcefully claims as its right. And by the same token they maintain, even while drawing upon officialese (its vocabulary, signs and symbols), the possibility of altering the place and time of this ratification.

The enumeration of the slightest educational achievement is one of the postcolonial codes of prestige, with special attention being given to distinctions attained in Europe. Thus, for example, people cite the number of diplomas with great care, they show off their titles – doctor, chief, president, etc. – with great affectation as a way of claiming honour, glory and attention. Displays of this kind have an effect beyond the contribution they make to state ritual. Such a display is transformative: by casting its rays upon the person installed it bestows upon him a new radiance. In the hierarchy of mock honours the description of scholarly achievements constitutes a marker of rank and status as well as of qualification....[26]

In the postcolony magnificence and the desire to shine are not the prerogative only of those who command. The people also want to be 'honoured', to 'shine' and take part in celebrations.

> Last Saturday the Muslim community of Cameroon celebrated the end of Ramadan. For thirty days members of the community had been deprived of many things from dawn till dusk. They refrained from drinking, eating, smoking, sexual relations and saying anything that goes against the Muslim faith and the law. Last Saturday marked the end of these privations for the whole Muslim community of Cameroon.[27]

From this one can say that the obscenity of power in the postcolony is also fed by a desire for majesty on the part of the people (*la plèbe*). Because the postcolony is characterised above all by scarcity, the metaphor of food 'lends itself to the wide-angle lens of both imagery and efficacy'. 'Food' and 'tips' (*pourboire*) are political,[28] 'food', like 'scarcity', cannot be dissociated from particular regimes of 'death', from specific modalities of enjoyment or therapeutic quests. This is why 'the night' and 'witchcraft', the 'invisible', the 'belly', the 'mouth' and the 'penis' are all historical phenomena in their own right....

Even death does not escape this desire to 'shine' and to be 'honoured'. The rulers and the ruled want more than ceremonies and celebrations to show off their splendour. Those who have accumulated goods, prestige and influence are not only tied to the 'constraints of giving'. They are also taken by the desire to 'die well' and to be buried with pomp.[29] Funerals constitute one of the occasions where those who command gaze at themselves, as Narcissus did....[30] It thus appears that those who command seek to familiarise themselves with death, thereby paving the way for their own burial to take on a certain quality of pleasure and expenditure....

As we have seen, obscenity – when regarded as more than a moral category – constitutes one of the modalities of power in the postcolony. But it is also one of the arenas in which subordinates reaffirm or subvert that power. Bakhtin's error was to attribute these practices to the dominated. But the production of burlesque is not specific to them. The real inversion takes place when, in their desire for a certain majesty, the masses join in the madness and clothe themselves in cheap imitations of power so as to reproduce its epistemology; and when, too, power in its violent quest for grandeur makes vulgarity and wrongdoing its main mode of existence. It is here, within the confines of this intimacy, that the forces of tyranny in black Africa have to be studied. Such research must go beyond institutions, beyond formal positions of power and the written rules, and examine the way the implicit and explicit are interwoven, and how the practices of those who command and of those who are assumed to obey are so entangled as to render them powerless. For it is precisely the situations of powerlessness that are the situations of violence *par excellence*.

The Postcolonial Constellation: Contemporary Art in a State of Permanent Transition

Okwui Enwezor

The Proper task of a history of thought is: to define the conditions in which human beings 'problematize' what they are, what they do, and the world in which they live.
Michel Foucault [1]

This flood of convergences, publishing itself in the guise of the commonplace. No longer is the latter an accepted generality, suitable and dull – no longer is it deceptively obvious, exploiting common sense – it is, rather, all that is relentlessly and endlessly reiterated by these encounters.
Édouard Glissant [2]

I

It is a commonplace of the current historical thinking about globalisation to say: there are no vantage points from which to observe any culture since the very process of globalisation has effectively abolished the temporal and spatial distance that previously separated cultures.[3] Another way this thinking has been expressed is in the form of globalisation as the mode and ultimate structure of singularisation, standardisation and homogenisation of culture in service of instruments of advanced capitalism and neo-liberalism. After such totalisation, what remains of the critical forces of production which throughout the modern era have placed a strong check on the submerging of all subjective protocols to the orders of a singular organising ideology, be it the state or the market? Thus expressed, what may immediately follow this teleological ordering is to ask: If globalisation has established, categorically, the proximity of cultures, can the same be said about globalisation and art? Many would wager differently on this question, arguing that culture, taken in all its vicissitudes – and also paying heed to the detemporalisation and despatialisation that occurs with its absorption into the maws of the capitalist logic of mediatisation and consumerism – is something else. As such, culture's propensity towards absorption into the 'ideological circuits'[4] of capital production lies in contrast to the uniqueness of art which for centuries has waged a fierce battle of independence from all cultural, social, economic and political influences. That is the given, if not sentimental idea of art's staunch integrity; the concreteness and uniqueness of art as a special category within the field of culture is partly where the logic of the autonomy of art rests....

Culture's vicissitudes is a necessary path through which to comment on the specificity of the idea of art, especially if we are to see art not just in relation to this specificity, but also its intersection with culture on the level of representation as well as in the economic field of reception and in the institutional ideology of the canon.

Unlike the apotropaic device of containment and desublimation through which the modern Western imagination perceived other cultures, so as to feed off their strange aura and displace their power, the nearness today of those cultures formerly separated by their distance to the objectifying conditions of modernist history, calls for new critical appraisals of our contemporary present and its relationship to artistic production founded on autonomy. Exhibitions of art provide us with one of the key fields that have attracted the most sustained appraisal with regards to how to evaluate the specificity and content of art. It is in the field of reception to which an exhibition belongs as a category of culture that the long-held principle of art's specificity or distinctness can be tested....

I start with these observations in order to place in proper context the subject of my analysis, which is the current conditions of production, dissemination and reception of contemporary art, now refracted, not just from the specific site of culture but in a more critical sense, from the standpoint of a complex geopolitical configuration that defines all systems of production.

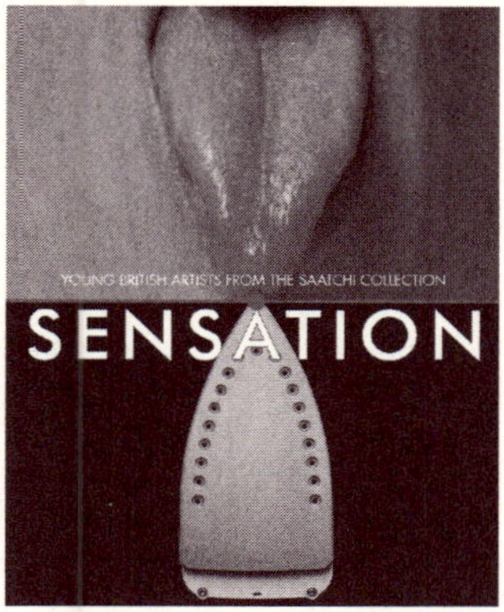

Published by Thames & Hudson.

Perhaps, bringing contemporary art squarely into the context of the geopolitical framework – between the so-called local and the global, centre and margin, nation state and the individual, trans-national and diasporic communities, audiences and institutions – in which its systems of legitimation are set, makes possible our ability to see the complex mechanisms of its distribution and discourses. Geopolitical discourses of power, however inimical they may be for a trans-cultural understanding of the present context of cultural production, nonetheless still elect a developmental discourse that relies on civilisational distinctions predicated on the tension between the developed and underdeveloped, reactionary and progressive, regressive and advanced for its efficacy. Such a discourse, however, is a legacy of classical modernity, which through these distinctions, furnishes the dialectical and ideological agenda for competition and hegemony....

From its inception, the history of modern art has been inextricably bound to the history of its exhibitions and the economic sphere that has accompanied its legitimation. To phrase it differently, fundamental to the historical understanding of modern art is the important role played through the forum and medium of exhibitions in explicating the trajectory taken by artists, their supporters, critics and the public in identifying the great shifts that have marked all encounters with modern art and advanced its claim for enlightened singularity amongst other cultural avatars. For contemporary art, this history is no less true. However, there has occurred a number of remarkable mutations in the growing discourse of exhibitions and in the public representations of art as something wholly autonomous and separate from the sphere of other cultural activities, that must be studied very carefully....

II

Today the critical content of most exhibition and curatorial projects concerned with contemporary art has come under increasing scrutiny and attack. More specifically, such projects have been called into question by two types of commentary. The first is generalist and speculative in nature and, to my thinking, lacks critical purpose. Therefore, we can dispense with it rather quickly. Its chief interest is its fascination with contemporary art as novelty, consumed by affects of reification – as a pure image and object of exhibitionism, i.e., with spectacle culture. It tends to equate the task of an exhibition with entertainment, fashion, new thrills and discoveries and seasonally tops up the depleted inventory of the 'new' exhausted in the previous season. The so-called mega exhibitions – such as Documenta, biennales, triennales, festivals, along with commercial gallery exhibitions of a certain type (and here I would include the sort of sensationalistic exhibitions that are the stock-in-trade of patrons like Charles Saatchi) – are normally the haunt of this kind of appraisal, which easily grows bored with any exhibition that lacks the usual dosage of concocted outrage and scandal. Impatient with historical exegesis, it contents itself with the phantasmagoric transition between moments of disenchantment and populist renewal.

The second type of commentary is more nostalgic. It usually takes the approach of a buttoned-up, mock severity: one based, as it is, on a pseudo-critical disaffection with what it sees as the consummation achieved between art and spectacle, between the auguries of pop cultural banality and an atomised avant-garde legacy. For such commentary, art has meaning and cultural value, only when it is seen wholly as art and autonomous. That is, any encounter with art must relate to that art scientifically, not imaginatively, in order to understand the objective conditions of the work in question. To the degree that it reflects the inner logic of its ontological status, art's removal from the realm of the social-life world that introduces it as an object of high culture comes with a price imposed by the formal constraints won through its autonomy from any accreted social or ideological baggage. For such critics, the curator's task is to pay the greatest fidelity to a restrained formal diligence and perspicacity as derived from immemorial values inculcated and transmitted by tradition, which can only be interrupted through a necessary disjuncture marked by innovation. The paradox of a disjunctive innovation that simultaneously announces its allegiance and affinity to the very tradition it seeks to displace is a commonplace of the entire history of modernity and its discourse of progress in the avant-garde. In any case, such paradox introduces a positive value to the nature of how certain types of art acquire their modernity. Modernity's model of constantly replenished innovation seems irrevocably tied to the past and tradition, even if such innovation holds steadfast to the historical idea of its promulgation as future-oriented. Yet, it can be allowed that such a view is the product of a social and cultural outlook, shared mostly by traditional scholarship. Traditional art-historical scholarship encumbers the view of modernity with a reified attachment to a tradition that goes back uninterrupted to antiquity, rather than as a patchwork of haphazard movements with many deviations, which it in fact is.

The trouble normally begins when there's a breach noticed between the supposed eternality of values that flow from antiquity to the present and the autonomy of art that suddenly has to contend with the reality of the secular, democratic public sphere which has been developed through a concatenation of many traditions.[5] This is all the more so, when such a breach appears, for instance, in the objective conditions of artistic production. One example is in the pluralisation of the concept of art, what has been described elsewhere as the 'Duchamp Effect'. Or, to take another view, Walter Benjamin's much referenced essay 'The Work of Art in the Age of Mechanical Reproduction' announced the changes in the medium of art that transform and question traditional notions of originality and aura. Or, in yet another view, a spirit of 'mutual' recognition of substantive development in other traditions feeds into new models of practice, the most obvious example being the encounter between modern European artists and African sculpture at the turn of the twentieth century that gave birth to cubism. The Duchamp Effect is the most traditional view to my thinking, because what it purports is the idea of the supremacy of the artist. It is the artist who decides what an object of art is or can be, not the progressive, formal, transformation of art from within the medium. Artistic genius emerges then from a subjective critique of tradition by the artist, against all other available data, not from an objective analysis of the fallacy of tradition. For Benjamin, mechanical reproduction expands the field and horizon of art, freeing it from traditional biases of originality and aura. Again this is about the shift in the medium, as well as in the reception of art. However, what the European artists' encounter with African sculptures did was to change the equation of the pictorial and plastic language of painting and sculpture based on the encounter. The remarkable aspect of this breach is that its historical repercussion has remained mostly consigned to formal aesthetic analysis and is not perceived as a true rupture with tradition, for European tradition cannot just simply claim and absorb African traditions just because it can....

Upon the opening of the Tate Modern in London two years ago, much discussion appeared in the press about the museum's 'radical' attempt to break with the outmoded chronological emphasis of modern art history for a more dialectical, hence discursive, approach

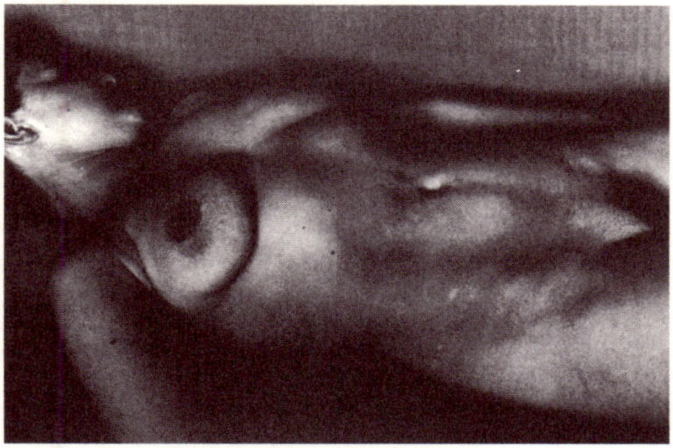

Craigie Horsfield, *E. Horsfield, Well Street, East London, August 1987*, 1995. Photograph on paper. © Craigie Horsfield, ADAGP and Tate, London, 2003.

according to genre, subject matter and form affinities. Divided into four themes – 'Still Life/Object/Real Life', 'Nude/Action/Body', 'History/Memory/Society', 'Landscape/Matter/Environment' – the idea was to break with a conception of modernist historiography long entrenched at the Museum of Modern Art in New York since its founding more than seventy years ago. The most memorable room in this dialectical encounter that is supposed to show us the necessary connections and continuity of an uninterrupted tradition is the one that combines one of Richard Long's typical mud wall paintings and one of Claude Monet's waterlilies paintings in the same room. What are we to make of this pairing? It certainly shows us that both Monet and Long are deeply interested in a primordialism that imbues spirituality into nature and in the conception of landscape as genre. That this pairing is a gimmick is not so difficult to see. For the rest of this exercise in dialectical and discursive historiography, rooms are divided like stage sets into the four themes that read much like a textbook. The surreal unmessiness of art's undisturbed progression in a newly founded museum of 'modern' art without contradictions, frictions, resistance, insurbordination, etc. (as if nothing else has happened within modernism beyond the 'standard' account) is in itself a historical conceit. Every possible position that could challenge this most undialectical of approaches has been sublated and absorbed into the yawning jaws of the canon.

One example, and by far the most troubling, of the curatorial reasoning behind this historical conceit will suffice. Typical of the cynicism towards any socially and historically determined analysis of the object of discourse in a museum of modern art is a room in the 'Nude/Action/Body' section. The theme suggests the idea of contingency, insofar as the category 'Nude' loses its classicism and formal modernist pedigree. With this image playing in my head, I hesitantly approached the gallery, but not before passing by one of Edgar Degas's ubiquitous *Petite Danseuse de quartorze ans (Little Dancer Aged Fourteen)*, 1880–81, cast in 1922 (every modernist museum must own one of these trophies) out at the entrance. This sweet little sculpture of a young ballet student, with its pose of propriety – left leg stretched out in front, her ram rod gait giving way to a small head thrust upwards and gathered layers of pleated muslin gauze around her small waist – reminds me so much of one of those Mkinsi ritual sculptures common amongst the BaKongo. From there, the first gallery which serves as some sort of introduction opens out to an eclectic cluster of paintings by Stanley Spencer, John Currin, Pablo Picasso and others. This is not an auspicious introduction. The selection and arrangement of the works strikes one more for its sensibility towards delectation than for authoritatively setting out a thesis of the nude. So we walk through the first gallery into the second gallery where we come upon two large-scale black and white photographic works by Craigie Horsfield and John Coplans facing each other. *E. Horsfield. Well Street, East London, August 1987* (1995) is in the tradition of the classical modernist reclining nudes reminiscent of Paul Cézanne's bathers and Henri Matisse's odalisques. It is an outstanding ponderous picture, heavy like fruit, while Coplans's *Self-Portrait (Frieze No.2, Four Panels)*, 1994, is typical of the artist's performative and fragmentary, multipanelled self-portraiture of his collapsing body. In a typical Coplans manner, the seriality of the depicted body reveals – though decapitated at the head and just below the ankle – a body that lays claim to its own sentient properties. Here, it should be said that the position of the contemporary nude finds formal echoes in relation to the classical modernist nude. What distinguishes the contemporary nude from its early modernist antecedents can best be summarised as the disjunction between the

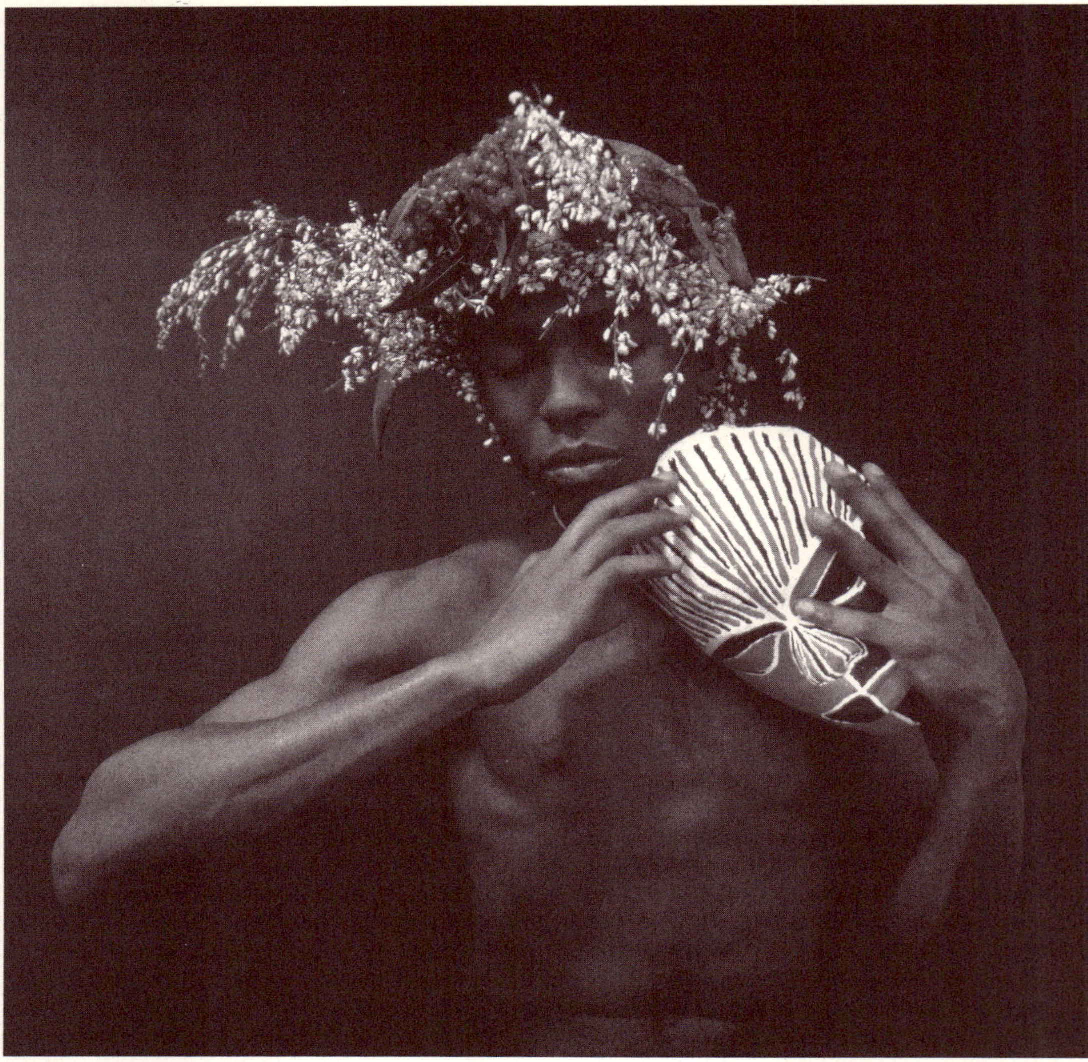

Rotimi Fani-Kayode, *Untitled*, *Communion* series, 1995. R-type colour print, 137 x 137cm. © the artist's estate. Courtesy of Autograph: Association of Black Photographers, London.

self-conscious subjectivity of the former and the formal idealisation of the latter. Looking at the contemporary nude facing the modernist nude, one could impute, correctly, that, in this regard, the dialectical framework does matter.

But what are we to make of what immediately follows this initial encounter with the body in the next gallery? What do we find? Just like that, a small ethnographic vitrine embedded into one of the walls of the room. To the left of the wall is a tiny LCD monitor containing extracts from two films: Marc Allégret and André Gide's *Voyage to the Congo* (1928) and an anonymous archival film, *Manners and Customs of Senegal* (1910). The two extracts evince a theme common to travel documentary. Though temporally and spatially apart, we can group these two films within a system of knowledge which belongs to the well-known genre of colonial, ethnographic film studies of 'primitive' peoples. (We already know much about the Western modernist fascination with 'primitive' peoples' bodies and material cultures along with their Orientalist correlatives, so I need repeat neither the fables nor the intense debates surrounding them here.) But Allégret and Gide's sentimental film and the more structurally open archival footage provide us with much to think about with regards to modernism, spectacle, otherness and degeneracy. In each of the two films, we see the setting of the village and its social life. They are mostly images of genre scenes: villagers self-consciously carrying out their everyday chores, such as grinding grain, tending fires, minding children, or participating in a village festival of dance and song. However, most striking about the films is that nakedness is what they mostly highlight, the nakedness of scientific specimens under imperial observation. Here, nakedness, as opposed to the nude, yields a structure of critical differentiation between the primitive and the modern, between objective knowledge, subjective intention and idealisation. According to James Clifford, these modes of differentiation, which is also a trope of distantiation, underline 'a more disquieting quality of modernism: its taste for appropriating or redeeming otherness, for constituting non-Western arts in its own image, for discovering universal, ahistorical "human" capacities'.[6] This observation taken *in toto* with modernism's relationship to otherness, the primitive and the abject bears on the distinction between the nude's formal, aesthetic stature within Western modernist art and that of simple nakedness that has no redeeming aesthetic value commonly found in ethnographic discourse.

However, if the Tate Modern was an institution working beyond the smug reflex of Western museological authority it would have found within the British context artists like Rotimi Fani-Kayode, the Nigerian-British photographer whose work – formally and conceptually – involves long, rigorous excursus into the distinction between the nude and nakedness as it concerns the African body. The analytic content, not to say the formal and aesthetic magnificence of Fani-Kayode's photographic work – and more substantially its awareness of the black body's conflicted relationship[7] with Western museum discourse – makes his absence in the 'Nude/Action/Body' section of the Tate Modern all the more glaring. This inattention to strong, critical work on the nude and body by artists such as Fani-Kayode is all the more troubling because it is precisely works like his that have brought to crisis those naturalised conventions of otherness, which have been the stock-in-trade of modernism throughout its history. It is also what should make it of dialectical and formal interest to the Tate Modern's attempt to address modernism's fascination with otherness. Without this view, the pornography of *A Voyage to the Congo* is simply allowed to stand. We should discount Tate Modern's monologue on the matter, both in its apology and self-abnegation for the film in a label accompanying the extracts. In a characteristic doublespeak the label expounds:

> European audiences in the early 20th century gained experience of Africa through documentary films. Generally these conformed to stereotyped notions about African cultures. An ethnographic film of 1910, for instance, concentrates on the skills and customs of the Senegalese, while *Voyage to the Congo*, by filmmaker Marc Allégret and writer André Gide perpetuates preconceptions about life in the 'bush'. However, the self-awareness displayed by those under scrutiny, glimpsed observing the filmmakers subverts the supposed objectivity of the film.[8]

It's best not to waste time analysing this unconvincing explanatory manoeuvre, for more than anything it entrenches a European modernist reception and appropriation of Africa in its primitivist discourse.

Still, our investigation has much to yield as we look further into the ethnographic desublimation taking place in the Tate Modern. Inside the vitrine, we find casually scattered postcards with the general title 'Postcards from West Africa' and an untitled, undated small, dark, figurative sculpture, identified simply as *Standing Figure*, but the label informatively tells us of its provenance – the collection of the sculptor Jacob Epstein. It is no use speaking about the lyrical beauty and artistic integrity of the sculpture so pointlessly compromised by the rest of the detritus of the colonial knowledge system in the vitrine. The sculpture's presence seems to connote not art – above all not autonomous art – just artefact or, worse still, evidence. Nearly a hundred years after the initial venture by Western modernists (and I do not care which artist 'discovered' what qualities in African or Oceanic art first), it would have been clear enough to the aestheticians at Tate Modern that, in terms of sheer variety of styles, forms, complexity, genres, plastic distinctiveness, inventiveness and complexity of sculptural syntax, no region in the world approaches the depth and breadth of African sculptural traditions. Let's take for example the Congo from where Gide and Allégret gave us the deleterious impressions of their voyage, as a point of illustration of this variety. In just this single region, we find distinct traditions of sculpture such as Yombe, Luba, Mangbetu, Kuba, Teke, Lega, Songye and Dengese. The expressive and conceptual possibilities in the language of artists working within each group have produced sculptural forms of such anthropomorphic variety and complexity of conception, whether of the mask or figure, that simple comparative study is not enough. But this is not communicated at all in the lugubrious gathering at the museum. It should also be noted that what this installation communicates is neither a history nor even a proper anthropology of modernism; rather the task of this 'historical' instruction is more a convention that has often been repeated in a variety of museums of modern art, that more obfuscates than enlightens us on the first proper rupture to occur within the Western tradition. In fact, along with museum collections, most Western modernist museology is predicated on the repetition and circulation of apocrypha and objects connected to this rupture.

As for the African conception of modernity in this depressing tale of museology, that would be for another place and time. Meanwhile, what we see in the rest of the vitrine is not the basis of a system of knowledge according to which the relationship of Western modernist art exists in correspondence to their African contemporaries, but rather, there are Carl Einstein's well-known book *NegerPlastik* (1915), Marcel Griaulle's accounts of the Dakar-Djibouti expedition published in the journal *Minotaure* and Michel Leiris's famous book

L'Afrique Fantome (1933) all performing a pantomime of the modern opposed to the primitive, which the Tate has now upgraded to the most astonishing form of ethnographic ventriloquism. Having emptied and hollowed out the space of African aesthetic traditions, the rest of the gallery is filled out – with customary care and reverence – with carefully installed 'autonomous' sculptures by Constantin Brancusi, Alberto Giacometti, works by Karl Schmidt-Rottluff and an Ernst Ludwig Kirchner painting of a cluster of nude figures which has a striking formal correspondence to Gide and Allégret's film of naked Congolese women and children. The strangeness of chancing upon the two film extracts of naked Africans (who seem naturalistically fixed in both habitat and habitus, making even clearer the opposition between nature and culture, savagery and civilisation) along with the unnamed sculpture and the ethnographic literature in a small cupboard in a museum of 'modern' art strikes a discordant historical chord. Moreover, it lays open to question the museum's dialectical frame. However, what is concretely conveyed is an attitude, a point of view, a sense of sovereign judgement. Put together, the limitations of the dialectical opposition between the aesthetic nude and mere nakedness to my view display a typical historical weakness of museums of modern art in their goal to serve as the memory bank of 'great' art. We should nonetheless concede that the Tate Modern is merely operating on well-trodden ground. A serious example of this sort was New York's Museum of Modern Art's important and influential *Primitivism in Modern Art: Affinities of the Tribal and the Modern* exhibition (1984–85), which limitedly was challenged by the Centre George Pompidou's *Magiciens de la Terre* (Paris, 1989). If the MoMA and Pompidou exhibitions responded to controversial and unresolved aesthetic and historical debates within modernist accounts concerning art from other cultures, Tate Modern, in its response to those questions, proves both unevolved and unreflexive. There is a sense of the entire set-up being ahistorical, bearing no semblance to the critical content of what Habermas calls the 'the philosophical discourse of modernity'.[9] After this encounter, I contented myself with looking at the rest of the collection without troubling further with its justifications, its subjugation of historical memory, in fact, its savage act of epistemological and hermeneutic violence.

III

If I have dwelled on elucidating this particular view it is only to frame what is at stake for artists and curators who step into the historical breach that has today opened up within the context of contemporary art. As regards modernist historiography, that's another matter. But we do know already that modernism has many streams that do not all empty into the same basin. Equally evident is the fact that the rising tide of institutional interest in other accounts of artistic practice will never lift all the boats into the dialectical position of comparison. And there is the nub of the current scepticism towards the globalised reception of contemporary artistic practices from far-flung places with little historical proximity to the ideas transmitted from within the legacy of the Western historical avant-garde. With regard to the complex conditions of production today, such a legacy seems inadequate to do the job of producing a unified theory of contemporary art. Because of its restless, unfixed boundaries, multiplicities and the state of 'permanent transition' within which it is practised, contemporary art tends to be much more resistant to global totalisation. Yet the last two decades have witnessed an exponential rise in the fortunes of curators who, with their portmanteau of terms neatly arranged – befitting of their status as the enlightened bureaucrats of modernist totalisation – travel the world scouring for new signs of art to fill the historical breach. Museums and academies – the secular churches of these travelling bureaucrats – have responded with equal gusto with themed exhibitions, blockbuster shows and curatorial studies programs.

IV

With institutions of art and their endless calculations, the effects can be identified as fivefold. The first is the proliferation and mutating forms of exhibition propositions – such as blockbusters, large-scale group or thematic exhibitions, cultural festivals, biennales, etc. – all of which have significantly enlarged the knowledge base of contemporary thinking about art and its commonplaces in museums and culture at large. This enlargement is crucial, because it has created new networks between hitherto separated spheres of contemporary artistic production – both in the everyday engagement with the world and its images, texts and narratives – and what I have called modernism's dead certainties. Even if this phase is still in a developmental stage, it has oriented the transmission of contemporary art discourse towards a deeper confrontation with what Carlos Basualdo has called the 'new geographies of culture'.[10] Basualdo's 'new geographies of culture' challenge curatorial and exhibition making systems with the fragility of their universalised conception of culture and artistic procedures in the typically bourgeois sense of their ordering in the twentieth century....

The second effect first appeared as an allegory of transformation and transfiguration, then subsequently as a mode of resistance and repetition. It is easy to underestimate today the force of the dissolution of colonial subordination and easy enough to mock the utopian niceties of self-determination and political independence that began to see off the imperial discourse that distinctly marked global modernity in its early phase. Similarly, global modernity, in the guise of the modern nation state that has furnished the political identity of the modern and contemporary artist, intercedes on behalf of a plethora of fictions that found the idea of a national tradition in art and culture. As such, decolonisation and national identity represent the bookends of two concomitant projects of late global modernity. On the one hand, decolonisation portends to restore sundered traditions, whilst the national identity works assiduously to reinvent and maintain them. Decolonisation, qua the postcolonial, transforms the subject of cultural discourse and the nation state transfigures the order of tradition for posterity. If the mode of the postcolonial is resistance through transformation, that of the nation is repetition through transfiguration. Out of each, the figure of the new becomes the emulsifier for either tradition and restoration or tradition and continuity. No doubt, contemporary issues of curatorial practice are keenly aware of the uses (and make use) of the fictions of a sundered past and tradition to produce a narrative of various invented histories of the modern and contemporary....

One reason for vigilance regarding multicultural and identity-based projects on the part of cultural institutions, of course, has to do with both the politics of self-interest and the changing of the cultural and social demographics of many contemporary societies due to immigration. In the case of the United States and Europe, the Civil Rights movement, anti-racist movements and the struggle for the protection of minority rights have increased the level of this vigilance. But also there is the recognition of the role of the market in the institutionalisation of national identity in recent curatorial projects, especially in exhibitions designed to position certain national or geographic contexts of artistic production, such as *Brilliant* (Walker Art Center,

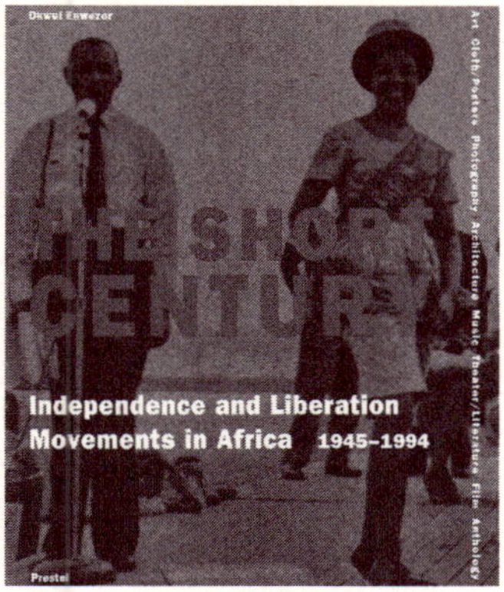

Published by Prestel. Courtesy of Gavin Jantjes.

New York, 1996) *Sensation* (Royal Academy of Arts, London, 1997), *Nuit Blanche* (Musée d'Art Moderne de la Ville de Paris, 1998), *German Open* (Kunstmuseum, Wolfsburg, 2000) and *Young American Colours* (Saatchi Gallery, London, 1996).

The speculative enterprise zones of national culture and authenticity are now pervasive in all kinds of curatorial projects from Africa to Asia and from Latin America to the Pacific zone. Hence, this effect has raised some significant issues and appraisals about prevailing paradigms of the inclusion and exclusion of non-Western artists within the mainstream of museum programming, acquisitions, and exhibitions in Europe and North America. However in the current political climate of the increasing intolerance of difference, institutionally, issues of multiculturalism have been difficult to confront seriously and critically, due to some of its ethical blindspots and excesses. Yet, the multiculturalist backlash and its debates falsify the issues behind it. Not all processes of inclusion and exclusion are necessarily multicultural in nature. If including the work of minority artists – such as African American, Asian, gay, female or any other category of the institutionally, and therefore socially and politically, marginalised – into the wider institutional framework of mainstream representation is merely multicultural, to my mind there is a tacit denial of their broader social, cultural, and political citizenship on the level of the subjective relationship of the artists to their practice and identity as artists. But on the other hand, if their exclusion is based on some notion of a sovereign judgement of quality and taste and purportedly blind to their difference (which by now must be viewed as suspect), the recourse of falling back to a unique minority aesthetic viewpoint that derives from a unique identity offers a counterpoint which equally makes the idea of the positive dimension of multiculturalism weak.

The third effect concerns the explosion and heterogeneous nature of artistic procedures immediately at variance with a historically conditioned and thereby conventional understanding of art within the logic of the institution. Such procedures have been propositionally theorised, quite correctly, as neo-avantgarde, rather than as a true rupture from its academic obverse. However, it can be said that institutional canniness has often found inventive ways to absorb the energies of even the most insurrectional positions in art. The emergence of new critical forces have all too often become cashiered as another instance in the positivist ideology of advanced art's discourse of *engagement* set forth by the institution.

The fourth effect is connected to the mediatisation of culture, especially in the transformation of the museum form into the realm of the culture industry of mass entertainment, theatricality and tourism. The most fitting expression of the passage of museums into the concept of mass culture has been achieved through the fusion of architectural design and the museum's collection. The objective reality of this effect is that discreet architecture no longer serves the purpose of the museum as a destination of culture. Rather, the fusion of the collection with the museum architecture is as much a value-enhancing feature as anything else, such that out-of-town visitors can either treat the Frank Lloyd Wright-designed Guggenheim Museum in New York or Frank Gehry's Guggenheim Bilbao as unique works of art in their own right or they may travel to see the buildings and visit the collections at the same time. Despite their universalist aspirations, most contemporary museums exist with the dark clouds of nationalism hovering over them. For, even if the aspiration of the museum is not specifically nationalist, in order to attract funding and state support its discourse in today's competition between global cities is decidedly nationalist in spirit.

Finally the fifth effect which I believe ultimately subtends the previous four is the globalisation of economic production and distribution, culture and the technological and digital revolution that has fused them. Two things make globalisation fascinating in relation to this discussion: its limits and reach. While the compression of time and space is understood as one of the great aspects of this phenomenon of modernity, there still appears within it, in such rampant forms, many anomalies that sometimes lead us to question even the reality of the idea itself. For in every moment where the wonders of globalisation are extolled, there are, in equal measure, those that remain sanguine about its effects. But for contemporary art this is crucial. Conditions of production and publics of art come in greater variety than the universalised domain of the contemporary art economy is willing to acknowledge. And with this great variety come further variables that shape distribution, transmission, translation and reception of contemporary art.

Having abandoned the strictures of 'internationalism', there is now the idea that the globalisation of artistic discourses opens the doors to a greater understanding of the complexities and motivations that shape contemporary art across Europe, North America, Asia, Africa and Latin America. Paradoxically, it is globalisation that has laid open the myth of a consolidated art world. Rather than a centre, what is much in evidence today are networks and systems of production, distribution, transmission, reception and institutionalisation. The development of new multilateral networks of knowledge production – activities that place themselves strategically at the intersection of disciplines and trans-national audiences – has obviated the traditional circuits of institutionalised production and reception.

V

For Foucault, of course, an object of thought could be anything, so long as we bring to bear upon its analysis a point of view that exposes it to all its historic and contemporary conditions (institutional, political, collective, individual, etc.). The museum within which many a curator operates or aspires to operate is such an object of thought, not least because it is also a political project deeply embedded in the relations of power that inhere in the history of imperial discourse. Still, the validity of the museum as an institution of modern and contemporary artistic imagination retains a great deal of critical credibility, even if museums are the least reformed and transformed by the legacy of the end of imperialism and colonialism. Paradoxically, the museum adopts the discourse of imperial sovereignty to defend its exclusionary and categorical power. It does just enough to assuage a few ruffled feathers, but never enough to question its own historical complicity in the constitution of an epistemological field that admits little difference and discordance. Therefore, the museum as an object of historical thought has a social life, as well as a political dimension, and its function cannot be dissociated from the complex arena of society and culture within which its discourse is imbricated. To that end then, it is of significant interest to see, in the curator, a figure who has assumed a position as a producer of certain kinds of thought about art, artists, exhibitions, ideas and their place amongst a field of other possible forms of thought that govern the transmission and reception of artistic production. It is also of interest to think reflexively about museums. Interestingly, it is artists who have interrogated the institution of the museum and its categorical exceptions of greatness with such propinquity. Even if 'institutional critique' has made itself redundant in light of the parasitic relationship it developed with the museum, it nonetheless opened up a space of critical address which few curators have ever attempted....

VI

Across the line from which the public faces institutions of legitimation, how does one reach this other figure of truth, especially in an exhibition context? With what aesthetic and artistic language does one utter such truth? And in what kind of environment, for which public? How does one define the public of art, particularly given the proliferation of what qualifies as public? Finally, in the circumstances of the contemporary upheaval of thought, ideas, identities, politics, cultures, histories, what truth? The upheaval which today defines our contemporary assessment of events is a historical one shaped by disaffection with two paradigms of totalisation: capitalism and imperialism and socialism and totalitarianism. If the disaffection with these paradigms did not shift significantly the axis and forces of totalisation, it did shape the emergence of new subjectivities and identities. However, the context and the reception of the news of this emergence has crystallised into a figure of thought that is radically enacted in oppositional distinctions made on civilisational and moralistic terms, such as 'the clash of civilizations',[11] 'the axis of evil',[12] the 'evil empire'.[13] During the late 1980s and early 1990s, the cultural wars in the United States were equally waged on these terms, which in time cooled the ardour of those institutions tempted to step beyond the scope of this limiting argument. I will not here rehearse the anguish of these debates for they are well known. Suffice it to say that my conception of the postcolonial constellation comes out of the recognition made clear by the current upheaval.[14] If, however, the postcolonial constellation is not the name of the site for new discourses of artistic practice, it is a name that echoes itself in a series of structural, political and cultural entanglements from the postwar movements of decolonisation, to Civil Rights, feminist, gay/lesbian, anti-racist, anti-essentialist, counter-hegemonic politics of a new global community. The postcolonial constellation is the site for the expansion of the definition of what constitutes contemporary culture and its affiliations in other domains of practice, the intersection of historical forces aligned against the hegemonic imperatives of imperial discourse.

Fatal Natalities: The Algebra of Diaspora and Difference after Apartheid

Sarat Maharaj

The affect proper to the natal is heard in the leid, in Holderlin or Thomas Hardy: to be forever lost or refound, or aspiring to the unknown homeland.... The ambiguity between the territory and de-territorialization is the ambiguity of the Natal.
Gilles Deleuze and Félix Guattari[1]

I

The scene of cultural translation and multicultural representation in the 1990s is shot through with two forces. They are, to use Adorno's words, not unlike the ripped-apart halves of an integral freedom to which, however, they do not add up:[2]

(i) On the one hand, across the art circuits and culture industry, we see difference treated less and less as flow and change – even if it is wrapped up in such lingo. In the culture industry's programmes especially, difference increasingly functions in terms of fixed cultural distinctions and ethnic demarcations filtered through a grid of contrasts and oppositions – a spook-lookalike of Apartheid logic – figuring out separate cultural identities and entities. It marks an emergent *multicultural managerialism*.

(ii) Against this, we have quite another understanding of cultural difference as the fugitive flash of différance – as something no more possible to pin down than an electron's vaporising trail in a Wilson cloud-chamber. From this viewpoint, cultural formations appear as dissolving, interpenetrating transitions and currents that cannot be represented without being whittled down into discrete, stand-still elements. Against tendencies towards multicultural fixity, différance strives to hold its own as the smoky, spreading flux of becoming.

The former is a calculus of difference. It identifies those who fall outside 'cultural visibility' sussing out how they might be counted in the arena of representation, how the excluded, 'the excremental other', might be rendered visible. It pictures cultural diversity as an array of separate, side-by-side places aiming to get those at the 'top end' to shift over so as to squeeze in upcoming minorities and marginals who are parcelled out as essential items and units – not least because of the game of quotas and quanta. The price of such managerialism is that difference institutionalises itself in terms of hard and fast compartments and divisions not unlike Apartheid's separating walls. The latter was not above fancying itself as a multicultural outfit: each ethnic group, fashioned as a self-enclosed identity, was allocated its segregated place in the sun – with the poisonous sting that one was more equal than the others.

The calculus's fatal limit is, however, bound up with its capacity to intervene in the world of representation, to bargain for difference in the rough and tumble of actual institutions. Its hard-nosed pragmatics are at odds with différance as an evanescent trace, which it tends to see as speculative and nebulous for being apparently unlocated in an action programme. Whereas the calculus tackles the condition of actual minorities, différance speaks of 'a pure becoming of minorities'[3] – the self-erasing sweep of another order.

II

But if the calculus gets bogged down in stereotypes of the given representational order, can 'pure becoming' be anything more than a nirvanic trip, anarchic, idealistic stuff? Or is the 'pure becoming minoritarian of everybody or everything' – like HCE or Here Comes Everybody, Haveth Childers Everywhere in *Finnegans Wake* – a matter of 'becoming imperceptible', becoming unreadable as this or that identity? Does it mark, at

2000, the genocidal century's cliff edge, the desperate urge to quit the ethnicised body, to rub out its apparently indelible cultural tattooing?

Churned up by storms off West Africa, equipped with the period's most advanced instruments of measure, Da Gama's ship – diaspora-making machine – first ducked out deep west into the Atlantic before heading back for the 'unknown continent'. Rounding the Cape in November, 1497, it sailed up the east coast before 'orienting' for the fateful touchdown off Calicut, India. At each stop, its signature was to brand the African body with the space of the slave-diaspora, to tattoo the Indian with that of indentureship. Where the spaces intersect on the South African east coast, at Christmas 1497, Da Gama named the land – Natal – the Nativity, birthplace, yearning for the anchorage of home. The machine's violating double-inscription – diaspora-home – would pass through several historical inflections from colonialism through to the Apartheid turbo-engine relentlessly removing people from ancestral territory and domicile for dumping in the 'homelands'.

In the 1990s, 'diasporic' covers a spectrum of people in drastically differing circumstances. At one end are the wretched of the transit camps and detention centres – refugees, 'illegal immigrants', deportees, asylum seekers for whom to be on either side of a border is to have ended up on the wrong side. At the other, the term serves as an all-too-positive celebrating of the crossed-wires and dislocations of contemporary life. Across the spectrum, however, the term harbours a surging counter-force, a hankering for belonging and birthplace – the refrain of the natal – it never manages to shake off. Even when dispersion and uprooting are cracked up as the exhilarating touchstone of the contemporary, they draw in their wake a conflicting quest for boundaries and borders. Scattering and homecoming remain shackled together, tugging at each other like a prisoner on his ball and chain.

In this tension of diasporising and natalising forces – which Aimé Césaire prefigured in the disquieting double-voicing of *Cahier d'un retour au pays natal*[4] – the latter force amounts to a slowing down process in which difference hardens into fundamental distinctions. It is the split image of the calculus's tendency towards the static – towards staking the ground of the birthplace and securing frontiers. Against this, the diasporic drive mirrors the self-dissolving flight of différance, restless motion that ceaselessly overshoots its own limits. The parallels might be put like this:

diaspora : the natal : : différance : the calculus

If the formula clarifies, it also risks casting the terms in a rather too tidy, stark form: the relationships between them are more inside out, more stretched and skewed. This is not least because the mix of accelerating and decelerating forces it strings together cannot be summed up as clear-cut oppositions, equivalents and equations – we have to take on board mutating transitions and twist-arounds.

At 2000, these cross-overs appear in an 'after Apartheid' perspective which we might understand in both the senses of 'in the wake of' and 'in the manner of'. Coming after its predecessor's absolutist cultural-ethnic segregation, South Africa's post-Apartheid Rainbow State 'follows on' as an open dispensation with a multicultural measure of its own. It fingers those 'left out', those who need to step forward into the arena of representation.

III

The calculus switches on straightway, sizing up, calibrating, computing the 'minoritised and marginalised'. The fact that the latter actually make up the numerical majority is not the issue. It is rather that

Alighiero e Boetti, *Mappa del Mondo* (Map of the World), 1989. Embroidery on fabric, 117.5 x 222.7cm. The Museum of Modern Art, New York, Scott Burton Memorial Fund. © DACS 2003. Digital image © 2002 The Museum of Modern Art, New York/Photo Scala, Florence.

the excluded have to be 'identified' as fixed entities – rendered legible as algebraic factors – to count at all in the Rainbow.

The business of 'rendering legible' is underpinned by a system of designations, signifiers and signs – a binary distribution dynamo intrinsic to language and discourse, something the Rainbow and its predecessor cannot but share. It is the sense in which we might say that the Rainbow calculus performs 'in the manner and style of' its Apartheid antecedent – informed by a logic of opposed and contrasting designations which 'live on' in its modes of depiction. This is less a case of language's 'imprisoning' walls than of sticky, resilient binaries that underpin everyday communication and the culture industry. But in acknowledging the shared binary dynamo should we necessarily conclude direly with Pseudo-Adorno that 'Apartheid, once thought defunct, lives on because the moment of its dissolution was missed?'[5]

What would a 'dissolution' have really looked like – given that Apartheid institutions have been formally dismantled and its surviving organs are on a terminal totter? Does it imply the meltdown of the arena of representation itself because of the cultural tagging and schematising it sanctions and replicates? In the face of the calculus's tendency to manage difference by natalising it, it does not seem unreasonable to want to turn our backs on it. But to go all anti-representational in favour of the direct conductivity of différance and becoming seems like privileging the 'anti-term' without stepping out of oppositional structuring – out of calculus *versus* streamsbecoming.

Streamsbecoming

In his *Green Box* notes,[6] Marcel Duchamp probed the 'collision and coupling' of speeding and static elements by expressing the relationship, perhaps not a little tongue-in-cheek, in letter-symbol form:

Algebraic comparison

$\frac{a}{b}$ a being the exposition
         b   "   the possibilities

the ratio $\frac{a}{b}$ is in no way given by a

(-)

number c $\frac{a}{b}$ = c but by the sign which separates

as soon as   are
a and b;   a and b   being '<u>known</u>', they become

new   relative
units and lose their numerical value (or in duration);

of ratio
: the sign ↙/ which separated them remains <u>(sign of the accordance</u> or rather <u>of</u> ......?..... <u>look for it</u>)

IV

His point is whether exposition through words and signs can square fully with the stream of experience it is summoned to represent? There is a lack of fit between verbal or visual representation and the swirl of streamsbecoming. But in acknowledging this difficulty, he stops short of its opposite, of positing the relationship simply in terms of non-fit. How to figure the ratio of non-accordance or find a sign for it? He leaves the issue open, something yet to be looked for – a search that goes on throughout the textual/visual exchanges of his *Large Glass* project.

He likens the plane of exposition to the camera's instantaneous exposure – it delivers up only a standstill

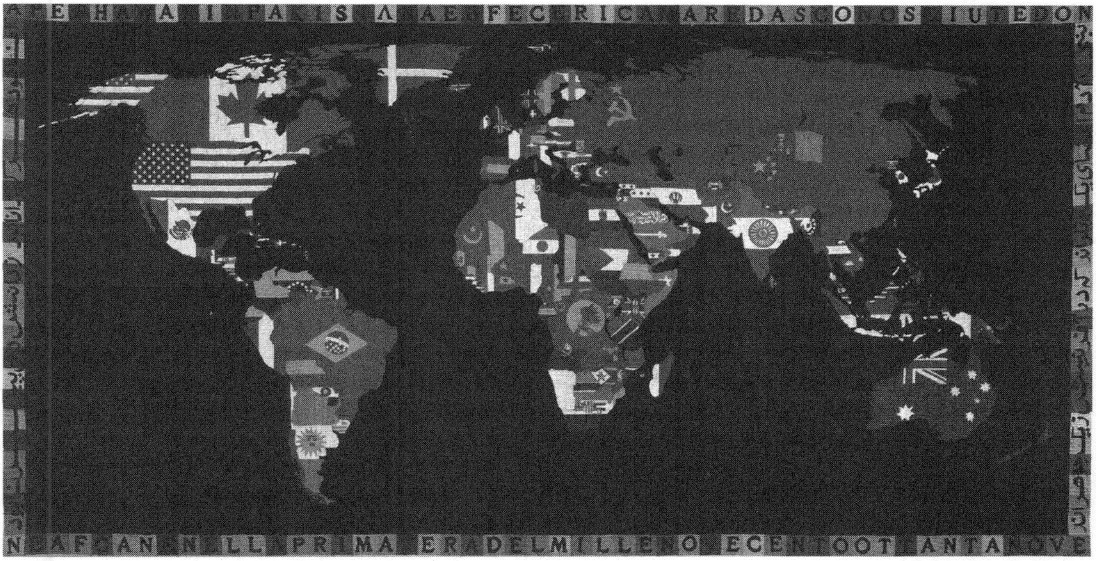

snapshot. How to capture the orgasmic currents and vibrations of the Bride and Bachelor desiring-machines of the *Large Glass* story, episodes of the Bride's stripping and cinematic blossoming when words and images can only give us freeze-shots and standstiff icons of such events-in-motion? His algebraic comparison retains more than a hint of Henri Bergson's critique of the 'cinematographical mechanism of thought'.[7] For the latter, the intellect's system of exposition gave us schematic, arrested moments of the streamsbecoming. Only by brushing aside the standstiff calculus of intellect and representation could one, through intuitive sympathy, tune into the play of difference and duration. But, as Adorno cautions with regard to this impossible dichotomy by referring to an earlier text of Bergson's, 'Intuition is not a simple antithesis to logic… it belongs to logic, and reminds it of the moment of its untruth.'[8]

Duchamp keeps on this side of Bergson's intellect/intuition divide and its devastating diagnosis of representation. He turns the latter's critique of the 'cinematographical method' inside out by sketching other modes of exposition more geared to the flow of difference. He proposed a lingo composed entirely of film blow-ups of sections and excerpts of large objects. These clips and celluloid snippets would take the place of words, sentences, static alphabet-letters. They would perform as liquid signs of a visible grammar replacing the components of ordinary language – substantitives, verbs, adjectives – which signify only by chopping up experience.[9] His drift is that a liquid grammar might make possible an 'ideal continuity' of exposition which approximates and matches the riverrun of difference.

His paragrammatic phrase – 'the extra-rapid State of Rest' – sums up the hi-speed switch-abouts and oscillations of his expositionary mode. As an undecidable – 'high-velocity standstill' — it goes beyond the Bergson binaries of either rest or movement, freeze-shot or flow, intellect or intuition. He warns that his made-up lingo is one-off, applicable perhaps only to the *Large Glass*. He resists setting it up as a catch-all principle or panacea – according to the spirit of his 'pictorial nominalism', each project should elaborate its own idiom and procedure of exposition as it goes along. In the singularity of the art event, calculus and flow, states of rest and the extra-rapid might all be grasped and experienced in one go – an expositionary machine for difference.

Duchamp's self-erasing model is an inspiration behind Alighiero e Boetti's soundings of the calculus and streamsbecoming in the post-Nuremberg, postcolonial space of identity and difference. Working with Afghan refugees in the Pakistan border-camps, his large-scale embroidered series *Mappa* (1971–89) pictures the world's nations strutting the global stage, jostling to be counted through their emblems as self-standing 'identities and presences'. The tightly packed needlework is filled in stitch by stitch, an assortment of disputed borders, flashpoints, no-man's lands, ethnically cleansed territories. Matter of fact and deadpan, the Apartheid-republic flag is embroidered in – the years during which *Mappa* was being made had seen the final wave of resurging opposition to the Apartheid regime. It is the normality of flag-waving fundamentalism, the self-glorifying natalities, the line-up of adversaries usually at one another's throats that quietly unnerves.

V

For his installation *Classifying the Thousand Longest Rivers of the World* (1971–80), Boetti approached government departments and worldwide bureaucracies for measurements of their rivers in order to draw up a league table. Facts and figures pertaining to each river, a sequence of entries, were put together as a book for consultation on a reading stand alongside the large canvas embroidered with the names of the top thousand rivers – an echo of how Duchamp's notes have to be read alongside the *Large Glass*. The statistics and data he collated were sometimes discrepant, often simply out-of-date or off the mark – but what would 'accuracy' mean in this instance?

Boetti was concerned with dramatising the tricky business of measuring a river – of pinning down its 'identity'. Where does the river begin, how exactly does one peg its source let alone define where it actually ends in the broad aqua-diffusion of the estuary mouth? At what precise juncture do the waters of Orange meet the Vaal – chalked up as numbers 50 and 122 on his list? Where do the fresh waters of the Orange end and the Atlantic salt waters begin? Where in the turbulent swell of the Blue Lagoon at Durban does the 'African' Umgeni become the 'Indian' Ocean?

The law of naming and measuring, he goes on to note, seldom coincides with the adventure of water.[10] For the point of the name tag is to 'identify', to delimit river-flow into standstill. This non-accordance of labelling and watery play might be algebrised in this way:

> law of naming : calculus :: adventure of water : différance

Boetti's response to naming, language and representation is at one with Bergson's critique of the 'cinematographical method'. In the latter's celebrated example, the mundane business of waiting for a cube of sugar to dissolve was an instance of the non-measurable, aionic flow of time – a glimpse of the experience of duration and difference.[11] Boetti spotlights a not dissimilar 'indeterminacy' at the fresh water/salt water meeting point. His Bergsonism centres on misgivings about measurement and mensuration – regimes of representation based on units of length that lay claim to precision though they are flimsy, fictional devices.[12] Both set off representation, in metrical, quantified terms, according to magnitude, size, dimension, against the non-metrical experience of streamsbecoming, against dissolving ripples of becoming. Here too we might watch out, as Adorno puts it, that the 'dialectical salt' is not washed away in a 'tide of intuitionism and anti-conceptualism'.[13]

But Boetti's misgivings have more in common with Duchamp's sceptical tone in dealing with measure. With his 'algebraic expression', the latter had mulled over Bergson's distinction between 'numerical relative value' and those 'in duration'. He had pointedly noted that in the *Large Glass* the principal forms of the Bachelor apparatus were mensurated while those of the Bride were not. The radius of her forms in representation were 'fictitious', rendered through the device of dots and dashes to highlight their provisional nature. Could anything as fugitive as the 'passage from Virgin to Bride' be gauged except by means that made themselves apparent as estimates, residues and traces of that movement?[14]

VI

The 'actual representation' of Bride and Bachelor elements, he emphasised, is made up of approximations – examples 'without representational value'. He applied the view to the *Large Glass* as a whole, describing it as a sketch-model, a papier maché standstiff of ever-changing configurations of desire and energy. He had staged these probings of measure in *Standard Stoppages* (1913–14, MoMA, New York): dropping three-metre-long pieces of thread from the height of a metre, he glued them down exactly in the chance squiggles into which they had fallen – an anti-measuring device or a skew-whiff ruler of sorts – as he put it, 'a new chance image of the unit of length'.[15] He and Boetti highlight

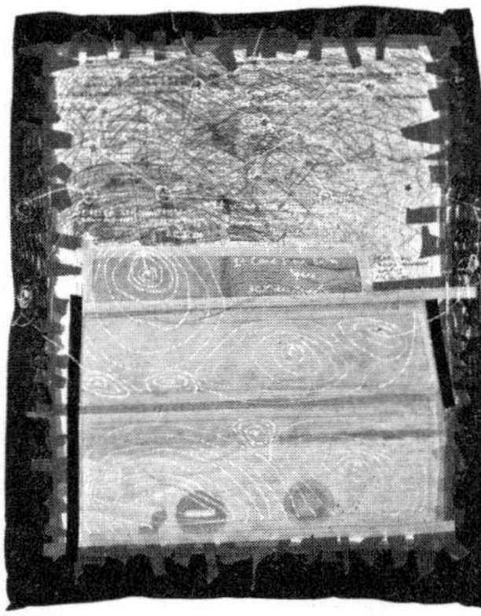
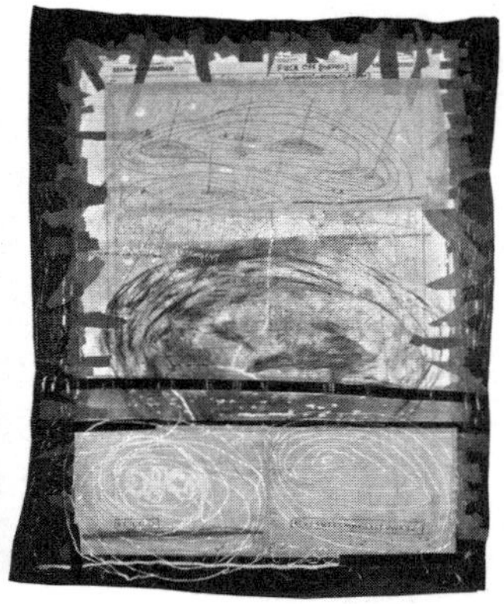

Right and far right: Moshekwa Langa, *Untitled*, 1995. Mixed media on paper, 113 x 97cm.

measure and representation as arbitrary datafiction. Both play-off the fixities of measure against chance free-fall and flow, turning them inside out to evoke the in-between of 'the extra-rapid State of Rest'.

Across the years of Boetti's *Thousand Longest Rivers* project, Deleuze and Guattari were working on *A Thousand Plateaus* in which the calculus of measure and representation is no less targeted.[16] In their Bergsonism, they distinguish between the metrical and mensurable and the flow of intensities, drawing a parallel with roughly two types of multiplicity. On the one hand is a 'denumerable multiplicity' – a grouping made up of countable items. In such a constellation, variety and difference are flattened because everything ultimately refers to or is derived from some implicit idea of an original One which subsumes the sense of the many and diverse. Against this, we have a 'non-denumerable multiplicity' consisting of disparate, singular items which hang together as a fuzzy aggregate. With the former we are obliged to think in terms of a process of totting up a string of digits expressed as (N + 1). With the latter we need to think not so much of a multiplicity composed of units but a congeries of non-totalisable factors and forces from which the sense of One is always subtracted (N – 1). The relationships might be expressed thus:

Calculus : denumerable minorities : :
streamsbecoming : non-denumerable minorities

To conceive of the 'minorities and marginals' along the lines of the first type of grouping is simply to treat them as a head count, a totting up of 'natal' entities. But to grasp the notion of a non-denumerable multiplicity is to see the minorities and marginals as ever-metamorphosing composites of disparate elements; with the change of any one element, a complete re-configuring, a different kind of hanging together comes into play. The former is a representation in terms of hard and fast 'natal' identities, as X = X (not Y) – something fixed. The non-denumerable multiplicity replaces this with an open equation of disparates – + y + z + a + – which expresses 'the pure becoming of minorities' as a constantly shape-shifting assemblage of elements, a de-natalising flow.[17]

After Apartheid Axioms

Zulu Richard Kumalo married Regina Brooks, a white Orange Free State woman. You know what she told the white cops? She wants to go and live with her husband, even if it means being classified an African. Can you beat that? The laanie wants to go and live in Orlando township.

Like a bolt from the blue, we heard that Singh and a laanie cherrie had been arrested under the Immorality Act. He married this sweet Afrikaner girl… one day the government allowed them to go and live in neighbouring Mozambique.
Jay Naidoo[18]

VII

Lovers across the colour-line, Sarap Singh and Rose, Richard Kumalo and the Orange Free State woman and innumerable other Bride and Bachelor desiring-machines were in head-on collision with the Apartheid turbo-engine. They had transgressed the Immorality Act forbidding cross-race sex, after which the Mixed Marriages Act sounded like a non-sequitur. Since neither partner was permitted to live where the other 'belonged' they fell foul of the Group Areas Act, after which the Race Classification Act could only be an inconsequential. Something other than a straight transgression of the regime's systems of representation was afoot. The love matches amounted to persistent leakage, a drip-dripping away that could not be contained by Apartheid

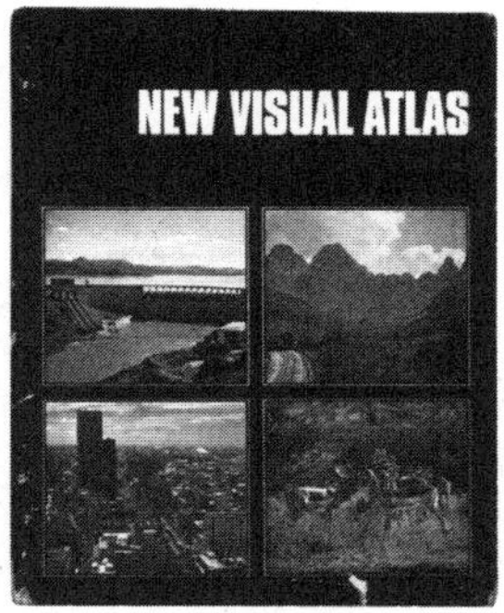

hydraulics and the network of conduits and sluits through which it sought to channel and represent relationships of desire.

Apartheid was not only a diaspora-making mega-machine – it was also an intensive natalising programme. It did not stop at casting out people from tribal lands, places of abode and residence to which it deemed they did not 'belong'. It took the further step of pronouncing on where they did 'fit in' and how this had to be lived. Not only did it devise and see through large-scale clearance of people from areas declared for 'whites-only', it also ethnically tagged the expropriated and dispossessed so as to oversee their confinement to new areas coded by colour, blood links and race – a calculated natalising.

The violence of this double production entailed the uprooting of people for re-location in the ethnic-tribal natalities of the 'homeland', the sham-independent Bantustans. At the other pole, it created city townships, shanty towns, satellite 'locations' to service the rural white towns with domestics, pockets of mixed race or 'coolie locations' in the white cities – soon-to-be-bulldozed municipal enclaves stamped with a bogus natality. The 'diasporic', normally restricted to exiles, exit permiters, émigrés, refugees and asylum seekers who left for the 'outside', should also be applied to those who remained 'inside' Apartheid – almost all Africans, Indians and Coloureds were at some stage pressed to get amoving and shunted around the country according to the plan of racialised re-location. The diasporic amounts to Apartheid's axiom – with a deadly corollary; dispersion was at the same time subordination to prescribed identity and belonging to a 'manufactured natality' – to one or another of the dozen official race categories, with those 'left-out' bluntly and bureaucratically classified as 'Other'.

The Apartheid axiomatic bolstered itself with laws to enforce the hi-speed removals of people, to regulate and anchor their re-location: the Group Areas Act which sorted, swindled and shipped out post-indenture communities in the province of Natal to 'Indian areas', shipping in Afrikaners and white immigrants in their place; the contract-permit-pass system fuelling the stop-go mega-circulation of labour between homeland and hostels of the industrial mining centres; the Influx Control laws monitoring the shuttle of blacks in and out of white areas. These laws of exclusion and expulsion expressed themselves in political punishment such as deportation, house arrest, exile, banishment. But in everyday terms they took the form of the unremitting dispersing logic of Apartheid with one proviso: no sooner had the axiomatic uprooted people, than it sought anxiously to fix and freeze them in its measure, to bring the streams of movement it had forcibly triggered to states of rest.

It is this overcoding – aimed at shoring up the territories Apartheid had carved up and stitched together – that Moshekwa Langa targets, scans and overrides in his collage series *Untitled* (1994–96). We catch him red-handed writing across pages ripped out of *Juta's New Visual Atlas*, a standard South African school textbook. An editing job, he glosses and emends the country's racial map. His word-ribbons, ink trails and scratchy doodles add up to a scattering of understated annotations, witty asides, quips, sniggers and swearwords. A low-wave running commentary on Apartheid's territorialisation gnaws away, defacing, cancelling, undercutting its representations. The map of Bophuthatswana, a Bantustan fashioned and fenced off according to Apartheid measure – site of a last-ditch shoot out at the birth of the Rainbow State by die-hards intent on maintaining the status quo – is scored over with acerbic, thick-fingered drawing. It obliterates the natalised map even as it sketches a fresh, pilot charting of the world.

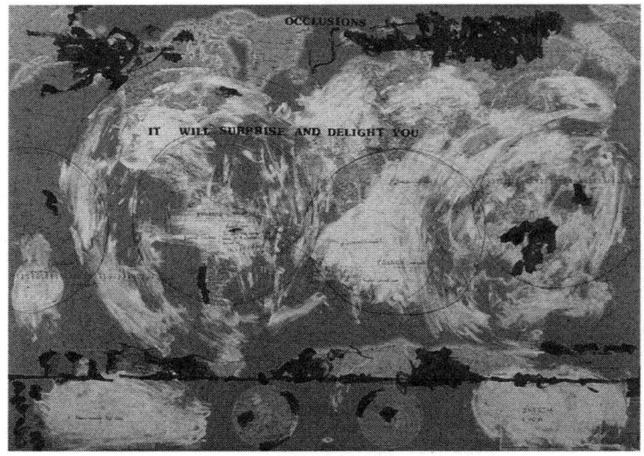

Moshekwa Langa, *Occlusions*, 1997. Typex and nail varnish on map.

VIII

Langa takes the measure of Apartheid's territorialising calculus by jamming its codes and units of measure. His scribbles and scrawls muck up the map-making conceptual devices of length, perspective and scale, the latitude/longitude grid. A jibe at the 'pleasant Afrikaners', expletives, snatch of a ditty, photo-cut-outs and sticky tape strips are plastered over pages of *Juta's New Visual Atlas* – old Apartheid cartographics – from the viewpoint of new South Africa. The extra-rapid switch over of modes recalls Duchamp's own speculations on a new atlas — an expositionary mode he called a 'geographic landscapism'.[19]

Across Langa's collages, grand schemes of calculation are played off against a personal, modest arithmetic: on one plane, the Apartheid state's macro-plan of counting up and classifying minerals and metals, enumerating and tabulating values, columns of figures, indexes of place-names, stock-exchange rates. On another, our glance pages through the bookkeeping of Mahlangu's *Butchery and Eatery* – a tally of assets and liabilities, income and outgoing, itemising of provisions and foodstuffs, the business of making ends meet. The juxtaposed registers impress a feeling of the lopsided and askew. In mock-exegetic marginalia jotted next to a map of the Bay of Natal, Langa dryly notes: 'approximate measurements, rates of discordance and deviance not accounted for…'. A sense of non-fit takes charge:

a being the overcoded Apartheid axiomatic
—
b " the decoding, denatalising, flow

The Apartheid map of homelands, racial areas, Bantustans – representations of fraudulent natalities — that Langa decodes and deterritorialises were the heavy-duty constructs of political policy. Debates over the last decade on re-conceptualising the historiography of the province of Natal have shown how Apartheid rationalised its manufacture of ersatz natalities by appeal to received, tendentious accounts of the 'mfecane' – the great blitz of the Zulu militarisation-migration under Shaka.[20] According to this myth the Zulu spilled out of their 'aboriginal heartland' in successive waves scattering neighbouring clans some of whom fled as far north as Lake Victoria. The shakedown and ensuing re-location of the clans was seized upon by Apartheid as the origins of the proto-homelands – as grist to its own design.

But, as has been argued, it is more than likely that the Zulu homeland was shaped defensively in the thick of struggles against a host of displacing threats – Portuguese slaving, British expansion, the Boer trek up from the south, enforced labour to meet shortages in the Cape colony – which was also to produce the 'excrementalised other' image of Shaka.[21] The point for us is that the natal – illustrated in the actual case of the province of Natal – surfaces not so much as a 'primal given' than as a focus emerging from the tussle with diasporising forces, in and through them.

The recoil from Apartheid's fake natalities triggers, perhaps not unexpectedly, the search for its 'true' opposite, for the yardstick of the 'authentically native place', an 'edenic aboriginality'. But in whatever mode 'the natal' is inflected, its thrust is to blur the divide between 'innate and acquired', 'crafted and natural' elements. Each element sits alongside and astride the other, each unravels and deterritorialises the other – highlighting its essential ambiguity.[22] On one front, if the natal is a refrain signifying a sense of location, it is also about the confines of a place that is always already-fraying, opening outward, dissipating. On the other, if it evokes the sense of diaspora, it is no less a displacing that is threaded and stitched to the 'homeland left behind or yet to be found'.

IX

The natal appears as a folding, involuting figure – 'its inside is outside' – the 'extra-rapid' flip-over of 'states of rest'. It tests and checks out the re-territorialising drives that riddle the multicultural milieu – questioning managerialist tendencies towards reducing difference to the standstiff, towards rendering the difference of the natal as 'aboriginal essence' and that of the diaspora as 'diasporic identity'.

At 2000, the tussle over difference and representation in the worldwide circuits of art and culture is mirrored in the clash of approaches in the Rainbow State. At one pole, Father of the Nation, Nelson Mandela argues from the basis of a heightened visibility of fixed 'natalities': 'the ordinary man, no matter to what population group he belongs, must look at our structures and see that "I, as a coloured man, am represented. I have got Allan Boesak there whom I trust." And an Indian must be able to say: "There is Kathrada – I am represented." And whites must also be able to say: "There is Gerrit Viljoen – I have got representation."'[23] At the opposite pole, Uncles of the Nation, 'members of the minorities', Allan Boesak and Mac Maharaj steer clear of such 'ethnicised' representation. The latter has pointedly observed that he did not wish to be referred to as an Indian claiming that as a third-generation South African without knowledge of an Indian tongue, his only connection with things Indian was his penchant for curry.[24] If his protestations sound a bit strenuous, they also have an idealistic ring.

However, it is not easy to decide which fares better – his attempt at 'becoming imperceptible' or Mandela's pragmatic calculus of representation. Both standpoints seem necessary to the uneven terrains and temporalities of contemporary multiculturalism and debates over difference. Each reflects something valid in its own right at the same time as each falls short of that 'liberty in the play of difference' they set their sights on. We are brought up short against another inflection of 'non-accordance'.

In this light, shifts in thinking 'difference' after Apartheid seem to be at once massive and minuscule. At Apartheid's highpoint, we saw Betsie Verwoerd, wife of the architect of Apartheid, exhorting white mothers to inculcate in their children a hard-nosed sense of distinction based on sheer visceral, odoriferous demarcations – of black body smell, of olfactory sensation and revulsion, as markers of cultural difference.[25] After Apartheid, we see her reading out an appeal for the creation of a white homeland – the volkstadt of Orania, for a separate space in the Rainbow. Mandela listens on, peering over her shoulders, gently prompting her as she falters without her glasses. As she looks up beamingly at him, the prickly question hangs in the air: can the multicultural calculus hold back from granting the volkstadt its own space in the Rainbow's arena of representation without defaulting on its principle of rendering 'difference' visible?[26]

The refrain of the natal is shot through with this play-off between deterritorialising drives and re-territorialising forces – which multicultural management is bent on stilling. Thomas Hardy's *The Return of the Native* (1878) is an exemplary site of this tangled play-off, its repetitions, mirrored returns and roundabouts. In the novel, Clym Yeobright returns from the metropolitan diaspora of Paris determined to turn his back on it and to settle into the rural natal ground of Egdon Heath. Heedless of the jagged electric forces that cut across and connect the two worlds – the extra-rapid state of rest – what he manages to set in train is ruin, disaster and pain summed up in his mother's pitiful cry: '*If you had never returned to your native place, Clym, what a blessing it would have been.....*'[27]

Issues Facing the African Arts: Interview with Adriano Mixinge

Landry-Wilfrid Miampika

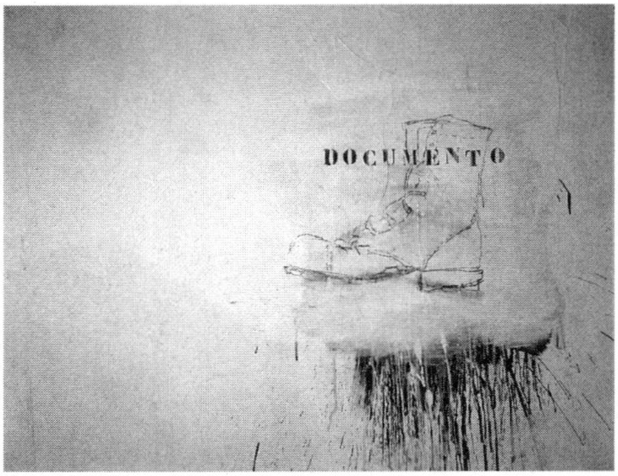

Fernando Alvim, *Documento*, 1994. Mixed media, 244 x 488cm.

Landry-Wilfrid Miampika: *With the advance of globalisation, you liken the African artist to a tortoise. Why?*

Adriano Mixinge: My likening of the African artist to a tortoise enables me to attribute him/her with the animal's inherent qualities and also to differentiate him/her from the rebel artist of the Western world, because the African artist is not an avant-garde artist in Western terms. The African artist is thus attributed with wisdom, reason, wiliness, creativity and resurrection, as described in African fables. This also shows how the African artist is capable of formulating a comprehensive postcolonial aesthetic.

L-WM: *So how does the African artist, or more specifically, the Portuguese-speaking African artist, as a tortoise, create his/her own modern identity in conjunction with an emerging postcolonial aesthetic?*

AM: A postcolonial aesthetic is becoming apparent right across the African arts, but the movement is still coming together. The postcolonial aesthetic was initially related to the independence of formerly colonised countries, most with policies focusing on regaining respect for local traditions. The postcolonial aesthetic comes as a challenge from the former colonies and African literature is still very much at the forefront of the movement. There are two main aspects to the new postcolonial aesthetic in the Fine Arts – the quest for images, icons and objects from the immemorial past and the construction or recreation of the present in relation to this past.

L-WM: *Given this new context, how does the African artist articulate, subvert and resolve the opposition between traditional and modern?*

AM: The European element has already become incorporated into our traditions. Everybody relates differently to this factor. Each artist's thought processes and creativity, the way he/she strings images together and the works of art he/she produces are intricately linked to his/her personal cultural context. This is quite distinct from the influence that his/her nationality, environment or the languages that he/she speaks (whether English, French or Portuguese) have on his/her work. However, the relationship between traditional and modern still bears the stigma of integration. As we know, integration plays an important role in Portuguese history since the indigenous peoples were obliged to forsake their cultural heritage. This then set a process of acculturisation in motion rather than *transculturisation* as defined by Fernando Ortiz. Although traditional culture is a constant backdrop to everyday life and the arts in Portuguese-speaking countries, modern culture almost always wins out over traditional culture.

L-WM: *African art has always gone hand in hand with historical disaster. How do the African arts currently depict this, especially in a country such as Angola that has been at war for the past thirty years?*

AM: In my opinion, there are two kinds of disaster. Firstly, there is the disaster that is war, and, secondly, there is the impact that war has on society. In places where there may be war – in a conventional form – there is, of course, a structural, social, economic, political and moral violence.

What's more, it must be noted that the decolonisation of the Portuguese colonies gave rise to a number of problems revealed through artistic and cultural creation. Angolan and Mozambique writers Pepetela and Mia Couto have shown several aspects of this catastrophe.

In the Fine Arts, Felipe Salvador, an Angolan artist currently exiled in Brazil, worked on the Cold War dichotomy during the 1980s. Rui de Matos, an army general working on the subject uses shrapnel and shells as material for his sculptures. Fernando Alvim, is behind the project *Mémoires Intimes: Traces*, which brings Cuban, Angolan and South African artists together. Frederico Ningi has created a sort of internal exile depicting the trauma of war in a city context. In

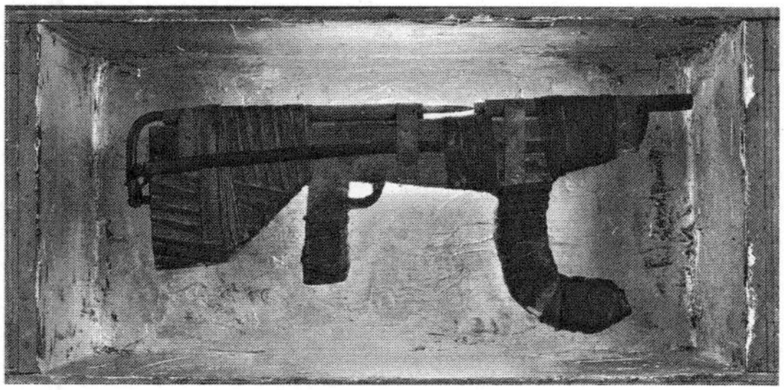

Fernando Alvim, *Mutinba*, 1994. Mixed media, 100 x 80 x 30cm.

Mozambique, Inacio Matsinhe also uses shrapnel and shells in his sculptures.

L-WM: *Art critic Jean-Godefroy Bidima puts forward the crossing as an epistemological and historical paradigm as a new foundation for the African arts. How do his 'art of the crossing' and the 'crossing of art' bring together the main threads of the African artistic sensibility?*

AM: Jean-Godefroy Bidima's idea of the 'crossing' is tri-partite. The first part is related to deconstructing influential myths, the second to the dialogue with modern culture and the problems of transcontinentality. The third and final part advocates the recycling of traditions in interaction with myth deconstruction. In this way, the art of the crossing does not make any reference to a static origin, other than a compromise with origin, with history, with traditions combined with a new reading focusing on the continuum.These ideas, drawn from Bidima's work, have contributed to my theory on the four tendencies of African sensitivity and logic already present in literature, dance and music. These are: the artistic sublimation of war and death; fictionalising history, myths and the universe; the portrayal of the subject, society, customs or nature; and lastly, the representation of time-space totalities like the reproportioning of the role of ancestral values and of a free imagination.

L-WM: *What are the essentials of each of the tendencies?*

AM: The artistic sublimation of war and death utilises war as a phenomenon in its own right and stresses the need for peace. This is depicted through the artists' appropriation of military papers, war-related objects, the idea of camouflage and the trauma that society has faced. According to the Christian Children's Fund, Angolan tribal chiefs insist that the war will probably continue in Angola until burial rites and ancient funeral ceremonies are performed. Strong socio-political statements of this kind go hand in hand with the artistic tendency. Art is currently performing a kind of purging process that society will eventually have to perform for itself. Artists following this kind of movement can also be found in Ethiopia, Rwanda, Mozambique and other countries that have been subjected to military or ethnic conflict.

Fictionalising history, myths and the universe is related to the way artists deal with myths. Artists like Mustapha Dimé and Viyé Diba from Senegal are part of the tendency. Another artist, Frederic Bruly Brouabré, has been creating a kind of personal diary of his view of the universe. Yinka Shonibare at one time produced a kind of personal diary of nineteenth-century Victorian England using photography as a type of theatrical space in which the artist dressed up as an Englishman of the time. His work is humorous, playful, slapstick and uses history not belonging to an African. However, since Yinka Shonibare lives in London, he takes on this history as part of his bicultural identity, so to speak, which means that he can move in English and African contexts at the same time.

The tendency of the portrayal of the subject, society, customs and nature dates back to the first half of the twentieth century with painting styles such as the portrait, still life, landscape and various ethnic group compositions which served as a supplement to anthropological studies. During the 1990s, four photographers were representative of this tendency. Seydou Keïta (Mali) portrayed the middle-class during the 1950s when Bamako was one of the most prosperous cities in Africa. The work of Oladélé Bamgboyé and Rotimi Fani-Kayode (Nigeria) focuses on racial (white/black) and sexual (male/female) identity within the context of the diaspora affected by cultural intermingling. Zwelethu Thetwa portrays South Africans living in shanty towns or townships. In short, the tendency depicts Africans of today as a subject or pretext for discussing social problems such as male homosexuality (still a taboo subject), poverty and the difficulty that the majority of

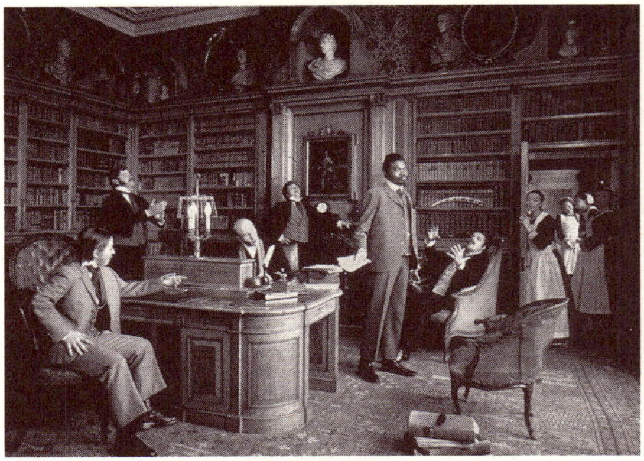

Yinka Shonibare, *Diary of a Victorian Dandy, 14.00 hours*, London Underground poster sites, 1–31 October 1998.

black South Africans have in gaining access to knowledge and high technology.

Lastly, the representation of time-space totalities such as re-assessing the role of ancestral values and of a free imagination refers to the integration of different types of art making use of the idea of time and space in connection with dance, theatre and music. Along these lines, Zaire artist Bodys Kingelez portrays a utopian Kinshasa in a post-industrial age and Tapfuma Gutsa from Zimbabwe is redefining African sculpture.

L-WM: *How does contemporary African art reconcile the need for a new pan-Africanism and what the President of South Africa, Thabo Mbeki, calls the 'African Renaissance'?*

AM: Lately, there has been talk of the need for a new pan-Africanism that runs parallel to what Thabo Mbeki has called the 'African Renaissance'. Historically speaking, pan-Africanism was postulated by William Du Bois in the late nineteenth century and early twentieth century to lay claim to the preconceptions of one Negro identity around the world. The 'African Renaissance', although recently reviewed by Thabo Mbeki, has previously been discussed in the *Introduction de la culture africaine*, published by UNESCO at the end of the 1980s to illustrate the relationship between political power and independence movements in sub-Saharan Africa. Thabo Mbeki no doubt talks about a 'second' African Renaissance related to the independence of South Africa and its rise as one of the centres of legitimisation of knowledge, old traditions and high technology. I believe that there should be a fusion between these two schools of thought. We will therefore come to talk about a 'pan-African Renaissance' in which all Africans, whether from Africa or elsewhere, will have a common identity and history – that of slavery, colonisation and decolonisation – at once uniting and differentiating them.

L-WM: *Could you then say that the African Renaissance is in some ways a fertile new utopia that follows the failure of the utopia of independence and the state of the current independence process constantly aggravated by ethnic conflict?*

AM: It is true that it could lead us to a real and new utopia. It is true that sub-Saharan Africa is a patchwork of cultures. Any discourse that goes beyond national boundaries is risky. The 'pan-African Renaissance' discourse makes it possible for Africans to dialogue with each other and also partake in other regional discourses in order to better combat the dangers of globalisation. Talking about a 'pan-African Renaissance' is therefore a necessary utopia.

L-WM: *Ousmane Sow's exhibition on the Pont des Arts in Paris, or the exhibition* 2500 Years of Nigerian Art *organised by the Fundación la Caixa were enthusiastically received by the public and art critics alike. Would you say that African art is being better accepted in the Western world?*

AM: Contemporary African art is gaining more respect on the Western circuit. There is a whole network of exhibitions, magazines and European and American institutions that are interested in it. Traditional African art, which was the subject of numerous colonial ethnological studies, is still the reference and is a historical fact. For example, the institutional system of art in Spain needs to be better structured and developed. Having said this, the system in Barcelona is an exception. There have been several exhibitions of traditional art, such as the exhibition *2500 Years of Nigerian Art* or an exhibition by South African artist William Kentridge, to name a few. All the same, it should be noted that the attention being paid to African art is partly because there are a great many African specialists in European universities and museums. This interest shows a change of attitude towards Europe and America's vast diaspora

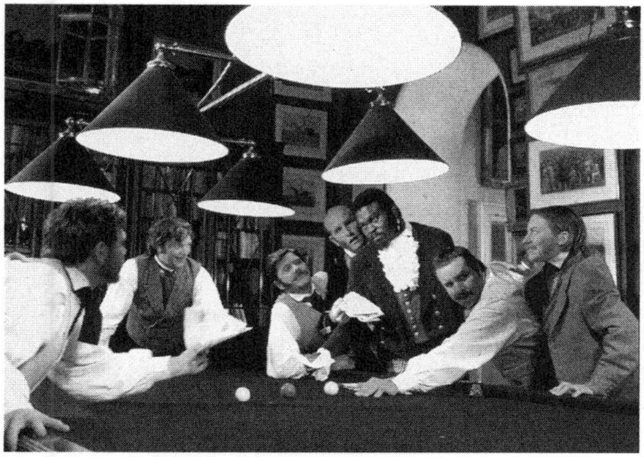

Yinka Shonibare, *Diary of a Victorian Dandy, 17.00 hours*, London Underground poster sites, 1–31 October 1998.

populations. In short, even though the West continues to speak in the name of the Other, it admits the possibility of the Other speaking for him or herself.

L-WM: *Will this acceptance have an impact on the power relationship between the centre and the margins?*

AM: Of course. Even though the centre-margin dichotomy has never really existed according to Eldridge Cleaver. Better still, two extremes have always existed – the have and the have-nots, the insiders and the outsiders, those who make themselves heard and those who are not heard. The dialogue between the arts makes it possible to go from one extreme to the other, from the extreme of forgotten or unknown art to the extreme of recognised art that has been studied and legitimised, or vice versa.

Untitled (A Way In)

Lisa Fischman

Laylah Ali's work is a complicated provocation, a dare that demands every viewer's complicity in the making of meaning. The works presented in *Fault Lines* include a selection from the artist's distinctive *Greenheads* series. In these spare gouache paintings, Ali renders brightly coloured figures with big round heads, in groups or alone, against distinctive sky-blue planes. Coded through precise articulations of physical form, gesture and costume, the figures struggle in circumstances that suggest complex relationships and uncertain ends. The work circulates, thematically, around issues of power, violence, indifference and the narrow possibility of redemption. Narrative is suggested but remains ambiguous.

Beyond the most basic schematic description, Ali's work insists on such self-reflexivity in the act of looking that even the distillation of meaning becomes culturally charged. Theoretical and adjectival choices that accrete into analysis become fraught with significance, an index of a given viewer's positionality – that accumulation of identity, experience and acculturated visual literacy that each of us brings to the act of looking. This is to say two things. First, that the deceptive simplicity of Ali's work cloaks a sophisticated strategic consolidation of aesthetic and semiotic signs into a form of active engagement. And second, while Ali's visual language employs familiar elements derived from American visual and material culture, it not only opens 'meaning' to a multiplicity of interpretations but makes each viewer responsible for its production.

Compositionally and stylistically, and in the figural evocation of action, the work refers to comics – a hybrid visual/textual medium of elastic conventions that invites endless innovation yet retains the egalitarian communicative power of its origins. Ali's images function like story-boards, presenting action either through sequential framing or encapsulating stills that read like amplified segments cut from larger sequences. Proportion, in the figures' relation to each other and to the ever-present blue sky, creates compositional tension; pictorial anxiety is further reinforced by the shallowness of the space, as a narrow white band grounds the tautly rendered characters. Although in large part absent, the linear framing device associated with traditional comics remains like a shadow, boxing in each plane.

Ali works in gouache (opaque watercolour), an old-fashioned, labour-intensive and tonally sensitive medium reminiscent of the inking applied to colour comics and illustration. It also calls to mind the stellar work of African American painter Jacob Lawrence (1917–2000), who favoured the 'hard, bright [and] brittle' qualities that lend the medium its robust graphic capabilities.[1] In Ali's hands, gouache is tightly, almost excruciatingly controlled, her line meticulous and unyielding. Tellingly, she speaks of refusing 'stray marks' and choosing instead to put 'the quixotic impulses of my hand into the motivations of the characters'. She prefers an 'austerity' of application that allows 'more unpredictability… to live in the paintings'.[2] Her shrewdly limited palette – black, brown, green, blue, red and white – and use of vividly saturated colour create a dissembling distraction of sorts, at a distance lending the work a cheerful buoyancy that transforms into something else entirely upon closer viewing. Even the signature blue of the skies against which her characters act is precisely nuanced, differentiated among pieces by exacting gradations of shade and tone. Painted meticulously over pencil outlines, her surfaces are paradoxical, retaining important evidence of Ali's hand while insisting on a cool anti-expressionism.

Capturing the graphic visual force of comics, Ali strips the figure to its barest humanoid essence, adds a gigantic head and excises the markers that we take for granted as sure signs of identity. The artist's reductive strategy is both mischievous and interrogative, a way of exploding simplistic binary categorisations – human/alien, male/female, good/evil, black/white – and forcing their reexamination. It also lends the figures a certain freedom, allowing them, as she puts it, to 'act like a question mark'.[3] They are simultaneously childish and brutal. Gender, race and age are fluid traces in these pictures, the integers of identity most crucial to Ali's power plays. I, for one,

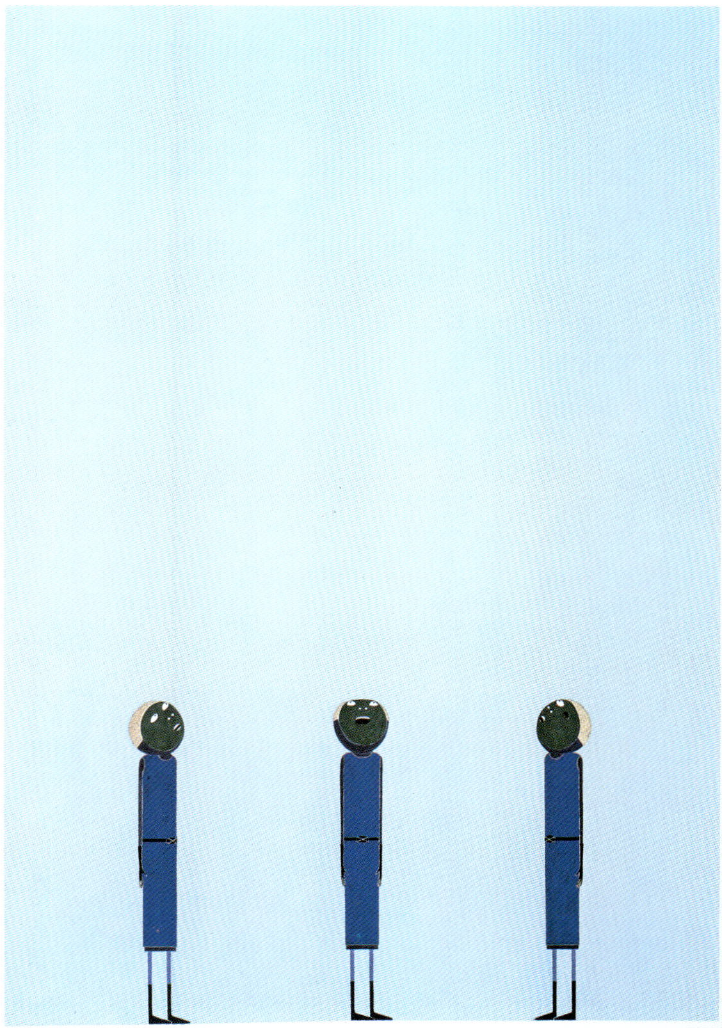

Untitled, 2001. Gouache on paper, 69 x 46cm.
Courtesy of 303 Gallery, New York.

cannot help but see most of the figures as male – although there are few signs to confirm this. Somehow, from the outline of a hairdo or a gesture, I think I recognise others as female. Then again, as Ali points out, to see her figures as human at all – remember their strange oversized green heads – is patently ridiculous.[4] The confusion and coercion are deliberate and precisely what makes the work so powerful.

Ali's images both evoke and undermine the nostalgic inflection of childhood innocence on to comics yet retain the inquisitive pleasures of early readership, particularly how we make sense of signs not yet fully known to us. While her earlier caped figures, for example, reference superheroes, they do so in ways more closely aligned with a comix sensibility (the 'x' signalling underground alternative publications that have thrived since the 1970s). They engage in behaviour that jars against the escapist power fantasies of traditional comics and unravels the familiar moral and narrative clarity of that genre. Through cunning reference, Ali's work raises pressing questions. Is masking a sign of power or vulnerability? Do uniforms connote strength or weakness of character? What does it mean to take sides?

Variants of capes, masks, ropes, belts, hats and uniforms of all sorts (plus bathing suits, vestments and shorts), elongated and dismembered limbs, green heads, big eyes and denture-like teeth are all components in Ali's unique system of signs, one that functions stylistically as well as symbolically. It is tempting to consider the figures typographically, as formal components of a visual language, to get at the subtle nuance of their evocation and their resistance to complete definition.[5] The figures also interact alphabetically and can be understood typographically, each piece as an element in a visual phrase, even given that content remains elusive. There is an intensely literary quality to the work, a boundless narrativity that rewards multiple considerations. Most of Ali's works are very small and invite patient solitary engagement, reminiscent of reading. (This is particularly effective at a moment when both art-market and advertising tastes run to the super-sized, preferring images digestible at a glance.) That Ali does not include text in the work – she eliminates speech balloons, for example, which give voice to characters and provide specific narrative direction in comics – is a strategic erasure, as is the choice to present her entire oeuvre *sans* title. Both decisions heighten rather than diminish her images' communicative power.

Three of the pieces presented in the exhibition include some of Ali's largest to date. Together with a fourth they comprise something of a mini-series, each setting a group of Greenheads against an unusually expansive blue plane. Costumed to suggest mysteries of affiliation, Ali's characters inhabit their panels as actors frozen in mid-script; mute and stopped, the scenes resonate with tantalising narrative implication. In one, a long tall figure stands faced by three progressively smaller ones. All are fully masked in black, with telltale emerald skin just peeping through around the eye and mouth holes. The tallest figure, in a long, blue robe with brown dots, has a head more ovoid than round. The others wear matching, belted uniforms, similarly patterned. Strangely stilled, they are differentiated by scale and subtle nuances of facial expression, which suggest great anxiety. Do they represent military or pedagogical alliance? Gradations of age or experience? A power relationship is clearly at stake, but what is it exactly?

Another (see p. 99) presents three equivalent Greenheads, each with a stubbled scalp that reads like a repulsively funny cap of rejuvenating skin. As parallel forms clad identically in cobalt suits, the trio stares intently upwards into an unmitigated blue. The middle figure, fully frontal, stands mouth agape... in a scream of pleasure or a wail of alarm? Two flanking figures, positioned at angles to the surface plane, are near mirror images, though one is disfigured by an emptied eye socket. What are their loyalties? What kind of violence has been done to them? What do they anticipate might descend from above? What meanings attach around such strained waiting?

A third large work is galvanised by more dynamic inter-relation. Like doctors rendered ominous behind their hygienic

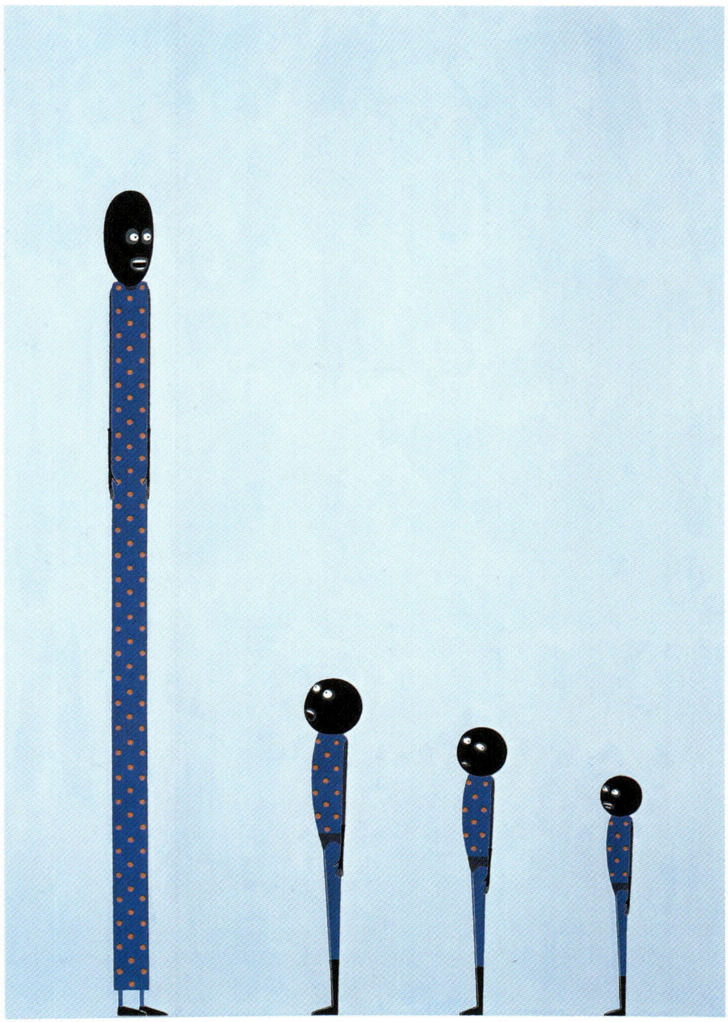

Untitled, 2001. Gouache on paper, 69 x 46cm.
Courtesy of 303 Gallery, New York.

protection, two larger Greenheads are tightly buttoned-up into blue overalls, their mouths shielded behind surgical masks and arms sheathed in long white gloves. They interact – touching, holding – with three creatures resembling mutant babies, squirmy beings akin to slugs or shrimps. Upper faces masked in black, their bodies bearing obvious hurt – with fleshy x-marked torso spots and legs truncated as though by amputation – these smaller Greenheads are clearly in distress. Wearing tiny sneakers on their hands, it would seem as though they've learned to manage; yet they remain essentially connected, either in circumstances of captivity or uneasy care, to the larger figures. The image eludes simple analysis, yet its obvious references to medicalised power suggest blurred lines between playfulness, nurture, dependence and control.

The final piece stages another trio. An imposingly attenuated figure, unmasked and adorned instead by a regal black nimbus that reads like an otherworldly Afro, is faced by two smaller figures. Dressed in hooded blue leotards and pale blue tights, the latter bend at the waist, speaking the body language of obeisance, their skinny brown arms thrust downwards in a gesture that implies entreaty under rule, fear or supplication in the face of power. Each is disfigured by a lumpy form, a hump at the upper back whose origins remain (protectively?) hidden, but for the tiny sneaker-clad feet that sprout like alien bug wings. Although narrative remains uncertain, Ali evokes the gestural signs of domination and submission, servitude and autonomy, through scale and form.

Ali's characters could be spacemen or aliens, kings or priests or servants, bandits or hybrid superheroes. Ultimately, they seem to be a species of doppelgängers, stand-ins for the human condition, embroiled in struggles and enacting gestures quoted from the pages of history and contemporary media coverage. Physically, they call to mind eugenics, the specious 'science' predicated on head shape and skin colour that effectively constructed race from the nineteenth century onwards in America. Perhaps they act out the social repercussions of

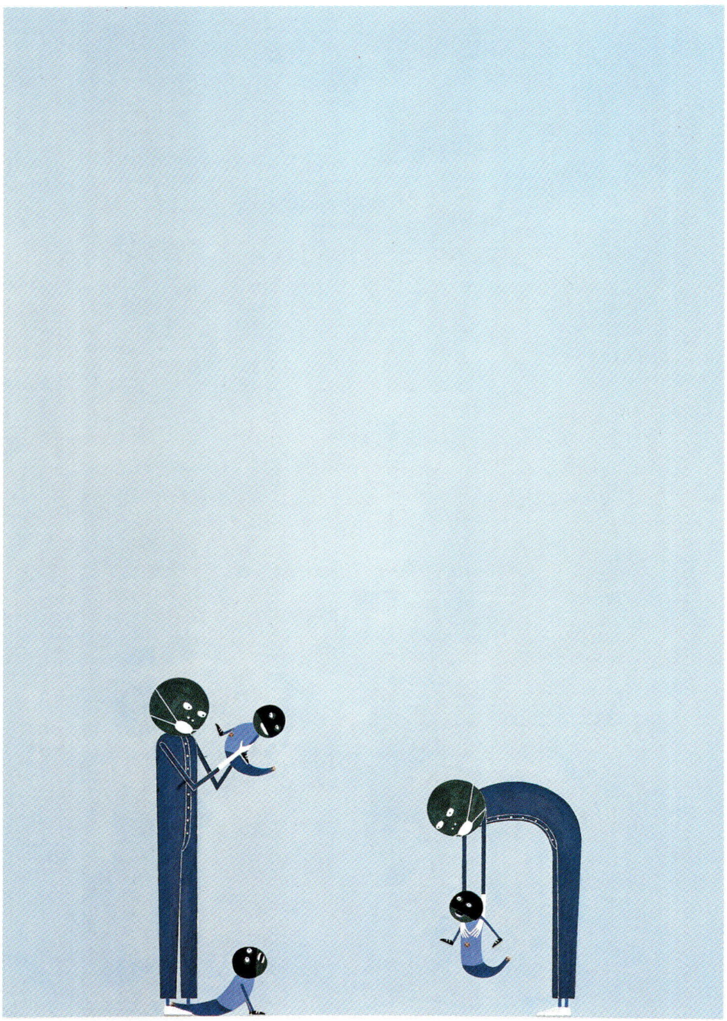

Untitled, 2001. Gouache on paper, 69 x 46cm.
Courtesy of 303 Gallery, New York.

such models writ large and distilled back down again, refracted through time and crystallised as permutations of possibility. Whatever their origin, these stories are clearly our own.

As forceful as Ali's artistic voice is in its independence, it is also generational in orientation. A child of the 1970s, the artist was raised on TV sitcoms and network news coverage, which detailed as well as mediated intense cultural shifts – Civil Rights, feminism, space exploration, political corruption, Vietnam, etc. – for visual consumption.[6] For her generation (also mine), radical social change was posed as a promise rather than a struggle, as evidenced by the revolutionary transformations of the Black Power movement and the dorky post-hippie assurances that we were all 'free to be, you and me'. We were guaranteed beneficiaries of a utopian dream. The betrayal of that promise is a defining element of a generational consciousness and the anger it produced has generated a distinctive energy. Like Ali, many young African American artists possess a confidence born of that era – an empowered optimism – but cast a critical eye on the course of history since.[7]

Although her practice is still young, Ali has honed a visual language that is intimidating in its originality. On first encounter, I was impressed by the bright menace of her work, a fierce threatening quality that commands closer inspection. Today I see the work as a force of defamiliarisation, a challenge to our acceptance of the ways things are, the ways things are run, the way the world has gone – an indictment of promises diluted and ideals betrayed. Pushing further beyond one critic's contention that 'visual literature begins where language leaves off; it extends mankind's abilities to identify, describe, analyze, evaluate and extol the ineffable',[8] Ali's work demands that art declare its own integrity, stand its ground and incite transformation. In ways that are particularly resonant at this historical moment, given the global sweep of political instability, Ali's work is both an act of faith and a critical intervention into the violent certainties of human relations.

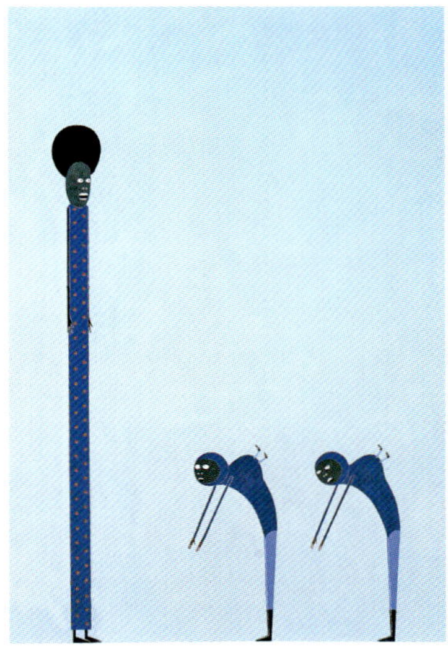

Untitled, 2001. Gouache on paper, 69 x 46cm.
Courtesy of 303 Gallery, New York.

The Right Position: An Interview with Kader Attia

Jérôme Sans

Jérôme Sans: *In your work, you make frequent reference to the identity of the Algerian community in which you were born, and to that of housing estates on the outskirts of cities.*

Kader Attia: The culture from which I am descended (my Algerian roots) has nothing in common with the culture in which I live. This is a fact of Arab life that is often misunderstood in France. You move from the culture of the *bled* (the North African village) to that of a housing estate. They're far from similar. On the estate, you eat at Pizza Hut or McDonald's, girls wear thongs and listen to R&B, and everyone shops at Foot Looker or H&M. Every day is another struggle for survival. On your own, you're nothing. You only exist as part of a gang and you have to put up with anything from them. When I borrowed art books from the library everyone thought it was a weird thing to do, totally devoid of interest.

In contrast to the ancient culture of the *bled*, the culture of the housing estates is still under construction (through graffiti, street wear, rap, break dancing, etc.). Speaking Arabic in Algiers is meaningful, especially as it's a language with strong links to the oral culture there. The people of the *bled* don't have the same gaping holes in their culture as the kids on estates. When you've grown up among the *beurres* (French-born Algerians) on an estate, you know that every estate will have its Elvis double, like my friend Mohamed, and its Elvis fans who don't ever give it up and who never will. It's a phenomenon that typifies a culture that has been cut off from its roots. Twenty years on, I came across a character from Garges-les-Gonesses who had stayed faithful to himself, Eddy le Rocker. Straddling two cultures means that I can keep a certain distance. African cultures are more accepting of difference and eccentricities (look at Algerian transvestites or Zaïrian *sapeurs* or dandies). In these cultures people have a need to express themselves through dressing up and show.

JS: *Is this why you have always been interested in portraits?*

La Piste d'Atterrissage (The Landing Strip), 1998–2000. Slide installation.

KA: That's what a portrait is: a way of promoting the best image of yourself.
JS: *But what is it that fascinates you in portraits, a photographic genre that has largely fallen out of fashion?*
KA: In photography I'm fascinated by early photographs of ordinary people, especially those by August Sander, where the subjects are shown full-length and in their own surroundings, as in Africa. Or grocers all got up in their Sunday best and pretending to be members of the bourgeoisie. Finery and display play an important part in North African culture. Hence the present culture of the right look: designer labels, gold jewellery, make-up, hairstyles, etc. And everything drenched in perfume. The effort we put into constructing the image we want for ourselves is always evident.
JS: *Do you photograph people in your own circle, or people from a particular community?*
KA: Some people have said that mine is a humanist photography. To photograph people, to take their portraits, is to meet them. A portrait is the faithful image of the individual you are photographing. It gives concrete form to your relationship with them, to the time it takes to get to know someone: their clothes, their sexuality, their daily routines, which is the reason why I have chosen characters from my world. They are all people with different backgrounds. When you photograph one of your friends, they never give you a picture of their everyday problems but immediately convey an aura of happiness, when often the reality is the opposite of this smiling idyll.
JS: *Curiously, although your family plays an important part in your life, until recently you have not included them in your photographic world.*
KA: I used not to want to picture people who were friends or family. I preferred to focus my work on rich, complex personalities with multilayered lives. People who are out of kilter or who live double lives. Sandrine, one of my ex-girlfriends, for example, wanted to be depicted according to one of her fantasies. Coming to terms with yourself and your fantasies in front of the lens

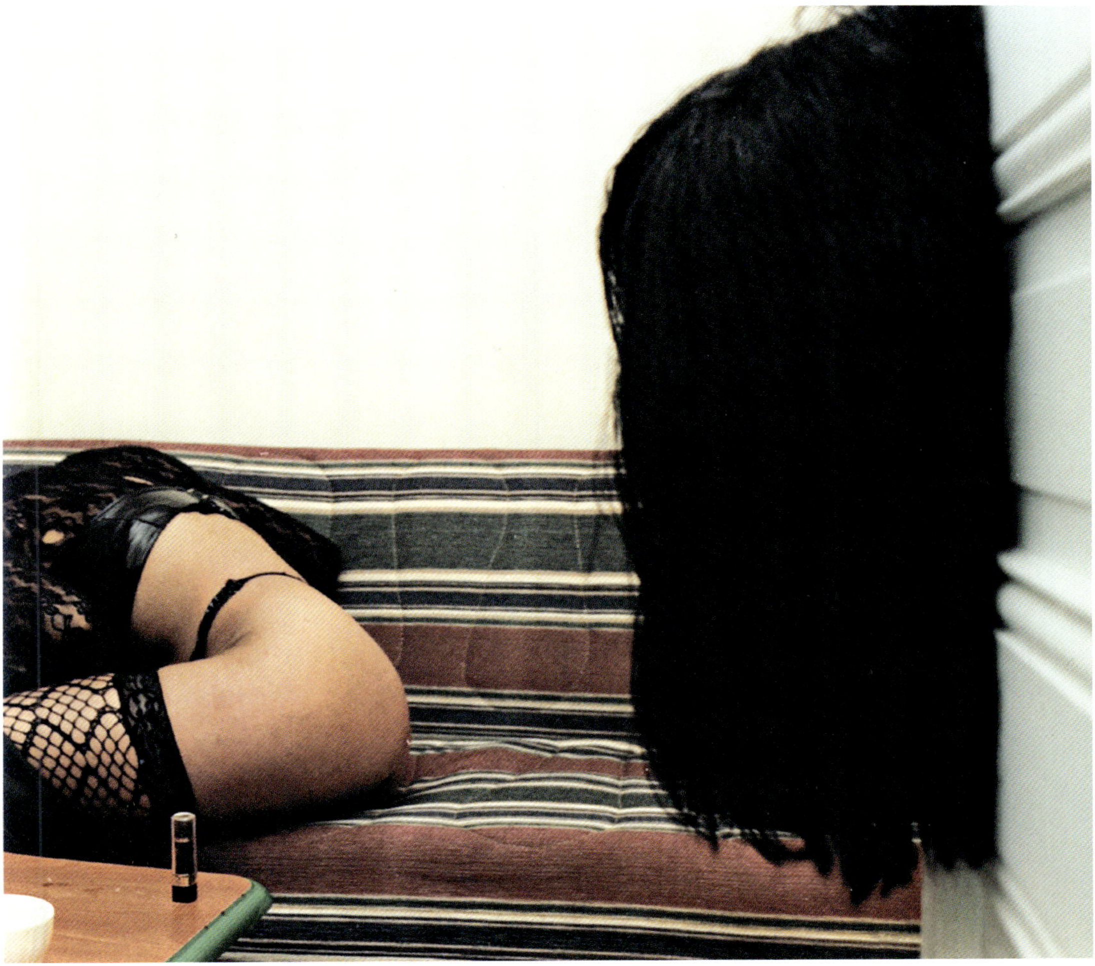

reveals an element of sordidness. Latent in the image is a sort of sexual impoverishment. It is as though the model is offering three seconds of immortality to her fantasy. Perhaps we are fascinated by this imbalance, by the fleeting nature of what we want to present as an image. But in reality we are all impoverished.
JS: *What is the significance of reviving portraiture now?*
KA: Portraiture is group therapy. It's healing. People with extreme personalities who lay themselves bare in front of the camera, facing up to their fantasies.
JS: *So should everyone take portraits?*
KA: Taking portraits is a natural, instinctive, human gesture. It is a dialogue between two people which develops as the encounter progresses. You never stop making portraits. When you meet someone new in your life, you naturally create their portrait. Since first impressions are often deceptive you frequently get it wrong, but that's inevitable.
JS: *Was this the motivation behind* Alter Ego *(2001–2)?*
KA: *Alter Ego* was conceived in Africa, at Brazzaville in Congo, where I was doing two years of military service in 1997. I had been talked into taking someone's photograph. When I gave him his photograph, showing him from the waist up, it frightened him. In that culture, the image of a person without legs is believed to be a bad omen. I then understood why African photographers always take special care to depict the whole person, with no parts of the body cut off. It was at that point that I started work on a series of full-length portraits, with the idea of depicting the subjects fully and as they saw themselves in their fantasies.

We tend to forget that smiling for the camera has become a natural reflex. Why do we smile? Because the resulting photo is passed round from person to person and others form an idea of whom we are on the basis of that image. Our immediate relationship with the camera lens is a fantasy of what we believe ourselves to be – our self-image. It is the principle of narcissism. I like the notion of this fantasy, of something we can never actually

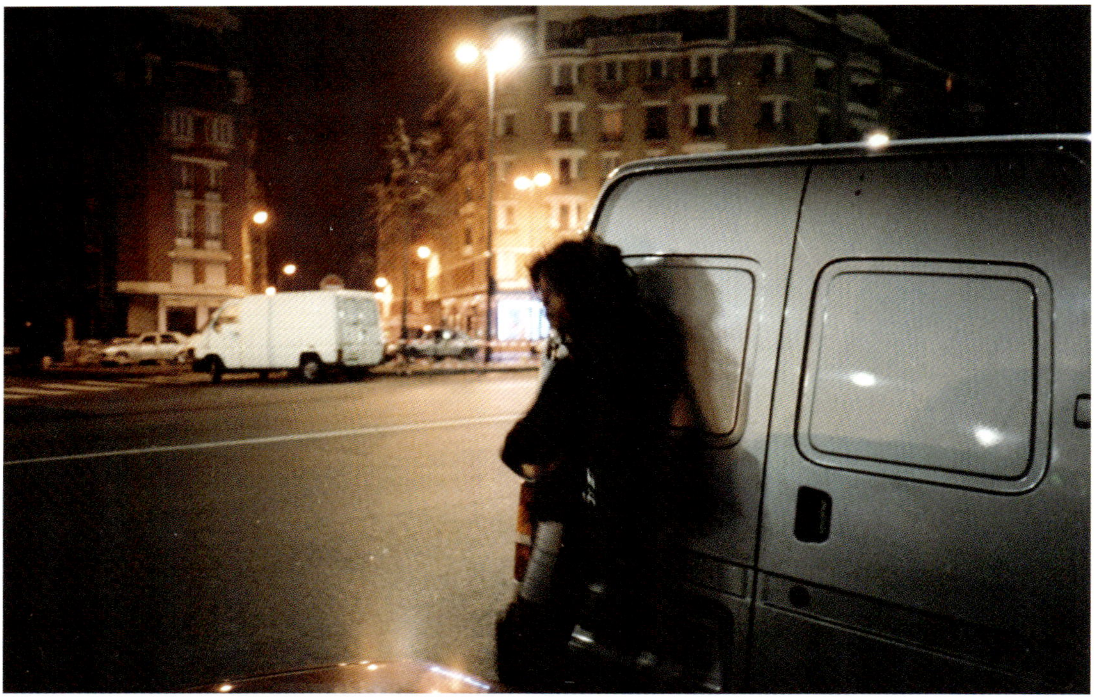

La Piste d'Atterrissage (The Landing Strip), 1998–2000. Slide installation.

achieve. We never manage to fulfil our fantasy and we never succeed in controlling the image that people form of us.

JS: *What in your view links* Alter Ego *with* La Piste d'Atterrissage *(The Landing Strip, 1998–2000), a slide installation of 160 photographs, the result of two years spent in the world of Algerian transsexuals living in Paris? Does your interest in this underground community lie partly in the fact that it is doubly marginalised?*

KA: Unlike photographs of daily life, *La Piste d'Atterrissage* is a quasi-ethnographic project in which the images form a link with a world that we don't even know exists and into which I found myself plunged. I immersed myself completely until I became part of it. Virtually all the characters were unaware they were being photographed. Both the setting up of the shots and the sequencing of them were important, as they tell a story. We are all part of a scenario in time, somewhere between fiction and reality. The work consists of horizontal images presented in the form of a slide installation, with the ending left hanging in mid-air. I wanted to stress the idea of reverence before these saints for the year 2000. For me they are the modern-day equivalent of medieval saints, people who take everything upon themselves, who are persecuted, abused, ridiculed and finally adulated. This is what happens to transvestites. Everyone heaps scorn on them while at the same time offering them adulation. It's the same for old eccentrics, such as rockers. In general, I believe that people who live on the margins of society represent our fantasies in some way. They enjoy a certain freedom by simply being themselves, regardless of how they may be ghettoised by society. Human beings spend their lives struggling to accept themselves. So when they come across someone who is not afraid to express themselves they are jealous and cast stones.

In *Alter Ego*, it was the subjects who chose how to present themselves. We find ourselves in a reality that hits us head-on. The photographs are life-size (110 x 210cm). The viewer is confronted by things he cannot see, by things that lie outside the frame. There is a spatial rather than temporal relationship with the image, which calls on the imagination. These are fixed, vertical, iconic images which communicate on a hieratic level that could never be created by a slide installation and its accompanying soundtrack.

JS: *Is the slide installation of* La Piste d'Atterrissage *a way of making a static film, of approaching the personal diary aesthetic of artists such as Jonas Mekas and Nan Goldin?*

KA: I admire Jonas Mekas and Nan Goldin, but in my work I try to avoid dwelling on the trashy or seedy glamour of the subjects in order to concentrate on the social and political weight of the images. Unlike the work of Nan Goldin, *La Piste d'Atterrissage* and *Alter Ego* do not constitute a personal diary. I select my subjects in the same way as an ethnographer. They are examples of the society in which I live and, to me, they are not that marginal. I was drawn to them, despite not being particularly sympathetic at the outset. But then they became my friends. In other respects, I remain influenced by my early years as a press photographer. Unlike Nan Goldin, I have an objective relationship with photography; I never take photographs of my girlfriend or of things that make me happy or sad.

JS: *Do you feel that in* Alter Ego *the social and political aspects are less obvious?*

KA: That's inherent in the subject matter. Certainly the political aspect is missing from *Alter Ego*, but it is replaced by a more psychoanalytical dimension. It is above all a socio-cultural work, in that all the people photographed come from African cultures and experience less difficulty in coming to terms with themselves. Mère Malou, for example, was the presiding genius of Congolese nights in Kinshasa and is hugely respected by numerous musicians (including Papa Wemba and Kofi Olomidé). Despite her age and the massive amounts of whitening products she has used to lighten her complexion, she retains all her glamour and style.

JS: *What are the limits of this series?*

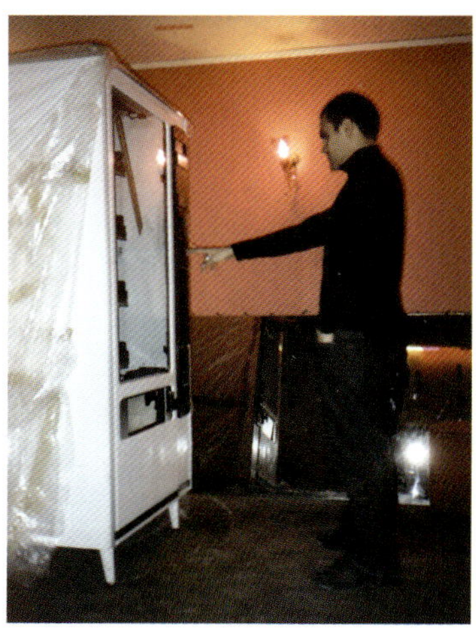

Left and right: *La Machine à Rêves* (Dream Machine), 2002–3. Vending machine.

KA: Even if I edit down the selection of characters, *Alter Ego* will always be unfinished, to the extent that there are still so many other personalities that I hope to meet who are at once complex and frivolous. For this work, I wanted to stay within my own immediate environment, which is why I have displayed only twelve portraits. They represent my world. Eighteen months ago, I went back to live with my parents at Garges-les-Gonesses. That made me want to photograph my friends' brothers, all kitted out and ready to go clubbing.

JS: *At your private view, everyone had to bring a photograph of someone they loved. What did you do with all this material? Was this part of the same process that is at work in* Alter Ego*, where the photographs represent a fantasised reality of oneself or someone else, their alter ego?*

KA: Everyone takes pictures of other people and keeps images of those they love. It's a natural thing to do. Once again, to meet someone is to form your own idea of them: to make their portrait. At parties, we usually put our everyday concerns to one side. Providing a photo of a loved one as an entrance pass for my private view was also a way of offering a fantasy image of someone dear to us. It is our favourite image, the one we always keep with us to the point where it ends up becoming part of us. To give this image away is to give away one of our fantasies. Nothing could be more natural than to begin a celebration with the idea of fantasy. Over four thousand people took part in the event that night. There wasn't room for everyone, but I managed to collect over two thousand photos. In the end they formed an installation as all the photos were pinned to a white wall like pictures of the latest stars on a teenager's bedroom wall. Everyone pictured there had their own fifteen minutes of fame – like the subjects of *Alter Ego*.

JS: *Your latest project,* La Machine à Rêves *(Dream Machine, 2002–3), deals with the clichéd lives that young people lead in the urban hinterland.*

KA: When you inhabit a social world such as these estates, whether as a teenager or

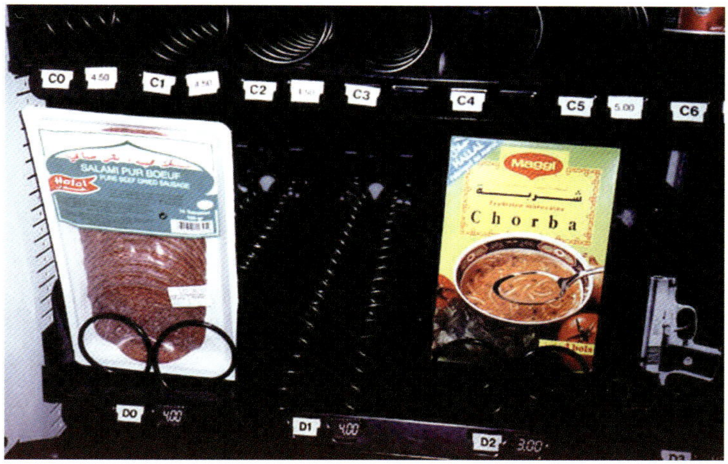

not, the symbols of success imposed by the consumer society take the form of pretty girls, smart cars, nice clothes – of affluence. If none of these is your thing, then you're left with proselytizing religion, whether Jewish or Muslim. On the estates, there aren't that many choices for survival. Either you attach yourself to a gang or group and conform to their distinguishing signs, wearing the right logos and designer names, or you go for a cosy and comforting pseudo-religiosity, the option favoured by the overwhelming majority of both young and old believers in both Islam and Judaism. The geographical shifts created by immigration have led to excessive religious practices, applying principles that are fifty years out of date. In the *Machine à Rêves*, I explore the concepts of kosher (for Jews) and halal (for Muslims).

I grew up in the largest Jewish community in France, at Sarcelles. Like Jews with kosher products, Muslims are now developing their own consumer society based on halal products. And it's not only meat. You can get kosher anything, from medicines to toothpaste and from crisps to prawns, even though prawns are forbidden in the Jewish religion. The Muslims have not yet reached this point, but thanks to products such as Mecca Cola (coca-cola for Muslims), they are catching up fast. These 'pure' products compensate for the contact they miss with their native countries, bringing them closer to their cultural and religious roots.

In this age of mad cow disease, of meat pumped full of hormones and of the ostentatious consumption of organic products, of a throw-away society and of countries which flood world markets with uniform products, when soft drinks taste the same from Los Angeles to Brazzaville and when the individual has become nothing more than a vessel of consumption, I am trying to tell my community that it's time to stop dreaming. Whether that dream be the consumer society described by Andy Warhol or that criticised by Osama Bin Laden.

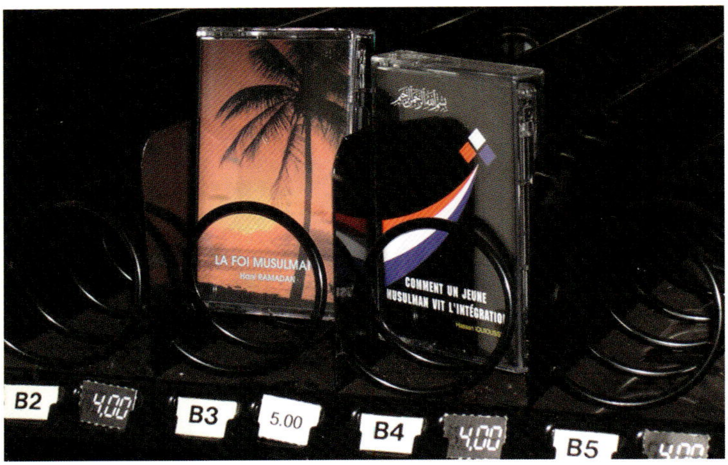

Left and right: *La Machine à Rêves* (Dream Machine), 2002–3. Details of vending machine.

We live in a world where the globalisation of trade and power affects the taste of the meat we eat. The quality of a product depends ultimately on its marketing (halal, kosher, 'product of the year', 'red label', etc.), rather than on its intrinsic properties. The moment industry enters the discussion – whether it be food, farming, music, textiles or cinema – we are sold the quality of a product as a function of the scale of its world distribution. When in fact the opposite is true. The less a product is duplicated, the better its quality. I'm not trying to return to the work of Andy Warhol or Marcel Duchamp in the *Machine à Rêves*, but it does seem to me that the shockwaves of the three most recent industrial revolutions are far from over.

The *Machine à Rêves* synthesises the fantasies of the kids on estates and, by extension, those of kids in ghettos throughout the world. It embodies the accessibility of all these dream attributes, which is why the first element of the project will be an automatic vending machine. Nothing could be simpler than buying a chocolate bar from a vending machine. Near to where I live there is a giant vending machine that sells everything, which has been there for a year now. The vending machine is the meeting place of ghetto culture and globalisation. It's a bit like the gates of heaven. By appropriating the vending machine and the industrial products it contains for artistic aims, I hope to demonstrate to the viewer that they need to keep their distance. All of us – French-Algerian kids on a Paris estate and American citizens alike – are puppets, with the consumer society pulling the strings.

If Andy Warhol had lived on a Paris housing estate, there's no doubt he would have used vending machines. We are machines for consumption. Vending machines occupy an increasingly prominent place in today's world, whether we want to buy cigarettes, newspapers, DVDs, drinks or sandwiches, wash our clothes or withdraw cash. And that's without mentioning the internet, which

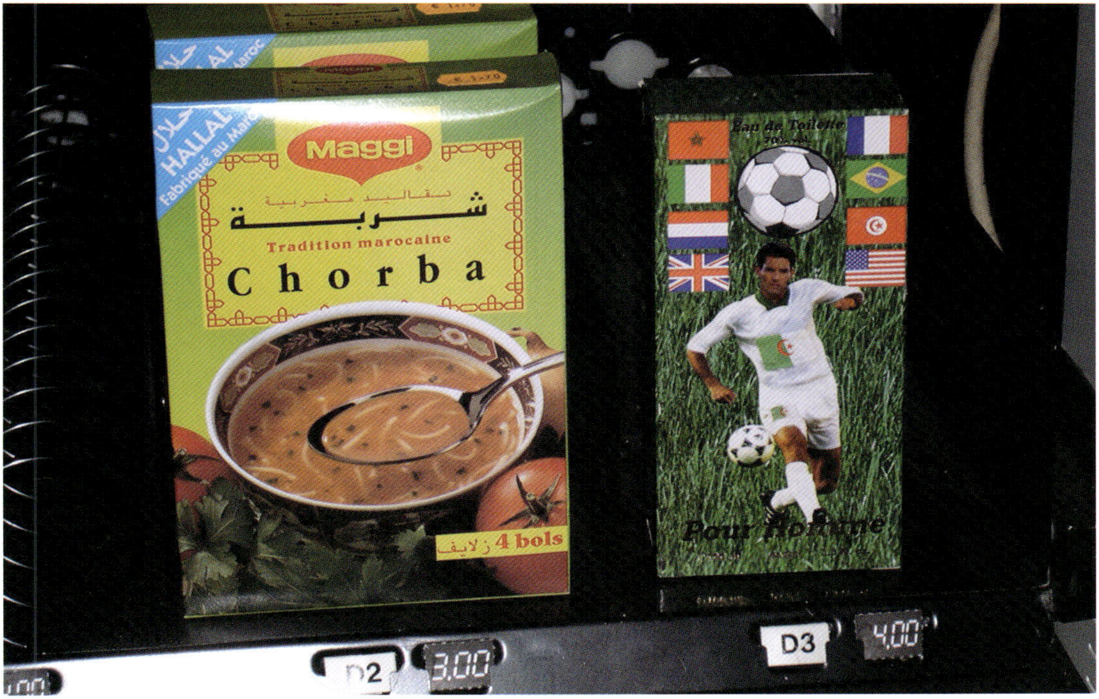

will lure us still further down the path of frenzied consumption.

The era of the image is unforgiving. We may believe that we are progressing towards a more modern world, but in fact we are regressing. The rigid laws of medieval heraldry anticipated today's hallowed signs, brands and labels. Crazier still, the scarifications practised by certain indigenous peoples as a sign of belonging to a particular ethnic group demonstrate just how fundamental it is to us to show our allegiance to a socio-cultural group, whether through designer labels such as Nike, Lacoste or Louis Vuitton, or whether through markers of religious purity such as halal or kosher.

***JS:** Is the* Machine à Rêves *a work in several stages?*

KA: Depicting the *Machine à Rêves* with one or two vending machines is frustrating. The world in which my struggle takes place consists of this dream peddled continuously by the mass media. Every day, each one of us is targeted by on average three hundred advertising slogans. The *Machine à Rêves* is a work capable of a multiplicity of interpretations.

One of the first marks of success for a kid on a housing estate is to become a pizza delivery boy. Many take-away pizzerias on the outskirts of French towns and cities now describe themselves as 'halal'. So do many of the kebab shops. But having seen the other side of the story – the market at Rungis, meat mecca of Paris – I know that this is simply a marketing ploy. You only have to think about it, after all. How could a chicken that has been killed by ritual Muslim slaughter methods sell for as little as four euros? It would have to command at least three times that price.

I'm working on a project in which a delivery boy on a moped will deliver messages such as 'Islam in 30 minutes (delivered to your door)' and 'Get out of the ghetto (in 30 minutes)'. Although I am not religious, my intention is not to ridicule Islam, a religion which I respect as much as any other. Rather I want to demonstrate how certain 'right-thinking' or 'God-

Correspondance (Connection), France, 2003. Slide installation.

fearing' people do and always will take advantage of human misery and poverty in order to make a profit, exploiting the thing that remains most dear to us: our belief in something (a better life). They persuade us that it is attainable. We live in an age that is obsessed with achieving and with the symbols of power that go with it.

JS: *Another of your recently completed works is* Correspondance *(Connection, 2003*). Does this address the area of overlap between your personal life and your artistic life and is it intended to set up a dialogue between your two lives?

KA: *Correspondance* lies within a notion of duality. It presents a series of images of Garges-les-Gonesses, projected in alternation with images of the village where I grew up in Algeria. It was a connection that I wanted to explore, as it was eleven years since I'd been back there on holiday. You have to understand that my father was the only member of my family to emigrate to France. As each side of the family only had old, dog-eared photographs, I assumed the role of a messenger bringing news to scattered family members on both sides of the Mediterranean. So I photographed our home environment on the outskirts of Paris, with my family and friends, and I took these images to my family in Algeria, in the Atlas Mountains. In the same way, I took photos of them and sent them to my mother at the end of every week.

The project gained even greater significance for me when one of my cousins who is the same age as me, old enough to come and work in France, told me that he didn't want to come to Paris. It didn't interest him. Then I understood that I was the product, on the one hand, of a French urban culture that was still in an embryonic state and, on the other, of a solid ancestral culture. I wanted to set up an air link between these two worlds.

The soundtrack that accompanies the slide installation consists of a wavering ballad on FM, as though someone was trying in vain to find a particular radio station, sliding through the frequencies from one pirate radio station or licensed channel to another, stopping on the way at

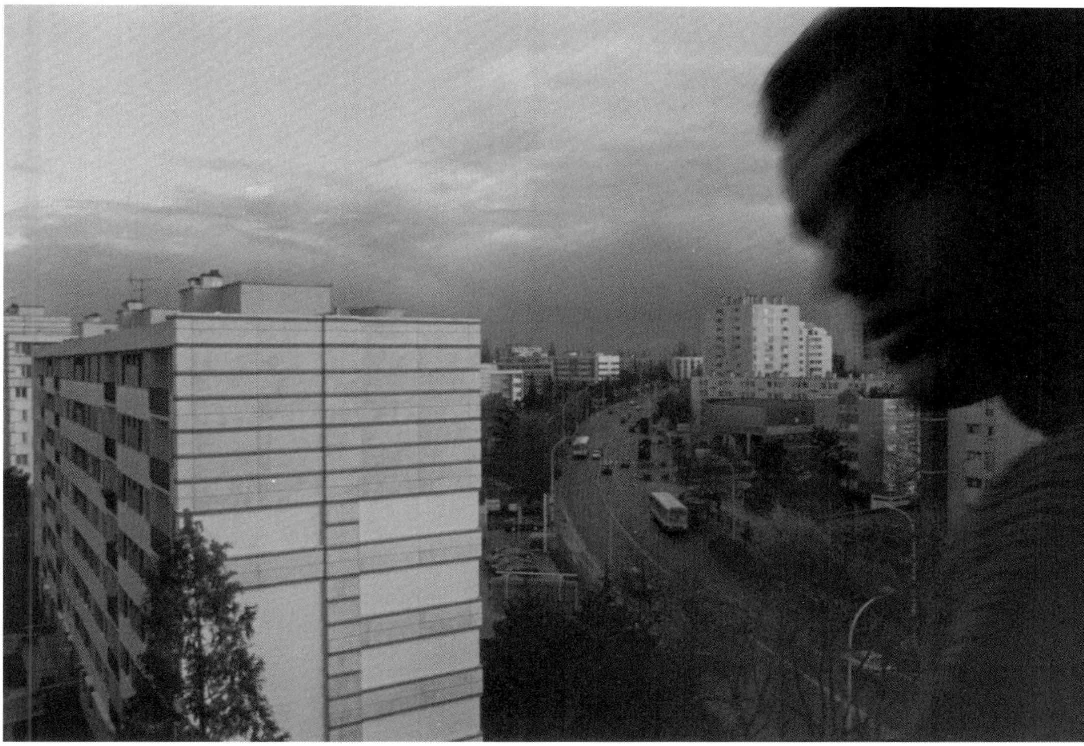

electronic, African or Muslim stations. It tends to make us feel that all cultures are accessible, but in reality they remain profoundly ghettoised, insular and protective of their own identity.

JS: *Is* Correspondance *an extension of your ethnographic approach to photography?*

KA: A bit like *La Piste d'Atterrissage*, *Correspondance* as a work is both aesthetic and ethnographic. It's a slide installation in black and white, based on a projection of still images intercut with video sequences in which – as in Chris Marker's *La Jetée* (The Pier, 1962) – the story emerges through a fixed image. When you compose a scenario it's difficult to avoid movement and it's the same with sound. The animated sequence comes at the end, placing back to back Chris Marker and Marc Garanger, who in the 1960s created work prompted by a trauma in the local community to which I wanted to respond. Garanger photographed women, standing rigid and face on to the camera, unveiled for the sake of documenting their identities. I film the members of my family, full-length and immobile. Instinctively, they freeze. In remote areas of Algeria, people's response when faced with a camera is reminiscent still of early ethnographic films made in Africa. Full-length is the only format they know. Don't move and watch the birdie. It goes back to the time of Nadar, when people had to pose for fifteen minutes. It's a pushing to the limits of the attitude of the individual to the camera that has always existed. In addition to this formal approach to photography in the remoter regions of Algeria, there is also a historical dimension. In Brazzaville, I learned that the first photographers to come to Africa were not journalists or artists, but rather ethnographers, who for technical reasons always had to ask their subjects not to move while their photographs were being taken.

JS: *Besides your artistic activities, you have also started the Café Chéri, a combination of designer bar and local café in Belleville. Was it simply that this was the best way of meeting or bringing together the characters that you would like to include in your work? Is it not*

Correspondance (Connection), Algeria, 2003. Slide installation.

ultimately a living project that falls completely within the parameters of your work as an artist?

KA: For an artist, and a humanist moreover, owning a bar is a fantasy. A bar is a place where people congregate naturally and in incredible variety, with all the different types of people you could wish for. That's what it's all about. The Café Chéri is a traditional bar serving coffee in the morning, while in the evening it welcomes DJs in one of the most popular areas of Paris. One day an elderly Kabyle turned to me and said, 'Now we've got a bar that's like us.' It's a place that's open to everyone and which will eventually become an autonomous work as soon as I've found the 'right position'.

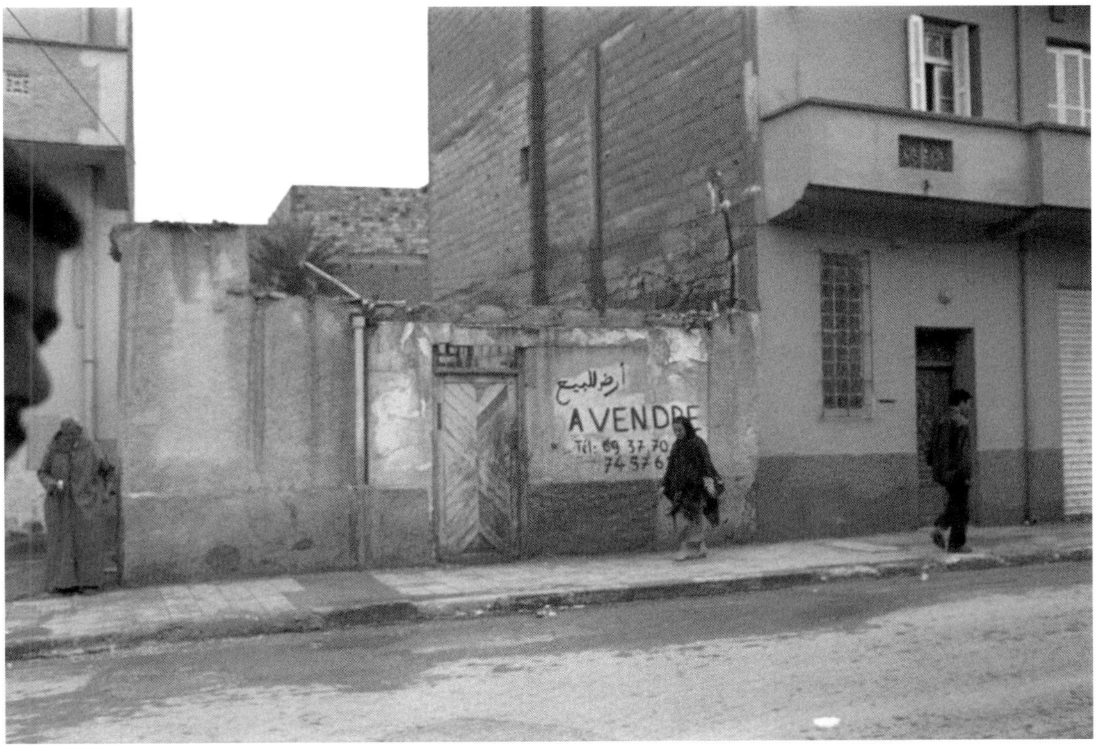

Through the *Mashrabiyya* and Other *Jalousies*

Ramon Tio Bellido

In any examination of the themes that Samta Benyahia has developed in her work over the past few years, it is difficult to ignore the signs they contain, signs that are at once both deeply personal and acutely topical. It would be impossible – and above all absurd – not to relate these works to her own experience as a woman born in Algeria, within a context that is itself fragmented into a number of different cultures, in terms of both ethnicity and upbringing. At the same time it is equally impossible (and probably equally debatable) not to consider the extent to which these signs concern questions that are present, both typologically and aesthetically, in our own daily lives.

Certainly, the sudden attention paid to these concerns prompts many questions, especially in the light of the work of other artists, which has led to a tendency to classify and categorise them in a slightly exaggerated way. What could be more long-awaited, more legitimate and yet more conventional than to see Benyahia's work exhibited alongside works by Zineb Sedira, Shirin Neshat, Ghada Amer and Ghazel? It is as if her work, or that of any other of these artists, cannot stand alone to inform us and give us the opportunity to share, through Benyahia's own language and in her own words, intrinsic realities, to which she provides her own unique commentary and point of view. For several years now, Samta Benyahia has deliberately included in her work an element that is both specific and recurrent, an easily recognisable object which, in its various forms, seems to offer answers to the questions it raises, like an index that can change its form to suit varying modes of presentation.

That element is the *mashrabiyya*, an architectural feature which, far from being limited to Muslim countries, is widespread throughout the Mediterranean world. Like a grille, it fills an opening in the exterior wall of a house, marking the passage from the interior to the outside world. Not really a window, and certainly not a railing or bars prohibiting communication or access, the *mashrabiyya* enjoys a complex and changing status. Not the least of its merits is the way in which it prompts and permits

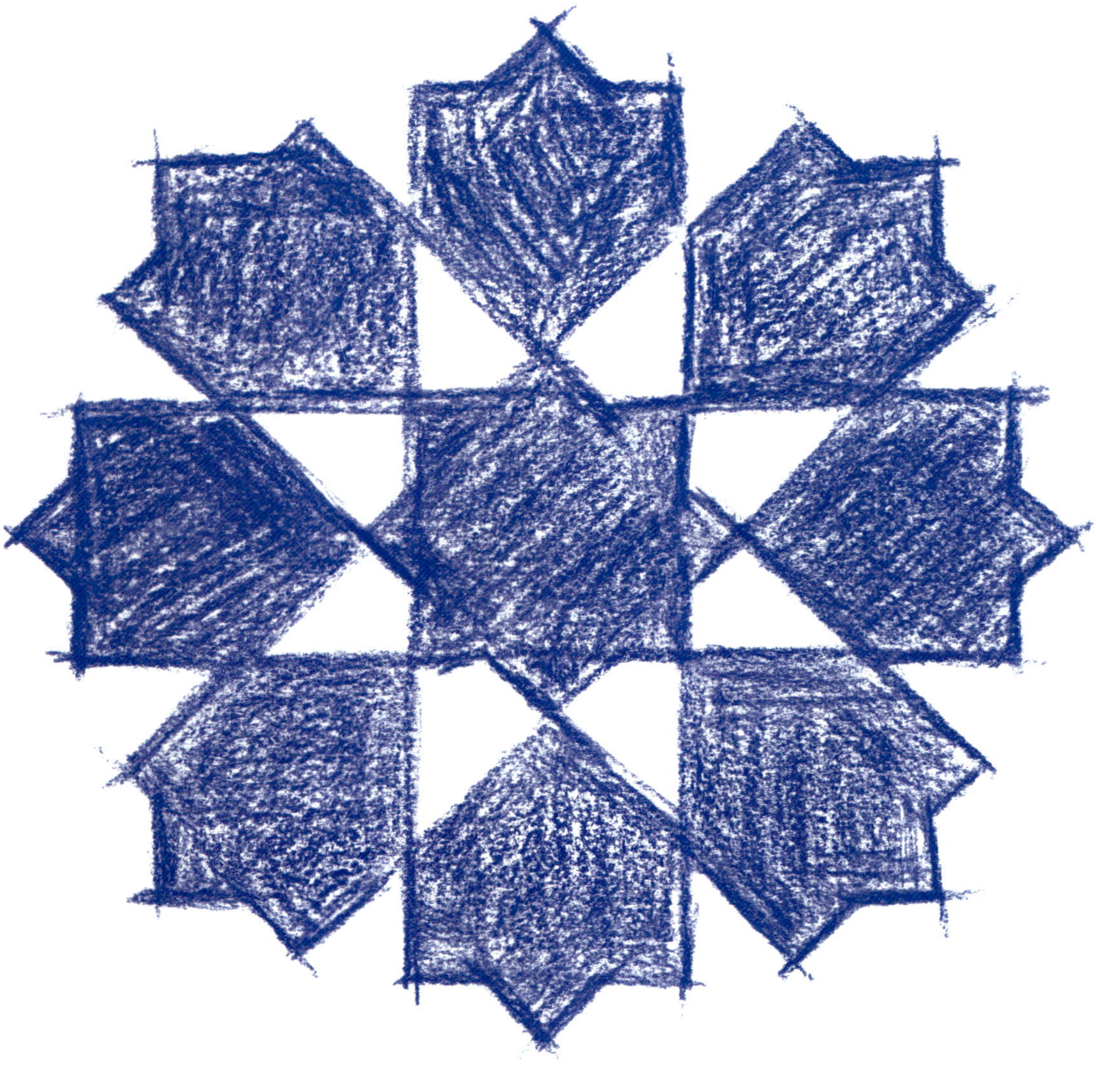

many different interpretations and functions, including and especially those for which it does not at first appear intended.

Samta Benyahia recalls some of the *mashrabiyya*'s functions, starting with the obvious: that it separates the interior from the exterior, the private space from the public, while at the same time offering protection against both heat and light, casting welcome shade in just the right amounts. In so doing, it plays on the opportunities it provides to observe the outside world from within and without being seen properly, creating an agreeable sense of intimacy. It is a separation that has shaped women's lives, creating a cloistered seclusion in which women themselves have played a more or less willing part; however, it has also prevented women from enjoying a more public role, from taking the first, far from easy, steps towards appearing and being visible in public, as they might wish or desire to do.

Faced with these shadowy façades, it is the image of this condition (in the etymological sense of the word) of abused or forbidden femininity that – for good or ill – is impossible to shake off. But it is a response that we should nevertheless reexamine and reassess, adjusting and reconstructing it in such a way as to prompt new perceptions, new questions, new dialectics.

I believe that this is what Samta Benyahia sets out to do – and is successful in achieving – for one very simple but irresistible reason. In her work, she uses tools of artistic expression, which are essentially alien to her chosen frame of reference, while at the same time explicitly employing them to target that same alien frame of reference. In other words, rather than seeking any kind of cross-fertilisation, she sets out to find connections that are *a priori* antithetical and to reveal the possible outcomes of such unions, which are often considered 'against the norm'.

This she achieves firstly through her use of technology-based methods, such as photography and silk-screen printing. She uses different processes of reproduction to intervene in the spaces created by her installations; these visible places are

Le Polygone et le Dédale (The Polygon and the Maze), work in progress, 2003.

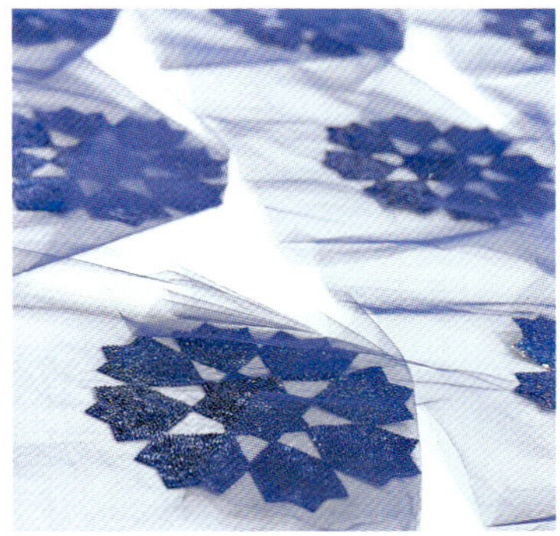

La Vie en Paillettes, 2003. Installation using material, sequins, beads and wood. Musée d'Art Roger Quilliot, Clermont-Ferrand. Photograph: Régis Nardoux.

occupied by layer upon layer of images forming thresholds, with permeable screens that we are required to both look at and – mentally – move through. Secondly, there is the mnemonic aspect of her work. Not only do the rosace motifs that are so characteristic of North African *mashrabiyyas* recall Benyahia's origins, but these same motifs were also presented recently in Clermont-Ferrand, stitched by embroiderers from Constantine. By putting their skills at the service of the artist, these women brought to the work a new and meticulously thought-through form of cooperative approach.

The systematisation of the concept of 'passage', of leading us from one world to another and from one state of being to another, has already been touched on in other discussions of Benyahia's work. What could be clearer, indeed, than this play of points of transition, these articulations of identities that are as complementary in their organisation as in their meaning? What seems exceptional in this case is the fresh approach to a subject that is as ancient as Western art itself, which here we see newly resourced, and transposed – with great judiciousness – into problems of a highly topical nature. I am referring to the motif of the window, which has served as the pretext for so many questions in modern art, both because of its significance as a locus of transition and demarcation – used to represent the passage from one space to another – and because it lays the ground for the casting off of the strictures of mimetic art in order to approach the unfathomable depths of a language of abstraction.

The decision to work with elements such as these is clear in works such as *Inside Memory* (1992), in which Samta Benyahia laid out precise lines demarcating the space of the installation on the floor, creating a powerful analogy of a room (perhaps a bedroom?) and separating the external world from an internal one. On the wall hangs a life-size photograph of a woman in 'traditional' dress but not wearing a veil, which is in fact a portrait of the artist's mother when she was younger. Opposite it, at a distance, rises a vertical wooden structure; with its grid-like structure and its play on notions of framing,

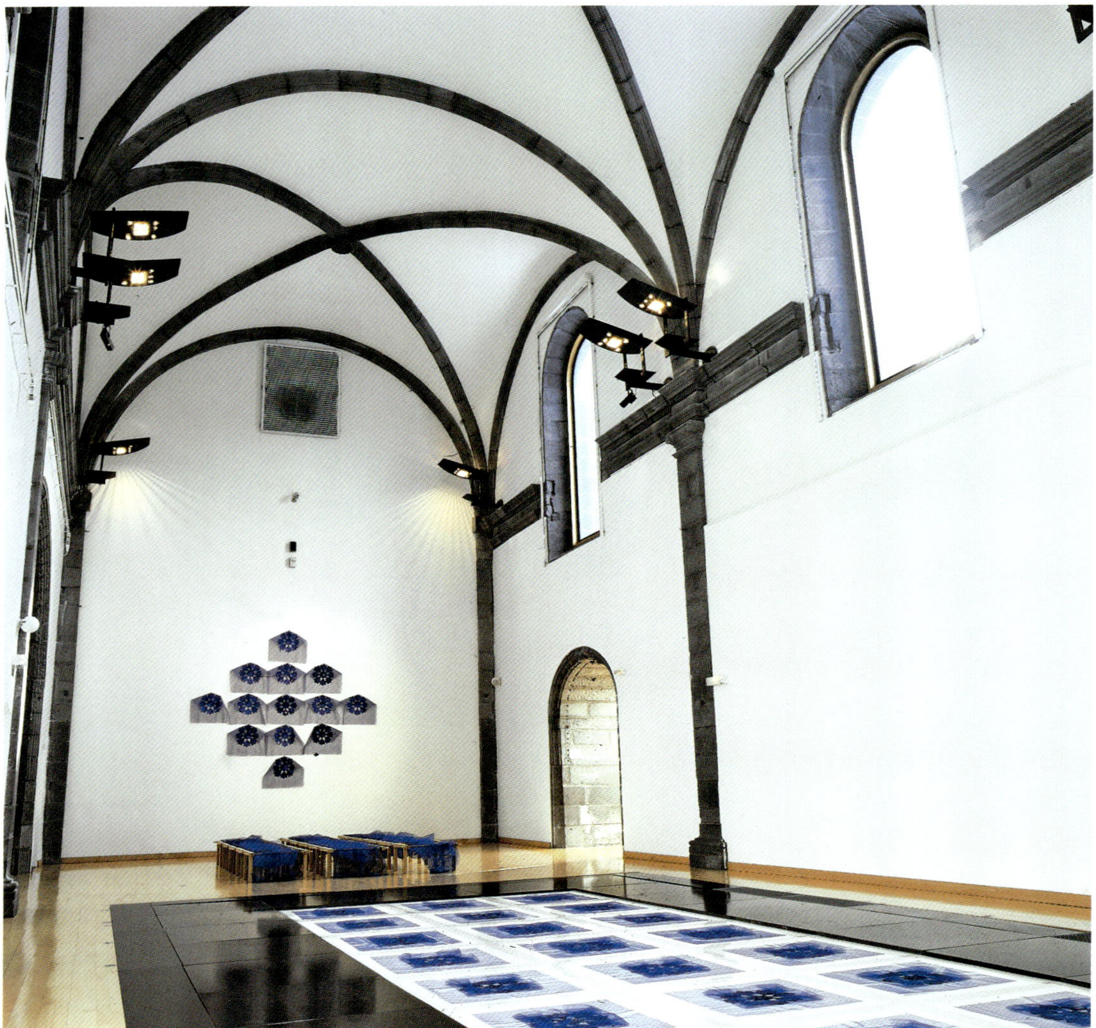

it evidently represents the famous *mashrabiyya*, or at least a generic transcription of it. Lying between these two facing images and separating them is a ceramic pavement, also comprising geometric motifs. Beyond the multilayered signals offered by these elements – and also thanks to them – we are invited not only to observe but also to participate in the presentation of a reality and the forms of behaviour associated with it.

We have to pass through, or at least traverse, the physical landscape presented here, moving both physically and mentally from one point to another. We have to imagine ourselves penetrating, almost breaking into, the private space that lies concealed behind the *mashrabiyya* as we walk the streets. Once behind it, we immediately come face to face with the image of this woman, almost too composed, hieratic, frozen; it is as if she is shying away from the processes of reproduction and recording which rob her of her identity. She is at once present and absent, clearly communicating that the act of casting off the veil is quite alien to her. It is all the more paradoxical given that Berber women never traditionally wore the veil and that this withdrawal of the self has been imposed on them by Muslim laws brought from Arab lands. But *Inside Memory* has yet more to say, indicating as it does that in order to pass from one self to the other, to make that journey, we must cross a no man's land, a courtyard or other antechamber, which is revealed as the true point of transition between the internal and external worlds. It constitutes a transitory space, in which we may establish relationships, meetings, dialogue or contact.

In this way, the space takes on form and meaning, bringing us back to a concrete reality in a sense. Perhaps it recalls the demise of the confrontational approach and the establishment of the questioning, participatory manner that informed the minimalist aesthetic and performance art of the 1970s, when works of art became theatrical spaces requiring us to inhabit them as much as to confront them. But here, because the motifs invoked offer such a clear challenge to the complex

La Vie en Paillettes, 2003. Installation using material, sequins, beads and wood. Musée d'Art Roger Quilliot, Clermont-Ferrand. Photograph: Régis Nardoux.

exchanges between modes of expression that are extrinsic (notably the photograph) and those that are intrinsic (the recurrent theme of the *mashrabiyya*), it is hard to recognise the stranger in the other person.

Thus appended, complemented, described, the operational process itself becomes clearer, more explicit, bringing together two states – not fusing them but on the contrary comparing them face to face – which are henceforth inseparable: the making and representation of images and the nature of those same images, their identification and their original reality.

A space such as this, transient and transcripted, brings with it other processes which require us to position ourselves in relation to the work in all senses of the term. How should we interpret it, in fact? What use should we make of it?

Clearly, developing as it has from two different origins – both Oriental and Western – that were mutually unaware of each other, the work has attained the authentic and universally verifiable value of *mashrabiyyas* and their Mediterranean counterparts – *jalousies* and other *celosias* – to become a potential space for communication. The work succeeds in establishing a dialogue – an exchange of words and encounters – between the two sides, in the way that the transparent nature of these screens intended. In realising – and above all feeling – the truth of this, we cannot help but find ourselves facing a space for reflection, in which we too observe our own ways of being. Unless this probability in fact operates in the opposite direction, and our observation is confirmed in its reciprocity, leaving much to say and almost as much to do.

Le Polygone et le Dédale (The Polygon and the Maze), work in progress, 2003.

The Artist Inhabited (The Polygon and the Maze)

In conversation with Jacques Berque and Jean Duvignaud

Jacques Berque: Throughout the Mediterranean Muslim world, one ornamental motif recurs with a haunting power that verges on the obsessive. You will have seen it on the stucco surfaces of the Alhambra in Granada, in the vestibule of the mosque of Le Barbier in Kairouan and on woodcarvings everywhere.

I am referring to a rosace of a particular type, since the rosace is a concentric motif that recedes from a central point, the diametric opposite of a polygon, which pushes its aggressive points outwards. Generally the rosace consists of one square superimposed on another and rotated through an angle to form eight points, but there are also other and much more complex variations....

Jean Duvignaud: *One thinks of [James] Joyce's spiral, which represents both the street plan of Dublin and the internal movements of* Ulysses, *or, in* Portrait of the Artist as a Young Man, *the labyrinth that is the central image of Western literature, be it Christian or not....*

JB: The arabesque is itself a maze, an Arabic form of maze; but it is a maze that leads somewhere.

Afrique Action, Tunis, 26 June 1961

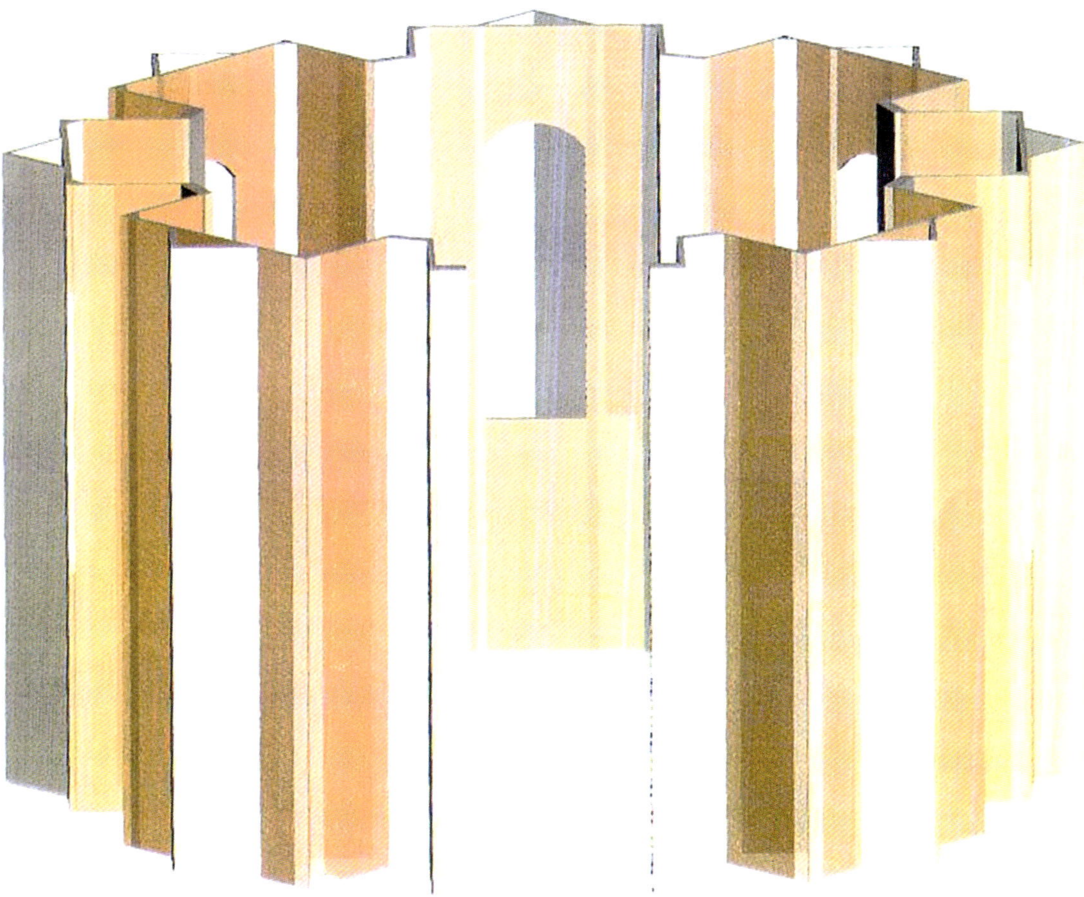

All of Algeria in the Taxi

In conversation with Nicole Muchnik

Kateb Yacine: When things are not going well and I start to write, my whole childhood resurfaces. In our country, childhood is a privileged world apart. We bask in a female universe. The women do not go out, are cut off from time and tell stories. They talk all the time. To each other, to their children. They are bearers of an enchanted world, inaccessible to men after the age of twelve or thirteen. Occasionally I meet people who have unhappy memories of their childhood and it always startles me. Then I try to imagine the life of children in the city, who spend all day at school. The only stories these children hear are those told by their teachers, impoverished tales that have been hashed and rehashed, or stories by famous authors that have been adapted, bowdlerized and gone through with a fine tooth comb. The imaginations of these children are starved of nourishment.

Le Nouvel Observateur, Paris, 10–16 April 1972

Rebirth of a Tragedy

In conversation with Jean-Marie Serreau

Kateb Yacine: There is a lesson in this for us North Africans plunged into a revolution which is without end or beginning, since it lies at the origins of another lost continent: liberated Africa, which is just as much of a hotbed as Asia. You would only need to approach the sacred flame, to create a spark, in order to unleash in Africa the explosive powers of the greatest theatre. The most liberated of all. This is why I refer to a 'poetic explosion'. North African theatre has affinities with [Bertolt] Brecht, but it is even closer to Chinese theatre, which has managed to create a harmonious relationship between tradition and revolution.... Because we have been living under a colonial power we have been cut off from our traditions. Our way of being in the world has been stolen from us. On the other hand, it is equally true that there is no living tradition in North Africa, and that this has nothing to do with the effects of colonialisation, which systematically tears people away from their deepest roots. In our country, the Quran has exerted a certain power of censorship over poetry in all its forms. Elsewhere, Marxism has fulfilled the same role. All doctrines, whether religious or philosophical, always lead to the castration of poets, who then become leaders of the chorus. Even in a progressive climate, true poets should manifest their divergent views. If they do not fully express these views, they will suffocate. That is their function. They create their own revolution within the political revolution; at the heart of trouble, they are perpetual troublemakers. Their tragedy comes when they are made to serve a revolutionary struggle, they who neither can nor should base their work on passing appearances. A poet is the revolution stripped bare, the very movement of life in an unending explosion....

Jean-Marie Serreau: *Lakhdar exists, virtually motionless, at the centre of a universe which revolves around him. You could almost have him standing on one spot throughout the play, at the side of rue des Vandales, a fixed character at the centre of a world that is constantly fragmenting and reconstructing itself. Thus he is – in the broadest sense of the term – encircled.*

KY: To me the circle is of fundamental importance. Lakhdar's initial monologue unleashes a whirling force which does not stop until the end of the play. The image of the circle, the reality of the circle around Lakhdar, is the reality of the revolutionary world, the freedom of men who are always on the move, freedom in both space and time. My play could equally as well have started with the third act or the second, as the events are not linked by a chronological order, but rather by a rotation in time, which constantly brings them back

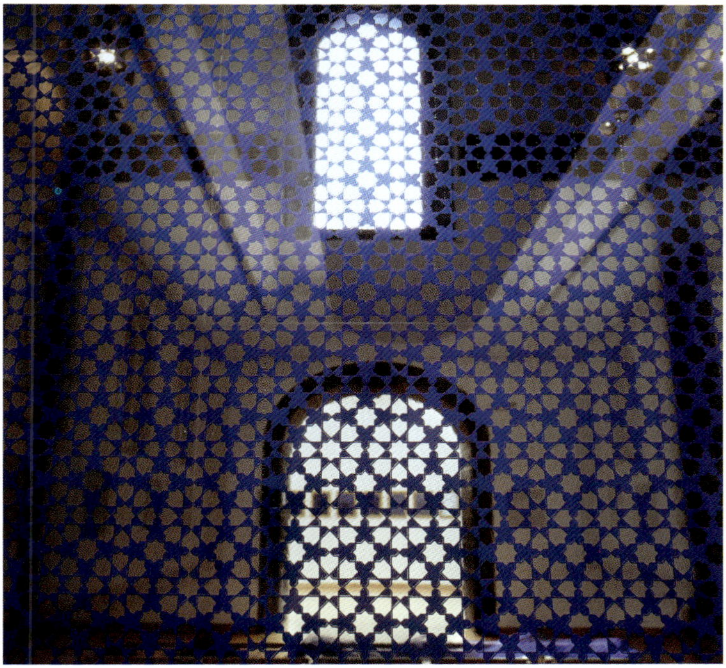

La Vie en Paillettes, 2003. Installation using material, sequins, beads and wood. Musée d'Art Roger Quilliot, Clermont-Ferrand. Photograph: Régis Nardoux.

to their starting point and sets them in motion again, each time harnessing new energies. My novel *Nedjma* is constructed along similar lines. The plays on which I am working are together entitled *Le Cercle des représailles* (The Circle of Reprisals), and my work as a whole is called *Le Polygone étoilé* (The Starry Polygon).

L'Action, Tunis, 11 August 1958

The Whole World as a Subject

Hence I began to question why the Greek tragedies had never been translated into Arabic. This is all the more surprising because it was the Arabs who introduced Greek culture to Europe; they translated virtually everything – the sciences, philosophy, etc. – but never Greek theatre. This was when I came to understand the opposition that exists between the language of religion (the Quran) and the language of freedom (poetry). It is an opposition that is irreconcilable and insurmountable, for this is the eternal reproach of prophets to poets. In the Quran, Muhammad characterises poets as people who talk but do not act, meaning people who express themselves but do nothing. The same condemnation of poetry is found in Plato's writings: his *Republic* had no place for poets....

Poetry must therefore not merely have a subject; it must have the whole world as its subject. With all its strength, poetry must vie with the constraints imposed by other forms of language, by powers of expression which weigh so heavily on men and which stem from religious powers and the terrible orgies of religious persecutions that stretch back into the mists of time. Against these, poetry is a force for freedom, a hugely important weapon in the struggle. And this is where the question of the audience's role comes in, this is where the transition into theatre is made. In the theatre, poetic language finds its audience, and the audience gives it material form. The poetic act becomes almost literally tangible, it becomes human; you see an audience, people listening. This is no longer the desperate abstraction of poetry turned in on itself, reduced to a state of powerlessness; this is the complete opposite.

France-Observateur, Paris, 31 December 1958

A New Sun Sheds Fresh Light on the Potential Richness of the Ruins
In conversation with Djamal Amrani

Over there, in our own country, is a people apparently plunged into total darkness. But with a glimmer of light – and dawn is just breaking – a new sun suddenly sheds fresh light on the rich potential of these ruins, it becomes clear that there is a place in Algeria for a genuine open-air theatre. Instead of ushering members of the so-called élite into plush auditoriums, complete with cosy upholstered seats and velvet-lined boxes, we should be bringing these ruins back to life, reviving a new Maghreb from Carthage to Cirta. And we cannot do this by offering the same old repertoire of foreign classics; rather we should offer work by the Maghreb's own people, performed in spaces on a scale befitting their stature; for the immensity of infinity is the very least that we can offer to a people who for centuries were thought to have been crushed.

El Chaâb, Algiers, 8 February 1963

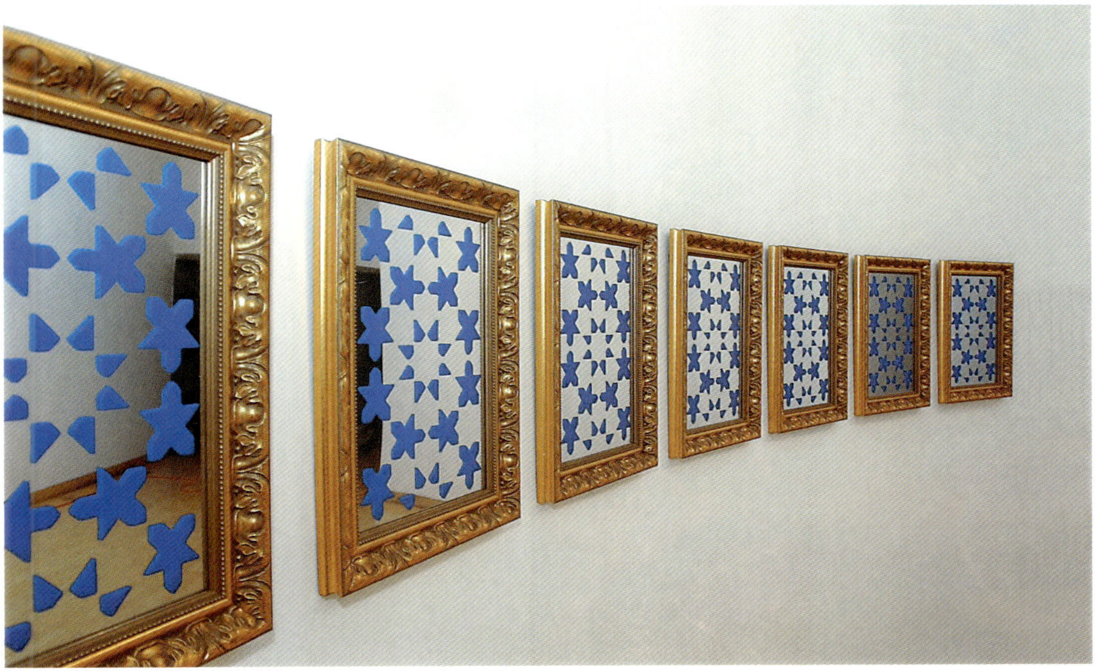

Le Chiffre Sept (The Number Seven), 2001. Seven screen-printed and framed mirrors, installed in Exeter Cathedral as part of Spacex Gallery's multi-site project *Patterns*. Photograph: Barbara Steele.

Tender Metaphor: The Art of Zarina Bhimji

Deepali Dewan

Ranging from installations to photography and film, Zarina Bhimji's work is carefully and deliberately composed to evoke an emotional response. Like poems compiled with visual forms, her work operates on multiple levels. While narrating stories that defy textual articulation, the images use beauty and history in such a way that form and content become inseparable. Never didactic, the work stays true to an emotional journey through complex and contradictory sensations of human experience.

Practising as an artist since the early 1980s, Bhimji has explored the politics and poetics of power and history through images rich in colour, texture and content. A 1987 installation, *She Loved to Breathe – Pure Silence*, consists of photographs and muslin sandwiched between Plexiglas panels hung from the ceiling. The frailty of the cloth parallels the imagery of a dead bird, evoking a sense of loss that serves as a metaphor for general human experience. A 1993 installation, *1822-Now*, presents black-and-white and colour photographs of mixed-race people on bookshelves flanking a scholar's desk and chair. The work uses as a starting point the 1822 study of racial purity by Francis Galton, eugenics. The library-like environment hints at the relationship between knowledge and power in that era, but as the title indicates, the present is implicated as well. Each photograph has a half-hour exposure time that echoes nineteenth-century techniques of long exposure, yet the sitter is not asked to remain perfectly still. The resulting image is blurry and the photographs look more similar than different to each other. The orderliness of the composition is ruptured by what the photographs do not reveal. The enduring effect is one that is haunting and rhythmic, leaving the work open in a way that allows the viewer a very personal response.

The coexistence of beauty and harshness is explored in subsequent work. In a series of photographic images from the late 1990s, Bhimji juxtaposes sumptuous fabric with substances such as pubic hair, dead flowers, an octopus. The rich colours and textures, intensified

Howling Like Dogs, I Swallowed Solid Air, 1998–2003. Transparency in light box, 130 x 170 x 12.5cm.

in a light box, evoke a response of both repulsion and attraction. Similarly, in an installation from 1994, commissioned by the Public Art Development Trust's Art in Hospitals programme, Bhimji juxtaposes images of medical specimens from a hospital's study collection with vibrantly coloured fabric and material. Textures and colours in the specimens and the fabrics seem to parallel each other – a wrinkle here and fold there. It is with prolonged looking that the objects reveal themselves. For example, the breast of a black female floating in formaldehyde evokes the unequal power relationships along lines of race and gender that are inherent in the medical sciences and based on notions of difference. The history of power, its translations in the present and the visual poetics of the aesthetic composition are inseparable. Form and content seemingly clash, yet softly. The rational intellect is rendered insufficient and the only way around the work is by using the senses and the emotions. In this way, the fine line, or even absent line, between horror and fascination, repulsion and attraction is exposed and explored.

In the latest body of work created over the course of three trips to Uganda since 1998, Bhimji has produced a 16mm film and numerous photographs of landscapes and architectural spaces. In some ways this work comes full circle with one of Bhimji's early works, a 1992 multiroom installation, *I Will Always Be Here*. Bhimji's first exploration outside of the photographic medium, the work examines the language of pain without compromising ideas of visual pleasure. In one component of the work, child-size *kurtas* (Indian shirts) dangling from the ceiling with burn marks around the edges serve as visual metaphors for terror, vulnerability and loss of innocence. The gap between what is fabric and skin collapses in this investigation of the emotional landscape of childhood.

Out of Blue (2002) is a 16mm film exploring landscape – streets, graveyards, domestic spaces, airports, military barracks and prison cells. The camera's eye traces a journey seemingly over the course of an era, from village streets at

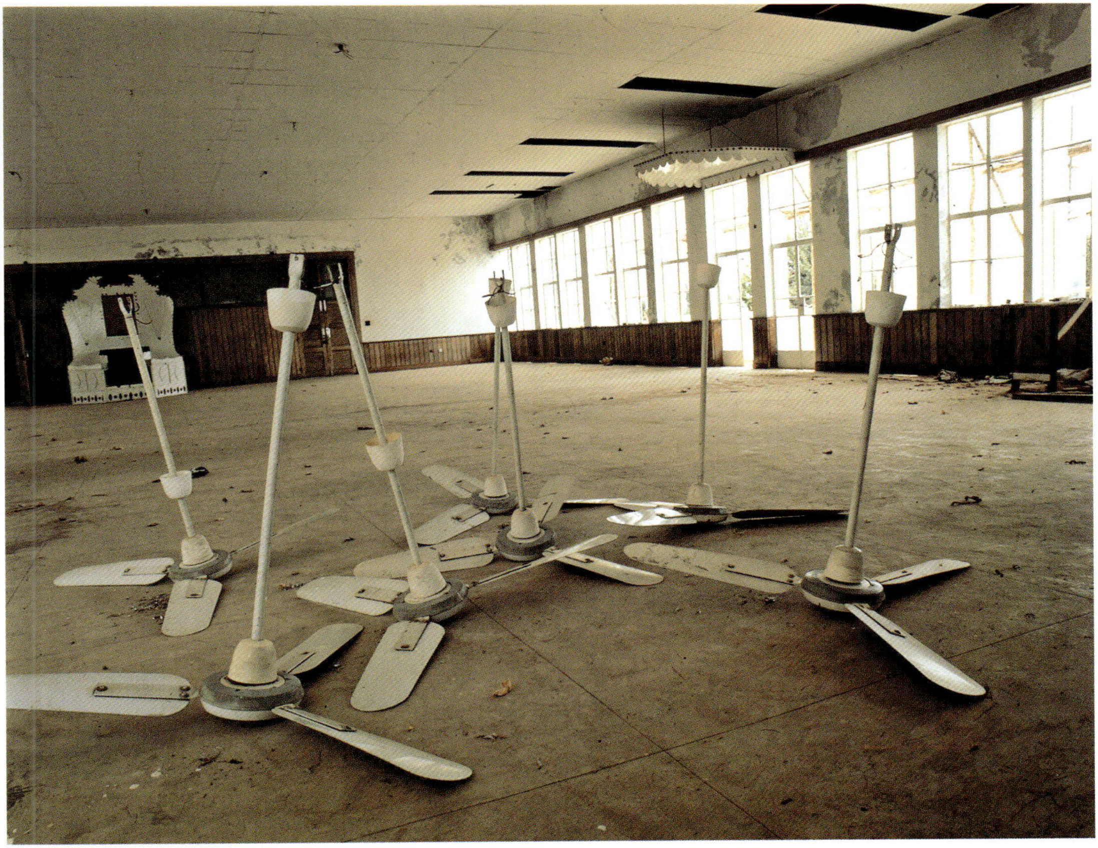

dusk to the remnants of 'Britishness' and the eerie emptiness of abandoned houses at the end of the day. Using research on Uganda during Idi Amin's regime in newspaper and print archives as a point of departure, the film is not about the factual data contained within those documents. Rather it stems from the layered experiences of different people at different points in time that reveal how any sense of 'what happened' is far more complex that anyone of us could have imagined. At the same time, the film is not a history lesson. The specific is reduced to its essentials and abstracted in such a way that allows for a clarity and simplicity that seem to penetrate more deeply into the subject. The film follows an emotional process without knowing where it is leading. Fusing facts and the subliminal, the artist universalises the subject and allows a more open interpretation. Camera movement and angles complement the soundtrack in such a way that sounds become visible and the visual can be heard. In the end the viewer is not left with a clear political or personal message. There remains an ambiguity, which, like a mirror, deflects the focus of the work on to the viewer. The enduring effect is one of tenderness and beauty, conveying the complexities of human experience and emotion.

The photographs in this latest body of work are featured in the 2003 Venice Biennale. Almost all focus on either empty interiors or architectural structures situated in the middle of a barren landscape or empty street. A pervading sense of quiet abstracts any narrative content and intensifies the metaphorical potential of the photographs. They give a sense of unspeakable horrors that may be momentary but also a sense of long-term decay. At the same time, they evoke a sense of beauty in colour, tone and texture and a stillness is exuded by the landscape whose daily changes become imperceptible over millennia. The effect is an abstraction of the present moment in a way that allows little separation between experience, memory and imagination. The images juxtapose tragedy with visual poetics – a patch of light, a dangling wire,

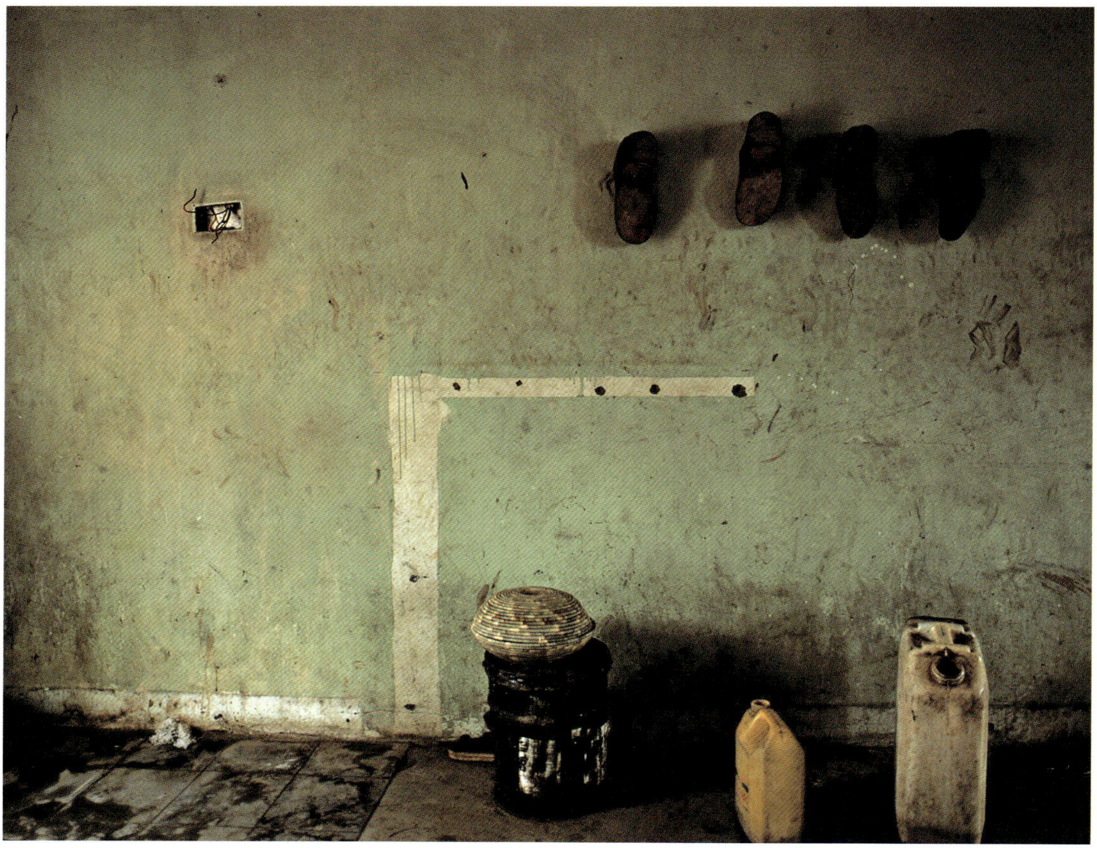

cell windows along the façade of a prison. The repetition of windows, guns leaning against a wall, a pattern on fabric, or yellow plastic water jugs like islands scattered about an empty room create a rhythm that is audible. The past resonates in the peeling paint, the crumbling plaster, the dust on prison bars, but these details transcend the particulars of time and place and address the poetics of the past as an abstract concept. Ultimately the images are not about Uganda and operate in a way that is not dependent on their historical, cultural, or geographical context. Rather, they convey a psyche of decay, loss and grief through a tender, almost lyrical, visual language, the translation of which is left up to the viewer.

Throughout Bhimji's work the body has been a recurring motif both through its physical presence and its obvious absence. A medical specimen, an abandoned shoe, pieces of hair, a garden, an empty kitchen – all index a variety of bodies: female, the exile or immigrant, the colonised, the slave. Further, the archive, the hospital, a wealthy residence, military barracks reference the abstracted body of institutional power and authority. In the current work, the body is indexed by the mark of a hand on a wall, by the drip of paint long since dried. Yet it is also present in architectural spaces, such as walls that serve as a metaphor for the skin and the landscape as a metaphor for the human psyche.

Scale is important as the size of the work creates a sculptural effect that implicates the viewer physically, making it difficult for them to remain neutral in the dialogue. Projected on to a gallery wall, the film is meant to be seen as a large-scale installation. Similarly, the photographic works are monumentalised and demand attention. Further, the compositions are spare yet full of minute detail. Abstracted, they reflect the geometric shapes of a modernist visual vocabulary. The white of a sky, red of a brick building and green of the grass create bands of colour across the picture plane. Moreover, a patch of light seems three-dimensional, carrying weight and taking up space on the picture plane like

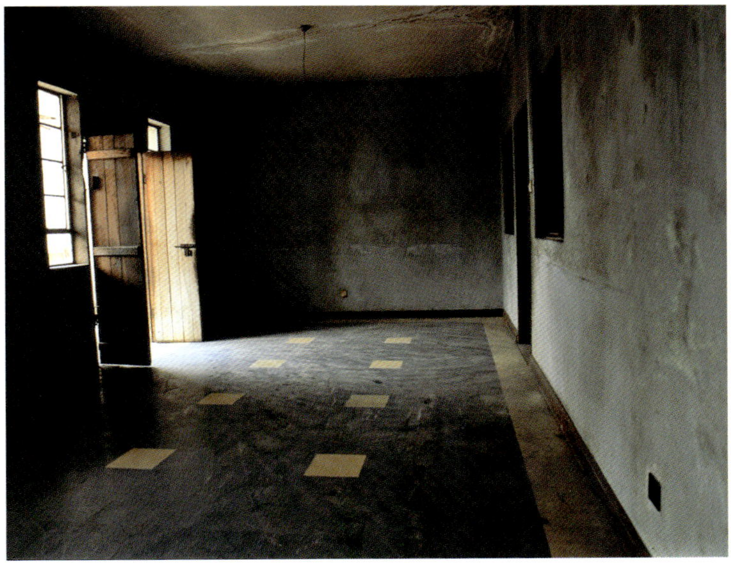

Memories Were Trapped Inside the Asphalt, 1998–2003. Transparency in light box, 130 x 170 x 12.5cm.

Grenade, 1998–2003. Transparency in light box, 130 x 170 x 12.5cm.

an object, such as a chair or water jug. Negative and positive spaces are somewhat equalised and the image is heavy with physical, and by extension metaphorical, substance.

In one way, this body of work is about making different images of Africa than have been seen thus far. Rather than being dominated by war or famine, the images evoke a sense of intimacy with the African landscape. Further, while recording spaces of institutional power, the images index stories of human lives that never make it into official histories. Although void of people, the images index human presence through a shoe hung on a wall, a bed and graffiti that evoke subaltern stories. For example, the window in a prison wall providing ventilation for a cell references human breathing, which is then associated to the body of the prisoner and, by extension, to personal histories. Yet unlike documentary photography, Bhimji's images exploit the technologies of the photographic medium to create compositions of objects arranged within the camera's frame. These are not 'found' scenes but rather images in which Bhimji has carefully arranged props to maximise their metaphorical resonance. The props are like physical gestures motioning to an emotional and psychological landscape that in the end defies representation. Save for a few visual clues, such as a decorative pattern on a building or a stray word left behind on a largely torn-down poster, the images transcend the specifics of time and place. In this way, they are like anti-documentary images that evoke a timeless realm occupied by the human psyche.

The notion of difference is explored on a number of levels. Visual difference – in the shadows, colours and shapes of an image – translates to subtle differences in the general atmosphere or tone of each image. In this way, the viewer is meant to hear with their eyes and listen to 'difference' on macro- and microcosmic levels. The work instigates the question of difference on a creative level as well. For so long, metaphoric images of human emotion and psyche have been confined to the Western canon or to the Western

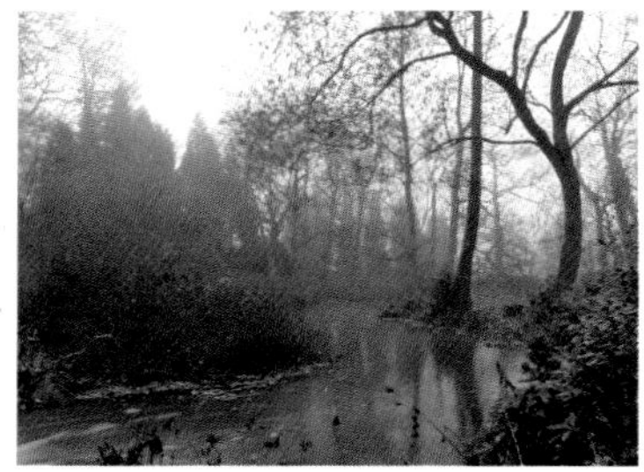

Above: *Whereas a Black Servant Boy*, 1998.
Cibachrome on aluminium, 122 x 120cm.
Right: *Female Government*, 1998.
Cibachrome on aluminium, 122 x 173cm.

world. This work quietly and gracefully inverts this art history and challenges the genealogy of Enlightenment thinking.
The images operate on a general level that expresses universalised concepts of grief, loss, tenderness and beauty that trace the contradictions and complexities of human emotion and experience.

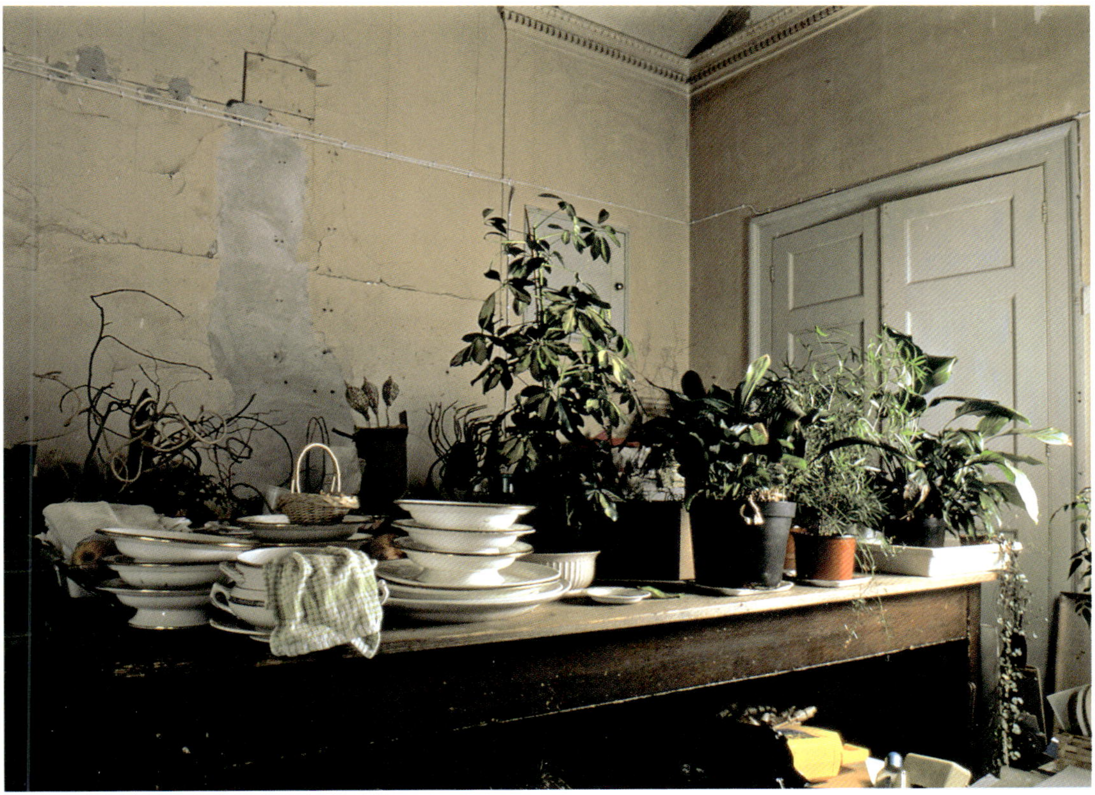

Frank Bowling's Map Paintings

Kobena Mercer

There is a strange shape floating above the stencilled edging of Latin America. At first, I thought what I saw was Nova Scotia. Some moments later, looking at another painting, I was aware that something was coming back at me from the corner of my eye. Just behind the surface of *Mother's House in South America* (1968) is a silkscreen print, whose grey and pale blue colours glow beneath the russet brown continental land mass by virtue of a photographic polarisation in the template, which switches areas of shadow and light. The ghostly tracings of palm tree fronds and colonial architecture, which had come into my eye from such an oblique angle, had been quietly waiting there all the while.

Frank Bowling's map paintings come from a key moment of transition. Produced between 1967 and 1971, the works have been acknowledged as a distinct strand in his oeuvre that arose out of a shift from figurative painting to post-painterly abstraction during the artist's relocation from London to New York in this period. Numerous writers agree that the map paintings are significant, but it is perhaps only now, belatedly, with the contemporary re-exhibition of the works, including the red, gold and green colour fields of *Who's Afraid of Barney Newman?* (1968) and the stunning deep mauve and black washes of *Marcia H. Travels* (1970), that the broader significance of Bowling's map paintings can be recognised. Where postcolonial perspectives have transformed our understanding of contemporary art and culture, it could be suggested that it has taken over thirty years for Frank Bowling's map paintings to reveal their hidden riches. Possibly by virtue of a temporal logic of deferred action, the full implications of the map paintings have been patiently biding their time, waiting for the moment to make their presence felt.

Maps featured frequently in advanced art of the 1960s. Artists working out of all sorts of paradigms came to the iconography of world maps with wide-ranging enquiries. In the period bookended by Jasper Johns's *Map* series (1960–65), which explored

South America Squared, 1967. Mixed media (silkscreen, acrylic on canvas), 221 x 114cm.

cartography as a system of signs, and *Mappa* by Alighiero e Boetti (1971–73), an embroidered fabric panel produced by the Italian artist in collaboration with weavers in Afghanistan, one can see artistic convergence around the motif of the globe as a response to the social and political turmoil of the time. Frank Bowling's trajectory through this moment shares the sense of searching, questioning and journeying evoked by other artists who also approached maps as a critical surface upon which new uncertainties had emerged. While paintings such as *From Africa to Australia* (1971) featured prominently in Bowling's solo exhibition at the Whitney Museum of American Art in that year, the distinctive concerns he brought to bear on the map motif had been registered earlier in one of his most important paintings, *Night Journey* (1967–69), whose sombre darkness evokes the unrepresentable terror of the Middle Passage. Whether exploring the historical violence that inaugurated the experience of diaspora – which transported bodies and cultures out of Africa into the Americas – or giving over the vast expanses of his canvases to an almost geological enquiry into the imperceptibly slow time of continental drift, Bowling was fully part of a cultural moment whose cumulative effect was to decentre the planisphere projection of the globe that had been taken for granted ever since the Renaissance.

One needs an ability to juggle multiple time scales when approaching Bowling's map paintings, for although they have now been brought out of storage and recovered from the recent past to be re-viewed among contemporary audiences, entering into their imaginative spaces entails a passage through deeper, slower, and stranger temporal zones.

Starting with the shifting biographical context in which Bowling created these paintings, what comes to light are both the dilemmas that diaspora artists encountered when facing the edifice of abstraction in twentieth-century art and the distinctive points of departure that were made available by aspects of the postcolonial experience of displacement.

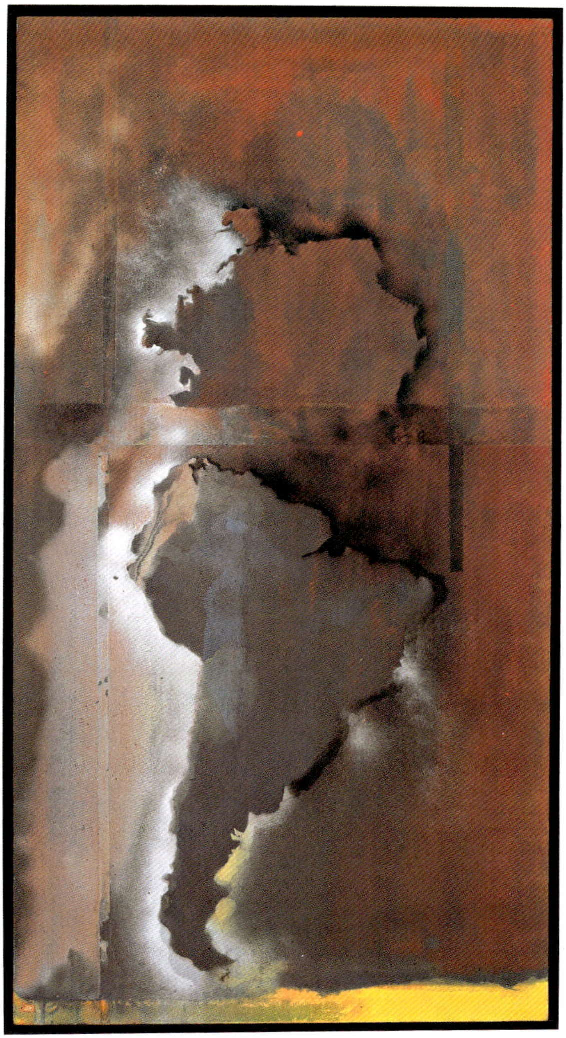

Marginal Modernists/Multiple Locations

Bowling began the map paintings while living in New York and following a 1967 visit to Long Island, when 'he stayed... in [Larry] River's house where he made the first stencils... with the aid of Rivers's epidiascope'.[1] Far from being remarkable, this anecdote shows that artists have always borrowed ideas, equipment, even wives and lovers, throughout modern art history. It is only in a social world governed by the political fiction of 'race', which abstracts European and African ethnicities into an overarching white/black dichotomy, that such interaction seems remarkable at all. Where perception comes to be coded by an either/or outlook, reality is limited to a monologic view of the world, and this, to put it baldly, was more or less how matters of cultural difference were dealt with among art world institutions for the first seventy years of the last century. With a monocultural world view, only one term in each dichotomy really matters, even though it requires the presence of the other to establish a contrast. The marginality of minority artists in modern art can be understood, then, not so much as the consequence of outmoded ideologies of Eurocentrism, but as an outcome of a monocular system of vision. When the creative value of cross-cultural mixing cannot be percieved as an enriching plus, but only as a subtractive minus, black artists have historically ended up in one of the several blindspots of the monocular gaze.

Featured in *Private View* (1965), a book of photographs by Lord Snowdon, with texts by curator Bryan Robertson and critic John Russell, Bowling was thrust into the epicentre of London's 1960s milieu after studying at the Royal College of Art from 1959 to 1962.[2] Initially dubbed by David Sylvester as a figurative expressionist wrestling with Francis Bacon's influence, Bowling, who was born in Guyana in 1936, had graduated at the same time as the Young Contemporaries generation, even though his broad interests were quite distinct, having set up a discussion

South America Squared, 1967.
Acrylic on canvas, 234 x 274cm.

group at college that included a scientist dealing with the chemistry of colour.

Images of Patrice Lumumba – Congo's prime minister assassinated in 1961 – and Othello appeared in his early paintings, and several awards, including the Shakespeare Quarto-Centenary commission given in 1963 and the Grand Prize for Contemporary Art at the First World Festival of Negro Art, held in Senegal in 1966, encouraged Bowling to make contacts with artists and galleries in New York. Exhibiting widely and writing on art as well, Bowling found himself propelled into the hotbed of controversy surrounding the 1969 exhibition at the Metropolitan Museum of Art in New York entitled *Harlem on My Mind.* Asked to write an editorial for *Arts* magazine, Bowling entered the debate that came about when African American artists protested the oversight of contemporary black visual arts from first-time institutional surveys, such as the Met's exhibition of Harlem Renaissance archival material. While arts activism resulted in a spate of all-black shows among prominent institutions, such as *Contemporary Black Artists in America* (1971) curated by Robert Doty at the Whitney Museum of American Art, Bowling's intellectual orientation as a formalist placed him at odds with the cultural nationalist demand for a pictorial manifestation of black identity. 'Is black art about colour?' he once impishly asked.[3]

Looking at the zigzag shape of his life story, what stands out is the restless quality of Frank Bowling's movement through multiple locations. Travelling between studios in London and New York City since the 1970s, Bowling has also navigated various paradigms in late modernist painting that stem from the double routes of organic and geometric abstraction. Equally 'at home' among the post-1945 generation of British painters selected for the *Hayward Annual* (1980), as among African American abstract artists featured in *The Search for Freedom* (1991), one might have thought that Bowling's cosmopolitan travels would be an asset rather than a liability.[4] However, in a monocultural value system where the

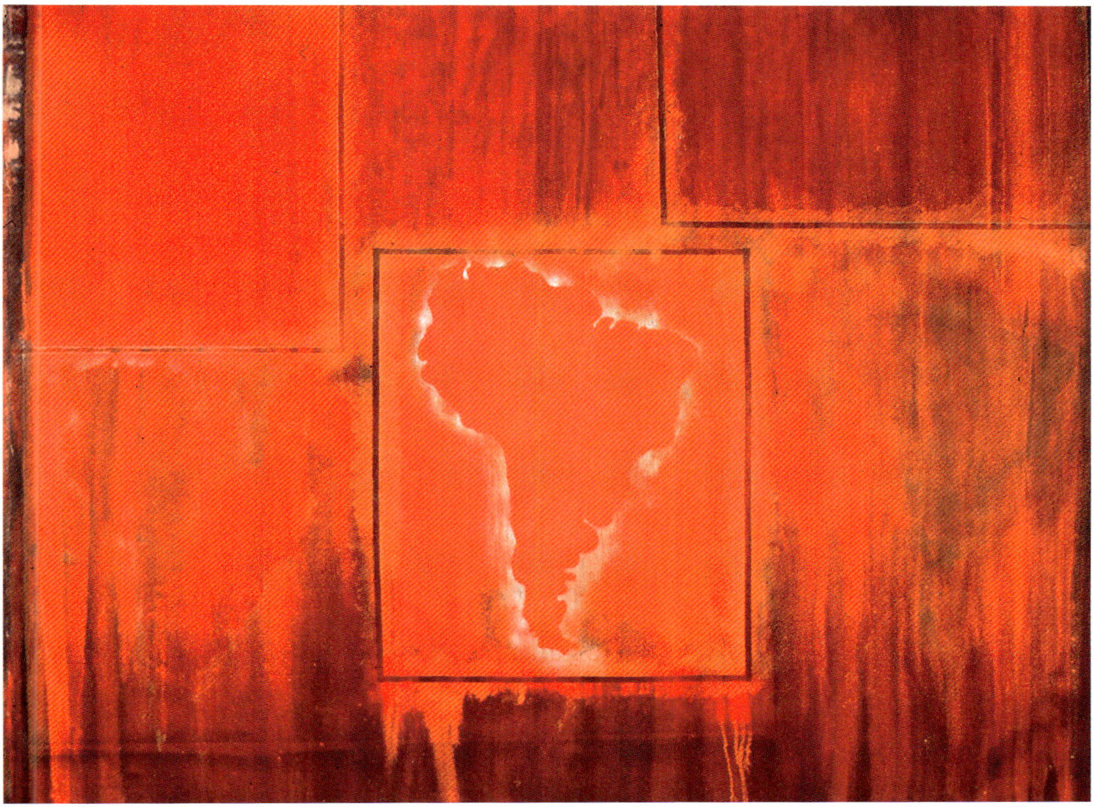

achievement of one signature style is prized above all as a sign of artistic originality, the practice of stylistic variation is regarded as a deficit that detracts from an artist's authorial identity. Where the underlying rules of canon formation tend to reward values of unity over multiplicity, the shape of Bowling's career can be grasped not as a result of institutional exclusion but as a consequence of a rift or discrepancy between the monologic codes and values of the metropolitan art world and the decentring ethos of displacement associated with diaspora consciousness.

To the extent that the map paintings were created out of a dynamic encounter between such centripetal and centrifugal forces, a closer look at their context confirms the view that black artists working in abstraction often ended up isolated, invisible and unseen. This was the result not of a lack of originality but because their choices were made in the shadow of a monocular system of vision in which cross-cutting dialogue between different cultural spaces could not be valued or rewarded as such. In such a visual realm, where one-ness wins out over two-ness, Bowling's differential abstraction was simply 'blanked'.

Diaspora Artists and Discrepant Abstraction

Against the grain of the reductive dichotomy of exclusion/inclusion, Ann Gibson's art historical studies reveal the ideological double binds facing African American artists of the 1940s and 1950s who attempted to negotiate a point of entry into abstract expressionism.[5] Where artists such as Hale Woodruff, Charles Alston and Romare Bearden retained aspects of figurative inscription in a practice of 'directed abstraction' that sought to anchor painterly process in a specific cultural context, critics mostly interpreted the work as a form of 'stylistic centrism' that stopped short of the expressive freedom promised by the rupture from representation into full-blown abstraction.

Taking account of the importance of primitivism in the high modernist doctrine

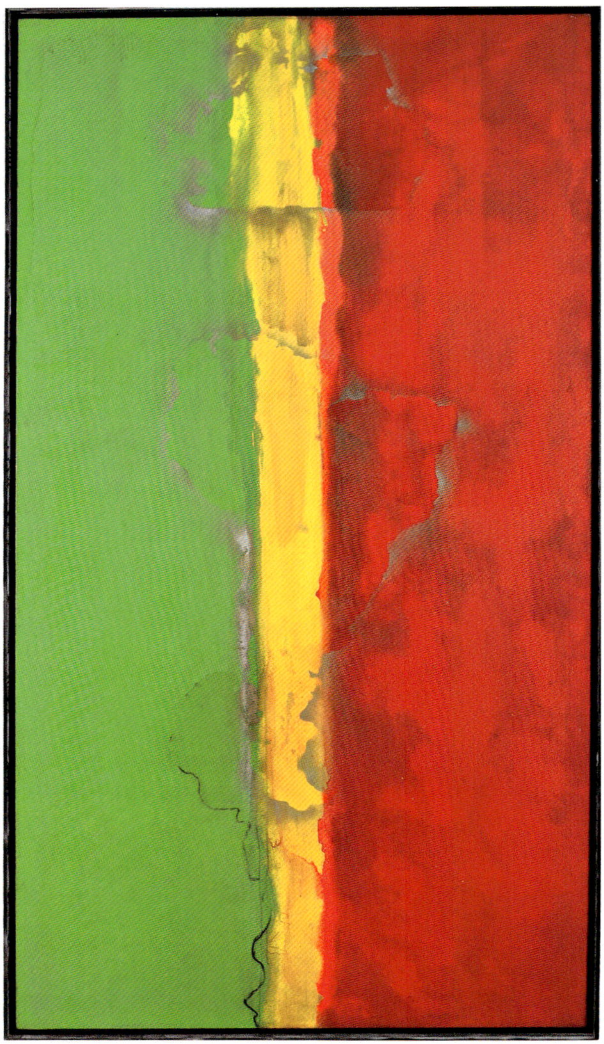

of 'significant form' – which had divorced perceptions of non-Western tribal objects from their ritual contexts so that artefacts were primarily valued for their plastic properties alone, a model consecrated by New York MoMA's exhibition of *African Negro Art* (1935) – Gibson illuminates the bittersweet paradox of cultural difference in the mid-century heyday of abstract art. While Piet Mondrian's *Broadway Boogie Woogie* (1942–43) openly acknowledged the influence of jazz, whose improvisational dynamics were highly valued by Jackson Pollock and Franz Kline as a generative model for action painting, when black artists such as Norman Lewis put forward his *Jazz Musicians* (1948), the presence of a representational or mimetic dimension was seen to fall short of the view that 'expressionistic brushwork was an authentic index of an artist's emotional honesty'.[6] Moreover, while European modernists fully embraced the otherness of various 'folk' cultural symbols as a point of access to unconscious creativity, or so they believed, the ancestralist paradigm advocated by critic Alain Locke – which sought to reconcile modernist freedom of expression with the affirmation and recovery of a historically devalued ethnic heritage – further inhibited minority artists from making a total break with depiction. Caught between the pressure to assimilate to painterly purity and the duty to depict their difference, black artists were blindsided by the underlying codes of abstract expressionism. By virtue of a philosophical dichotomy in the view that the role of abstraction was to interrogate the formal properties specific to the medium of painting – as formulated by critic Clement Greenberg, who was a friend of Bowling's – questions of ethnic or cultural particularity were regarded as irrelevant to the search for the universal 'truths' of art's essential condition.

Although Gibson's account underplays the Caribbean contexts in which, for instance, painter Aubrey Williams explored Carib, Arawak and Mayan motifs in his practice of directed abstraction, her analysis reveals patterns of conflicted inclusion whereby black artists were

Who's Afraid of Barney Newman?, 1968.
Acrylic on canvas, 234 x 123cm.

present at the very centre of modern art movements even though their work subsequently went missing in the margins of art history. Such patterns help to explain the discrepant timeline whereby it was not until the late 1960s that African American artists, such as Al Loving, Mel Edwards and Alma Thomas, could reconcile their equal commitment to abstract aesthetics and the ethics of difference. Locating Bowling's journey in a broader conception of diaspora culture, we can see his stylistic travels as cutting a critical passage through the lived experience of a 'discrepant cosmopolitanism'.[7] He had arrived, through the map paintings, at a place in which to creatively undo the double binds of blackness and abstraction. I want to suggest that it is only now, with the concept of the Black Atlantic,[8] that we too can enter this imaginative place, even though it was very much unchartered territory during the 1960s.

Dub Spaces of Other Modernisms

Bowling's characteristic layerings, pourings, stainings, stitchings and accumulatings all activate optical agency. Across his canvases, such processes draw attention to the constitutive elements of painting. However, equally important to the 'all-over' quality of multiple surface incident, that gives the eye no fixed place to rest, is the gradual activation of affect, which engages the viewer's inner world with subjective thought and feeling.

Critics have observed Bowling's intimate relationship to British landscape traditions, in both the atmospheric hues of his palette and in the often strong horizontal axis of large-scale works such as *Traingone* (1996), which has been read as gently alluding to J. M. W. Turner's *Rain, Steam and Speed* (1844).[9] In the light of Paul Gilroy's convincing reading of Turner's maritime world as a visual inscription of an Atlanticist imagination that was aware of the connective links between the different spaces brought together by imperial power, it is tempting to take this line of enquiry further. Where Aubrey Williams enacted an

Mother's House in South America, 1968. Mixed media (silkscreen, acrylic on canvas), 264 x 123cm.

archeological investigation into the traces of lost and unknown ancestral figures buried in the soil of the New World, Dennis de Caires suggests that it is the quality of light reflected off the mudflat surfaces of Guyana's Essequibo, Mazaruni and Cuyuni rivers that is key to understanding the emotional response activated by Frank Bowling's work.[10] Taken together, the aquamarine imagery of rivers, streams and oceans which characterises the glacial acrylic mass seen in works such as *Iceni* (1975), also flows into the Atlantic iconosphere found in parallel works by the Bermuda-born abstract painter Norman Lewis, such as *Ebb Tide* (1975) and *Seachange XIV* (1976).

It was in the map paintings that Bowling first plunged into the aquatic mood that came to suffuse his later practice. In the darkening vertical stains that threaten to engulf the outlines of Europe and the Americas in *Marcia H. Travels*, it is possible to suggest that the world picture imprinted by the Empire project was being placed 'under erasure'. By virtue of the ways in which they tackle the subject of postcolonial history, the map paintings were critically rewriting the Eurocentric projection of the globe that was installed in modern consciousness when Albrecht Dürer 'engraved the first representation of a hemisphere according to the laws of perspective and the system of latitudes and longitudes'.[11] The order of knowledge implicit in maps as documents of Europe's global power was cancelled out but still barely visible in the Black Atlantic spaces of Bowling's oceanic abstraction. In the sense that this was a painterly act of postcolonial re-vision, producing a critical difference in our 'mapping' of pictorial space by decentring the planisphere projection system, the paintings disturb the underlying codes of representation embodied in maps as documents of Europe's modernity.

Some writers felt troubled by these 'more or less monochromatic'[12] paintings, as if the encroaching darkness of the blackening stain threatened to render the figure/ground relationship unreadable. Perhaps such a response reveals the

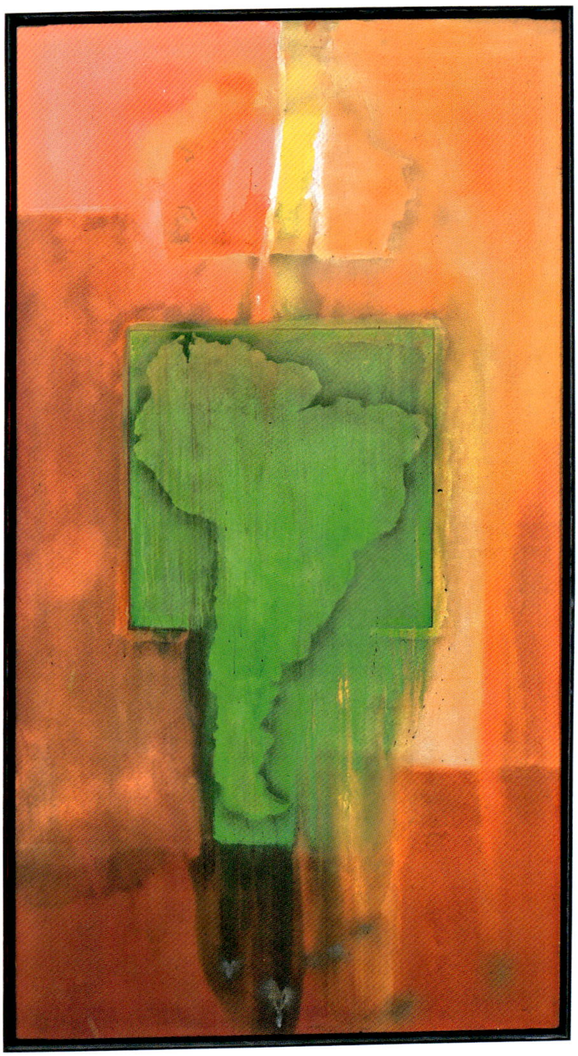

subjective underside to the paintings' oceanic dimension. Indeed, where the key fault line of the period in which they were produced seems to fall between the visual and the verbal – for Bowling himself conducted a fierce polemic against black art politics in such articles as 'The Rupture'[13] – the mood of his map paintings is contemplative rather than confrontational.

With a quality of openness and gentleness towards a receptive state of feeling, the melancholic or even sorrowful atmosphere of the deep monochromatic staining in *Marcia H. Travels* evokes a pre-symbolic space in which edges merge and lines blur in a kind of oceanic enjoyment of colour for its own sake. One ego's bliss, however, is another ego's anxiety at the loss of boundaries. Describing Bowling's 1980s works as 'relief maps of an emotional terrain', one writer perceptively observed that 'sometimes "wounds" open up in the skin' of the painting[14] and thus pinpointed the place that joins the optical agency of surface incident to the psychic depth activated in the viewer's affective response. I suggest that such 'wounds' mark the inscription of an oceanic abstraction that re-crosses the Atlantic as a space of traumatic rupture and potential healing, where the spatial politics of world history meet the transitional spaces of psychic life.

Breaching the boundaried world through acts of abstraction that signify upon the map motif as an emblem of a desire for global mastery, the Black Atlantic spaces of Frank Bowling's map paintings resonate with the eerie logic of dub versioning. Dub aesthetics practise a form of critical repetition in which new spaces are opened up by the subtractive 'cutting' of blank passages. Little pockets of nothingness are sculpted into the song structure or melody and the drop – a sudden rim-shot or clash of cymbals – marks the echo that reveals where the engineer has taken something out of the master or original. It is not so much that abstract art is like 'a narrative painting without the lyrics',[15] but rather that the dub factor reveals a creative logic of differential repetition. As James Snead once put it, 'in black culture, the thing (the ritual, the dance, the beat) is "there for you to pick it up when you come back to get it". If there is a goal in such a culture, it is always deferred.'[16] In this sense, blackness is never just a sign of absence or lack in Western culture, even though it has served the symbolic function of the 'other' in the Eurocentric imagination; it is also a sign of 'difference' in the Derridean sense of intervening in the codes of a culture to delay and postpone the closure of the signifying chain. Frank Bowling's map paintings activate an awareness of the agency of something that is not there anymore.

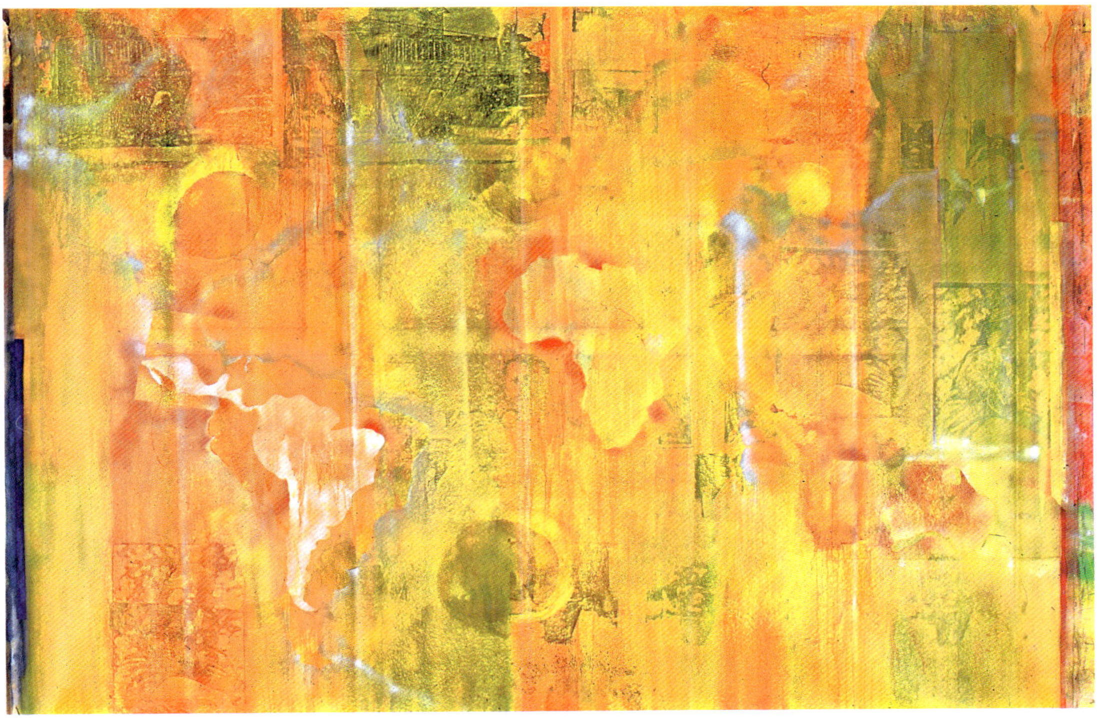

Where is Lucienne?, 1971.
Acrylic on canvas, 320 x 340cm.

Clifford Charles and the Pleasures of Contemplative Insurgency

Bheki Peterson

The work of Clifford Charles is another reminder that compelling art exacts a prize, a commitment from both the artist and the audience. It does not present itself as surface beauty, simply there to be viewed, grasped and just as quickly forgotten or mounted as décor. Nor does it pander to the well-intentioned, but ultimately fickle and prescriptive, notions of what the thematic and aesthetic prerogatives of black artists in South Africa should be. Always against the grain of convention and expectation, the paintings of Charles possess a startling energy that invigorates them in a manner that constantly teases the viewer into new, and hopefully, fuller ways of perception. Upon each viewing, the observer is challenged with whether to add on to, refine and even reassess their initial encounter and apprehension of the images.

My initial sense is that the ink paintings that form Charles's contribution to the Venice Biennale 2003 are likely to evoke differing responses that are either going to praise or fault the seeming flight away from the themes generally associated with any evocation of the word 'post-apartheid'. If this is the case, then both polar readings are not only false, but wrong as well. Since the late 1980s, the work of Charles has retained a strong sense of continuity and a preoccupation with a number of aesthetic and thematic questions and challenges. This underlying thread is still discernible in the current work in spite of the deep twists and turns that have also marked the creative phases through which Charles has passed. I would like to tease out just two key tropes or signposts that, in a way, are constants in Charles's past and present work.

Firstly, there is the journey motif. Charles is obsessively preoccupied with matters of form, always striving to interrogate and refine his own command of craft. On the other hand, the impulse towards journeying results from Charles's integrity and lifelong pursuit of a textured artistic vision that will enable him to chart the trails and tribulations of life on the southernmost tip of Africa. These quests impinge on each other in complex ways such as when, as in the ink paintings, the politics are as much in the formal methods and processes followed as in the ideas evoked. I would suggest, for

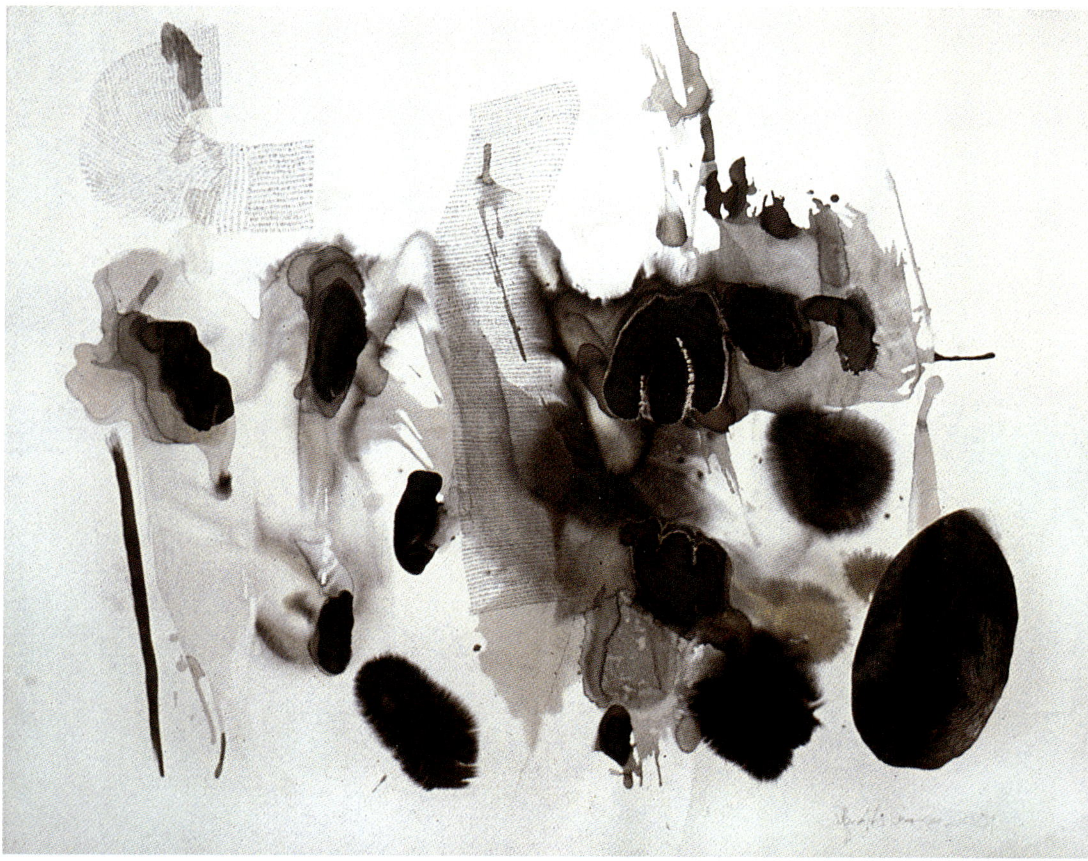

instance, that the incisions on to the paper which are then layered with ink upon ink resonate beyond the imperatives of the technique used. I say this because incisions upon the body, as it was literally scarred, tortured and reconfigured under the violence of apartheid, were a powerful focus of a series of oil paintings Charles produced in the 1980s under the composite title of *Metamorphosis*. Huge in scope and intent, *Metamorphosis* was an audacious intervention. It shifted the focus away from the then common representations of urban squalor and of black people as passive victims of apartheid; instead it privileged an unflinching examination of the dehumanisation within the forces of oppression. Moving between the body and the landscape, Charles increasingly explored and drew our attention to the landscape and its markings, scratches and representations imbued with memories that contested and recast the distortions of colonial narratives.

The second motif that is prevalent in the work of Charles is that of memory. Very much aware of the ambiguities and complexities of memory work, Charles has sought to do more than merely bear witness. His approach seems to thrive on unsettling whatever orthodoxies both black and white South Africans hold on to for whatever personal or social reasons. Charles is always drawn towards the fissures in the grand narratives of apartheid and post-apartheid South Africa. It is the fragments that he finds compelling in his reflections on and representations of the paradoxes and contradictions of South Africa's past, present and future. His *Carrier Bag* series (1989) looked simultaneously in a number of directions. It examined the ways in which the lives of black people were packaged and commodified by racial capitalism and, in response, the manners in which black people internalised or resisted the identities forced upon them. *Masks* (early 1990s) teased with its colourful recreations of African masks that, despite their beauty, called upon the viewer to look beyond the stereotypes and clichés associated with African masks and see instead the insurgent carnivalesque and spiritual energy that is staring back. In the

Rhythm and Blues, 2001.
Ink on paper, 123.5 x 153cm.

Healing series (1996), the fascination was on the significance of materials such as cloth, mud and ink, on how – almost as instruments of ritual associated with *sangomas* (traditional healers) – they come into play in resolving the tensions between the sacred and the profane; in the beautification and preservation of space and place; in the representation of experience; and in negotiating dreams for the future. *Mapping* (1997) tried to strengthen the connections, casting the artist as an archeologist of sorts, retrieving and reconstructing lost 'topographies' of self from as far back as the rock paintings of the San to the contemporary pursuit of resistance and redemption. The latter focus was underpinned by an unapologetic celebration of blackness that was far removed from the delusions of post-1994 'Rainbow Nation'[1] mantras, a theme that was to be revisited in *B(l)ack In Town* (1997–98).

The purpose of my brief guide to Clifford Charles is to establish two facts: that innovation is a constant burden and, despite its current unfashionable status in South Africa, so too is the intent of producing work that is engaged. Unlike the work of many artists, although Charles's practice is deeply inscribed with historical specificity, it also stubbornly refuses to be reduced to, solely defined by, or more correctly, confined to the exigencies of time and place. It demands that it be approached and assessed within its own terms, which it fortunately also eloquently suggests to the attentive viewer. Charles had the following to say about some of the impulses behind the ink paintings that are being exhibited at the Biennale:

> Finishing new work is a pausing moment – a punctuation, a realisation or maybe the last step where effort ceases. It becomes for me both a culmination of experience and a dilution of conformity. An uninhabited space of not being yet being, a contradictory and ironical motive, since the action of painting becomes an act of nothingness. Unbundled by the known. An active meditation and contemplation. Attempting not to defy or define – just

being. Trying to move to a thoughtless moment of listening to oneself till one exhausts words. Working with water as the basic medium throws further challenges since its nature is liquid, uncontained, fluid, and transparent – is nothing yet everything.

There are a number of tricky ideas that need to be unpacked in the statement by Charles. There is the acknowledgement that each step in the journey is both a retracing and a charting of new paths. There is, in a sense, nothing remarkable or paradoxical in such a gesture. African artists across a variety of genres have insisted on the need to look both ways at once. To mention just two, Dub poet Lesego Rampolokeng has championed 'end-beginnings' and novelist Dambudzo Marechera has written, somewhat obsessively, about 'stitches' on the body as the reconnection of what has been ruptured, in ways analogous to the articulation between re-membering and dis-membering. Stitches, in a move similar to Walter Benjamin's anecdote about borders,[2] mark not simply the beginnings and ends of territories or flesh; the incision/border in itself speaks of a much more complicated history, often of fissures that are the consequences of violence and conflict. This, of course, suggests some overlap with the notion of fault lines and all that is implied in the idea of shifting landscapes. While I can allow for the exigencies of an 'uninhabited space of not being yet being' that thrives on the premise of being 'unbundled by the known', I am reluctant to regard it as 'an act of nothingness' or a 'thoughtless moment' of listening. Charles is, of course, merely stating the importance of entering the creative process without any debilitating presuppositions. My fear, to be upfront, is to guard against the appropriation of such strategies by the orthodoxies of the metropolitan theories in vogue that thrive on infinite deferment and dispersal, where everything and, ultimately, nothing is up for grabs in the area of identity and politics.

From the preliminary work that I have seen, the ink paintings represent another turning point in the creative mission of

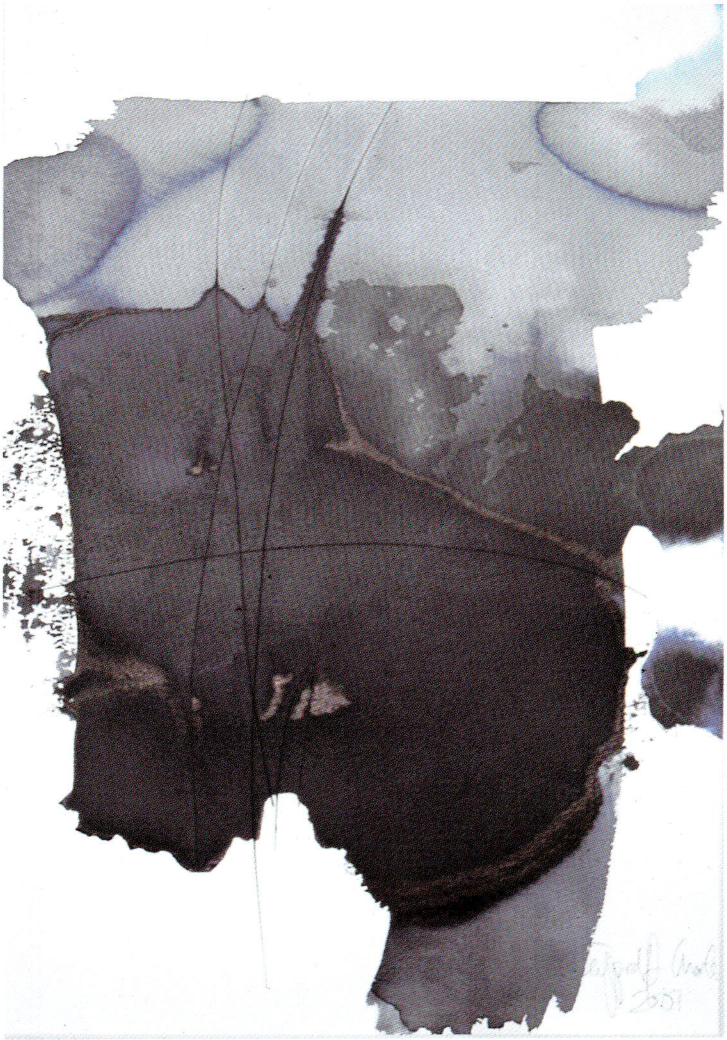

Interaction, *Haiku* series, 2001.
Ink on paper, 30 x 42cm.

Charles. Fundamentally, they are a provocatively ingenious response to South Africa's 'altered states'. By 'states', I am referring to the changes that have taken place in the areas of, especially, governance and consciousness in South Africa. It is no surprise that almost ten years after the first democratic elections in South Africa, the artistic pulse behind the ink paintings feels as if it is overwhelmed by the need for introspection and meditation. As if trying to flee from the disillusionment and cynicism that many artists and activists bear towards what they see as present-day South Africa's colluding with the individualistic and consumptionist agendas of globalisation, the ink paintings at a glance appear to yearn towards a somewhat hesitant neo-primitivism and mystical symbolism. Charles elicits the allure and perils of minimalism in the ink paintings – exciting the imagination by avoiding the naturalistic and figurative as well as all the seductive images of mass culture that currently overwhelm us. Also, the large scale of some of the paintings and Charles's use of colours – in their starkness and contrasts – evokes a somewhat mythical and ironic sense of beauty. Even when the opaqueness and the dark thematic currents behind some of the work are taken into consideration, I was still left with the tranquillity, wry smile, acceptance and resolve that a thorough knowledge of the past engenders as it reminds us of the challenges of the future.

Contemplation in Charles's hands is, therefore, nothing less than a dimension of the journey and memory motifs. It signals a desire to reclaim the self on personal, creative and social levels. Again, the creative impulse encompasses the modes of ritual that Charles's work often revisits with all the attendant ambiguities. For instance, in some of the ink paintings, the incisions that are cut into the paper can be deflected away from the violence of and associations with repression. Instead they can be viewed from within the ambit of the making of African identities; circumcision and bodily markings as markers of rites of passage are two obvious examples that come to mind. The scarified paper is then steeped with watercolours, allowing the

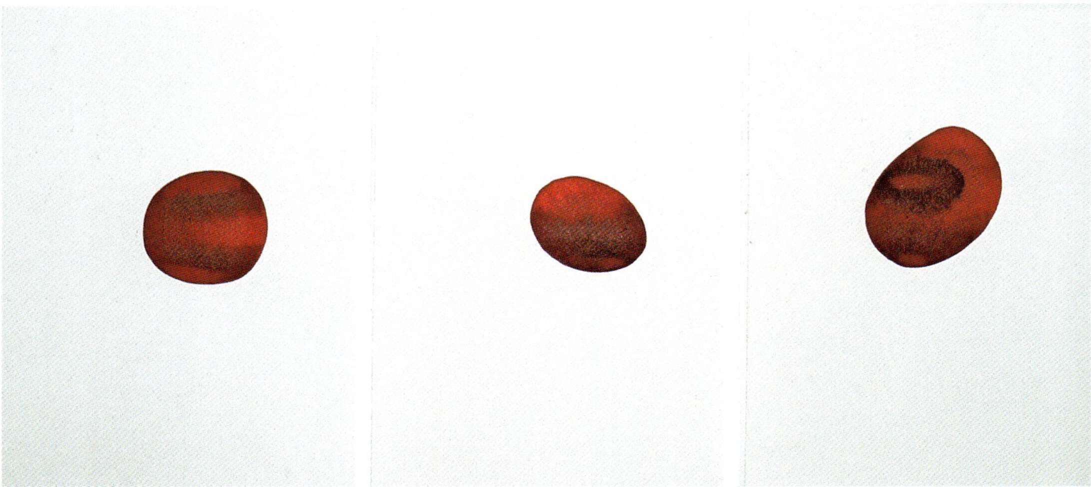

A Breath, *Painting on Water* series, 2002–3. Ink on paper, each part of triptych 37 x 27cm. Photograph: Thandi Grenville-Grey.

different contours to suck in the colours in the drying process, often in an uneven manner. The other ink paintings are, often, the result of deep meditation and focus where Charles's creative and living experiences are called upon and released in a single, quick gesture of ink upon the canvas. Again, the cracks that appear in the ink as it dries stir up feelings of earthiness, of landscapes that are dry in many senses of the term.

Although there is clearly an element of a self-conscious, structured use of technique in the ink paintings, once initiated, Charles calls upon considerable spontaneity and improvisation as he responds to the energies of the material used and tries to put them into the service of his thematic intentions. The end result is that the viewer is sensitised about the material and techniques used, allowing for a more critical appreciation of the different elements and dimensions that have gone into the work. In short, the ink paintings are imbedded in the tussle with form as much as they continue to explore the journey and memory motifs.

It is important to realise that for all their evocations of palaeontology, of San rock paintings, of ritual, Charles's ink paintings also speak to contemporary influences and issues. As far as their dialogue with contemporary black South African art is concerned, for me the ink paintings nod to the oblique influence of, in particular, the works of two contemporary masters: Ernest Mancoba and Thami Mnyele. Thematically, the ink paintings are another, necessary archival project – one of many such interventions that are currently underway in South Africa, the most well-known being the Truth and Reconciliation Commission (TRC). For all its numerous flaws, the TRC was also a moment for ordinary black people to speak the truth to whiteness, to valorise and institutionalise their experiences, narratives and hopes.

The ink paintings, for me, are a thoughtful and humorous displacement of whiteness with the intricacies of blackness. In their minimalism and dense imagery, they restate the obvious (but for many still difficult to accept) premise that black existence, thought, spirituality and artistry is as complex as any other and can be

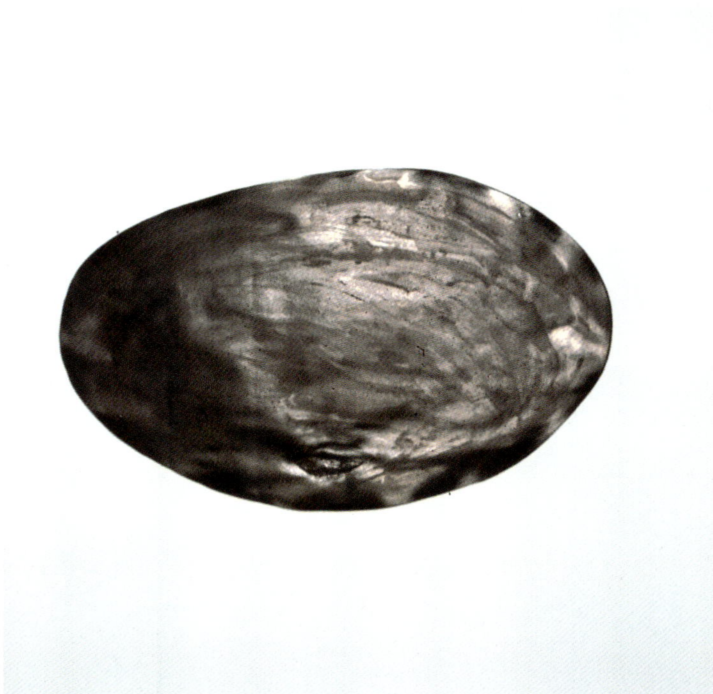

Quietude, *Painting on Water* series, 2002–3. Ink on paper, 139.6 x 153cm. Photograph: Thandi Grenville-Grey.

expressed in as many forms and styles as any other. The thick and, at first glance, impenetrable shapes of black against white tease the eye to come forward and see if there is, indeed, anything else beyond the 'dark abyss'. In this sense, they recall the black marks (usually blocks) that apartheid censors used to hide faces and material that was considered subversive. Of course, the black blocks (like a veil) intrigued and tantalised the imagination and desire as much as they concealed. One peered at the blocks intensively, hoping to catch a glimpse (or even fault line if you wish) of the face blotted out or desperately scanned the permitted lines of prose or of a poem, trying to find clues in order to retrieve the prohibited content. Let us also not forget the sardonic humour of apartheid that euphemistically described areas populated by black people outside of the homeland reserves, as 'black spots' that needed to be removed from white South Africa.

At any rate, once I was captivated by their black shapes, the ink paintings elicited an emotive response. I was drawn in by their evocation of the warmth of the colour black, the tenderness of the night, and of the infinite pleasures of blackness. In short, the ink paintings, consistent with Charles's oeuvre, retrieve marginal memories and animate them under new contexts as part of the larger project of displacing whiteness and inscribing the complexities of the African heritage and experience as the basis for a redemptive future.

We've Also Been to Soweto

Prince Massingham

At exactly 9.30am on an oppressive sunny Saturday morning Morena, a *mpinchi* and reformed *gintsa* turned taxi driver whom I hijacked from the local taxi rank in my ghetto, brought the *skaftin* to a screeching halt next to the main entrance of the Witswatersrand University Medical School, Parktown, Johannesburg.

We waited for Rudolf – a Danny DeVito lookalike, Austrian medical student, who was part of a group I took on a tour the previous week – and his four colleagues to take them on a five-hour tour of Soweto with a local dish of chicken stew served with *morogo*, pumpkin, *maxonja, chakalaka* and beverages included. Like all tourists, they wanted a firsthand experience of the real *makoya, Msawawa*. In reality, it was an opportunity for Rudolf to collect *ivusa nduku* from Sophie, a local traditional healer, because the main ingredients hadn't been available the past Saturday. He complained to her that his 'main switch' was not functioning well. Shame.

After ten minutes of waiting, Morena spotted an open-air *chisa-nyama* on the pavement and nagged me to buy him a plate of *pap* and steak and a *collie* to wash it down. We both alighted and sauntered to the *chisa-nyama*, where we purchased his order and a 500ml bottled juice for me.

Whilst Morena gobbled his *pap* and steak voraciously, I reflected on the tongue lashing that *Bra* Zakes – a short, fifty-something visual artist and staunch patron of Aunt Lettie's *shebeen* – had given me the

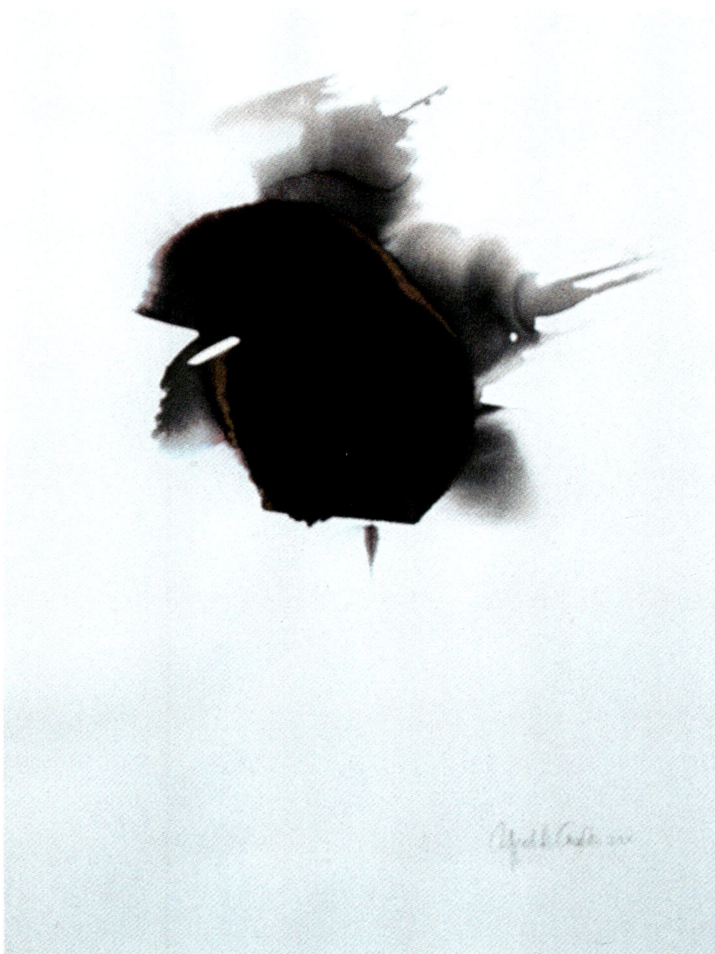

Ignite, *Haiku* series, 2001. Ink on paper, 56 x 41.8cm.

previous evening at the cabin. I was busy imbibing the waters of immortality all by myself in the corner, when without any provocation he attacked me verbally.

'People like you, my *laaitie*, are a disgrace to the black masses', he said, pointing his index finger at me, 'you should be ashamed of yourself'.

'What have I done *Bra* Zakes?' I asked perplexed.

'You are a sell-out, a black Judas Iscariot.'

'That is a serious allegation, *Bra* Zakes. *Hoe meen jy* I'm a sell-out?' I enquired, still confused.

'You bring these *larnies* to look at our poverty, squalor and *mkhukhus*. Sies! *Uyangi dina*! Tell me! What are your *ngamlas* going to change? *Fokkol*, absolutely nothing. The reason why they come to *Msawawa* is because of sheer curiosity to see how darkies can survive under severe conditions. In fact it is like a visit to a zoo for them and a reassurance that they are better off.'

Suddenly I registered Rudolf tumbling and bouncing towards the *skaftin* like a *diski*, with his colleagues in hot pursuit. *Abo shwee* were sporting different coloured shorts, t-shirts, designer sneakers and eyewear, equipped to the teeth with top of the range digital Minolta and Pentax cameras. Morena, who gallops after everything wearing bloomers, like a chihuahua on heat, was smitten by the ladies.

'*Bheka lo slenda ufana no Julia Roberts*', he said amusingly as we hasten to the *skaftin*.

'*Ja, ufana naye*', I confirmed.

'*Eish, uyangi shaya ding dong*', he said looking at her amorously and rubbing his palms against each other.

'*Hayibo unga zophupa la, si sem sebenzini*', I said jokingly.

'Hey *wena* dreams do come true and it is *pashasha* to mix business with pleasure. Just imagine me, Morena, married to a *ngamla*', he bragged.

'Good morning master Prince', Rudolf greeted me folding his hands Buddha-style.

'Good day everybody', I responded. The others mumbled their greetings.

Lackadaisical, *Painting on Water* series, 2002-3. Ink on paper, 153 x 90 cm. Photograph: Thandi Grenville-Grey.

'I brought you tourists. I must become your partner', he said with a broad smile endowing his round face.

'Thanks Dolf', I said opening the sliding door.

Morena and myself exchanged pleasantries with his colleagues. Zwaam. The doors closed and we were on our way to *Msawawa*.

'My name is Prince as you all know and my pilot's name, nodding in Morena's direction, is Morena. It is a Sotho word meaning 'king'. You should feel very honoured to be chauffeured by royalty.'

'*Kua! Kua! Kua!*' they laughed.

Ah, got them. They at least laughed at my stale joke. Ice broken, I consoled myself.

Our first stop was the old Forte Prison in Braamfontein. 'Guys, this was a former prison called the Forte Prison. It was notorious for its ill-treatment of black prisoners until its closure in the late 1970s. It is now a heritage site. It hosted Nelson Mandela, Mahathma Gandhi and a number of other political prisoners', I explained. While I was explaining to them, my mind went on a fantasy flight to nowhere. I imagined Mandela and Gandhi doing the *tauza* jive to the delight of the warders who were a law unto themselves back then. Just imagine *buntu* two great people jumping up and down *kaalbezozie.*

'Prince, was Gandhi held here?" Barbara asked giving me dagger looks.

'Yes', I answered.

'What was he doing in South Africa?' she continued with her interrogation.

'Gandhi practised as a lawyer in South Africa in the early 1900s, after studying in England, and staged numerous passive resistance marches against the discriminatory laws before he returned to India in 1914. He had his first taste of racism, when he was ordered off a whites-only train coach', I answered.

'Yes! Yes! I saw it in the film *Gandhi*', Rose, the squeaky-voiced Julia Roberts lookalike British woman chipped in.

'Yes you're right', I confirmed.

'I didn't know that he once lived in South Africa', said Barbara startled.

She then conversed in her native *scamto* to Rudolf and her compatriot Johanna, a tall slim, hourglass-figured, oval-faced brunette with big shifty eyes, who did her internship at Baragwanath/Chris Hani Hospital, Soweto, a former military base. Baragwanath is the biggest hospital in Africa. Some argue that it is the biggest in the world. It was at Bara, as the locals affectionately call it, where the greatest number of youths with bullet wounds were arrested by the system during the Soweto uprising.

As we drove through Hillbrow, the place was, as usual, busy like India during rush hour. Taxis and cars were zigzagging through the congested traffic defying road rules. Morena was making full use of the opportunity to impress the *mlungus* with his *kasie* driving skills. *Magoshas*, whose curves were bulging out of their xxx-small miniskirts, and street vendors were enticing potential customers with their wares. Two glue-sniffing urchins standing next to Nandos, a chicken outlet, blew kisses and made indecent movements to the ladies. *Batung!*

'This is Hillbrow, popular for its nightlife, vice and influx of African immigrants. This place is busy twenty-four hours a day. It also housed immigrants from Europe from the early 1900s until the abolishment of the Group Areas Act. White people started moving out when blacks moved in.'

'Is this place safe?' enquired Rose, starry-eyed.

'It is very dangerous if you don't know the place well. There is what we call "no-go areas", which are where a lot of muggings take place.'

'My colleagues who are based at the General Hospital said they get more than four gunshot victims from this place on weekends', she said.

Rudolf also mentioned that they learn to treat gunshot wounds in *Umzansi* because in their countries they seldom treat gunshot victims. Shoo! That means we are a violent country *mos*. I also told them about the pass laws and how black people had to carry and produce that dreadful document at every corner, when confronted by cops. It is the very same document that Mandela and his comrades burnt during the Defiance Campaign in 1960, which resulted in sixty-nine people being shot in Sharpville

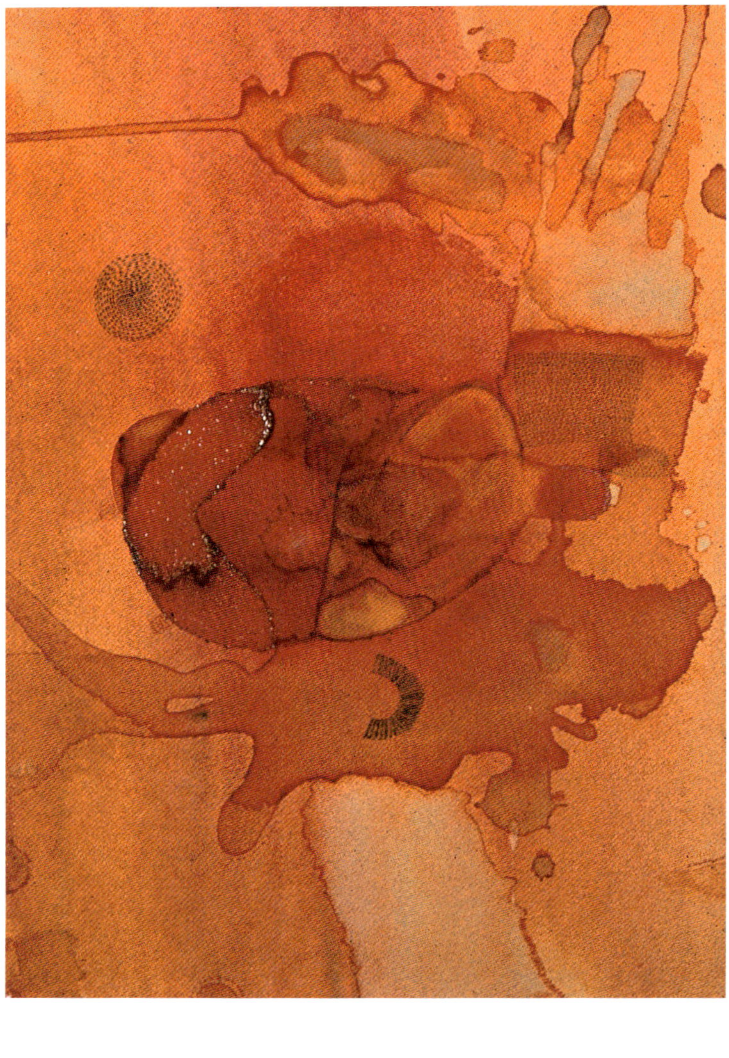

Filament, *Painting on Water* series, 2002–3. Ink on paper, 37 x 27.5cm. Photograph: Thandi Grenville-Grey.

on the 21 March 1960. I didn't forget to mention the 10pm to 10am curfew. If you were found in town after ten, you had to produce a night pass signed by your employer.

Jy ken, the hourglass-figured one seemed to be in a state of total paralysis. *Ke a o jwetsa. Mahlo a hae ane ale maholo jwale ka kgomo*. She resembled someone who has seen a *tokoloshe.*

On the M1 south, I showed them mine dunes owned by white mining houses and explained to them that *Mjondolo* was built as a result of the discovery of gold, hence the names *Igoli* and *Gauteng* both meaning 'the city of gold'.

'The sand is being removed to extract gold from it', I said.

'Prince, can we go and steal the gold', asked Rudolf.

'Yes, you can, but do you have the equipment to extract the gold?' I replied.

'WELCOME TO SOWETO' screamed a board as we approached Baragwanath Hospital.

'Are there white people living in Soweto?' asked Barbara.

'No, I don't think any white person would even dream of living or setting foot here. They are still privileged and Soweto is just a big ghetto.'

Morena emitted a loud guffaw, when Barbara asked, 'Is that a nuclear plant?' pointing at the Orlando Power Station.

'That is a former power station. It has existed since the late 1940s and yet Soweto only got electricity in 1982', I explained.

'Who then was it supplying?' asked Johanna.

'The white people', I said.

The *skaftin* became silent like a horror movie. The only sound came from the clicking and clacking of their digital toys, as they were snapping away at the locals who looked at them mysteriously.

'Those are four-roomed council houses built by the previous government. The locals call them matchbox houses. The new government is building houses even smaller than those', I said.

'What is the population of Soweto?' asked Barbara.

'It is estimated at five and a half million.'

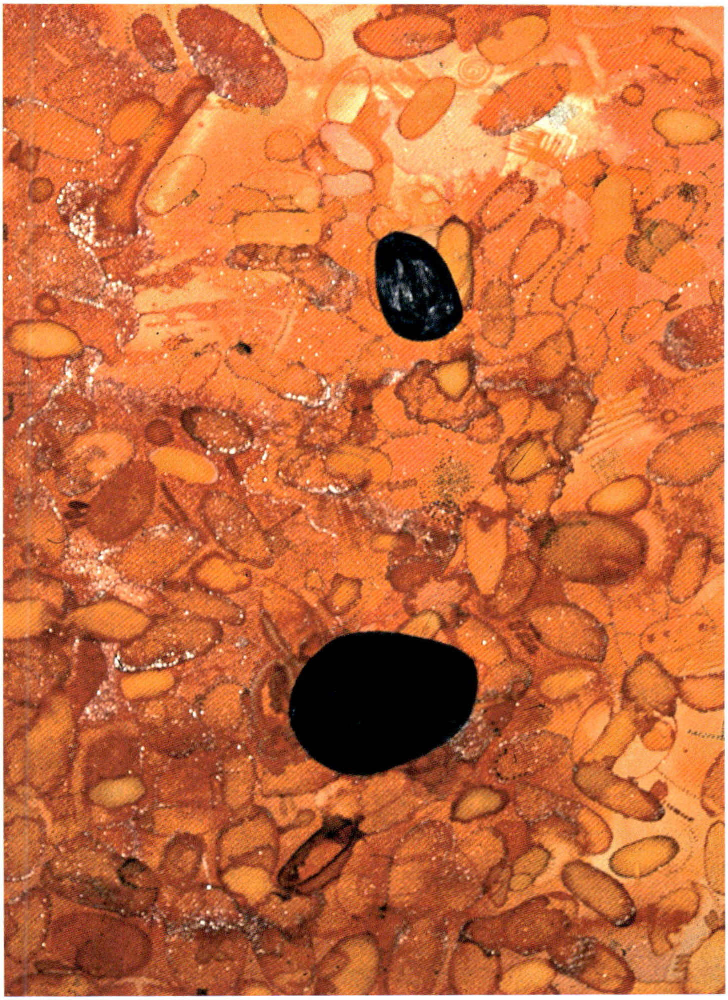

Fall, *Painting on Water* series, 2002–3. Ink on paper, 37 x 27.5cm. Photograph: Thandi Grenville-Grey.

'You know', said Johanna, 'I always thought that Soweto was a shanty town. Do you know what a shanty town is, Prince?' she asked. I nodded. 'I'm surprised that people live in nice houses and drive nice cars. Look at that one', she added pointing at a BMW 325i.

'We call that a *Gusheshe*. It means 'fast' in the lingua franca of the youth. In Soweto most brand cars have their own township names. For instance a BMW 535 is called *isandla SEM fene*, meaning monkey paw, because its gear lever looks like a monkey's paw. BMW 520is and 518is are called dolphins because of their shapes. The 518i and 520i 1990s models are called g-string due to the shape of their boot and any cabriolet is called *sihlahlamatende*, meaning "throwing the tent backwards". A mini is called Mr Bean.'

'Kua Kua! Kea!' they laughed.

'Because Mr Bean drives one. It sounds creative. Can you please write it down for me?', asked Rudolf.

We descended on Kliptown, Morena parked and we alighted for a walk through the marketplace. The girls zapped out their cameras and took *kiekies*. The marketplace, which attracts people from Soweto, was an *inqubevange* of activities. The pavements on Union Street were packed with traders selling everything from fresh fruit and vegetables, shoes, live chickens, tripe, trotters and *muti*. Pedestrians and motorists were competing for space on the road.

'This is oldest township in Johannesburg. It was proclaimed in 1904 and the Freedom Charter of the African Nationalist Congress was launched here in 1955.' I was still explaining when a tall petrol attendant with a light complexion called Chopper (in acknowledgment of his egg-shaped head) approached us. Nobody dares call him by his nickname within hearing distance, although he knows it. He asked Barbara, 'Madam could I please take a photo with you?'

'Why not?' she replied.

'I want international photo', he said, winking at me. I volunteered to take the international photo.

'*Uyabon*', he bragged. '*Ngi posa nabo tegen ase States. Hayi nabo darkie*.'

Gene, a freckled-face coloured man and curator of the photo exhibition at the Kliptown Community Centre *wietied* the group as they browsed through the exhibition viewing photos taken during the launch of the Freedom Charter. The Centre was a disused council building that was renovated and extended to attract tourists during the Earth Summit in 2002. It ceased to attract tourists after the summit. Next to it is a big squatter camp called Angola, where people live in abject poverty with a high rate of both unemployment and HIV/AIDS. Storks deliver daily babies infected with *Z3*. Instead of improving the plight of the community, money is spent on attracting tourists. I hope things will change now that the Rand has been imbibing *imbiza* and it's becoming strong enough to compete with the *nkalakatas* – the Dollar and the Pound. We need to address the issue of *Z3* because some ignorant people believe you can cure yourself of *Z3* by sleeping with a virgin.

We alighted from the *skaftin* in front of Mandela's old house – now turned into a museum – where Winnie Mandela used to sell soil to tourists for twenty dollars. I saw a snot-nosed *laaitie*, who was in goal for a street *diski* game, abandon it when he saw the *mlungus* and bolted like lightning towards us. '*Ngi cela ugu culela abelungu?*' he asked. He bursts into an impromptu rendition of our trilingual national anthem and spiced it with a Madiba shuffle when the crew started zapping him. He was also well rewarded for amusing them. This is a new phenomenon in Soweto. It is common to see groups of children at tourist sites galvanising into diluted and adulterated African dances with the hope of receiving coins.

Our last stop was the Hector Peterson Memorial, where a tour guide totally distorted the history of June 1976, telling the tourists that the students' action was spontaneous. *Ek was in die moer in* and I'm sure Steve Biko and all those who died on that day were turning in their graves. He totally marginalised an organisation that created a consciousness during that period and became an *imbongi* of the popular movement in our country.
HAI SUKA.

Glossary

abo shwee (slang): the ladies
batung (Sotho): people
bheka lo slenda ufana a ufana no Julia Roberts (Zulu): look at the slender one, she looks just like Julia Roberts
Bra: Brother (abbreviation)
buntu (Zulu): People
chakalaka (slang): hot chilli salad
chisa-nyama (Zulu): place where they sell meat or a plate of porridge and meat
diski (slang): ball
collie (slang): cold drink
eish, uyangi shaya ding dong (slang): she makes me crazy
ek was in die moer in (Afrikaans): I was very angry
fokkol (Afrikaans, slang): nothing
Gauteng (Sotho): the city of gold
gintsa (slang): car thief
Gusheshe (slang): fast
hai suka (Zulu): go away
hayibo unga zophupa la, si sem sebenzini (Zulu): hey, don't dream, we are at work
hoe meen jy? (Afrikaans): what do mean?
Igoli (Zulu): the city of gold
imbongi (Zulu): praise singer
imbiza (Zulu): a herbal drink that strengthens you
inquebevange (Xhosa): pot-pourri
isandla SEM fene (Zulu): monkey paw
ivusa nduku (Zulu): aphrodisiac (literally, stiffen the stick)
ja, ufana naye (Zulu): she looks like her
jy ken (Afrikaans): You know
kaalbezozie (slang): naked
kasie (slang): township
ke a o jwetsa (Tswana): I'm telling you
kiekies (Afrikaans): photos
kua, kua, kua: mimicking laughter
laaitie (slang): boy
larnies (slang): white people
magosha (slang): sex worker
mahlo a hae ane ale maholo jwale ka kgomo (Sotho): her eyes were as big as those of a cow
makoya (slang): genuine
maxonja (Tsonga): mopani worm
Mjondolo (slang): Johannesburg
mkhukhus (Zulu): makeshift dwellings
mlungus (Zulu): white people
morogo (Zulu): wild spinach
mos (Afrikaans): affirmation
mpinchi (slang): friend
Msawawa (slang): Soweto
muti (Zulu): herbs
ngamlas (slang): white people
ngi posa nabo tegen ase States. Hayi nabo darkie (Zulu): I'm posing with ladies from the United States of America. Not with darkies
ngi cela ugu culela abelungu? (Zulu): could I please sing for the whites?
nkalakatas (slang): brave ones
pap (Afrikaans): porridge
pashasha (slang): good
Sies (Afrikaaans): Sis
skaftin (slang): Mitsubishi 2000 minibus; lunch box
scamto (slang): talk
shebeen (Scottish): illegal pub
sihlahlamatende (Zulu): throwing the tent backwards
tauza (slang): prisoners had to jump up and down naked to show that they were not hiding anything
tokoloshe: evil spirit
Umzansi (Zulu): South Africa
uyangi dina (Zulu): you irritate me
wietie (slang): talk to
wena (Zulu): your
uyabon (Zulu): You see
Z3 (slang): HIV/AIDS.

At Least One Person Was Killed

Prince Mbusi Dube

I have been documenting the children of Iraq since 1998. Even at large hospitals in Baghdad, medicines have vanished from pharmacy shelves. Medical equipment is broken and unusable. When children are malnourished, even common diarrhoea or colds can lead to death. But the most alarming phenomenon is the enormous increase in deaths due to leukemia and other cancers. Iraqi hospitals are filled with children suffering from leukemia, cancer and physical deformities. To treat the enormous increase in patients, the two pediatric hospitals in Baghdad had to build special wings for leukemia patients. However, because of financial limitations, there is a severe shortage of medication. Doctors are overwhelmed with the number of severely ill patients. Deaths from cancer in Basra, the city in southern Iraq closest to the battlefields, increased from 34 in 1988 before the war to 219 five years later in 1996. Since then, they have continued to soar.
Takashi Morizumi[1]

This morning (13 February 2003) two residents from the Asherville and Umbilo areas just outside Durban were robbed. At approximately 04:15 five men stormed a house at Daintree Avenue in Asherville just as Mr A. Moosa had opened the front gate to allow his son in to pick him up for Mosque. The victims were threatened with AK-47 rifles and handguns before they were robbed of cash, jewellery and other valuables with a total value of approximately R500,000. The robbers fled in the victim's silver Toyota Corolla. A few hours later a group of four men forced their way into a house at Lamont Road in Umbilo. The victims were threatened with handguns before they were robbed of a firearm, cash and jewellery to the value of R250,000.
South African government website[2]

Veliswa Gwintsa's and Pitso Chinzima's presence at the Venice Biennale represent VOICE in the new South Africa. They regard their installation as social art in that it is about human and global problems rather than their own personal problem. Their work touches on a very critical subject: humanity. The installation talks about the

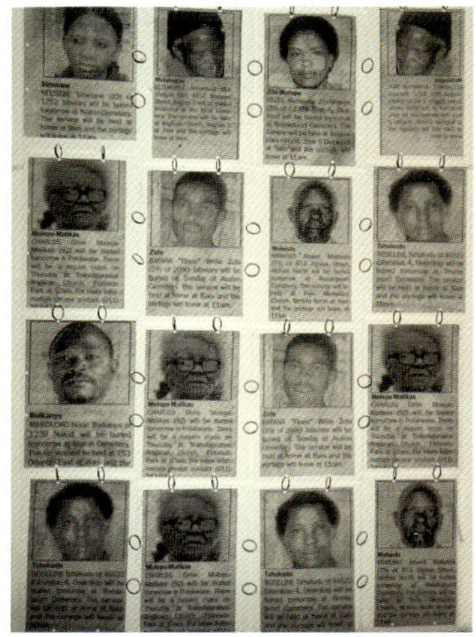

Above and right: Pitso Chinzima, *Archive*, 2003. Mixed media installation.

heartless brutality against humanity and also addresses the way the mass media uses death as a tool to propagate the supremacy of one section of humanity. Approaching death from a global perspective, the artists see their installation as a 'visual monument for the dead'. The work transforms the exhibition space into an arena in which to debate the critical subject of human orchestrated crimes against humanity. The quotations above reinforce what Gwintsa and Chinzima have experienced in their lives, respectively.

Children's furniture covered with newspaper clippings of the deceased and photographs of child victims of the Gulf War are intended to arouse the viewer's consciousness of the most shocking effects of death. Drawing from their own experience, the artists remind us that children are often helpless victims of death in one way or another. When contemplating the work, the viewer is moved to remember deaths that they have witnessed or experienced and thinking about children who are victims intensifies the viewer's emotional response.

This work represents human ideological contradictions at odds with humanity, which are not only peculiar to South Africa, but are also global. In addition to death, the work also looks at the value ascribed to human life. Depending on one's position in the unnatural human chain, one can more easily be made a victim.

Both Gwintsa and Chinzima have rubbed shoulders with death, but they have experienced it in different ways. Gwintsa was born in Lesotho where her parents were exiled after running away from brutal apartheid forces. As a child she lived with death only a foot away. The apartheid regime used its soldiers to invade camps of the exiled South Africans in neighbouring countries such as Lesotho, Swaziland, Botswana, Zimbabwe, Mozambique, Angola and Zambia. Gwintsa witnessed shock, depression and stress after every raid. Each time the South African Defence Force invaded camps she recalls how surviving parents brought children to their house for security. Gwintsa thinks they were half safe because they lived in a house

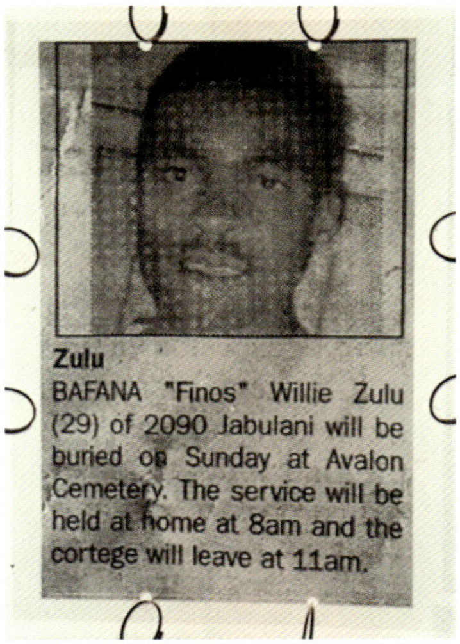
Zulu
BAFANA "Finos" Willie Zulu (29) of 2090 Jabulani will be buried on Sunday at Avalon Cemetery. The service will be held at home at 8am and the cortege will leave at 11am.

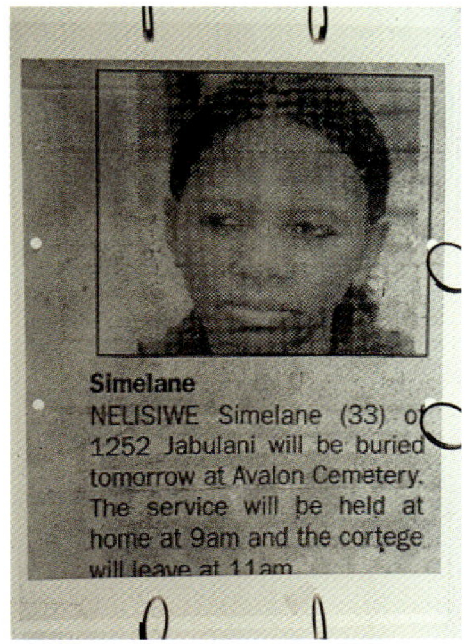
Simelane
NELISIWE Simelane (33) of 1252 Jabulani will be buried tomorrow at Avalon Cemetery. The service will be held at home at 9am and the cortege will leave at 11am

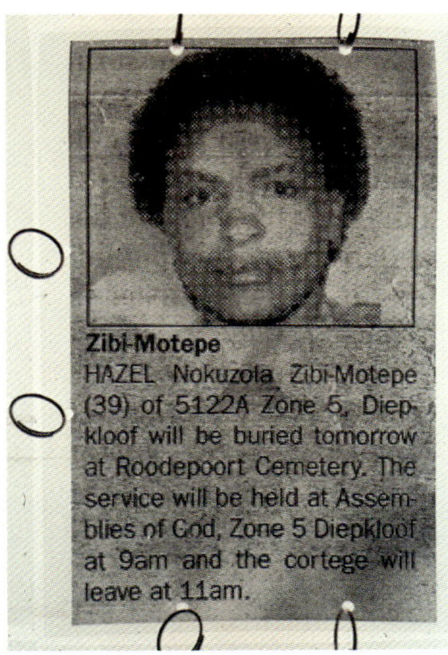
Zibi-Motepe
HAZEL Nokuzola Zibi-Motepe (39) of 5122A Zone 5, Diepkloof will be buried tomorrow at Roodepoort Cemetery. The service will be held at Assemblies of God, Zone 5 Diepkloof at 9am and the cortege will leave at 11am.

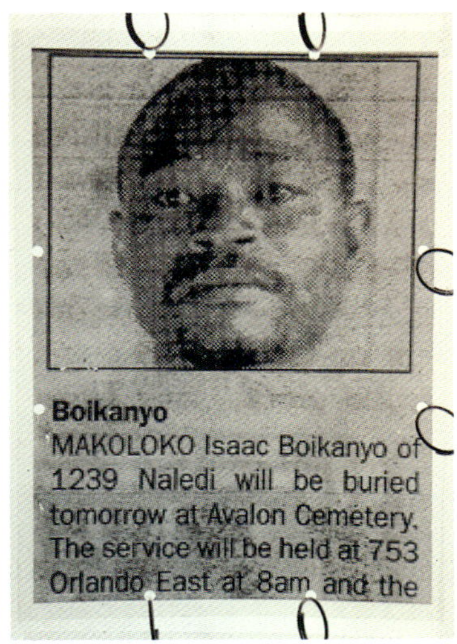
Boikanyo
MAKOLOKO Isaac Boikanyo of 1239 Naledi will be buried tomorrow at Avalon Cemetery. The service will be held at 753 Orlando East at 8am and the

that was away from the camps. She did not understand what was happening at the time, but she remembers that life was painful, economically and otherwise.

It was in 1994 that South Africa gained its freedom. Having denounced apartheid as a crime against humanity, the new challenge is to throw off the shackles of global apartheid. The new VOICE in South Africa addresses what happened to human beings who committed such gross crimes against humanity. VOICE emerges in various forms and tones, not least in the production of contemporary art. When a South African visits another country, they are generally met with curiosity by those who want to hear about their experiences under apartheid. The collaboration between Gwintsa and Chinzima therefore also inspires us to think about the artistic environment in which they grew up.

In most cases, South African artists received art education only at tertiary level, but Gwintsa was fortunate to study art at secondary school in Lesotho. After completing her secondary education, she was accepted to study fine arts at a South African university just before emancipation. Gwintsa has recently learnt that, there, she studied under professors who had also served in the South African Defence Force, some of whom had been deployed in cross border raids. Some may even have participated in the raiding campaigns in Lesotho that Gwintsa survived. Studying at this university exposed her to another possible discrimination based on her supposed place in a conceptualised human hierarchy.

Chinzima was born inside South Africa and did not have the opportunity to study art at secondary school since art was not offered to black children in segregated schools. He also registered for a fine arts degree at the same university where Gwintsa studied, but was only accepted after the emancipation of black people. Both artists were victims of apartheid. Even after the abolition of apartheid, the victimisation of black people continued. Both artists feel that it was particularly bad at their university, where victimisation was institutionalised; black students were awarded credits depending on the degree

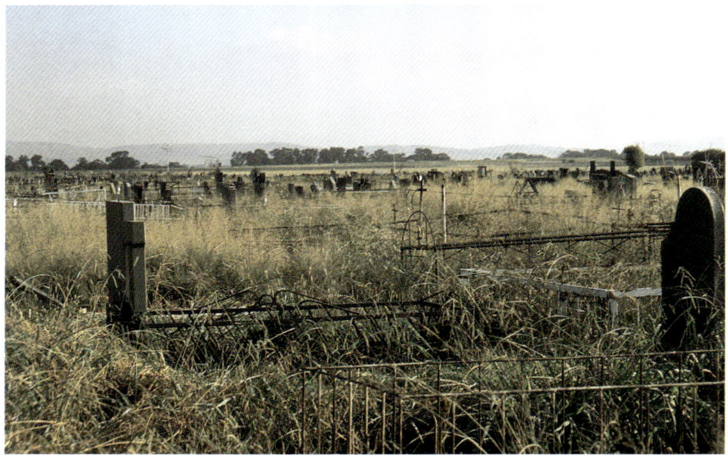

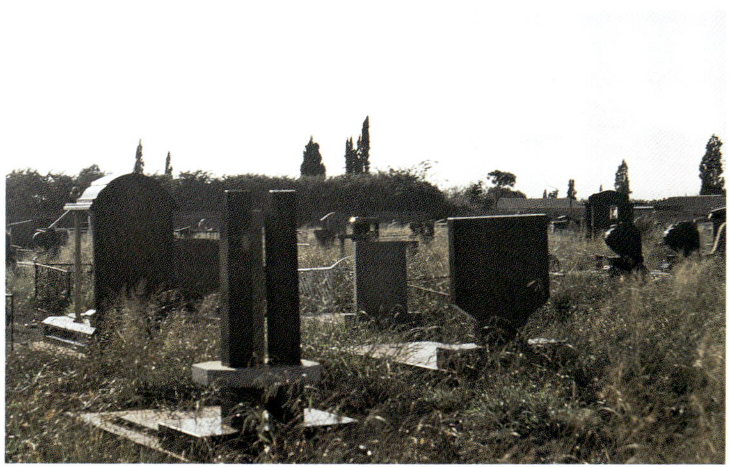

All images: Pitso Chinzima, *Exitzone*, 2003. Mixed media installation.

to which they surrendered to the theory and practice of social control. Black students were heavily harassed inside the campus and Chinzima recalls the many times that university security officers picked him up for trespassing. He feels the university was reinventing apartheid pass laws, as this form of harassment made him sense how his forefathers had been treated by apartheid police forces. Both artists also agree that the education offered at this university is colonial.

The thinking of both artists is affected by the daily activities of those around them. Chinzima grew up during the era of the 'People's War'. He was too young to understand what was happening, but recalls seeing the South African Defence Force terrorising people in the township where he lived. As a child, his parents tried to prevent him from seeing dead bodies in the streets, but after seeing the military trucks, the number of reported deaths tormented him. He was at least safer than Gwintsa, but still feared that his parents would one day be killed by the SADF and that he and his siblings would be left without food, clothes or money to go to school and with no one to look after them.

While the relationship between children and their parents is based on an absolute love, conflict between the two generations is soaring. Certain adults hate and oppress children and yet children trust, rely and love adults, but may feel betrayed by them. Atrocities committed by adults mostly affect children, who are hard hit by political decisions and economic programmes. When social order impacts negatively on their parents, especially their mothers, children are psychologically affected. They begin to plot for the future. The realisation that at their age they are powerless and oppressed can lead them to plan for revenge. Those who grow up in difficult social conditions are aware of atrocities and know what is required to improve that social order.

It has been confirmed through the Truth and Reconciliation Commission (TRC) that the apartheid regime used unsuspecting black people to wage war against other black people. When the struggle against apartheid intensified with growing

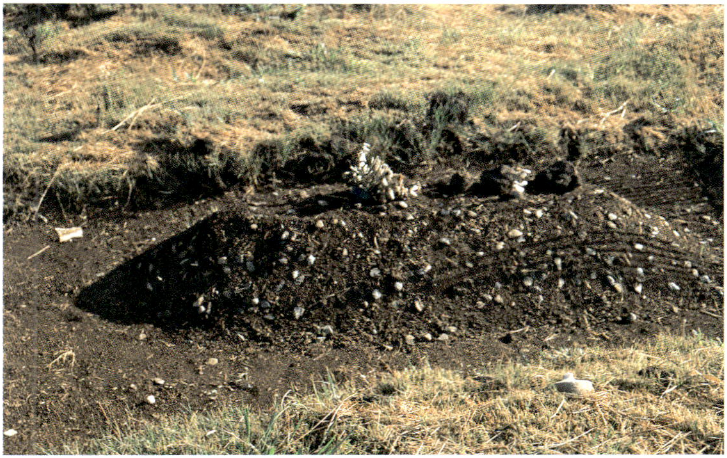

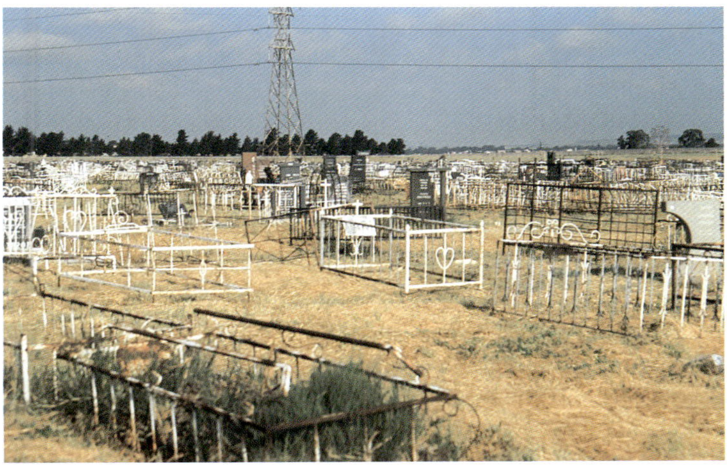

international support, the regime infiltrated many mercenaries into the liberation movements. One of their objectives was to taint the image of the liberation struggle to the outside world. Their strategies emerged in various forms, not least the 'necklace', a method of killing a person by putting a tyre around their neck, pouring petrol over them and setting them on fire.

Chinzima witnessed a number of these incidents as a child and talks of the nightmares he would have after seeing victims. His parents used to scream at him for looking at the dead, knowing that it would lead to sleepless nights. Monday morning was tough; on his way to school he encountered many people killed over the weekend. For Chinzima, the trauma continues to reinvent itself today and he still feels distressed by the images he saw as a child. He is not sure how to heal himself and feels there is no universal cure. However, addressing death in his artistic practice serves as much-needed psychotherapy.

Horrific activities were proliferated through the mass media. Chinzima still cannot forget the image of burning people that he saw on government-controlled television news and the photographs shown in pro-government newspapers. Death dominates the media, but art activities get little or no coverage. On this note, Gwintsa and Chinzima's installation also intimates the media's contribution to promoting inhumanity in our society. Open representation of African corpses by the media renders their lives valueless in relation to other sections of humanity. See, for example, the media's coverage of the victims of 11 September and of the war in Afghanistan, in which few images of dead people were shown. Media prejudice serves to promote crimes against humanity.

Today we believe there is freedom in the world. While supposedly celebrating and enjoying humanity, we find ourselves in the middle of the most difficult struggle, the desocialisation of human inequality. Under apartheid in South Africa, we bravely said that South Africa belongs to all who live in it, black and white. Now we are free from that bondage, but some of our fellow citizens do not accept that equality. Instead, they are driven by the racist

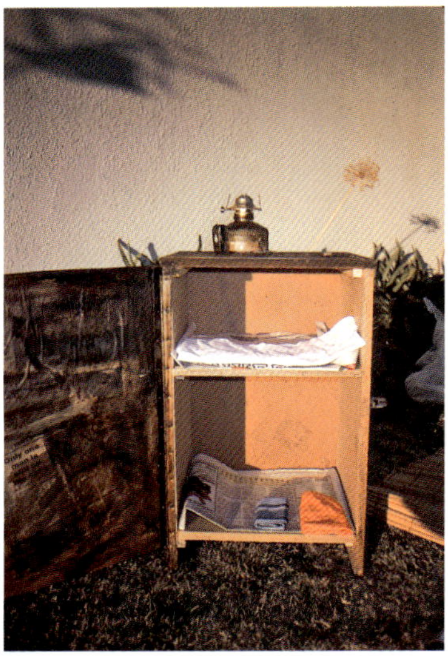

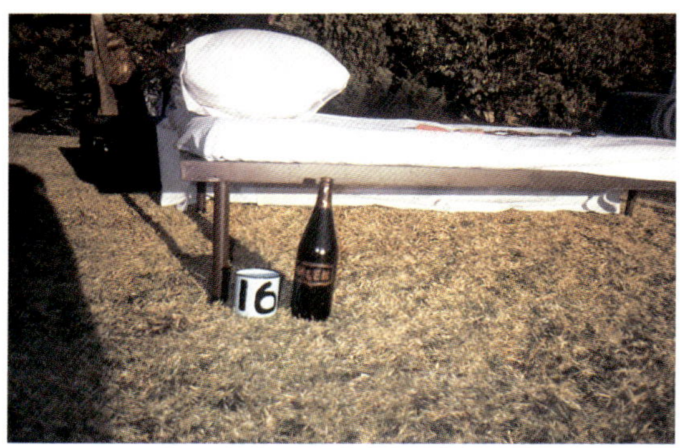

Above and right: Veliswa Gwintsa, *1913*
The Inception, 1997. Mixed media installation.

conviction that they have the right and duty to subjugate and exploit without mercy other people who do not look like them.

Chinzima has been the victim of crime a number of times, but refuses to accept such acts as crime. To him, they are acts of terrorism. While enjoying a night with his family, four men stormed his house and threatened them with guns. They put a handgun in Chinzima's mouth while others ransacked the house, taking whatever they wanted. Chinzima wondered what would have happened to his year-old daughter if the terrorist had pulled that trigger.

With the imminent threat of war on Iraq, Gwintsa replays images of South African exiled children after a raid in their camps. She wonders how children in Iraq will survive a cluster bomb dropped by an F-15 Tomcat. Gwintsa and Chinzima's installation is representative of the new South African paradigm, of a country that is making a significant contribution to creating a peaceful world and endeavouring to stop the war in Iraq. South Africa strongly advocates daring diplomatic intervention as other countries are preparing for war.

> We have done all this because we prefer peace to war. We have taken the positions we have, not to oppose any country, nor to seek any glory. We have done what we have because as South Africans and Africans we know the pain of war and the immeasurable value of peace.[3]

In the course of colonialism and apartheid South Africans resisted assaults on their dignity, but did not surrender to the temptation of advocating black racial domination. Instead they reached resolutely and optimistically for the antithesis of apartheid: the ideal of non-racialism. Their experience of racial oppression and non-racial struggle is expected to prove a valuable contribution to the ongoing global debate around racism and intolerance.

> I have seen our country torn asunder as those, all of whom are my people, engaged one another in a titanic battle. I have experience of the situation in which race and colour are used to enrich some and impoverish the rest. I have

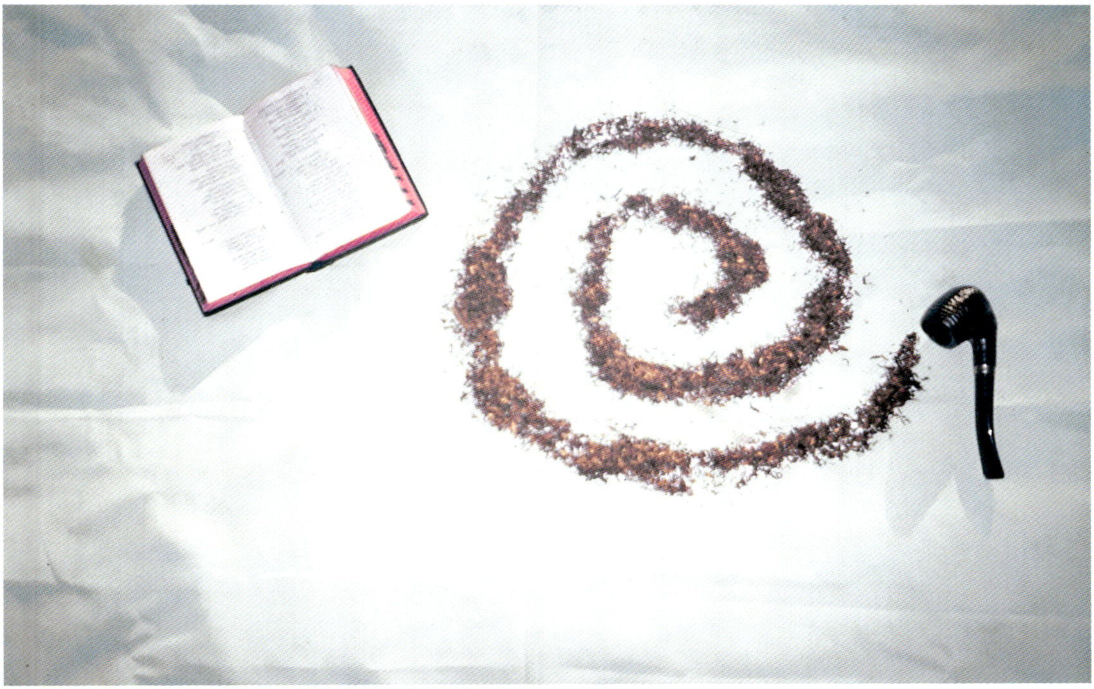

Veliswa Gwintsa, *1913 The Inception*, 1997. Mixed media installation at 2nd Africus Johannesburg Biennale.

> seen the corruption of minds and souls as a result of the pursuit of an ignoble effort to perpetuate a verifiable crime against humanity. I have seen concrete expression of the denial of the dignity of human beings emanating from the conscious, systemic oppressive activities of human beings.[4]

It is highly disturbing to ponder why fellow human beings, because they are physically different from others, behave in such a satanic manner. The world is divided into two unequal parts, one prosperous and the other poor, a division accentuated by the fact that United Nations resolutions are informed by the inhuman demands of the Super Powers.

Despite the developing white consciousness movement that wants to ensure that blacks remain objects for exploitation and systematically seeks to wipe out everything that would give black people a sense of identity and national pride, the majority of South Africans continue to contribute to the progressive transformation of Africa and the rest of the world. There can be no more urgent objective than to unite the peoples of the world against racism, to ensure and secure equality, justice and dignity.

South Africans place humanity before anything else. If anything happens to anybody, it affects everyone. Thus the slogan: 'An injury to one is an injury to all.' Crimes committed by the apartheid regime affect every human being anywhere in the world. The pain felt by people in Hiroshima and Nagasaki belongs to humanity just as much as the suffering felt by the victims of 11 September. With this in mind, Gwintsa and Chinzima's installation questions why humanity continues to destroy itself. This can only stop when we all see ourselves as equal, not as human and inhuman. Those who regard themselves as more human than others assume an absolute right to terrorise others, which results in victims being subjected to and tormented by the theory and practice of institutionalised social control.

As South Africans and Africans, Gwintsa and Chinzima teach us that, as human beings deliberating an effective response to any tragedy and crime, we must first reject the call for war. Militaristic responses that treat human life as callously as terrorists treat ours must be categorically rejected. As with any other crime, the perpetrators and their accomplices must be brought to justice, but not according to the fundamentalist 'an eye for an eye, a tooth for a tooth' precept. The world nations have made heartening progress in establishing and enforcing international norms for human rights and crimes against humanity. There will always be an avenue to forge a broader international coalition to bring disparate nations together in common determination to fight crimes against humanity.

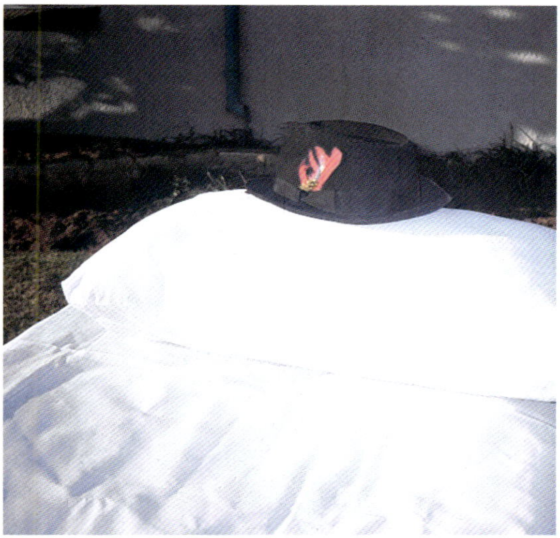

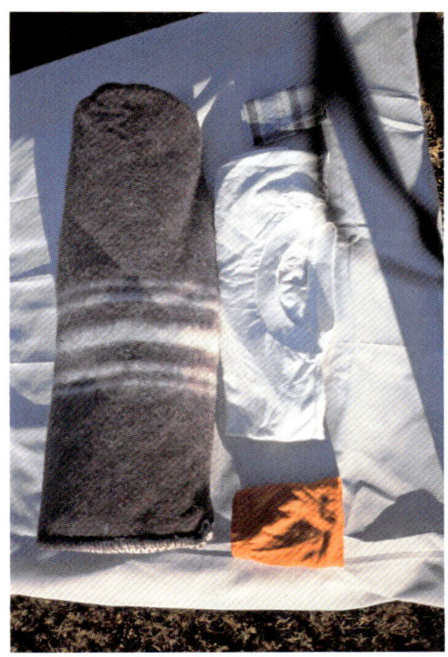

Above and right: Veliswa Gwintsa, *1913*
The Inception, 1997. Mixed media installation.

Traces of Ecstasy

Rotimi Fani-Kayode

It has been my destiny to end up as an artist with a sexual taste for other young men. As a result of this, a certain distance has necessarily developed between myself and my origins. The distance is even greater as a result of my having left Africa as a refugee over twenty years ago.

On three counts I am an outsider: in matters of sexuality; in terms of geographical and cultural dislocation; and in the sense of not having become the sort of respectably married professional my parents might have hoped for. Such a position gives me a feeling of having very little to lose. It produces a sense of personal freedom from the hegemony of convention. For one who has managed to hang on to his own creativity through the crises of adolescence and in spite of the pressures to conform, it has a liberating effect. It opens up areas of creative enquiry which might otherwise have remained forbidden. At the same time, traces of the former values remain, making it possible to take new readings on to them from an unusual vantage point. The results are bound to be disorientating.

In African traditional art, the mask does not represent a material reality: rather, the artist strives to approach a spiritual reality in it through images suggested by human and animal forms. I think photography can aspire to the same imaginative interpretations of life. My reality is not the same as that which is often presented to us in Western photographs. As an African working in a Western medium, I try to bring out the spiritual dimension in my pictures so that concepts of reality become ambiguous and are opened to reinterpretation. This requires what Yoruba priests and artists call a technique of ecstasy.

Both aesthetically and ethically, I seek to translate my rage and my desire into new images which will undermine conventional perceptions and which may reveal hidden worlds. Many of the images are seen as sexually explicit or more precisely, homosexually explicit. I make my pictures homosexual on purpose. Black men from the Third World have not previously revealed either to their own peoples or to the West a certain shocking fact: they can desire each other.

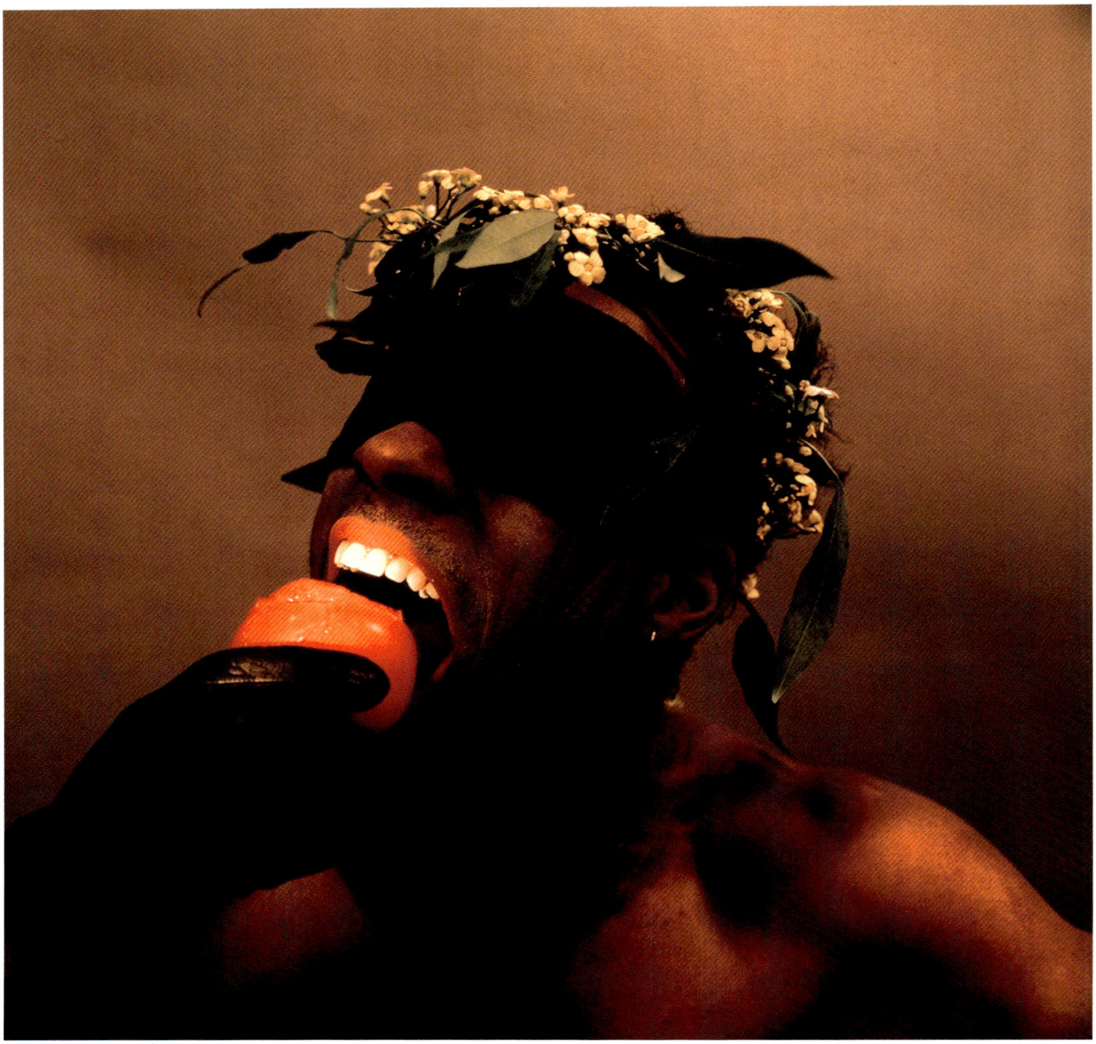

Some Western photographers have shown that they can desire Black males (albeit rather neurotically). But the exploitative mythologising of Black virility on behalf of the homosexual bourgeoisie is ultimately no different from the vulgar objectification of Africa which we know at one extreme from the work of Leni Riefenstahl and, at the other, from the victim images which appear constantly in the media. It is now time for us to reappropriate such images and to transform them ritualistically into images of our own creation. For me, this involves an imaginative investigation of Blackness, maleness and sexuality, rather than more straightforward reportage.

However, this is more easily said than done. Working in a Western context, the African artist inevitably encounters racism. And since I have concentrated much of my work on male erotism, I have also had homophobic reactions to it, both from the white and Black communities. Although this is disappointing on a purely human level, perhaps it also produces a kind of essential conflict through which to struggle to new visions. It is a conflict, however, between unequal partners and is, in that sense, one in which I remain at a disadvantage.

For this reason, I have been active in various groups which are organised around issues of race and sexuality. For the individual, such joint activity can provide confidence and insight. For artists, it can transform and extend one's Westernised ideas – for instance, that art is a product of individual inspiration or that it must conform to certain aesthetic principles of taste, style and content. It can also have the very concrete effect of providing the means for otherwise isolated and powerless artists to show their work and to insist on being taken seriously.

An awareness of history has been of fundamental importance in the development of my creativity. The history of Africa and of the Black race has been constantly distorted. Even in Africa, my education was given in English in Christian schools, as though the language and culture of my own people, the Yoruba, were

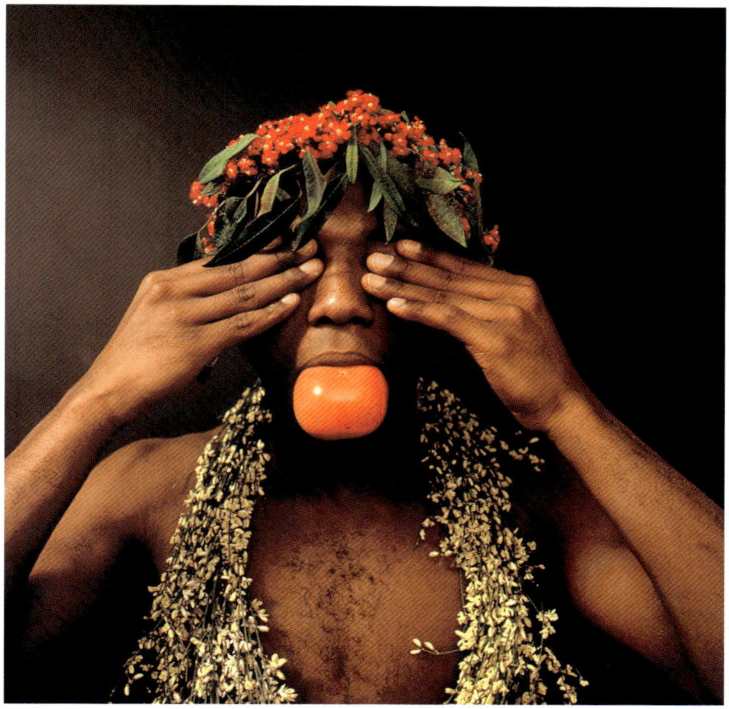

Untitled, *Communion* series, 1995. R-type colour print, 137 x 137cm. © the artist's estate. Courtesy of Autograph: Association of Black Photographers, London.

Untitled, *Communion* series, 1995. R-type colour print, 137 x 137cm. © the artist's estate. Courtesy of Autograph: Association of Black Photographers, London.

inadequate or in some way unsuitable for the healthy development of young minds. In exploring Yoruba history and civilisation, I have rediscovered and revalidated areas of my experience and understanding of the world. I see parallels now between my own work and that of the Osogbo artists in Yorubaland who themselves have resisted the cultural subversions of neo-colonialism and who celebrate the rich, secret world of our ancestors.

It remains true, however, that the great Yoruba civilisations of the past, like so many other non-European cultures, are still consigned by the West to the museums of primitive art and culture. The Yoruba cosmology, comparable in its complexities and subtleties to Greek and Oriental philosophical myth, is treated as no more than a bizarre superstition which, as if by miracle, happened to inspire the creation of some of the most sensitive and delicate artefacts in the history of art. Modern Yoruba art (amongst which I situate my own contributions) may now sometimes fetch high prices in the galleries of New York and Paris. It is prized for its exotic appeal. Similarly, the modern versions of Yoruba beliefs carried by the slaves to the New World have become, in their carnival form, tourist attractions. I am inevitably caught up in this.

Another aspect of history – that of sexuality has also affected me deeply. Official history has always denied the validity of erotic relationships and experiences between members of the same sex. As in the fields of politics and economics, the historians of social and sexual relations have been readily assisted in their fabrications by the Church. But in spite of all attempts by Church and state to suppress homosexuality, it is clear that enriching sexual relationships between members of the same sex have always existed. They are part of the human condition, even if the concept of sexual identity is a more recent notion.

There is a grim chapter of European history which was not drummed into me at school. I only discovered much later that the Nazis had developed the most extreme form of homophobia to have existed in modern times, and attempted to

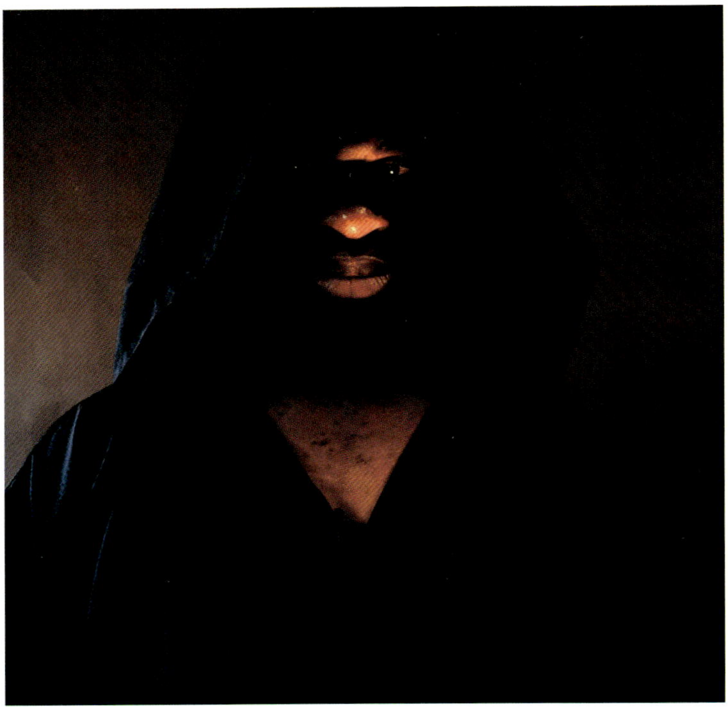

Untitled, *Communion* series, 1995. R-type colour print, 137 x 137cm. © the artist's estate. Courtesy of Autograph: Association of Black Photographers, London.

Untitled, *Communion* series, 1995. R-type colour print, 137 x 137cm. © the artist's estate. Courtesy of Autograph: Association of Black Photographers, London.

exterminate homosexuals in the concentration camps. It came not so much as a surprise but as yet another example of the long-standing European tradition of the violent suppression of otherness. It touches me just as closely as the knowledge that millions of my ancestors were killed or enslaved in order to ensure European political, economic and cultural hegemony of the world.

For this reason I feel it is essential to resist all attempts that discourage the expression of one's identity. In my case, my identity has been constructed from my own sense of otherness, whether cultural, racial or sexual. The three aspects are not separate within me. Photography is the tool by which I feel most confident in expressing myself. It is photography, therefore – Black, African, homosexual photography – which I must use not just as an instrument, but as a weapon if I am to resist attacks on my integrity and indeed my existence on my own terms.

It is no surprise to find that one's work is shunned or actively discouraged by the Establishment. The homosexual bourgeoisie has been more supportive – not because it is especially noted for its championing of Black artists, but because Black ass sells almost as well as black dick. As a result of homosexual interest I have had various portfolios printed in the gay press, and a book of nudes published by GMP [Gay Men's Press]. There has also been some attention given to my erotic work by the sort of straight galleries which receive funding from more progressive local authorities.

But in the main, both galleries and press have felt safer with my ethnic work. Occasionally they will take on board some of the less-overtly threatening and outrageous pictures – in the classic liberal tradition. But Black is still only beautiful as long as it keeps within white frames of reference.

I have been more disconcerted by the response to my work from certain sections of the self-proclaimed avant-garde, however. At the *Misfits* exhibition at [London's] Oval House (which happened to coincide with the unveiling of a plaque to commemorate the birth there of Lord

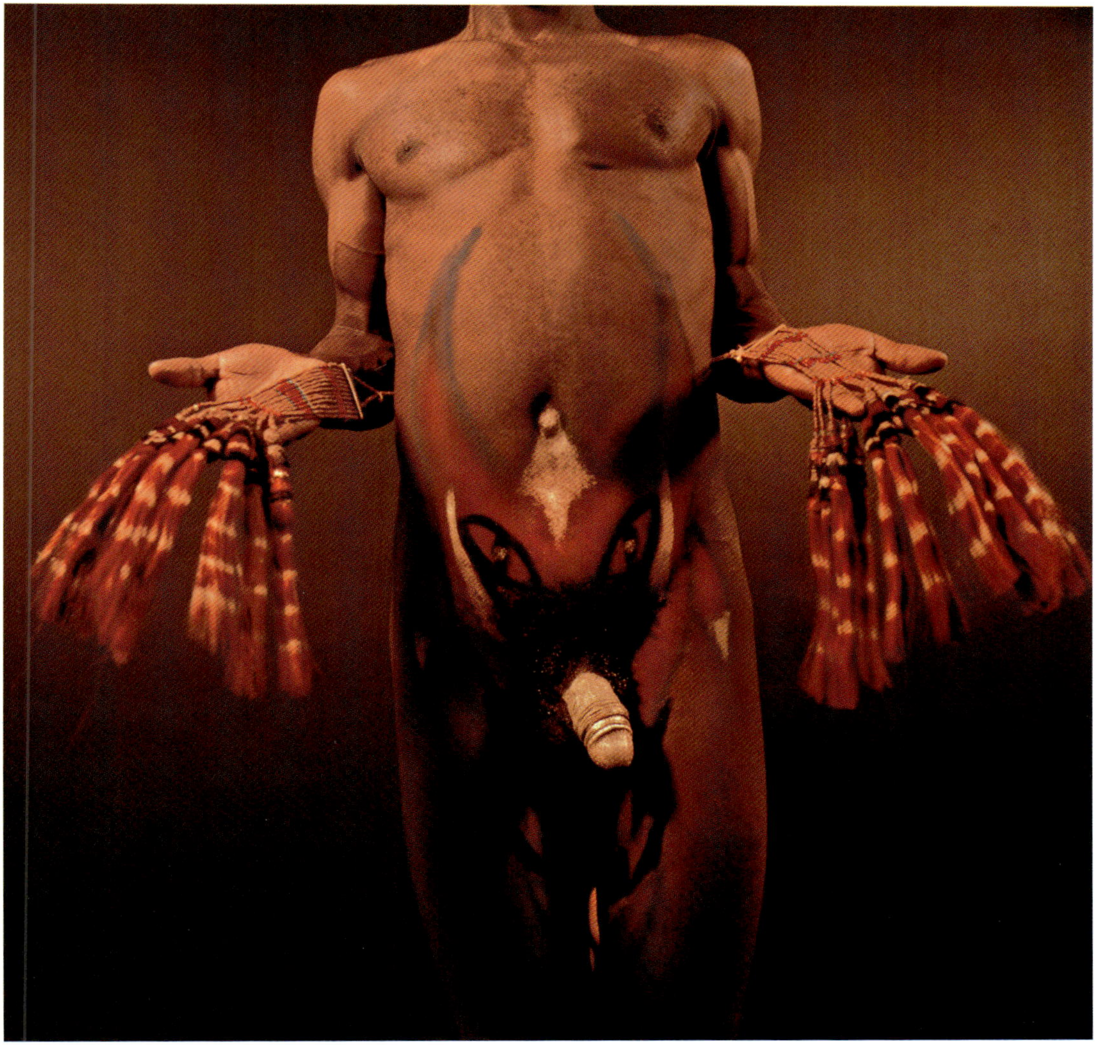

Montgomery of Alamein) I was asked, along with other artists, to remove my work in case it attracted unfavourable publicity. We refused, naturally. Unfortunately, the press were too busy paying homage to Monty so the national reputation of Oval House was saved, and we were denied some free publicity.

As for Africa itself, if I ever managed to get an exhibition in, say, Lagos, I suspect riots would break out. I would certainly be charged with being a purveyor of corrupt and decadent Western values.

However, sometimes I think that if I took my work into the rural areas, where life is still vigorously in touch with itself and its roots, the reception might be more constructive. Perhaps they would recognise my smallpox Gods, my transsexual priests, my images of desirable Black men in a state of sexual frenzy, or the tranquillity of communion with the spirit world. Perhaps they have far less fear of encountering the darkest of Africa's dark secrets by which some of us seek to gain access to the soul.

Untitled, *Communion* series, 1995. R-type colour print, 137 x 137cm. © the artist's estate. Courtesy of Autograph: Association of Black Photographers, London.

A Note from Outside on Rotimi Fani-Kayode

Mark Sealy

Kayode, along with many other black artists at this time, had no advocate or agent. Kayode wanted to make interventions. His version of *Olympia* entitled *(White Flowers) Olympe*, 1989, was not a simple reversal of gender and race roles. This work was a direct attack on the institutional canons. *(White Flowers)* is a challenge which reads: 'I have done my home work, I have read your art history. This is what I want to do with that knowledge – invert, subvert and appropriate it – to suit my own concerns and experiences.'

Kayode's references in many of his photographs offer more than just a representation of the exotic, or simply taking pictures for shock value. His photographs, as Wendy Grossman pointed out in her thesis on African photographers, were not produced in a vacuum. They are informed studies.

White flowers, in drawing upon a multiplicity of sources, displays the diversity of Fani-Kayode's work and background. In his use of montage and exploration of enigmatic visual occurrences, Fani-Kayode echoes the surrealistic style and illusive narrative of conceptual photographers such as Duane Michals and Jerry Uelsmann. Reflected in this image is the photographer's search for his own voice which led him through the fine and graphic arts to photography.

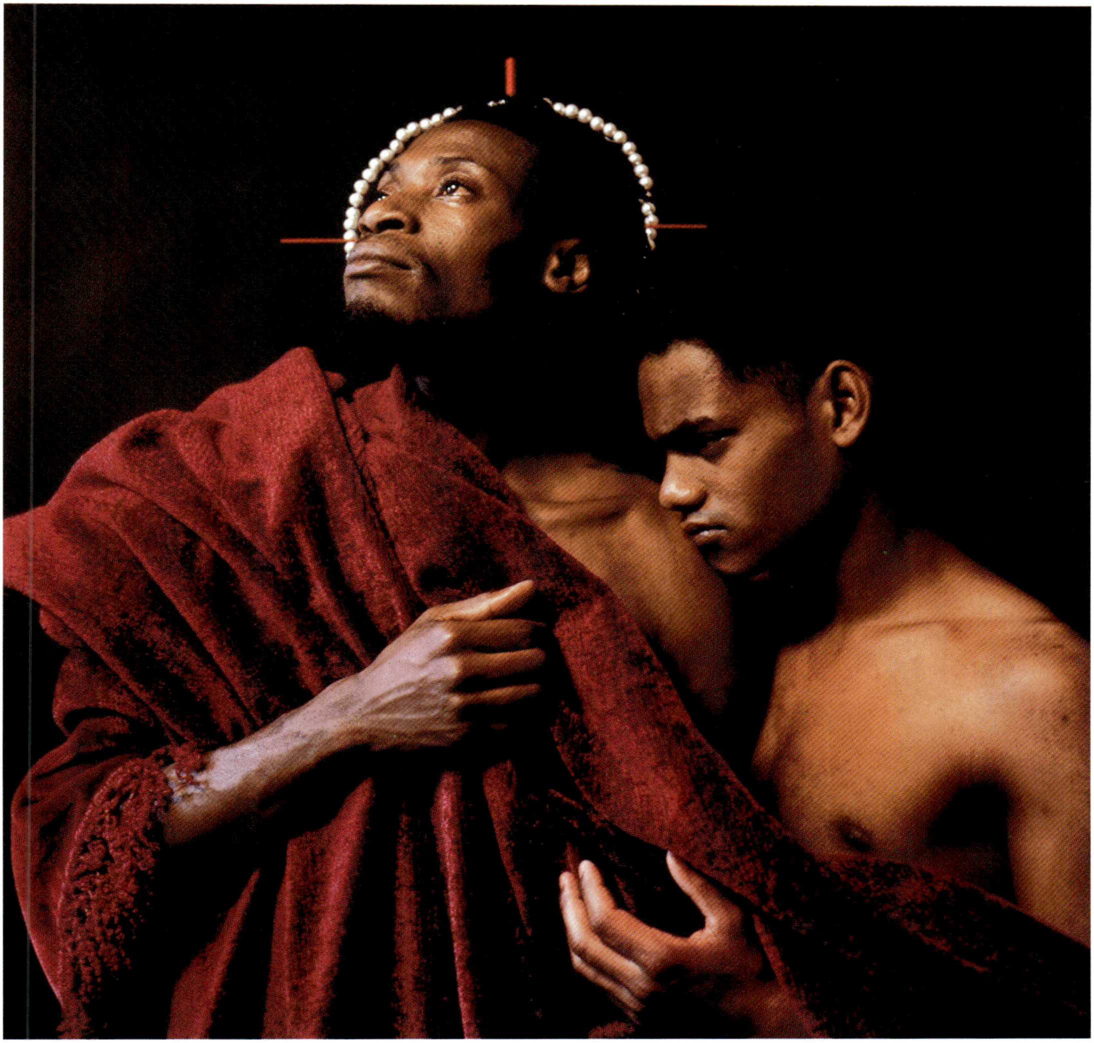

Few galleries had time for a photographer concerned with his own 'Africaness'. Few magazines were interested in work produced by indigenous African photographers, and if photographic works were published from African photographers the tone was, and generally still is, patronising. Books and journals are still dominated by works from the USA and European based photographers producing so called 'definitive stories' for the Sunday supplements, from some 'exotic' African location which, when published, often reproduce a racial stereotypical view that falls in line with the long history of mis-representation of African cultures.

It is only recently with the formation of organisations like Revue Noire and Autograph that progress has been made in redressing this situation by exhibiting, publishing and advocating work from Africa and the diaspora, that shows there is a vibrant complex photographic movement within the continent of Africa.

On occasion when curators and critics would attempt to decode Kayode's photographs they constantly fell into producing lazy and crude comparisons with Mapplethorpe's work. The assumption has always been that Kayode wanted the mantle of Mapplethorpe. This was never the case. These and similar attitudes to Kayode's photographs led Kayode to write: 'Working in a Western context, the African artist inevitably encounters racism.' Kayode was becoming more and more aware of subtle forms of post colonial racism that are endemic to eurocentric institutions.

Within the UK, little work was being done with and about black photographers and artists in general. (Although there was a growing sense of agitation at a grass roots level). This was being animated by artists such as Eddie Chambers and Sunil Gupta, to name but a few. (This situation was highlighted in the joint essay by Professor Stuart Hall and David A. Bailey for *Ten.8* magazine – *Critical Decade. Black British Photography in the 80s* entitled 'The Vertigo of Displacement'.) Institutions appeared to have little interest or inclination to research and develop an understanding of practitioners like Kayode and their terms

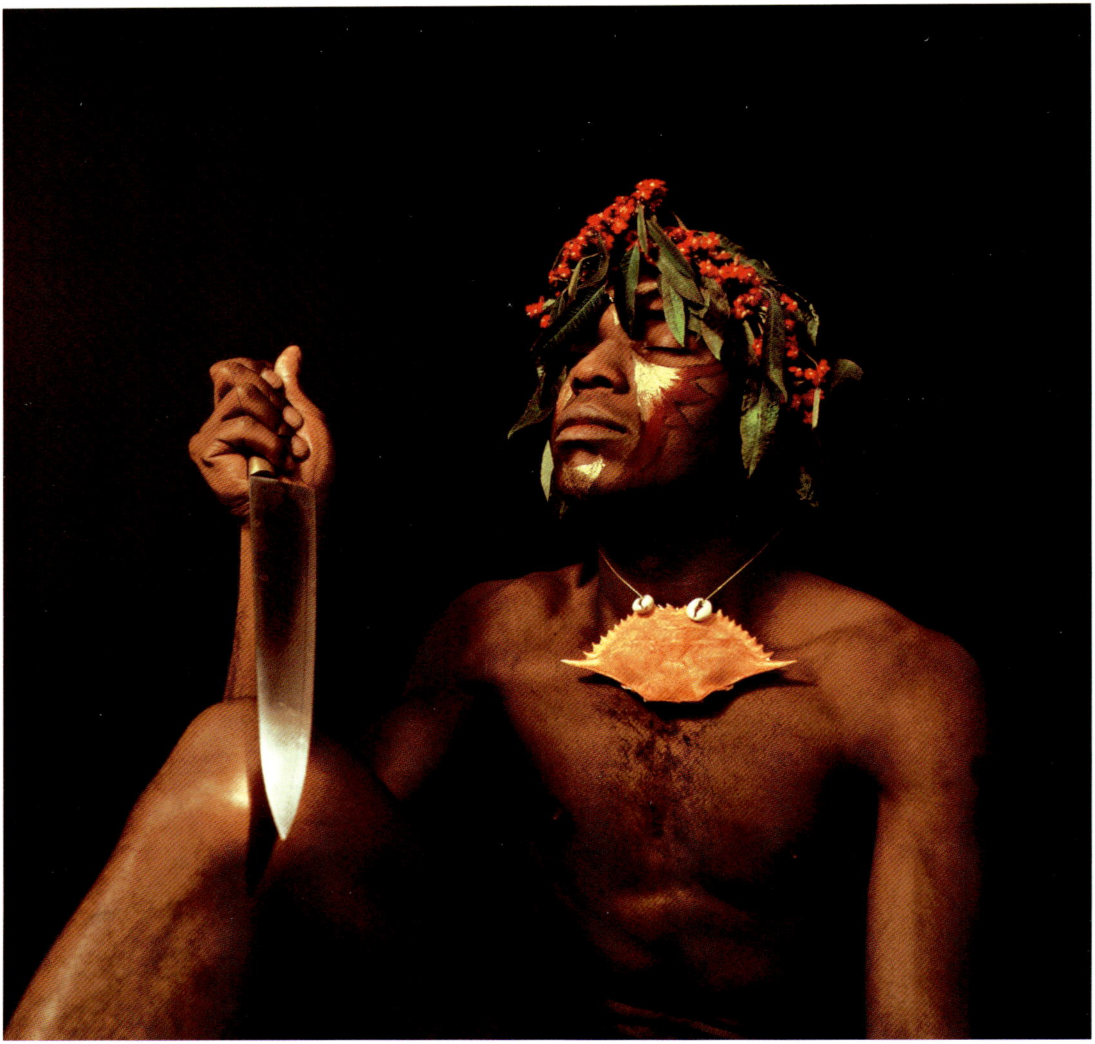

of reference. If black photographers/artists were to gain any ground, then supportive collaborations and relationships had to be formed. Alex Hirst, Kayode's friend and lover became such a collaborator along with several other artists who were experiencing similar problems.

Networks and lobby groups began to formulate ways of gaining visibility. Kayode was a key player within this formulation and was, indeed, the first chair of Autograph, the Association of Black Photographers.

All the photographs [presented in the *Rotimi Fani-Kayode 1955–89: Communion* exhibition, 1995] are created within the studio context using models. Kayode did not subscribe to the notion of a decisive moment.

Each photograph presents a small narrative. Kayode's use of mise-en-scene, chiaroscuro and saturated Rubenesque-like colours gives the works tragic, theatrical qualities, but at the same time offers us a reverential calm. The overted gaze of many of the models enhances this sense of calm.

This technique allows the viewer to feel comfortable within the act of looking. By not being presented with direct eye contact the viewer is seduced into holding the gaze. The dramas in Kayode's work could either be past or present. The work does not locate or signify a specific time or place. This is the land of fantasy and desire where date, time and location are irrelevant.

The photographs generally represent an act. They are fragments of plays that Kayode and Hirst constructed which relate to dislocation and disruption. The recurring presence of masks is essential within this series of photographs, suggesting to the viewer that the surface is there to be challenged but at the same time offering the subject a protective barrier.

The ethereal world was as important to Kayode as the tangible world. In his work he is inviting us to play with him in the grey zones between black and white, gay and straight, acceptance and taboo. This work was the beginning of a constructed twilight cross cultural zone. A kind of Never Never Land where 'reality' is a stranger.

Untitled, *Communion* series, 1995. R-type colour print, 137 x 137cm. © the artist's estate. Courtesy of Autograph: Association of Black Photographers, London.

Architecture for the Poor: An Experiment in Rural Egypt

Hassan Fathy

Paradise Lost: The Countryside

I had always had a deep love for the country, but it was a love for an idea, not for something I really knew. The country, the place where the fellaheen lived, I had seen from the windows of the train as we went from Cairo to Alexandria for the summer holidays, but this fleeting experience was supplemented by two contrasting pictures, which I had got respectively from my father and my mother....

These two pictures combined in my imagination to produce a picture of the country as a paradise, but a paradise darkened from above by clouds of flies, and whose streams flowing underfoot had become muddy and infested with bilharzia and dysentery. This image haunted me and made me feel that something should be done to restore to the Egyptian countryside the felicity of paradise. If the problem appeared simple to me at that time, it was because I was young and inexperienced, but it was and is a question that has occupied the greater part of my thoughts and energies ever since, a problem whose unfolding complexity through the years has only reinforced my conviction that something should be done to solve it....

After I graduated I went one day to supervise the building of a school at Talkha.... The town haunted me; I could think of nothing but the hopeless resignation of these peasants to their condition, their cramped and stunted view of life, their abject acceptance of the whole horrible situation in which they were forced to put up with a lifetime's scrabbling for money amid the wretched buildings of Talkha. The revelation of their apathy seized me by the throat; my own helplessness before such a spectacle tormented me. Surely something could be done?

Yet what? The peasants were too sunk in their misery to initiate a change. They needed decent houses, but houses are expensive. In large towns capitalists are attracted by the return from investment in housing, and public bodies – ministries, town councils, etc. – frequently provide extensive accommodation for the citizens, but neither capitalists nor the state seem willing to undertake the provision of peasant houses, which return no rent to

Gourna, Plan and Elevation with Hathor, 1948. Gouache on paper, 58 x 47cm. American University of Cairo Collection, Rare Books and Special Collection Library. Photograph: Philippe Maillard.

the capitalists and too little glory to the politicians; both parties wash their hands of the matter and the peasants continue to live in squalor.... Their state is shared by millions in Egypt, while over the whole of the earth there are, according to the U.N., 800,000,000 peasants – one third of the population of the earth – now doomed to premature death because of their inadequate housing....

Mud Brick – Sole Hope for Rural Reconstruction

Surely it was an odd situation that every peasant in Egypt with so much as an acre of land to his name had a house, while landowners with a hundred acres or more could not afford one. But the peasant built his house out of mud, or mud bricks, which he dug out of the ground and dried in the sun. And here, in every hovel and tumbledown hut in Egypt, was the answer to my problem. Here, for years, for centuries, the peasant had been wisely and quietly exploiting the obvious building material, while we, with our modern school-learned ideas, never dreamed of using such a ludicrous substance as mud for so serious a creation as a house. But why not? Certainly, the peasants' houses might be cramped, dark, dirty and inconvenient, but this was not the fault of the mud brick. There was nothing that could not be put right by good design and a broom. Why not use this heaven-sent material for our country houses? And why not, indeed, make the peasants' own houses better? Why should there be any difference between a peasant's house and a landowner's? Build both of mud brick, design both well, and both could afford their owners beauty and comfort.

Mud for Roofing, Bahtim: Trial and Error

Soon afterwards the war started.... Steel and timber supplies were completely cut off, and the army requisitioned such materials as were already in the country. Yet, still obsessed by my desire to build in the country, I looked about for ways of getting round the shortage. At least I still had mud bricks! And then it occurred to me that, if I had mud bricks and nothing else, I

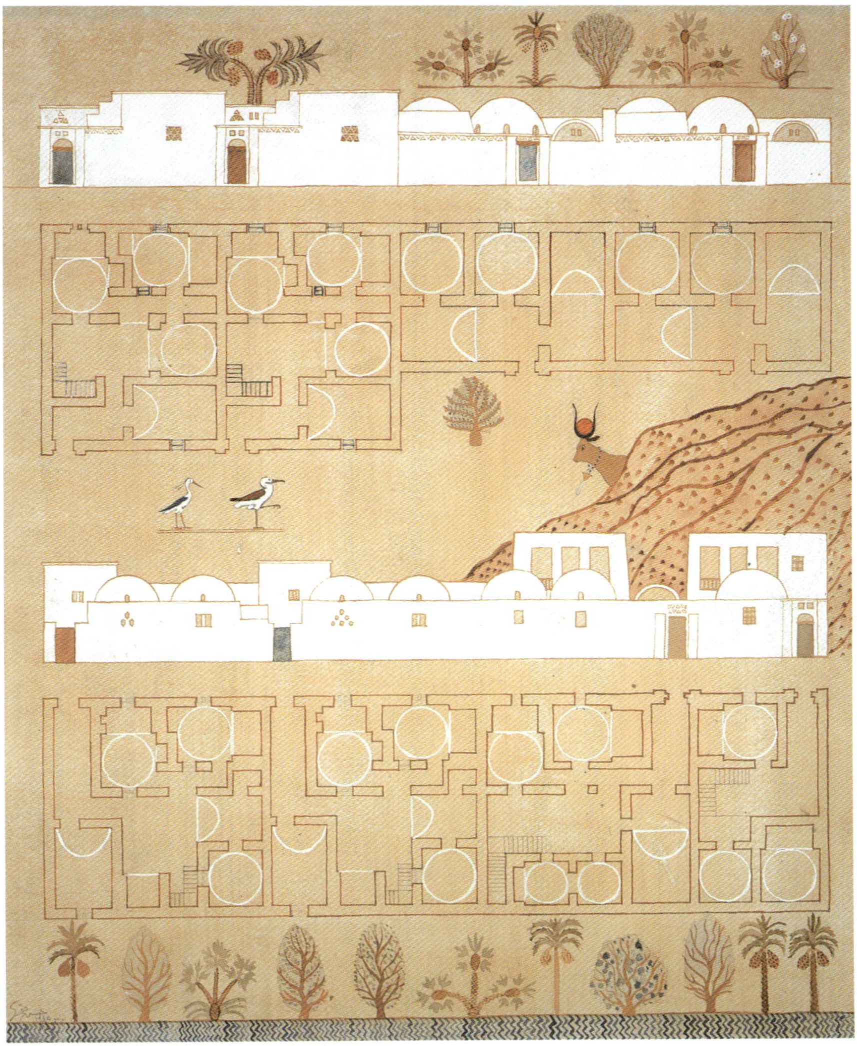

was no worse off than my forefathers. Egypt had not always imported steel from Belgium and timber from Rumania, yet Egypt had always built houses. But how had they built? Walls, yes. I could build walls, too, but I had nothing to roof them with. Couldn't mud bricks be used to cover my houses on top? What about some sort of vault?...

I explained my wishes to the masons, and they attempted to put up my vaults without using centering. The vaults promptly fell down.

Repeated attempts brought no more success. It was clear that, if the ancients had known how to build vaults without centering, the secret had died with them.

My elder brother happened at that time to be a director working on the Aswan Dam. He heard of my failure, listened sympathetically, and then remarked that the Nubians were, in fact, building vaults that stood up during construction without using any support at all, to roof their houses and mosques. I was immensely excited; perhaps, after all, the ancients had not taken their secret to their provoking vaulted tombs with them. Perhaps the answer to all my problems, the technique that would at last let me use the mud brick for every part of a house, was awaiting me in Nubia.

Nubia – Survival of an Ancient Technique of Vaulting

It was a new world for me, a whole village of spacious, lovely, clean and harmonious houses, each more beautiful than the next. There was nothing else like it in Egypt; a village from some dream country, perhaps from a Hoggar hidden in the heart of the Great Sahara – whose architecture had been preserved for centuries uncontaminated by foreign influences, from Atlantis itself it could have been. Not a trace of the miserly huddle of the usual Egyptian village, but house after house, tall, easy, roofed cleanly with a brick vault, each house decorated individually and exquisitely around the doorway with claustrawork – moldings and tracery in mud.

I realized that I was looking at the living survivor of traditional Egyptian architecture, at a way of building that was a natural growth in the landscape, as much a part

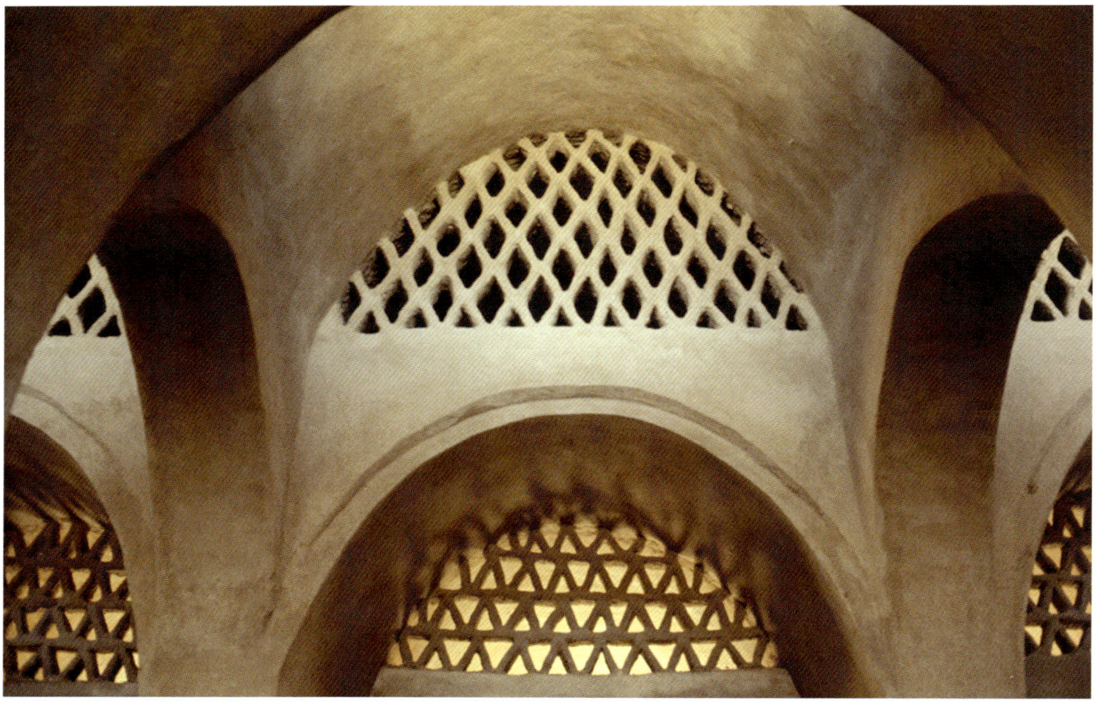

of it as the dom-palm tree of the district. It was like a vision of architecture before the Fall: before money, industry, greed and snobbery had severed architecture from its true roots in nature....

There is also, close to Aswan, the Monastery of St. Simeon, a Coptic building of the same period. Here too mud brick domes and vaults are employed, but the simplicity and humility of the monastic ideal is revealed in the architecture, which thus proves able to accommodate equally well the contrasting inspirations of the Moslem and Christian religion. Among other things, I noticed with great surprise and interest that the refectory held a broad gallery, supported entirely upon an ingenious system of main and secondary vaults to avoid a heavy filling between the curved surface of the vault and the horizontal floor above it. This showed the argument that mud brick buildings could go up to two stories and still be strong enough to survive for a thousand years. I was getting more and more confirmation of my suspicions that the traditional materials and methods of the Egyptian peasant were more than fit for use by modern architects, and that the solution to Egypt's housing problem lay in Egypt's history....

The Nubian Masons at Work – First Successes

Thus the whole vault could be built straight out in the air, with no support or centering, with no instrument, with no drawn plan; there were just two masons standing on a plank and a boy underneath tossing up the bricks, which the masons caught dexterously in the air, then casually placed on the mud and tapped home with their adzes. It was so unbelievably simple....

The simplicity and naturalness of the method quite entranced me.... My builders needed nothing but an adze and a pair of hands.

Within a few days all the houses were roofed. Rooms, corridors, loggias were all covered with vaults and domes; the masons had solved every problem that had exercised me (even to building stairs). It only remained to go out and apply their methods throughout Egypt....

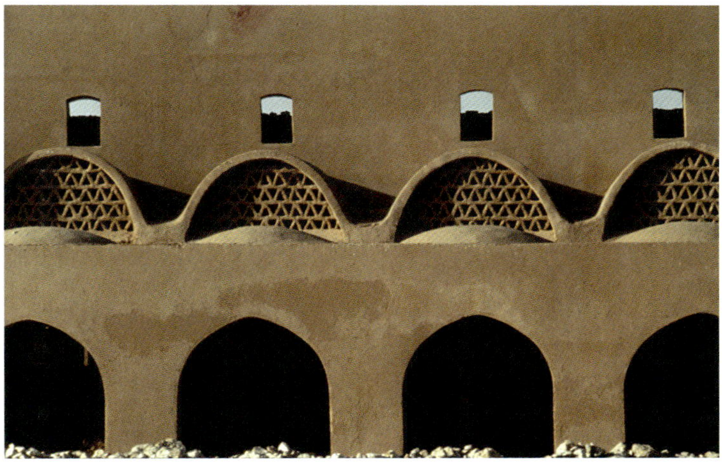

Left and above: New Baris Village, Kharga, Egypt, 1967. © Aga Khan Trust for Culture.

A Tomb Robbery Begets a Pilot Housing Project

The village of Gourna is built on the site of these Tombs of the Nobles. Here there are very many graves, some known, cleared, and cleaned, and some still unknown to the department and consequently full of objects of great archaeological interest.

There are seven thousand peasants living in Gourna crowded into five clusters of houses, built over and around these tombs. Seven thousand people living quite literally upon the past. They – or their fathers – had been attracted to Gourna some fifty years before by the rich graves of their ancestors, and the whole community had ever since lived by mining these tombs. Their economy was almost wholly dependent on tomb robbing; the farmland around could not support anything like seven thousand people, and anyway it belonged mostly to a few rich landowners....

This robbery caused such a stir that the Department of Antiquities had to take some positive action over the problem of Gourna. There was already a royal decree expropriating the land on which the Gournis' houses were built and annexing the whole area of the necropolis to the government as public utility land. This decree gave the Gournis the right to continue using the existing houses, but prohibited any further additions or extensions. So now another ministerial decree had to be issued expropriating the houses too, with the intention of clearing the whole antiquities zone of its undesirable squatters....

The only solution was to rehouse them, but hitherto this had been far too expensive a proposition. One million pounds was the estimate for an exactly similar village which was being built for the workers at Imbaba, just outside Cairo. It was then that my buildings came to the notice of the Department of Antiquities....

They had seen my two examples of mud brick building, the houses for the Royal Society of Agriculture and the house for the Red Crescent, and had been impressed alike by the potentialities of the material and the low cost of using it. Accordingly Drioton came to see these buildings and approved the suggestion, with the result that I was granted leave of absence from the School of Fine Arts for three years to build a village. So I was going to fulfil my childhood wish – I hoped somewhat more cheaply than for L.E.1,000,000....

Birth of New Gourna – The Site
However attractive may have been the project of at last building a whole village, it was also somewhat daunting to be presented with fifty acres of virgin land and seven thousand Gournis who would have to create a new life for themselves there. All these people, related in a complex web of blood and marriage ties, with their habits and prejudices, their friendships and their feuds – a delicately balanced social organism intimately integrated with the topography, with the very bricks and timber of the village – this whole society had, as it were, to be dismantled and put together again in another setting....

Architectural Character
Every people that has produced architecture has evolved its own favorite forms, as peculiar to that people as its language, its dress or its folklore. Until the collapse of cultural frontiers in the last century, there were all over the world distinctive local shapes and details in architecture, and the buildings of any locality were the beautiful children of a happy marriage between the imagination of the people and the demands of their countryside.... It follows, too, that no one can look with complacency upon buildings transplanted to an alien environment.

Yet in modern Egypt there is no indigenous style. The signature is missing; the houses of rich and poor alike are without character, without an Egyptian accent. The tradition is lost, and we have been cut off from our past ever since Mohammed Ali cut the throat of the last Mameluke. This gap in the continuity of Egyptian tradition has been felt by many people, and all sorts of remedies have been proposed. There was, in fact, a kind of jealousy between those who regarded the Copts as the true lineal descendants of the

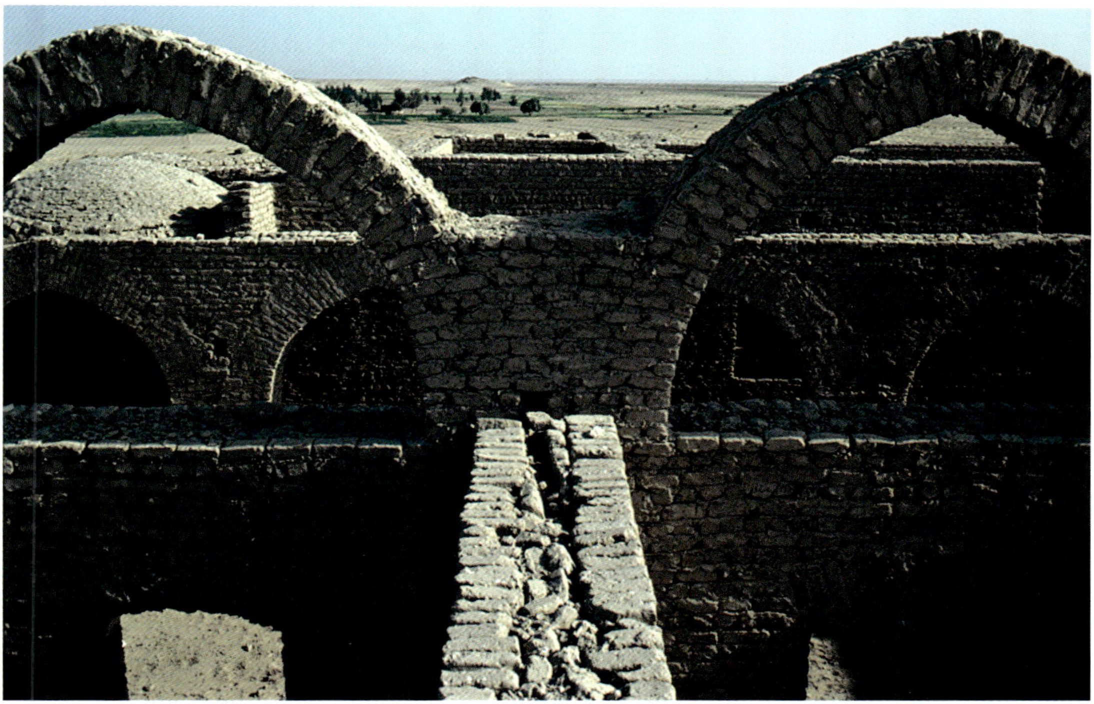

New Baris Village, Kharga, Egypt, 1967.

Ancient Egyptians, and those who believed that the Arab style should provide the pattern for a new Egyptian architecture….

But in the architectural schools they make no study of the history of domestic buildings, and learn architectural periods by the accidents of style, the obvious features like the pylon and the stalactite. Thus the graduate architect believes this to be all there is in 'style,' and imagines a building can change its style as a man changes clothes. It was thinking like this that led some architect to ruin the entrance to the classrooms at Gourna school by transforming the original archway into an Ancient Egyptian-style temple doorway complete with cavetto cornice. It is not yet understood that real architecture cannot exist except in a living tradition, and that architectural tradition is all but dead in Egypt today….

Tradition's Role

Tradition is not necessarily old-fashioned and is not synonymous with stagnation. Furthermore, a tradition need not date from long ago but may have begun quite recently. As soon as a workman meets a new problem and decides how to overcome it, the first step has been taken in the establishment of a tradition. When another workman has decided to adopt the same solution, the tradition is moving, and by the time a third man has followed the first two and added his contribution, the tradition is fairly established. Some problems are easy to solve; a man may decide in a few minutes what to do. Others need time, perhaps a day, perhaps a year, perhaps a whole lifetime; in each case the solution may be the work of one man.

Yet other solutions may not be worked out fully before many generations have passed, and this is where tradition has a creative role to play, for it is only by tradition, by respecting and building on the work of earlier generations, that each new generation may make some positive progress toward the solution of the problem. When tradition has solved its problem and ceased developing, we may say that a cycle has been completed….

There are, on the other hand, traditions which, although they have appeared only

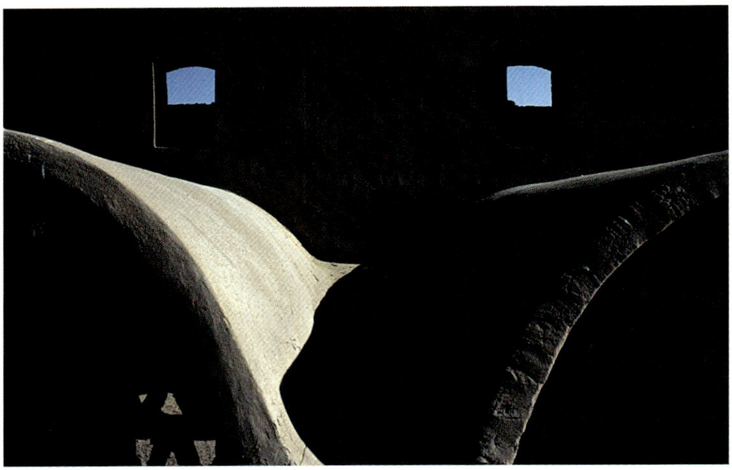

Left and right: New Baris Village, Kharga, Egypt, 1967. © Aga Khan Trust for Culture.

recently and ought to be in an early phase of their cycle, were in fact born dead. Modernity does not necessarily mean liveliness, and change is not always for the better. On the other hand there are situations that call for innovation. My point is that innovation must be a completely thought-out response to a change in circumstances, and not indulged in for its own sake. Nobody asks that an airport control tower be built in some peasant idiom, and an industrial structure like a nuclear power station may force a new tradition upon the designer.

Once a particular tradition is established and accepted, the individual artist's duty is to keep this tradition going, with his own invention and insight to give it that additional momentum that will save it from coming to a standstill, until it will have reached the end of its cycle and completed its full development....

Architecture is still one of the most traditional arts. A work of architecture is meant to be used, its form is largely determined by precedent, and it is set before the public where they must look at it every day. The architect should respect the work of his predecessors and the public sensibility by not using his architecture as a medium of personal advertisement. Indeed, no architect can avoid using the work of earlier architects; however hard he strains after originality, by far the larger part of his work will be in some tradition or other. Why then should he despise the tradition of his own country or district, why should he drag alien traditions into an artificial and uncomfortable synthesis, why should he be so rude to earlier architects as to distort and misapply their ideas? This happens when an architectural element, evolved over many years to a perfect size, shape and function, is used upside down or enlarged beyond recognition till it no longer even works properly, simply to gratify the architect's own selfish appetite for fame....

When an architect is presented with a clear tradition to work in, as in a village built by peasants, then he has no right to break this tradition with his own personal whims. What may go in a cosmopolitan city like Paris, London or Cairo, will kill a village.

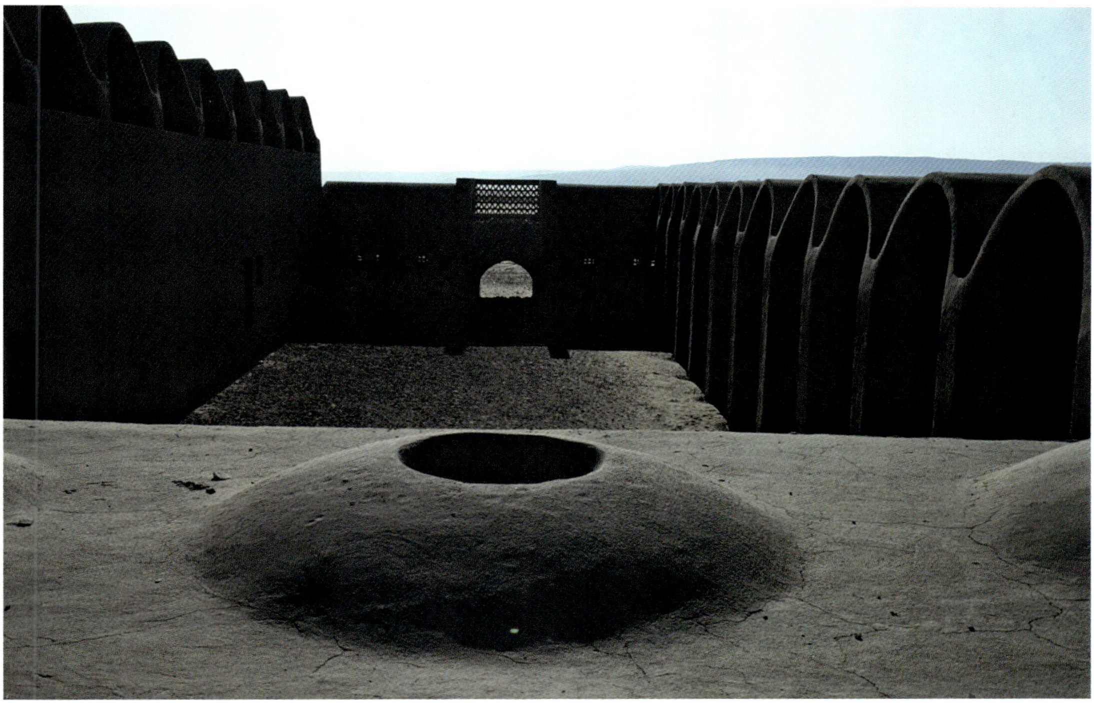

Hassan Fathy and the Identity Debate

Nasser Rabbat

In a field overwhelmingly dominated by famous names from the West, the Egyptian architect Hassan Fathy (1900–89) stands out as a rare exception. Not only was he an internationally celebrated architect and philosopher of architecture who hailed from the developing world, but he also lived, studied and made his name essentially building in and writing about the traditional architecture of his native Egypt. In fact, Fathy carved his distinct image out of a studied yet subjective – and at times downright idealistic – engagement with vernacular architecture, an engagement that he spent the second half of his life refining and expanding. His passionate identification with local building traditions, however, did not prevent him from seeing himself as an architect with a global mission. He tirelessly preached the simple principles of his design philosophy aimed at respecting the environment and improving the living conditions of the poor everywhere. He wrote relatively profusely in Arabic and English and wisely had his books translated into the main European languages. This allowed him to introduce his concepts to a large audience when his architecture itself had been too remote and too unassuming to compete with the great monuments of modernism. He taught in various institutions of architecture in Cairo and Athens and, in 1977, founded his own educational enterprise, the International Institute for Appropriate Technology. He also privately trained a group of talented and devoted

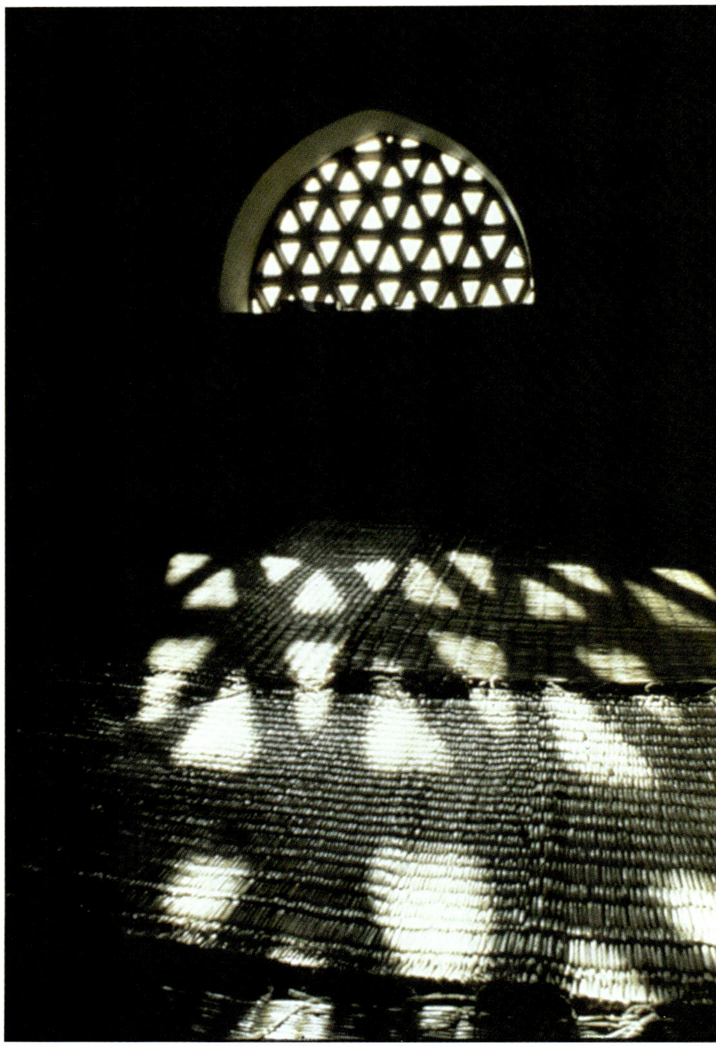

disciples/apprentices who worked with him, absorbed his teaching and spread his vision and his famous vernacular forms in their own designs, primarily but not exclusively in the Arab world.

Fathy's achievements translated into a worldwide exposure that had usually been reserved for architects working in the artistic metropolises of the world, such as Paris, New York, or Los Angeles. During the last twenty years of his life, but especially since his death in 1989, he and his oeuvre became the focus of numerous books and essays and many exhibitions. Most publications and shows, including those written by the man himself, emphasise a set of almost mythical notions about his work. Pre-eminent among them are his pioneering adaptation of the vernacular in the age of mechanisation and bland international modernism; his almost utopian environmentalism and socio-cultural commitment; and, most of all, his highly lyrical interpretations of Egyptian architectural traditions. Fathy's scholars, however, generally ignore the formative period of his career before his first important project in New Gourna (1948–61).[1] They rarely examine the considerable shift in the scope of his theories on the vernacular between New Gourna and his last grand project in Abiquiu, New Mexico (1981–86), when Fathy's trademark design crossed the Atlantic for the first and last time to be implemented in the south-western American wilderness.[2] They also fail to relate the man to the main currents of thoughts prevailing in his lifetime both within the field of architecture and in the context of the changing politics of Egypt and the Arab world in the age of decolonisation and nation building. Instead, we are presented with an image of a sui generis architect, emerging independently of his professional, ideological and social environments to single-handedly challenge the mainstream modernist architecture by advocating a return to the vernacular as a source of architectural and even social rejuvenation. Thus, despite the relative abundance of material available on Hassan Fathy, only a few incomplete critical reviews of his career have been written, and, more noticeably, fewer critiques of his ideas and designs.

Dar al-Islam Village, Abiquiu, USA, 1980s.
© Aga Khan Trust for Culture.

Improving the record requires the accumulated efforts of many scholars pursuing different lines of enquiry. After all, the man was a towering figure and his oeuvre was profoundly and decisively influential. What I will offer here is only a brief historical outline of one critical aspect of Fathy's career, that is how he revised the meaning of his vernacular type in light of the changing perception of Egypt's cultural identity in the second half of the twentieth century.

Initially trained in the classical, Beaux-Arts tradition, Fathy's early projects in the 1930s and 1940s followed many of the changes that contemporary architecture in Europe was going through from Art Deco to the Bauhaus. To judge from the various projects he designed during those twenty years, Fathy seems to have been a wanderer searching for a direction rather than a committed follower of a specific style or school of architecture. He tried his hands at every new or established style available to him or fashionable among the members of the aristocratic class of Egypt to which he belonged. He built eclectic and ornamented mansions, islamicising mausolea and modernistic and cubist villas. His conversion to indigenous architecture came slowly in the 1940s. He first revealed his revivalist ideas in a house design he exhibited in 1937 and built his first courtyard house in 1941 in Bahtim in Egypt for the Royal Society of Agriculture. This was followed by a series of courtyard houses commissioned by rich individuals who were mostly family friends and fellow members of the Egyptian intelligentsia. This stage culminated in the project of New Gourna in Upper Egypt (1948–61): a village of domed and vaulted adobe courtyard houses planned after a mixture of rural traditional and modern, utopian principles. The village for instance not only had a mosque, school and infirmary, but also a theatre. This was a totally alien innovation in rural Egypt which reflected more the architect's class background and utopian perspective than a well thought-out addition aimed at truly enriching the peasants' lives. Conversely, Fathy refused to use 'modern' building materials and opted instead to revive the

Right and far right: Dar al-Islam Village, Abiquiu, USA, 1980s. © Aga Khan Trust for Culture.

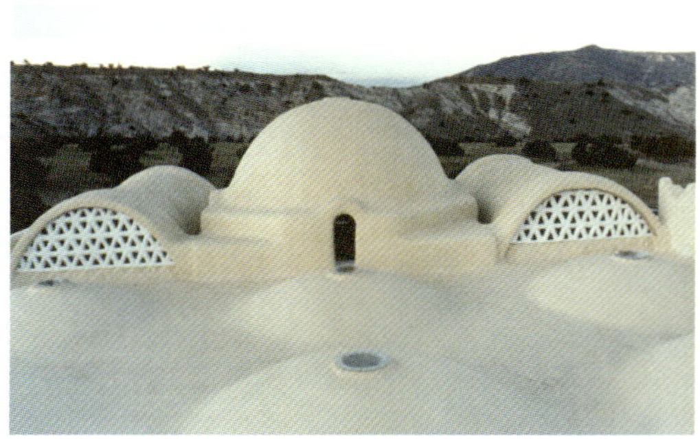

traditional material of rural Egypt, unbaked brick. He introduced vernacular ways of constructing domes and vaults that he had seen and admired in Nubia, a region in the south that was historically separate from Egypt proper, from which his family originally came. Fathy also imported some of the Mamluk and Ottoman Cairene forms, such as the *qa'a* (residential reception hall), the *malqaf* (wind catcher), the *shukhshikha* (open wooden cupola) and, most famous of all, the *mashrabiyya* (intricate window lattice). This mixture of traditional urban and rural forms was to become Fathy's hallmark design. It was to appear in a variety of combinations in all future projects for the rest of his life.

Fathy's architectural transformation was no different from many other conversions that contemporary Egyptian idealist and nationalist artists and intellectuals underwent at the same time. They had turned nativist and traditionalist as a way to reclaim the 'indigenous' Egyptian culture upon which they were to base their own modern identity. This process was fuelled by an awakened nationalism that swept across Egypt in the 1910s and 1920s and exploded in the revolution of 1919 against the colonial power, Great Britain. The revolution brought about a clear cultural articulation of an Egyptian identity that unified the two wings of the nation, Muslim and Coptic. It transcended other notions of belonging, such as Orientalism and Islamism, with which various political powers in Egypt toyed in the late nineteenth and early twentieth century. The emergence of an Egyptian identity was analogous to other nativist movements which sprang elsewhere around the Mediterranean and in Europe during the same period as signs of nations in formation. But in Egypt it was more a renascence than a birth, for a strong notion of Egyptian-ness had always pervaded the history of the country long before the advent of nationalism as we know it. From as early as Pharaonic times, Egyptians have possessed a strong conception of their homeland with its distinct character, its single source of wealth, the Nile, and its indisputable, fixed natural boundaries,

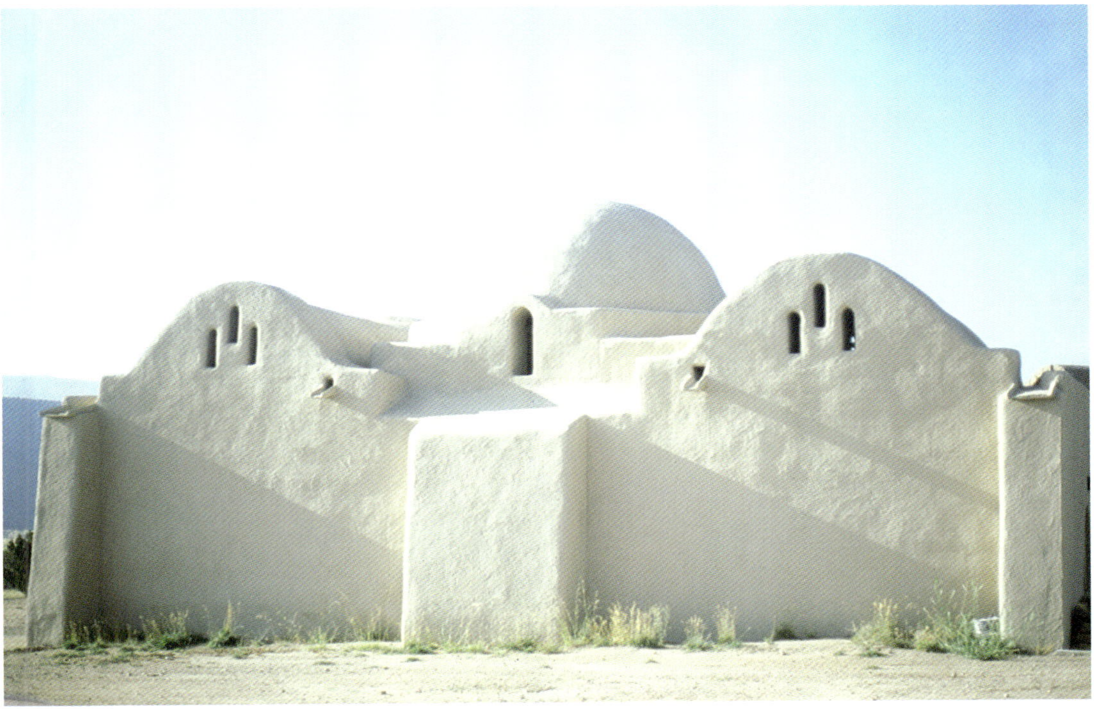

comprising desert barriers in the east and west, obstructive cataracts in the Nile in the south and the Mediterranean in the north. So solid was this perception that it permeated the artistic and literary production of the different epochs despite the various radical changes in religious, cultural and political outlook of the country that occurred throughout its history.

Beginning in the 1920s and 1930s, the outburst in the artistic expression of Egyptian nationalism became more extensive and more far-reaching than before for it had acquired tangible and urgent ideological and political functions. Poets like Bayram al-Tunsi and 'Abd al-Hamid al-Deeb began experimenting with the colloquial language and idioms of working-class people and the *fellaheen* (peasants) as the authentic voices of Egypt. Novelists like Yahya Haqqi and Naguib Mahfouz looked for topics and images in the popular milieu and adopted the street language to lend their fiction a realistic tone. Painters like Mahmoud Said and Youssef Kamel searched for artistic inspiration in the accumulated traditional wisdom of the common people and turned to the daily lives of the working poor and the destitute for painting subjects. In the field of architecture, Fathy was not alone. Other contemporary Egyptian architects went native as well. Most notable among them was Ramses Wissa Wassef, another visionary architect with a socio-religious mission which he translated into an arts and crafts centre constructed in stages in the village of Harraniya outside Cairo (1957–74).

For Fathy, New Gourna was a turning point despite its ultimate failure in solving the immediate problem of housing the inhabitants of old Gourna. The project took many years of bureaucratic haggling to complete, and even then, it was never completed as planned. The Gournis, who lived off robbing old tombs, refused to relinquish their old site with its access to hidden Pharaonic treasures. They also hated what they considered a waste of space in the courtyard houses and felt uneasy about the unfamiliar domes and vaults which they associated with funerary architecture. Fathy became very frustrated

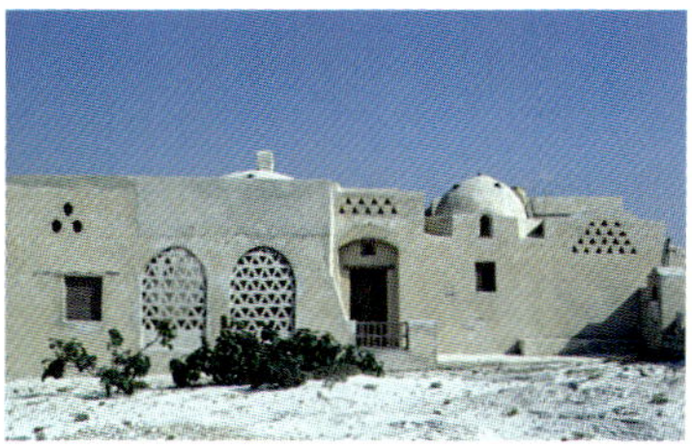

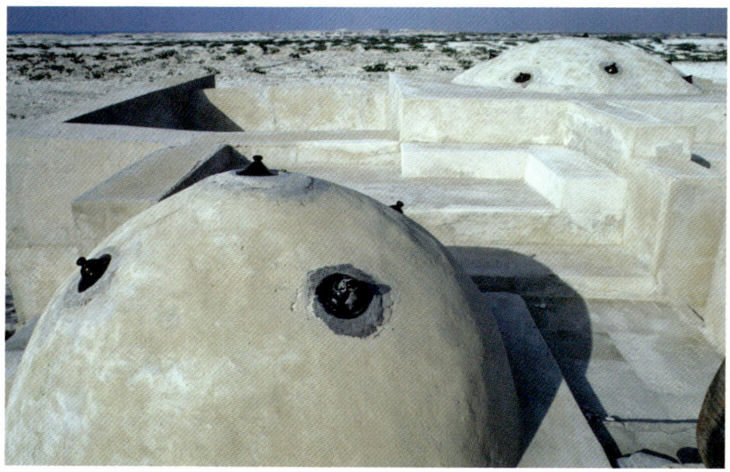

and considered quitting many times. Then came the revolution of 1952 with its half-baked programmes of national liberation and social and agricultural reforms. Fathy seems to have evinced a strong alienation from the new regime whose main goal appeared to be to strip the aristocratic class, with which Fathy fully identified, of its wealth and privilege. He thus accepted an offer from Constantinos Doxiades and moved to Athens in 1957 to join Doxiades Associates, an innovative planning firm which was then developing new and scientific methods for international development. Fathy spent five years there essentially as the expert on traditional and vernacular architecture of the Arab world where Doxiades had many commissions in Lebanon, Syria and Iraq. The experience of working for a multidisciplinary firm in which he had to negotiate every decision with a group of visionary planners and managers compelled Fathy to systematise his design principles and to sharpen his holistic approach to architecture. At the same time, he sensed a growing divergence in opinion between himself and Doxiades about the role of the architect which finally drove him to quit and return to Egypt in 1962.

Fathy's standing improved after his comeback, which may have been urged by President Gamal Abdel-Nasser himself. The publication of his book on the project of New Gourna, *Gourna: A Tale of Two Villages* (limited edition, Cairo: Ministry of Culture, 1969), in which he recounted his conversion to indigenous architecture, established the theoretical, ideological and environmental underpinnings of his philosophy. Fathy's architectural beliefs caught on in the late 1970s with the translation of his book into European languages (the expanded English edition under the title *Architecture for the Poor* was published by the University of Chicago Press in 1973). He became an inspirational master to be emulated and copied by countless young architects in Egypt and elsewhere who espoused his principles and his forms, sometimes dealing lightly with the former and leaning heavily on the latter. In 1980, Fathy received the first Chairman Award of the Aga Khan Award for Architecture, the most prestigious

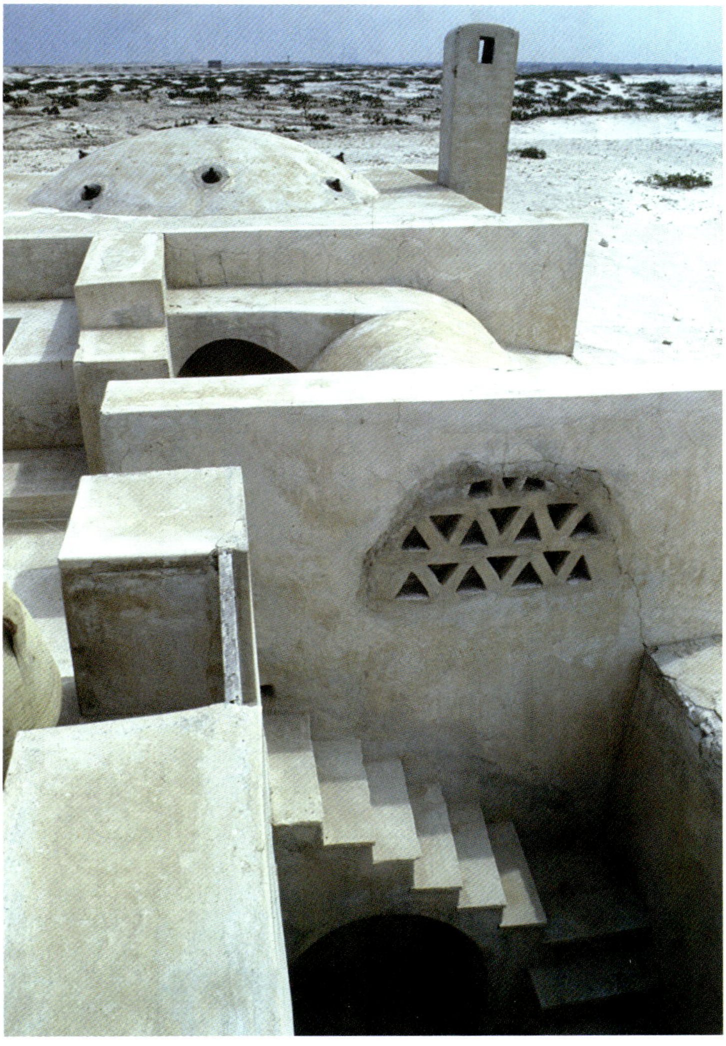

All images: Development of the Northern Shore at Sidi Krier, Egypt, 1971. © Aga Khan Trust for Culture.

architectural prize available for architects working outside the West. The last decade of his life was basically a time of recognition. Fathy became the wise old master living in the shadow of the Citadel of Cairo. He opened his house to visitors and disciples who came to see him as a kind of spiritual and educational pilgrimage.[3]

Fathy's career obviously had its own dynamic. But it had also more or less mirrored what was happening in Egypt, a country undertaking the long and torturous journey from colonialism to independence to development and its aftermath entangled with grand dreams of regional supremacy during the same time period. Fathy's conversion to the vernacular had its ideological roots in the mounting grumbles against British colonialism in the 1920s. But what started as an expression of an Egyptian cultural identity – admittedly of an unlikely mix of Cairene and Nubian styles – was transformed at least twice after Fathy's return to Egypt in 1962. Fathy himself modified the interpretation of his architecture in his own writing from a manifestation of a primeval Egyptian model to an essentially Arab and later an Arab-Islamic one with ambiguous universal applicability. He began to write about the introverted Arab house and its spatially ingenious response to its harsh desert environment as the model for his own courtyard houses. A few years later, the model became the Arab-Islamic house. References to an Islamic conception of the serene and protected family life, in addition to a more symbolic register dealing with the conception of the unique God and the images of His promised paradise, were added to the normative paradigms of Fathy's architectural model. This process paralleled the changing ideology of Egypt from 1920s and 1930s Egyptianism, to Nasserist pan-Arabism in the 1960s, to Islamism in the 1980s. But here too, Fathy's case was not unusual. Many artists, authors and architects expanded their frames of reference during the same time period and under the same circumstances. They resorted to Arabism and Islamism successively without necessarily abandoning the earlier nationalist identity. In fact, the Egyptian intelligentsia was at the

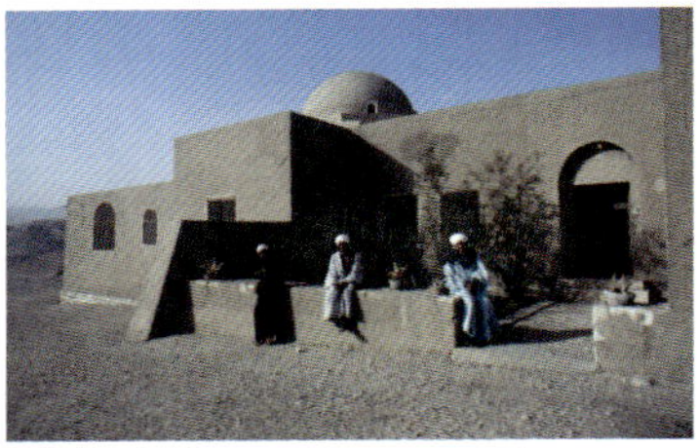

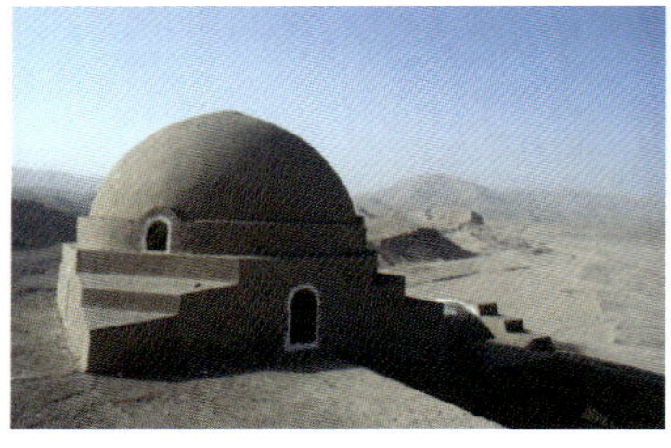

same time instigating and following in the transformation of the cultural identity of Egypt which was initiated and underwritten by the ruling regime for clear political ends.

What makes Fathy an exceptional man is how passionately, gracefully and, most importantly, seamlessly he accomplished the crossing from the national to the pan-Arab and then to the universal dimension of architecture. Indeed, as he himself knew when he wrote his first book, he was in transition, anticipating his own transformation, which he grasped but still did not have the convincing ideological vehicle to express. The fervent debate on national identity that erupted in the aftermath of liberation and independence suggested a path which Fathy readily adopted in his continuous striving to articulate his own architectural language. To him, vernacular architecture became the equivalent of folklore to the artist: a symbol of the vitality of the native culture before and beyond the tarnishing colonial experience. But as the trajectory of his career illustrates, the changing ideological context within which he operated inspired him to transcend the narrow confines of nationalism and to invoke vernacular architecture as the foundation for a passage from the local to the universal, from the past to modernity and from patriotism to humanism.

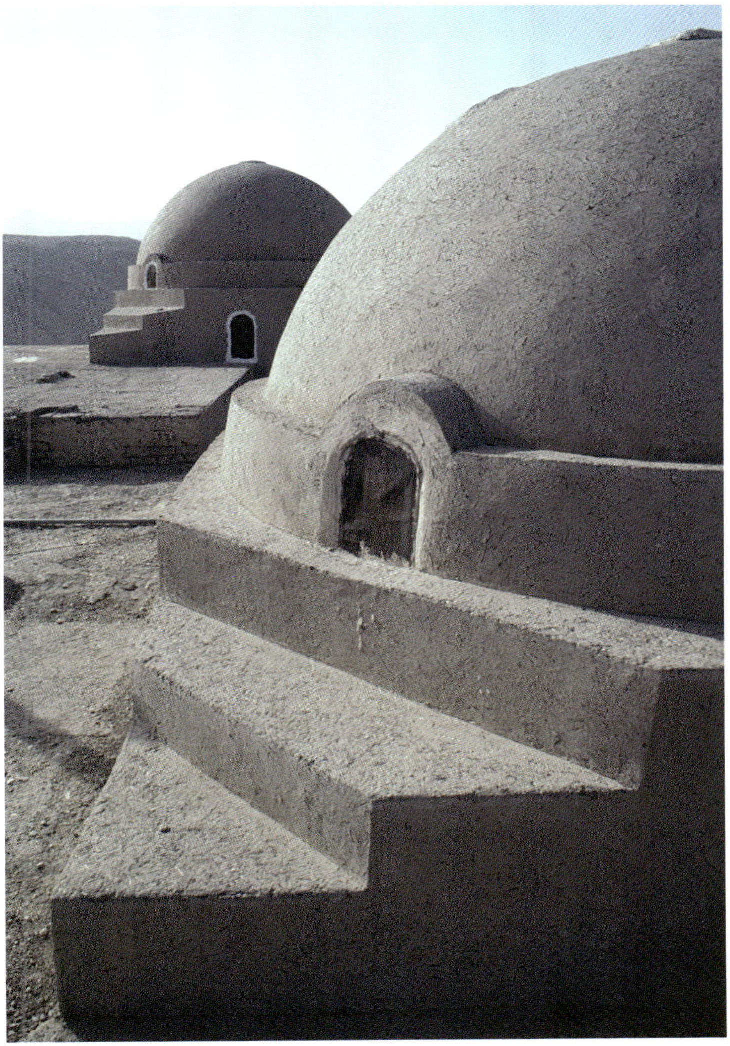

All images: Stoppelaere House, Luxor, Egypt, 1950. © Aga Khan Trust for Culture.

The Global Village Revisited

Hamza Walker

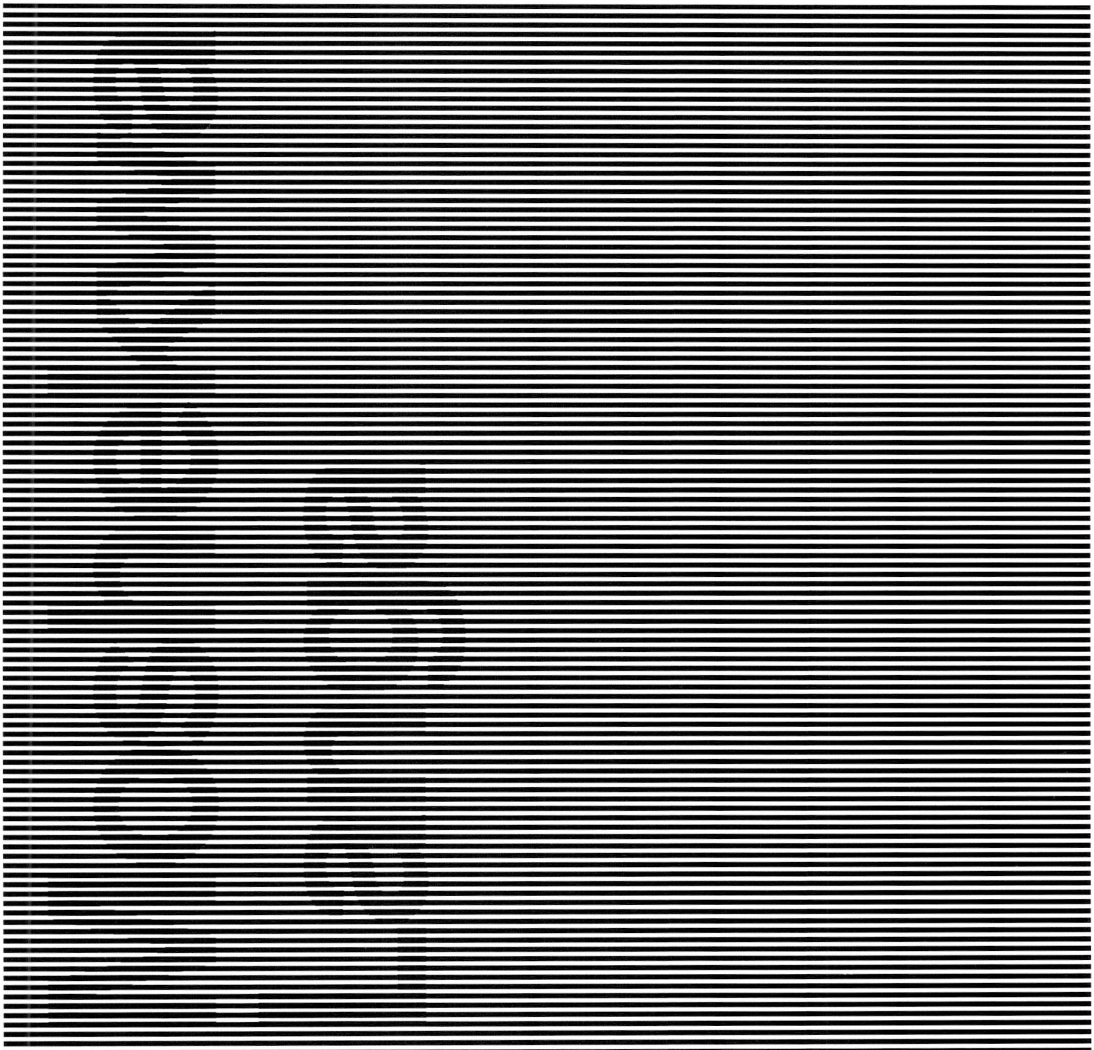

New Babylon ends nowhere (since the earth is round); it knows no frontiers (since there are no more national economies) or collectivities (since humanity is fluctuating). Every place is accessible to one and all. The whole earth becomes home to its owners. Life is an endless journey across a world which is changing so rapidly that it seems forever other.
Constant, *New Babylon*, 1974 [1]

From 1958 to 1966, Dr. Hendrik F. Verwoerd served as Prime Minister of South Africa. His vision of apartheid was distinguished by its scope. Whereas apartheid proper involved the segregation of races, Verwoerd wished to separate them into newly created, self-governing states. 'Grand apartheid', as it was known,... called for establishing a small white republic to coexist alongside a series of black tribal states or homelands.... In March of 1960, after riots in Johannesburg, a state of emergency was declared. Opponents to Verwoerd's plans were jailed and the principal black political organizations, notably the African National Congress (ANC), were outlawed.... Maps were eventually drawn-up and communities were bulldozed and resettled according to new boundaries. At the same time, the migration of blacks into the industrialized cities had to be halted and reversed. Factories were encouraged to relocate. Already existing pass laws were stiffened. All blacks, including those born and raised in the city, were assigned a homeland.

Although Verwoerd died in 1966, grand apartheid had enough momentum to see it through successive administrations before its dismantlement in 1989. By 1977, four out of ten homelands were granted independence. Although homeland chiefs could liken their independence to liberation struggles elsewhere on the continent, the homelands exemplified neo-colonial rule. Massive land reapportioning complicated by tribal bickering resulted in the relocation of upwards of 3.5 million blacks. The shanty towns and resettlement camps... were now a permanent fixture. The homelands were characterized by corruption, exploitation, widespread poverty and a substantial number of internally displaced persons.

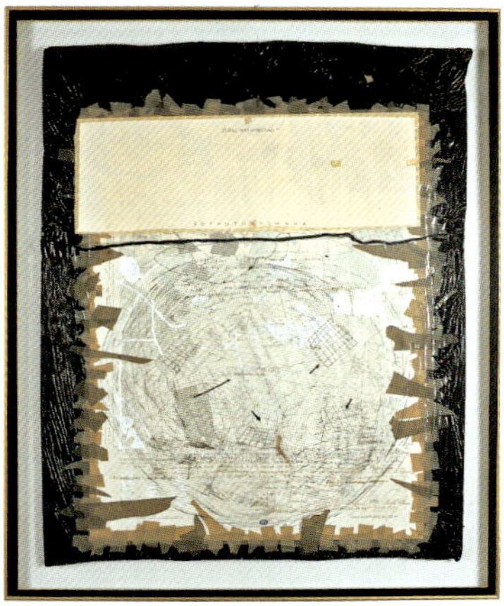

Untitled, 1995. Mixed media on paper, 113 x 97cm.

In an untitled assemblage made in 1996, Moshekwa Langa taped a map of Bophuthatswana to a trash bag, but not before scribbling on what was already a masterpiece of gerrymandering. The drawing features a roughly sketched circle accompanied by a few stray grids, arrows and fragments of hand-rendered text. One reads 'They Lived Happily Ever After' and another 'State Copyright'. In the context of Bophuthatswana, the circle is not so much a symbol of unity as it is of containment. In light of apartheid, the text is purely and painfully ironic.... The state can not only copyright what it has created, it literally and systematically copied, i.e. repeatedly exercised, its right to move and remove people as it drew and redrew boundaries. In general, however, Langa's language is consciously cryptic. Making sense of this work is no doubt like trying to follow the logic of apartheid which, in the case of this map, is the illogic of dispersal. Langa's rough, desperate line and emphatic use of tape reek of force – an effort to fix and rationalize displacement in a homeland whose creation involved the redistricting and reapportioning of several far flung regions in the Northern Province. Having learned from the mistakes of previous homelands, Bophuthatswana was to be a model independent state. Instead it only illustrated the advanced stages of grand apartheid's moral and political bankruptcy.

Langa hails from KwaNdbele, a homeland adjacent to Bophuthatswana.... Considering when and where he was born, Langa witnessed revolutionary change from a regime in the last and perhaps cruelest stages of its maintenance to the coming of a democratic and unified South Africa. He is a radical scavenger. While living in South Africa, he worked almost exclusively with found materials, particularly those imparting a sense of impermanence. The untitled Bophuthatswana assemblage is one in a series of thirteen works formally linked through the use of trash bags and maps. These materials, along with scraps of corrugated metal, fishing line and tarp-sized pieces of paper that were crumpled and smeared with household goods (tea, coffee, soap, sugar, syrup), seem to have been his favorites. The works were often installed in a

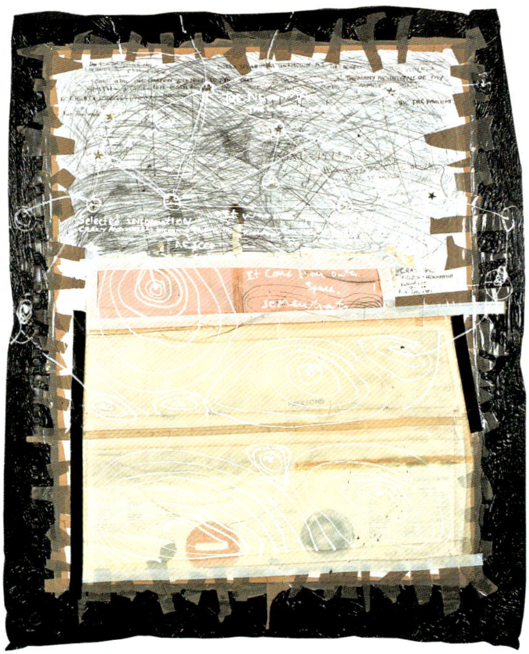

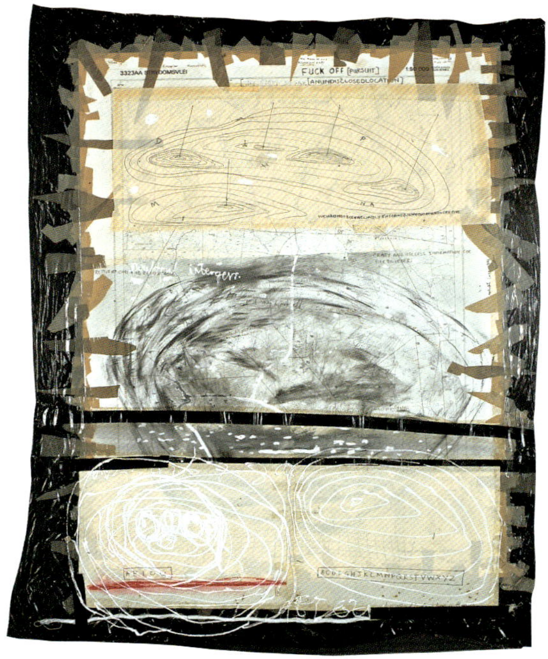

Above and right: *Untitled*, 1995. Mixed media on paper, 113 x 97cm.

transient manner – leaned, hung, clipped or draped – coming across as disparate fragments of happenstance. Whatever holistic, personal sensibility Langa brought to bear on this work found itself disassembled and reapportioned much like KwaNdbele's makeshift environs. Indeed, Langa's formative years were marked by conditions in which the dichotomy between the personal and the political was an imploded binary whose remnants were indistinguishable. Biographical and political content had become one and the same. This is confirmed throughout his notebooks in which maps of South Africa's provinces are squarely juxtaposed against family photos. In another related work from the previous year, Langa draped several homeland phone books over white wire coat-hangers and permanently sealed them in black plastic to prevent their being opened again. It is tempting to read this work as an acknowledgment that the historical chapter of the homelands had drawn to a close since those independent states were absorbed into Nelson Mandela's government. But by then, dislocation had become an inextricable part of South Africa's foundational narrative – from its colonial origins, with its celebratory tales of treks, voyages, frontiers and settlers, to the rampant displacement of blacks under grand apartheid, and finally in the biographies of numerous dissidents and exiles. For a vast amount of northern South Africa's black residents, the journey to Johannesburg from the immediately surrounding townships and underdeveloped homelands still remains all but mandatory. If anything, Langa, through his own travails (moving from KwaNdbele to Johannesburg), cultivated a sense of internal displacement already endemic to South Africa's polyglot national identity.

Langa has produced videos, banners, photographs, drawings, paintings and installations. No medium is privileged, yet all are distinct, as the eclectic hanging of his exhibition makes clear. Langa's heterogeneous mix of artistic media ultimately recapitulates two contradictory artistic paradigms: namely, modernist art's aspirations for universal legibility, i.e. 'the prospects of an emancipatory

Marta, 2002. Video stills, 8 mins 40 secs.

transcendence of regional and national artistic conventions',[2] notably through abstraction, and post-modernism's investigation into the basis of subjectivity and identity formations as they reside in autobiography, performance and figuration. Although each of Langa's works, ranging from the sizable monochromatic paintings to the photographs prominently featuring the artist engaged in role-playing, may be considered individually, the paradigms they represent when taken together pose a set of interesting questions regarding the development of an aesthetic articulating the conditions of displacement and exile. Given that mass migration is an inextricable aspect of modernity, one could, as art historian Benjamin Buchloh suggests, begin documenting such an aesthetic so as to yield a 'typology' of formal characteristics corresponding to displacement as a global condition. But what, if any, would be the relationship between an aesthetic articulating global conditions of displacement and modernism's utopian aspirations for an art of universal legibility? Tellingly, Langa engages modernism's universalist paradigm as someone whose experience is that of displacement. According to his work, the key characteristic of an aesthetic articulating displacement as a global condition is one of universal illegibility. This is born out in Langa's most consistent practice, drawing. Langa's drawings are a mixture of styles resembling the twentieth century's best scribblers (Cy Twombly, Jean Michel Basquiat, Bill Traylor, Louise Bourgeois). Many are executed with unorthodox materials, including nail polish, ball point pen and White-Out used to delete fragments of appropriate text. They are strange, idiosyncratic acts of communication belonging to someone in search of a private Esperanto. This is hardly surprising since his native South Africa has eleven official languages.

Whereas it would appear that Langa's earliest work reflected circumstances unique to South Africa, the conditions of displacement specific to that country no doubt greatly inform larger, global conditions of displacement. Although places such as Bophuthatswana,

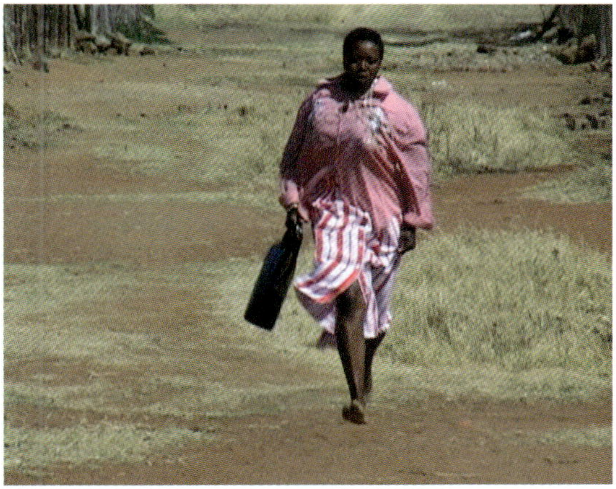

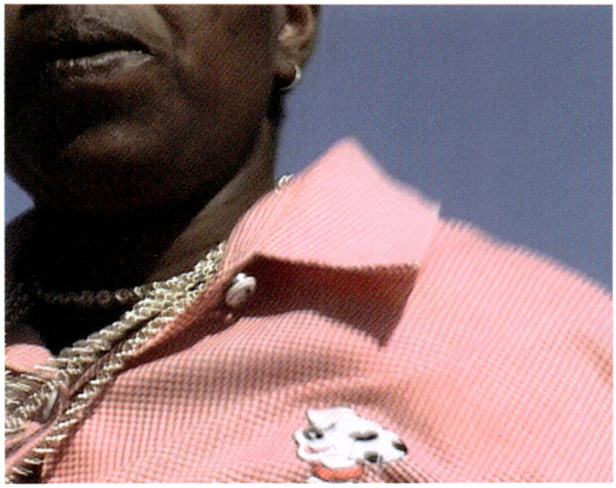

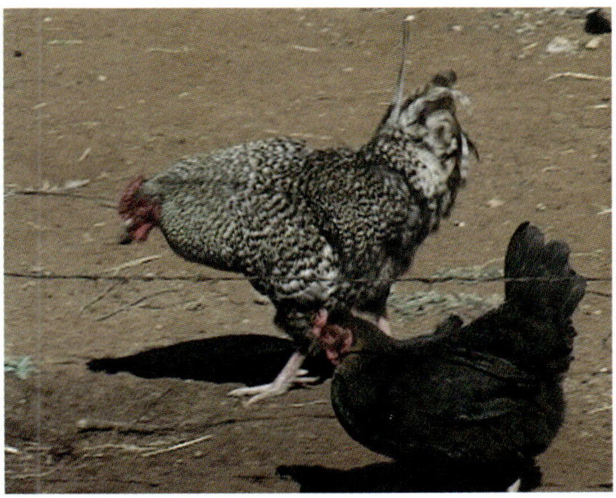

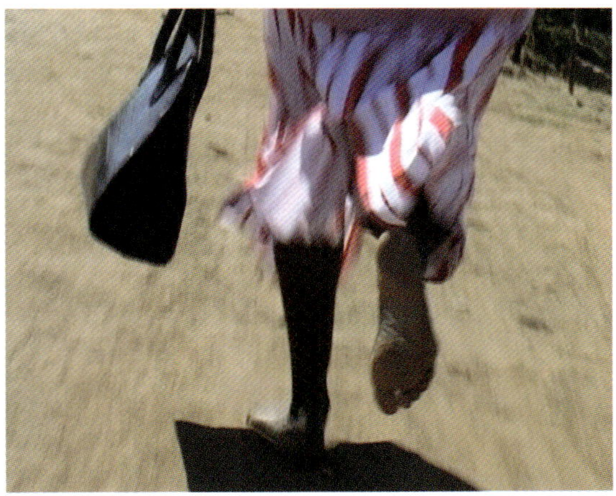

KwaNdbele and Kwazulu Natal, all of which have been featured in Langa's map-based collages, are neo-colonial tribal constructs, under a rubric of global displacement they become as cosmopolitan as any place else whose population is essentially a transient ward of the nation-state at the mercy of global capital. In this respect, Langa's work is hardly region-specific. Without ever leaving the confines of his native South Africa, Langa could have assumed the status of 'world citizen' and his work could rightfully lay claim to being 'cosmopolitan' insofar as that word is commensurate with the term 'global village'. Paradoxically, Langa's emigration from Johannesburg (the new world) to Amsterdam (the old world) would threaten to reduce his status from 'world citizen' to that of 'native' since his work – based on the artist's identity, as manifest in his name, race, and country of origin – was in all likelihood expected to reflect regional specificity. Its ability to participate in a global or universalist discourse would then be denied unless the modernist paradigm for universal legibility was disrupted.

Langa moved to Amsterdam in 1996 to pursue two years of study at the prestigious Rijksakademie. During that time he produced a sizable body of work in all media, much of which constitutes his dual exhibitions at the Center for Contemporary Art, Geneva, and The Renaissance Society [Chicago]. Langa notes although he had no intentions of producing paintings, he was not immune to pressure to study the craft upon which the Rijksakademie most prides itself. His response was a series of several large canvases, some monochromatic, and others drawing-based. Together, this body of work represents opposite poles of painting's universalist discourse as it was developed early in the twentieth century. On one end of the spectrum, abstraction's claim to universality was bolstered by the monochrome that transcended (or obliterated) reality through its reductivist, formal rigor. On the other end was the rhetoric of primitivism advanced by several strands of the avant-garde (Expressionism, Cubism, Surrealism, and later L'Art Brut), all of which found inspiration in a category of cultural production (ethnographic objects,

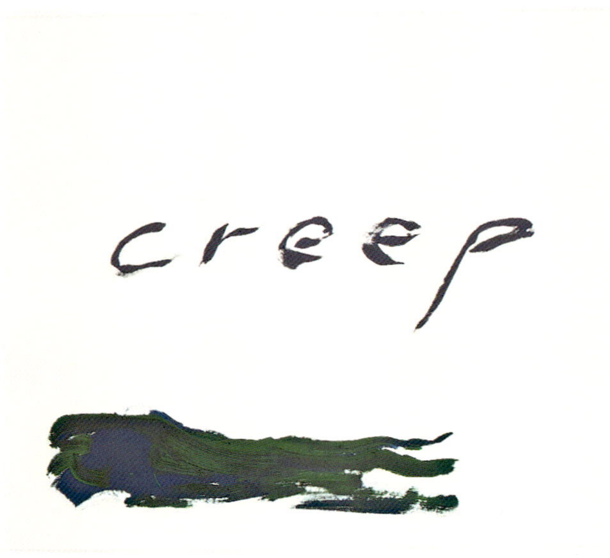

Creep, 2000. Mixed media work on paper, 140 x 100cm.

cave drawings, children's art) taken to represent nascent states of human development common to all individuals and societies. Langa's large-scale canvases indulge both extremes. The densely layered scribbles and sheer painterliness reveal an integrity to each approach, suggesting that both languages – primitive and transcendental – are not simply tropes but fully operative. A universalist discourse as expressed in the medium of paint, however, was also an absolutist discourse that had achieved historical closure. On both primitivist and transcendentalist terms, figures such as Paul Klee and Ad Reinhardt could be said to have already spoken on Langa's behalf. Both painterly languages, even when employed by the likes of Langa, only serve to reiterate the exclusion of non-Western individuals from a universalist discourse already predicated on their absence. If the universalist discourse were to be re-opened so as to register inclusion of the 'other', painting would have to be joined by another medium. This required that Langa expand his assemblage sensibility to encompass the installation of his exhibition so that his paintings could inform and be informed by other bodies of work.

Although Langa pursued paintings with the utmost integrity, it was never his intention to exhibit these works separately. For Langa, the absence of the universalist subject in painting would equal its very presence in photography.... In this instance, the universalist subject being conjured is none other than Langa himself. Parallel to his painting practice, Langa executed several series of photo-based self-portraits. Sans shirt and shoes, Langa captures himself in a variety of action poses. Shameless, silly, sexy, sentimental or just plain non-sensical, Langa's computer-enlarged Polaroids have no production values to speak of. In the series *How I Left the Couch*, Langa sports only crisp white briefs and socks. Two of these photos feature Langa suspended in the air, a large portion of his upper body cropped out of the frame making it impossible to tell how he is suspended. While airborne he fully contracts his lower legs in one photo. In the other, they are thrust out. Between the

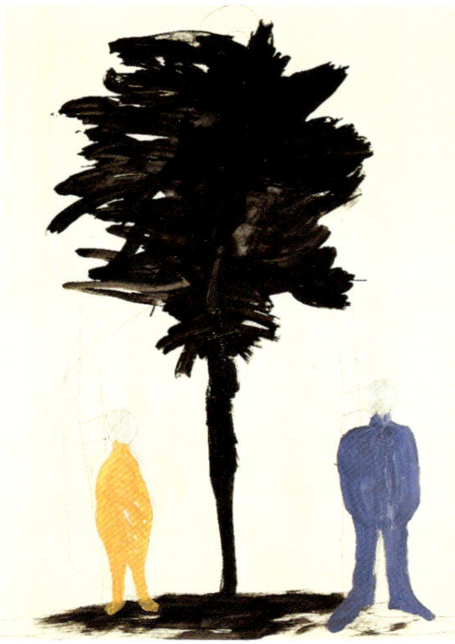

Adam and Eve, 2000. Mixed media work on paper, 140 x 100cm.

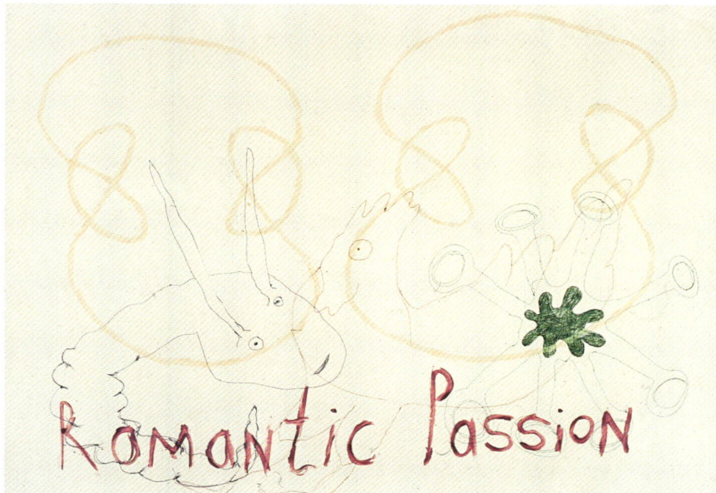

Romantic Passion, 1998–99. Mixed media drawing on paper, 100 x 140cm.

contraction and release, it is a striking and extremely expressive gesture, but even before Langa's body can assume the form of an expressive grapheme, it speaks through the inescapable matrix of race. In short, his body speaks while at the same time it is already spoken for. His attempts to defy gravity can be read as a rather humorous but futile effort to transcend narratives of self and other played out through the cultural fetishizing of a skin tone set in stark contrast to his white undergarments.

Langa's self-portraits can be linked to an older tradition of African studio portraiture through the figure of Samuel Fosso whose self-portraits, dating from 1977–78, are likewise filled with a playful sensuality. One in particular features Fosso churlishly posed, hands on hips, in white briefs and tank-top. As Hall and Sealy note of Fosso's role-playing, 'These images are consciously constructed around or across the traditional/modern dichotomy: they are "playing" on both a certain desire for the modern, and on certain dissonances in the idea of "modern" Africa.'[3] Unlike Fosso, Langa has largely dispensed with props in what is a non-descript, makeshift studio so barren as to be labeled primitive and so primitive as to be considered modern, or post-modern for that matter. With the exception of a black leather couch which he occasionally straddles, the only other prop is a microphone that appears in the triptych *My Life as a Disco Queen, as told to John Ruskin*. In one image, Langa offers the microphone to his make-believe audience in a gesture that is unabashedly erotic and at the same time an endearing invitation to sing along. The honesty and aggressive charm behind this performance is a surreal view into the sparsely populated karaoke bar of the artist's mind. No costumes and no make-up, these photographs are a critical camp redux, the 'passionate failure to strive for a compulsory identity'.[4] Stripped of any options as to how his corporeal self is to be perceived, this is 'Moshekwa! Unplugged' and literally 'playing' at the presentation of an essential self unable and unwilling to hide behind name, gender and race.

Graced with a billowy pair of parted curtains at the entry, Langa's Renaissance

Where do I Begin?, 2001. Video still, 4 mins 20 secs.

Society exhibition announced itself as theater. Needless to say, the metaphor of life as theater is central to any definition of camp. Langa's image is omnipresent throughout the exhibition as he is engaged in all manner of role-playing, borrowing poses from a variety of discreet sources (pornography, Weegee homicide photos, crucifixion scenes). In this respect, the relationship to an ongoing tradition of African studio portraiture, in which the sitter borrows available clothing and accessories to better express how they would like to be perceived, is quite clear. Role-playing becomes synonymous with self-determination. So the question is not 'Why role-playing or theatricality?' The question relevant to Langa's work as it was phrased by Susan Sontag in her now classic essay 'Notes on "Camp"', is 'When does travesty, impersonation, theatricality acquire the special flavor of camp?'[5] The answer to this question becomes apparent when comparing Langa's self-portraits to the dignity found in the work of Seydou Keïta, the excessive romanticism of Rotimi Fani-Kayode's photographic tableaux, the irony of Iké Udé's parodies of fashion photography, or the stern, masculinist identity-politics of Oladélé Ajiboyé Bamgboyé. Playing against this context, Langa's self-portraits harbor camp's essential element, namely a seriousness but 'a seriousness that fails'.[6] To use Sontag's words, Langa's self-portraits contain 'the proper mixture of the exaggerated, the fantastic, the passionate, and the naïve' to be considered prime examples of camp.[7]

This becomes even more obvious when Langa's work is considered within a trajectory of staged photography that developed in the 1980s as a critique of earlier documentary and photo-journalistic practices. The photograph no longer simply registered an available reality. Instead, the photograph was viewed as complicit in the construction of subjective codes involving race, gender, class, sexuality and ethnicity. Photographic truth was interrogated, often beginning with the self and the body, particularly as it posited notions of difference and beauty. However, by the time Langa reached the decision to interrogate identity it was something of an exhausted

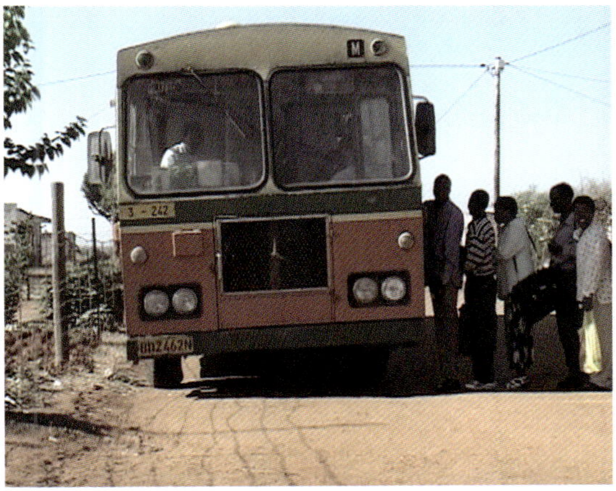

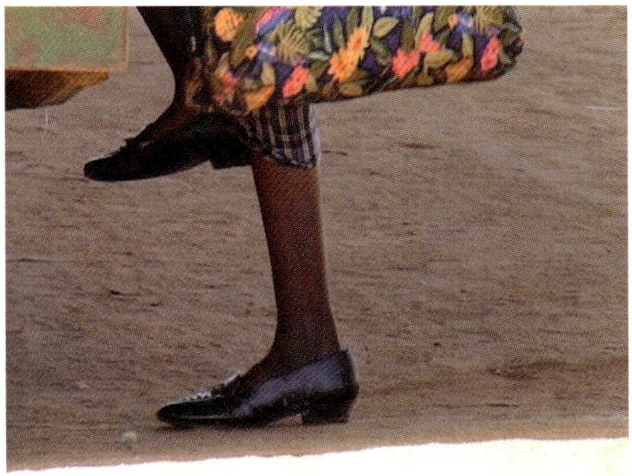

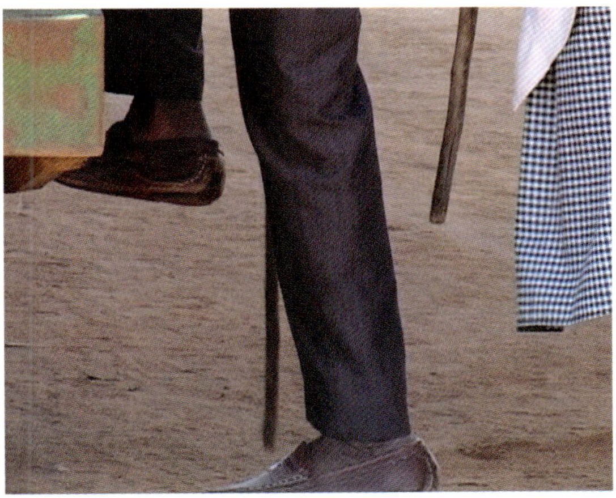

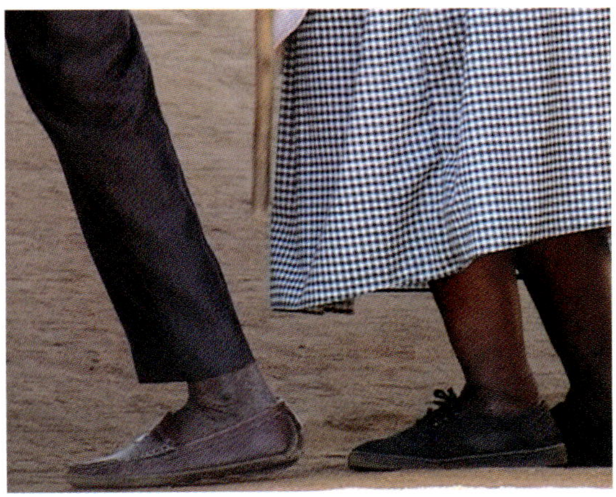

topic. When Langa began his series of photo-based self-portraits, staged photography, at the hands of Lyle Ashton Harris, Catherine Opie, Iké Udé, and Yasumasa Mori Mura, to name but a few, had run much of its course. As early as 1990, cultural critic Kobena Mercer noted that the neutralization of leftist political movements was 'paralleled by the cultural appropriation and commodification' of identity politics, 'many of whose radical slogans (such as "the personal is political") have been hijacked, objectified and sold back to us as an ever-widening range of "lifestyle" options for those who can afford to pay'.[8] Langa's photos could hardly be said to appear at a moment of crisis, one lacking in representations of blacks. If anything it is just the opposite. The photos appear at a moment dubbed 'hyperblack', allowing Mercer, in a later essay, to restate his earlier position more emphatically.

> Surveying the contemporary mediascape in which the drag, kitsch and camp iconography of a Ru Paul is about as transgressive as the Muppets; in which supermodels like Naomi Campbell and Tyson Beckford seek to subvert nothing more than their previous salaries; and in which hyperstylized blackness resold by Karl Kani, Tommy Hilfiger, Nike and other logos and labels demonstrates the frenzied commodification of diversity, we are faced with the paradox whereby the apparent proliferation of freedom of choice is undergirded by the gothic social horror of resegregated demographics.[9]

Despite the accuracy of Mercer's assessment, his expectation that camp iconography transgress the very conditions that bring it into being – namely, the recycling of an exhausted commodity fetishism – is misgrounded. Camp can mock, not transgress, the subject it lovingly imitates. It is problematic precisely because it is a solvent of the morality being raised by Mercer. In Susan Sontag's words, camp 'neutralizes moral indignation', sponsoring a playfulness that is a defining characteristic of Langa's work....[10] Market demographics

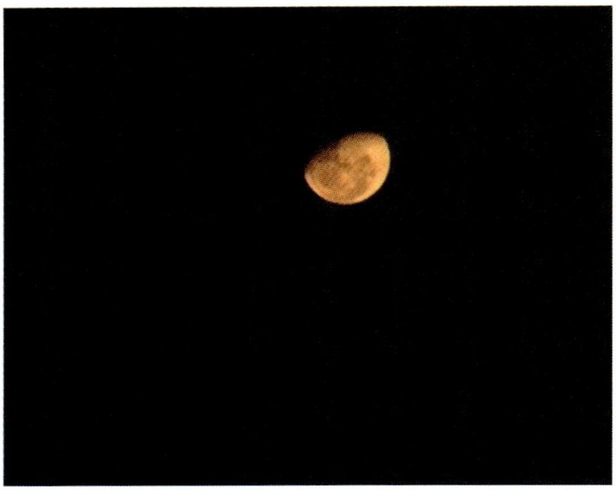

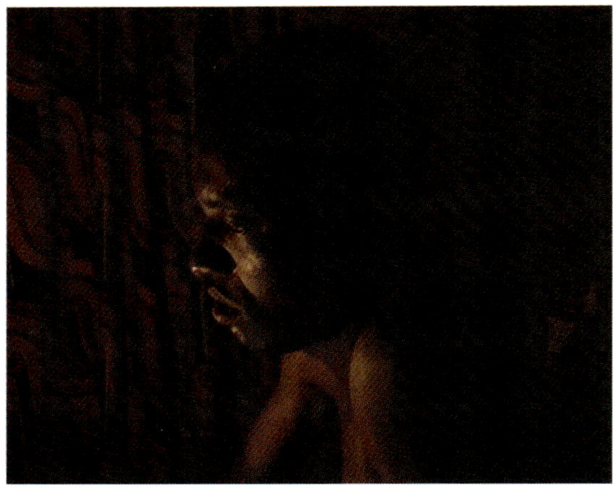

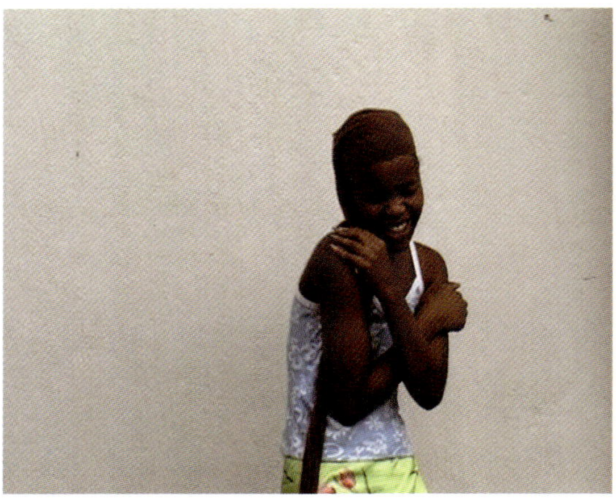

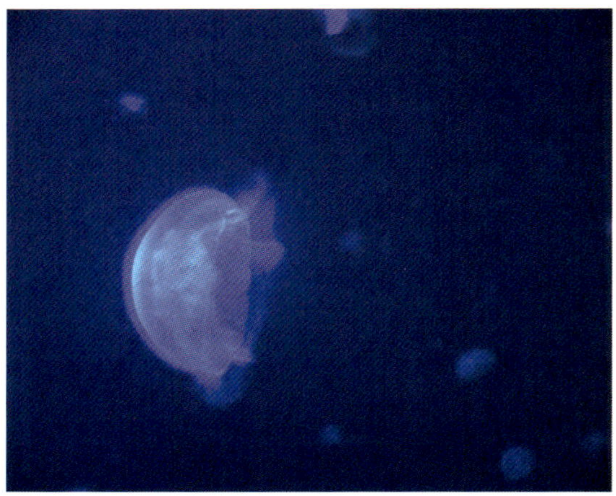

pale in comparison to the state-sponsored 'gothic social horror' Langa has witnessed. As much as it is the byproduct of an assemblage aesthetic, Langa's crypticism, his decontextualized iconography, his deployment of any and all media, is a willful obscurity meant to disrupt readings overdetermined by a political context. All this for the sake of play, which is not to say that there are no stakes. Camp is not only a solvent of morality. It is also a solvent of an authenticity that artists in Langa's position are no doubt expected to bear. The bona fide African subject who would speak for an entire village cum continent cum world is re-instating a universalist discourse as an exclusionary master narrative to which ultimately no one belongs. The failed seriousness at work in Langa's photographs is also at work (or play) in his monochromes, for it is not an essential Africaness that is being subject to camp but the universalist discourse itself. Langa is merely exploiting its inherent hyperbole. Now that the world is a global village who else but Moshekwa Langa should speak on its behalf? Although this question is rhetorical, the point being that which camp cannot transgress, it may be able to redeem. What is at work in Langa's use of camp is nothing short of the reprisal of humanism. Fully applicable to Langa's exhibition is Sontag's extraordinary insightful observation regarding camp's ability to re-animate whatever universalist discourse remains latent in humanism through fragmentary practices.

> This [camp] sensibility also insists on the principle that an oeuvre in the old sense (again, in art, but also in life) is not possible. Only 'fragments' are possible.... Something is good not because it is achieved, but because another kind of truth about the human situation, another experience of what it is to be human – in short, another valid sensibility – is being revealed.[11]

Under those circumstances, who would want to transgress the Muppets? Certainly not Langa. Theirs is a sensibility that is vital to the imagination, which is why he has appropriated it, as in his use of toys for variations on his signature string installation, *Fieldwork* (1997).

Moon, 2001. Video stills, 4 mins 20 secs.

A temporary installation exhibited during the end of his studies at the Rijksakademie, *Fieldwork* has been reconfigured for numerous venues including the Offenes Kulturhaus in Linz, Austria, the Johannesburg Biennial, and The Renaissance Society. Spilling hundreds of yards of string across the floor in a gesture reminiscent of Jackson Pollock's manner of painting, Langa converted the ground plane into an elaborate map. The metaphor was completed with the occasional toy car and through the use of spools and bottles as stand-ins for buildings, monuments or significant topographical features. Despite the simplicity of means, the results varied greatly, occasionally warranting a new name. The poetic nature of the piece was reinforced by Langa's literary flair, which he often reserves for his titles. In Linz, the work was entitled *The Mountains of My Youth – A Novel*, a ridiculously sentimental title in which nostalgia is bred by chronological as well as geographical distance. By contrast, The Society's version was more compact and baroque, filled with toys, including a plastic tank, rubber mice and spiders, and replete with a mirror ball at its center. Yet, Langa offset its playfulness with a gothic, if not downright sinister, title, *Temporal Distance (with a criminal intent)*; *You will find us in the best places*, a version of which was shown at the Johannesburg and Havana Biennials. In any and all cases, these installations gave new meaning to the term World Wide Web.

Part of this installation's critical success lay in the playful manner it reinscribes Marcel Duchamp's famous installation *mile of string* within the rubric of globalization. Not surprisingly, Duchamp, as part of the 1942 *First Papers of Surrealism* exhibition, in which *mile of string* was included, encouraged Sidney Janis's children to play loudly and excitedly during the opening reception – a gesture Langa has subsumed through his use of toys. Given *Temporal Distance's* delightfully haphazard resemblances to a metropole, the installation has an even deeper affinity with the Situationists' ideas regarding city planning about which they wrote numerous tracts. Inspired by the writings of Johan Huizinga, in particular his concept of Homo

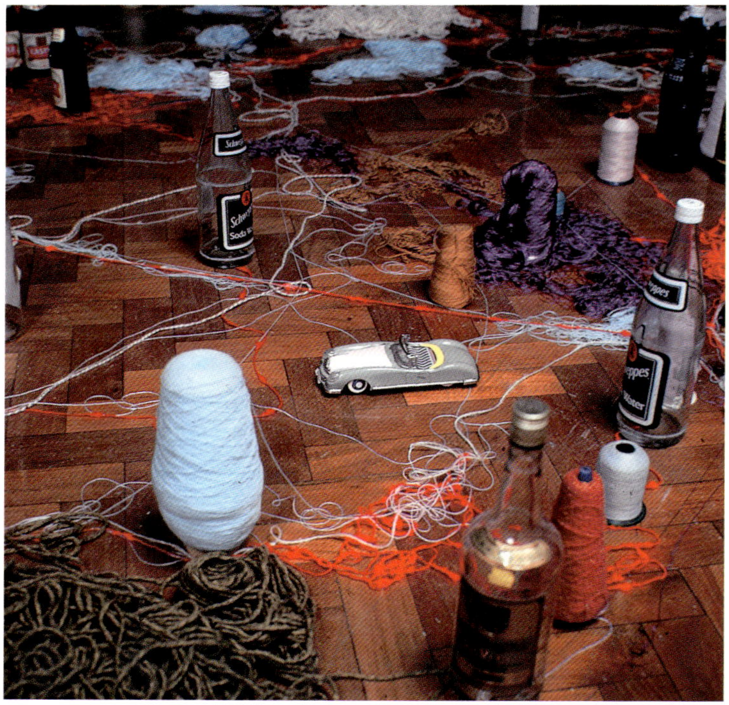

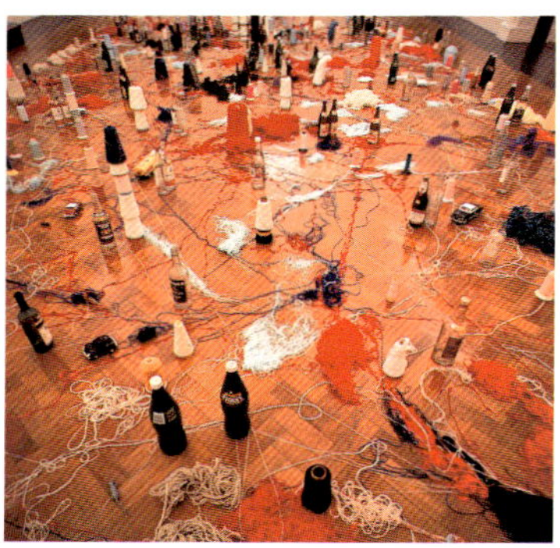

All images: *Temporal Distance (with a criminal intent): You will find us in the best places*, 1997. Mixed media installation, South African National Gallery, 2nd Johannesburg Biennale. Photographs: Werner Maschmann.

Ludens, man as player of games, the Situationists rooted the motives for their architectural theories in 'a passion for play'.[12] Their grandest scheme was Unitary Urbanism and its most vocal proponent was Constant, whose installation, *Yellow Sector* (1958), which utilized toy cars, is also a seminal precedent for *Temporal Distance*. Unitary Urbanism was a combination of all the Situationists' thought and strategies, the dérive and détournement, brought to bear upon ideas of urban planning. In no way whatsoever was Unitary Urbanism pragmatic. It was a critique of a functionalist, post World War II urban environment stripped of joy. Guy Debord and Constant were keen to stress Unitary Urbanism as a game that emphasized continual movement. 'Unitary Urbanism is opposed to the fixation of people at certain points of a city. It is the foundation for a civilization of leisure and play.'[13] Constant, however, persisted with Unitary Urbanism well beyond the Situationists, incorporating it into his concept for a utopian civilization called New Babylon, which was his preoccupation from 1956 to 1974, becoming the basis for hundreds of models, paintings, and collages.

> The Culture of New Babylon does not result from isolated activities, from exceptional situations, but from the global activity of the whole world population, every human being engaged in a dynamic relation with his surroundings. There are no a priori links between anyone.[14]

Reveling in the ecstasy of communication as described by Constant, Langa is perhaps New Babylon's first citizen. Having abandoned a sense of mastery and master narratives, his robust laughter serves as his passport. For him, the world is a ball of string with neither its beginning nor its end anywhere in sight. It is a monotonous series of windings creating elaborate connections between people and places accompanied by an equally elaborate set of thoughts and longings. If Langa's disparate and desperate practices constitute an atlas of the difficult world, then his is an invitation to join him 'in the streets of the universe, now'.[15]

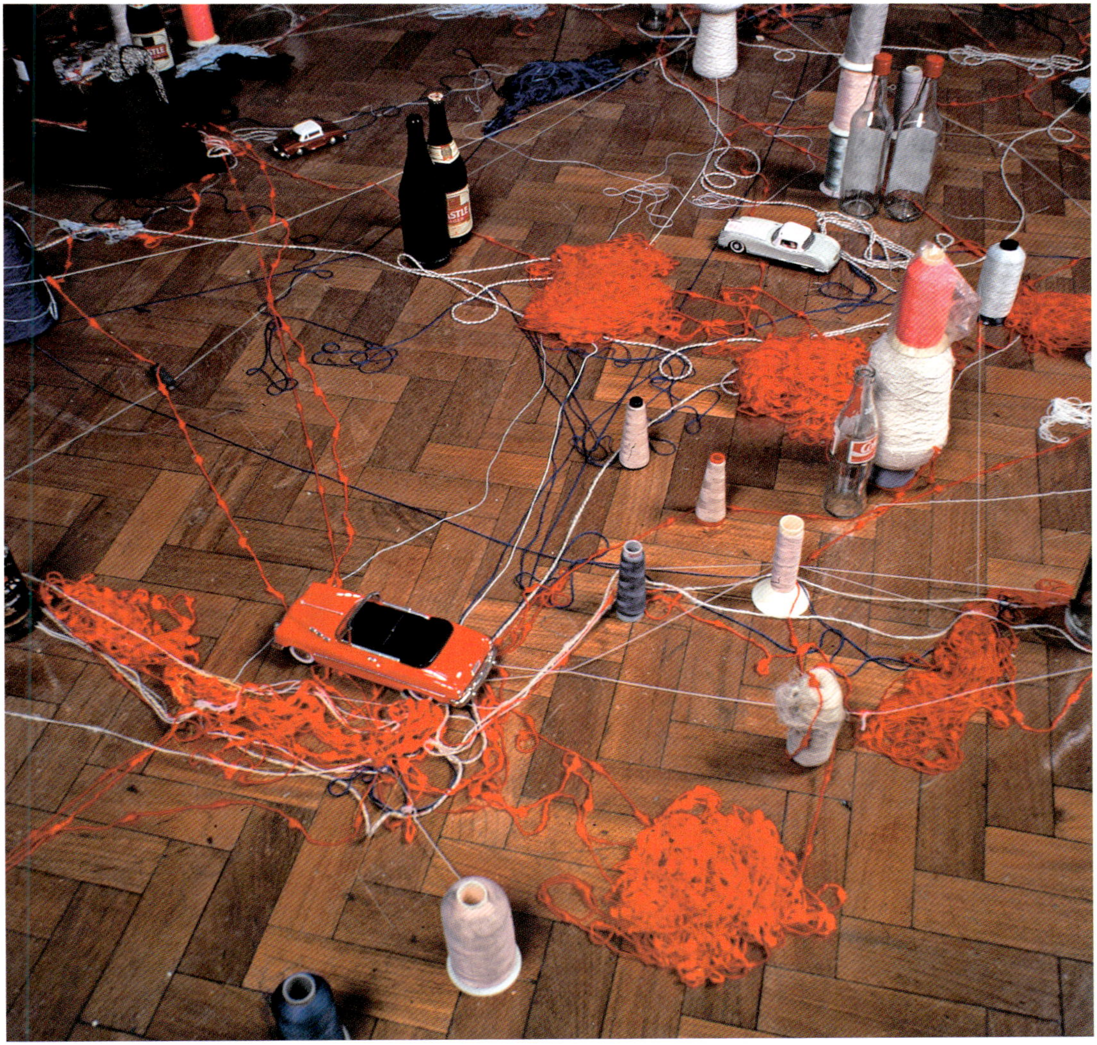

Salem Mekuria
Elsabet W. Giorgis

The Orthodox Trinitarian Theology reveals the divinity or the essence of God as the Trinity of persons existing one in another, in a unity of being; the Father is the unique source, the Son is begotten of the Father and the Holy Spirit proceeds. The creation of the world establishes a borderline between God and His creation. This imaginary boundary between the two is neither the one nor the other but something completely atypical, simultaneously connecting and separating the one and the other.

The triptych in Salem Mekuria's video installation refers to this iconic representation of the Trinity in the Ethiopian Orthodox faith. Her work proposes the pervasiveness of this representation in the praxis of Ethiopian art and life. Mekuria challenges the universal and linear narrative of Ethiopian history; her work acknowledges the varieties and complexities of Ethiopian culture and questions the ability of any single philosophical rationalisation to be the primal context of conventional value. It insists on a dialogue as a solution to the ongoing conflicts, recurring famines and repressive governments that make up the existential dilemma of the Ethiopian's meaning and being.

The dominant narrative of Ethiopian Orthodoxy obscured and/or annihilated social, religious and ethnic differences and denied multiple views of identity. For centuries, it forged an ensemble of myth and fact to undergird the founding stone of Ethiopia's 'national identity'. A deeper comprehension of Ethiopian Orthodoxy inscribes the founding myth of Ethiopian nationhood, postulating an ontology of interchangeable sanctity and divine election. Conquest and integration have facilitated this sense of collective 'national culture' regardless of ethnicity and many have adorned the nuances of Orthodoxy with a repertoire of pagan culture.

Ethiopian art has been described as Byzantine Art in an African setting, dedicated to Biblical themes, and manifests itself in icons, wall paintings and manuscript illustrations. Often painted on wood as triptych panels, icons are regarded with great reverence. Paintings

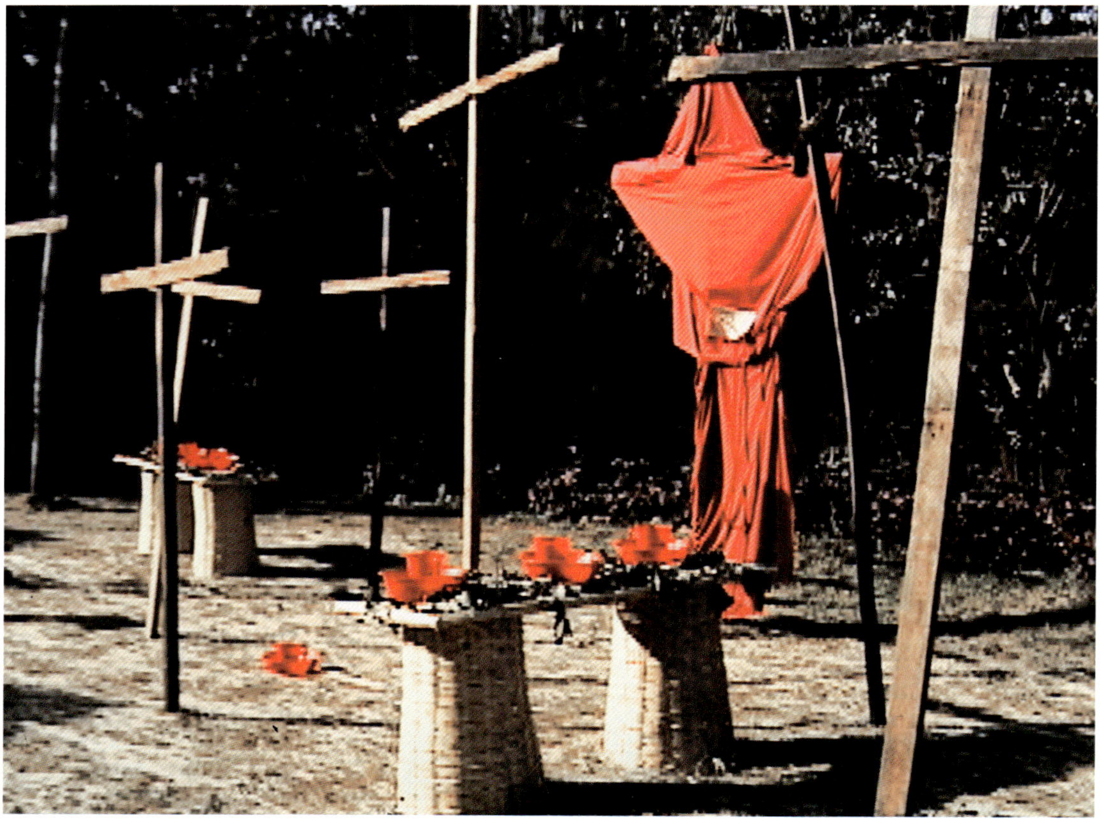

were seldom signed as the artist worked for the glory of God and would consider such action as both blasphemous and audacious. There is little acceptance for progress and evolution in the Orthodox mentality. Mekuria refers to the triptych of the Orthodox icon as a ubiquitous presence in all facets of traditional art and as an ongoing influence on both art and life in present-day Ethiopia.

Mekuria problematises the restrictive parameters of Western modernist/postmodernist aesthetics as governing conventions for formal experimentation. The evolution of social movements has been a cyclical process in the history of Ethiopia; no element can be removed without the collapse of the cycle. However, the historicisation of Ethiopia operates within a dialectical dynamics where one system of government aspires to be different and unique by its irreconcilable negation of the past and yet finds itself in the elusive flow of its antithetical past. 'In Ethiopia today', Mekuria says, 'the past, the present and the future coexist on the same plane and are experienced simultaneously in the present. Time is circular; one is never too far from encounters with the prehistoric, the pre-modern, the modern and the postmodern in the course of a few moments. Even as new images appear in the triptych, the old presences are never far from the surface. The triptych motif provides me with the opportunity to explore this existential fact.'[11]

Adaptation and resistance therefore have been contradictory influences behind the adoption of a particular symbolism. While there is an incessant search for modern political culture to contribute to liberal democracy and structural social change, there is also a continual need to re-establish the distinctive marks of national identity. Flanked with globalisation, modernisation and postmodernisation, poverty remains a hideous reality. The modernist/postmodernist movements of the Western avant-garde are only significant for Ethiopian cultural and social history in as much as they prepare the ground for a rethinking of the links between tradition, modernity and postmodernity.

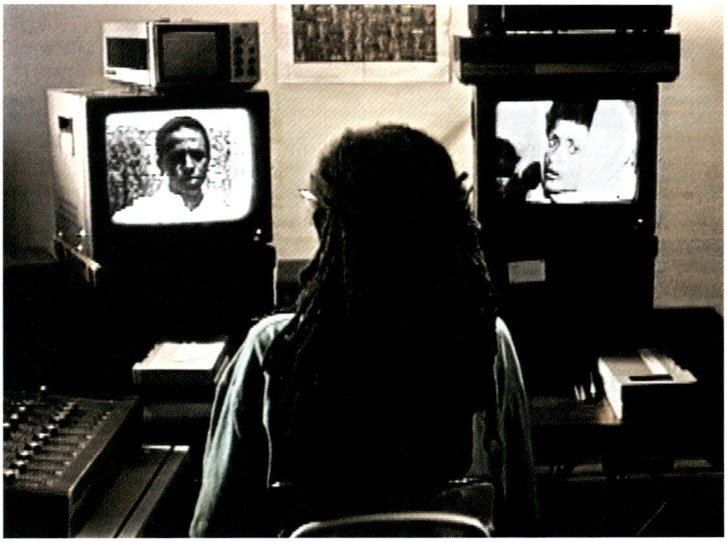

RUPTURES: A Many Sided Story, 2003. Video still of 2003 installation by Bekele Mekonnen.

DELUGE, 1997. Video still.

Dysfunctional modernity that fails to reach industrialisation and fails to enter the mechanical age has often been equated with unstable or chaotic economies and is characterised by ethnic conflicts.

In view of Ethiopia's current political and economic crisis, it is difficult to imagine that this country was once politically significant and had attained great notoriety as a distinctive hallmark of pan-Africanism. The quest for continental unity and integration took its root in Addis Ababa on 22 May 1963 when heads of African States convened for a historic meeting to form the Organisation of African States. It is important to situate Emperor Haile Selassie's pivotal role in the movement for African unity. The signing of the charter of the Organisation of African Unity (OAU) in Addis Ababa was the culmination of years of efforts during which President Kwame Nkrumah of Ghana and Emperor Haile Selassie of Ethiopia played particularly prominent roles, with Emperor Selassie advocating independence within existing boundaries. He was strongly committed to multilateralism and collective security and was an active supporter of national liberation movements across the continent.

Unfortunately, it was also the emperor's subsequent autocratic rule that led to the popular uprising of 1974. The fascinating history of the ancient Axumite civilisation, the legend of the Queen of Sheba and the Solomonite Dynasty that began with Menelik I (son of Solomon and Sheba) ended in 1974 with the overthrow of Haile Selassie, the Lion of Judah, King of Kings, Elect of God. In the end, the royal epithets had a hollow, mocking ring, dismantling the myth of Ethiopia.

There is a diverging discourse among Ethiopian intellectuals on the inception of Ethiopian modernism, or rather its 'dysfunctional modernism'. While historian Bahru Zewde acknowledges the great efforts made by the Emperor Haile Selassie towards education, telecommunication and cooperative farming to implement social modernisation, Messay Kebede in *Survival and Modernization* describes the policies of Haile Selassie 'as meant not so much to modernize the country as to

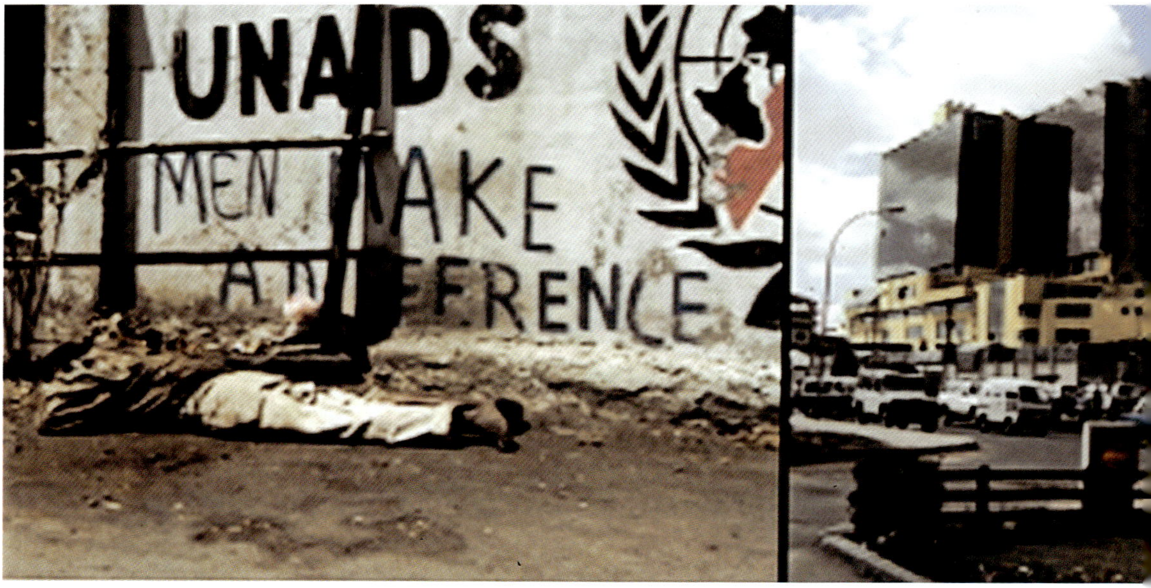

RUPTURES: A Many Sided Story, 2003.
Video stills of scenes in Addis Ababa.

establish autocratic rule.... It is the centralization of power, rather than modernization, that defines his regime.'[2] Nevertheless, Haile Selassie's reign signified a period of uneven modernist development in the socio-political history of the country. The triptych articulates this reality and the outcome of what Messay Kebede calls 'the point of departure of Haile Selassie's autocracy'.[3]

Mekuria focuses her fragmented lens on personal reflections of loss that mirror the national and individual experience under three regimes spanning over forty years: Emperor Haile Selassie, deposed in 1974; Mengistu Haile Mariam, whose dictatorship ended in 1991; and the present government of Meles Zenawi. She critically reveals decentred episodes and the monstrous paradox of the continuity of interrupted pieces.

Perhaps the most poignant stories in the triptych are drawn from Mekuria's most recent documentary *DELUGE* (1997) in which she meditates on the traumatic rupture of a nation and a collective grief that parallels her own. Located between the fall of Emperor Haile Selassie and the demise of Mengistu Haile Mariam, *DELUGE* captures the youth of the nation's heroic attempt to enter modernity and the misguided and hasty actions that led to the horrific loss of human and national resources. For those of us who escaped the human slaughter, the history of the events were part of our upbringing, a cruel initiation to our adolescence that had lost vitality; they contribute to our amputated spirit that has yet to be healed. The word 'deluge' is particularly appropriate to that period, a time when famine and war had ravaged the country and despair had crippled all hope. The 'reasoned doctrine' of Marxism prevailed in the guise of a revolution for the disenfranchised. Hence, the beginning of an unhappy saga, of mutual annihilation and the genocide of a nation.

During this apocalyptic period known as the Red Terror, Mekuria's brother Solomon and her best friend Negest were among the thousands whose lives were obliterated by the military Marxists who appropriated power from the monarchy. Solomon and

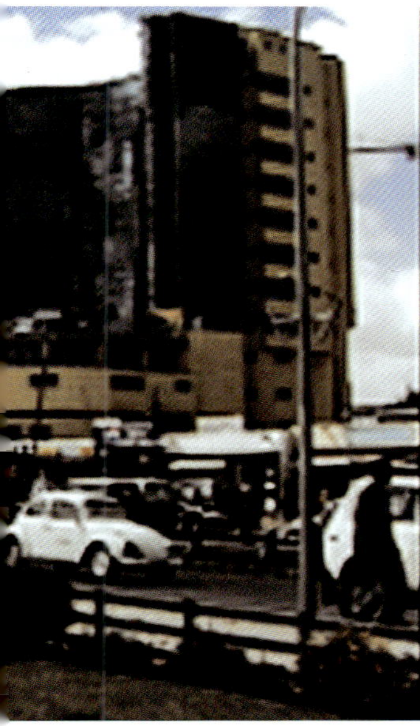

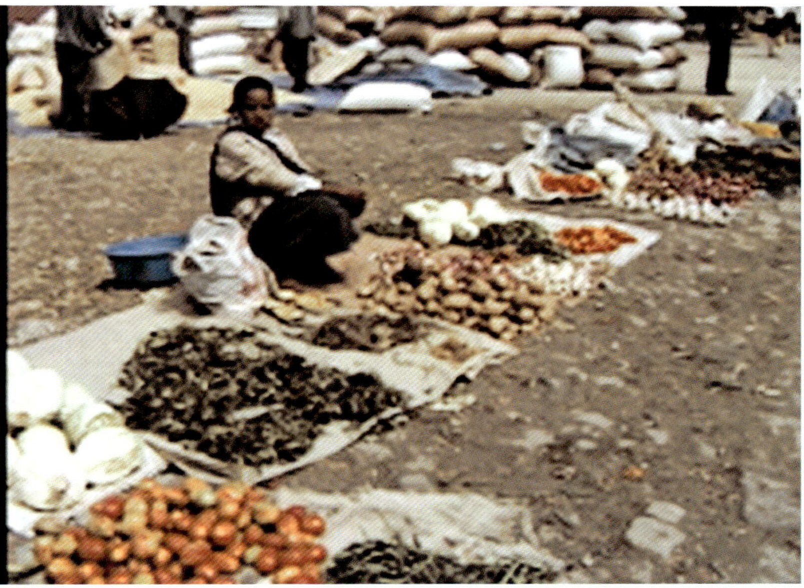

Negest, friends at one time and antagonists later, were Marxists who feuded with each other over an oxymoron of an ideological difference within the larger ideology of Marxism. They became ironic adversaries, both immersed in the affairs of the oppressed while other Marxists, led by the military, came to power.

The banality and dehumanised quality of life under industrial capitalism paved the way for Marxism in the West. Marxism and modernism are strongly connected in that Marxism summed up the sense of disillusionment with the world and embodied a disenchantment with material wealth. In the fervour for rapid change, Ethiopians were ambushed by a Western truth that addressed only a token of our reality and failed to articulate the context of our social and political construct. Mekuria contextualises this critical paradigm of Western epistemology into the cultural valuation of complex moments in Ethiopian history.

In *DELUGE*, Mekuria opens her story with the myth of the Queen of Sheba.

> She shall rise up in the judgment with this generation and shall condemn it: for she came from the utmost parts of the earth to hear the wisdom of Solomon: and behold, a greater than Solomon is here. (Matthew12:42)

It is said that Ethiopia was the first African nation to worship the one true God of the Old Testament and adopted the Judaic element in 1,000BC. According to legend, the worship of the true God was officially established by Queen Makeda, also known as Sheba. Makeda's union with King Solomon of Jerusalem produced Menelik I, the first emperor of Ethiopia and founder of the dynasty that would rule Ethiopia for most of its history and into the 1970s. It is said that after visiting his father, King Solomon, in Jerusalem, Menelik I brought the Ark of the Covenant to Ethiopia. The Ark is believed to be kept at the Cathedral of St Mary of Zion in Axum, the holiest shrine in Ethiopia.

Mekuria grew up in the city of Axum, the crossroads of antiquity, the social base of the old Semitic civilisation of Saba that spanned southern Arabia and the coastal areas of the Horn of Africa. Her father was the 'Nebure Eid' of Axum, a religious and secular position specially designed for Axum and another holy site in Addis Alem. Axum's famed architectural ruins, burial catacombs and granite stelae stand as a root metaphor for glory and are seen as the pinnacle of Judaism and Christianity. Mekuria renegotiates the symbolic control of a cultural point of reference and confronts the unfathomable darkness of desolation, tragedy and uncertainty by problematising this binary relationship of pride and mayhem. She reunites ideas and objects, diverging parallels of past events perceived in the present by transposing current themes into an imaginary past.

The triptych installation also contains the story of dislocation, of exclusion and the creation of the undesirable Other. It is a story of postcolonialism rather than of postmodernism that Mekuria addresses in her film *SIDET: Forced Exile* (1991). The film addresses the huge displacement of Ethiopians following a pandemonium of ethnic warfare, famine, political persecution and the social and economic dynamics of structural dependency. In terms of identity, Ethiopians are lumped as second-class foreign Others lacking historical and contextual ground. In *SIDET*, Mekuria conveys notions of identity where identity becomes a negotiated construct within the interplay of the social, cultural and political conditions of a society.

Modernism exists in the political and economic arena that has privileged its various discourses. Modernity and modernism in Ethiopia, both as a historical stage and as a cultural process, are unpleasant metaphors for the fact that underdevelopment assumes the contradictions of dependency and a postcolonial dominant culture. No doubt, the intervals between actions are infinitely variable in duration and content. Mekuria talks about a present of unresolved pasts, an ambivalent future, a disorderly coexistence of tradition and contemporaneity and nuances of modernity that are appropriated and debased.

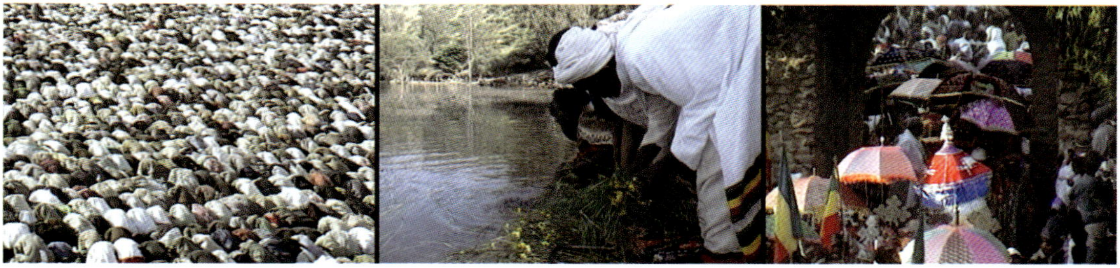

RUPTURES: A Many Sided Story, 2003.
Video stills of prayers.

Fault Lines and Shifting Landscapes in Contemporary African Art

Solomon Deressa

Fault lines: a metaphor borrowed from geology and used here to suggest the range and depth of fractures in the continuity of contemporary African art. The second metaphor – shifting landscapes – suggests a static spectator in front of changing tableaux, or, conversely, a spectator hurtling through space-time in a vehicle under someone else's control. In either case, the spectator's relation to the process remains ambiguous; (s)he is neither subject nor quite passive object. It is perhaps this sense of ambiguity that foists on fault lines a threatening appearance when they can just as easily be perceived as flexible vertebrae that facilitate dynamic play. In less self-conscious periods, African art has in fact responded energetically to shifts in the landscape, rearranging form until form is sacralised by the matrix that supports it. Private and public collections throughout the developed world are full of examples of this supra-formal response to the creative urge, a response that in part inspired Paris-based early twentieth-century Western art to break out of its exaggerated preoccupation with Euclidean niceties and prettified rationality. Until it met post-Renaissance Western art, African art had instinctively resisted seductive comeliness and melodrama.

Europe discovered African art from top down and partook of it as a cleansing and rejuvenating sacrament. Africa discovered Western art from bottom up and continues

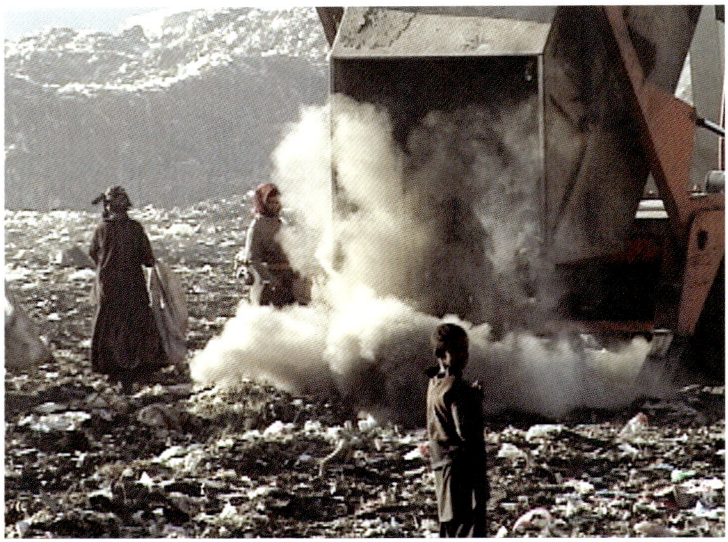

RUPTURES: A Many Sided Story, 2003.
Video still of Addis Ababa city dump.

to choke on it. Since all originality is an astute recycling of somebody else's notion, image, form, or turn of phrase, what might the source of Africa's problem with assimilation be?

The bedrock on which inter-generational alienation rides may be the continent's repeated tangles with slaving empires (Arab, Portuguese, French, British, Belgian, Spanish, American or Marxian) which have left Africans with a skewed sense of reality in which they perceive themselves through the eyes of the Other, yet perceive the conqueror according to the conqueror's narcissistic self-idealisation. That there have been equally ruthless intra-African conquests, and that some of these conquests were by slave-holding monarchies, does not exculpate the non-African imperial powers. After all, a black slave in a black society can, at least in principle, escape into the larger free society much in the same way that despised white immigrants who arrived as recently as in the post-glasnost era have melted into mainstream American society well ahead of African or Ojibwa or Sioux Americans who have been there from four hundred to ten thousand years. External appearance is a power to reckon with.

Claims to the contrary notwithstanding, even Ethiopia, the one African country that was never formally colonised from the outside, displays the tell-tale signs of victimisation by empire. (In passing, the same can be said of most Asian cultures.) This willingness to look up to Western, or, *faute de mieux*, Islamic cultures, dates back to the days of Christopher da Gama and Suleiman the Magnificent. Corroborative evidence is plentiful, but one example suffices. The break-up of Ethiopia and Eritrea into two nations, first in 1896 and then in 1991, has roots not in Asmara or Addis Ababa, but in Berlin, in November 1884 where, in the absence of any non-whites, Congolese interests were represented by the humanitarian Leopold II of Belgium. Clearly, this is not to argue for a backward re-imposition of Ethiopian hegemony over Eritrea, but it is to argue that, whether in politics or in aesthetics, marginal areas respond to dictates from the centres of empire.

Having said what needs to be said about empires, a cursory glance at the last five or six decades of African affairs suggests that it is not the empires that failed Africa, and consequently, African art. Empires do what empires have to do. After all, conquest is hardly practicable unless the conqueror is willing to fulfil the first duty of empire – more or less to dehumanise the Other. More as in the Tasmanian case, in which myth, art, language, poetry and Tasmanian flesh all permanently disappear off the face of the earth exactly eighty-eight years after the first white Christians settled in Australia. Or as in the Salvadorean example, where as recently as 1932, some thirty thousand Indians are rounded up and gunned down for the audacity of looking Indian or speaking their native tongue.[1] Goodbye form, goodbye texture, goodbye poetry. Less in cases like the Ethiopian, where one empire after another is invited in because Ethiopia, a peripheral, small-scale collection of cultures, is untutored in the ways of empire and ignorant of the context in which she operates. And finally, there is the test that all marginalised societies fail: giving up the assumption that their imperial interlocutors accept them as equals in a way that they do not accept other marginal or peripheral societies.

Although never paralysed by its weakness in the linear analysis that is the mainstay of European world hegemony, the African artistic tradition continues to pay a price for not recognising the value of after-the-fact analytic response. Analysis has served European civilisation by facilitating early detection of, and subsequent coming to terms with, tectonic shifts rather than allowing them to be amplified into fault lines of cataclysmic proportions. This has in turn cut down to size the seemingly unscalable peaks and unfathomable chasms that uninformed imagination tends to exaggerate into menacing demons. In the African case, not only do these peaks and chasms continue to sunder one generation from its predecessor, but they also render the act of looking back at one's point of departure

DELUGE, 1997. Video still by Mark Gunning showing a toppled statue of Lenin.

a futile exercise. Futile because the younger generation, instead of rebelling against its elders and thus acknowledging their authority, simply dismisses them. Consequently, any looking back, analyses and forecasts that do take place, come about courtesy of alien largesse.

But since all analysis is in part self-analysis, the foreigner's will remains, at least partially, foreign. Also, in art as elsewhere, imported maps to salvation tend to proceed down the proverbial primrose path, if not to the bonfire, then to Tennyson's Land of Lotus-eaters.[2] Savvy contemporary saviours tend to be invited, or even hired, by the Africans themselves and know to leave the Bible (if not the Qur'an) at home. But these are niceties that have little impact on inter-generational African discontinuities.

Succinctly put, the older, more traditional, generation is in deeper contact with the creative muses of the people, as well as with the day-to-day linguistic magic, but lacks the comprehension of the larger non-African world. And new technologies and techniques, ever the handmaidens of art, are predominantly the domain of the young – a situation not uniquely African. What makes it more of a problem in African art is the fact that Western education scuttles any chance of apprenticeship of the young to their elders and imbues the young with magical power that they are not ready to handle. The current AIDS crisis, by decimating a large proportion of the adult population, is bound to exacerbate an already bad situation.

Ethiopia's Marxist revolution turned into a nightmare not only because a functionally illiterate soldier took control of the affairs of state and chose to wing it on not much more than native wit, but also because even the learned theoreticians of the revolution did not mind a few basic facts, namely that Hegel's university tenure, Marx's university enrollment and the Scramble for Africa all took place in Berlin in the first forty years of the 1800s. They failed to mind that despite the inequities of Tsarist Russia, Lenin and the Bolsheviks hijacked an economy that in 1917 was growing faster than that of the

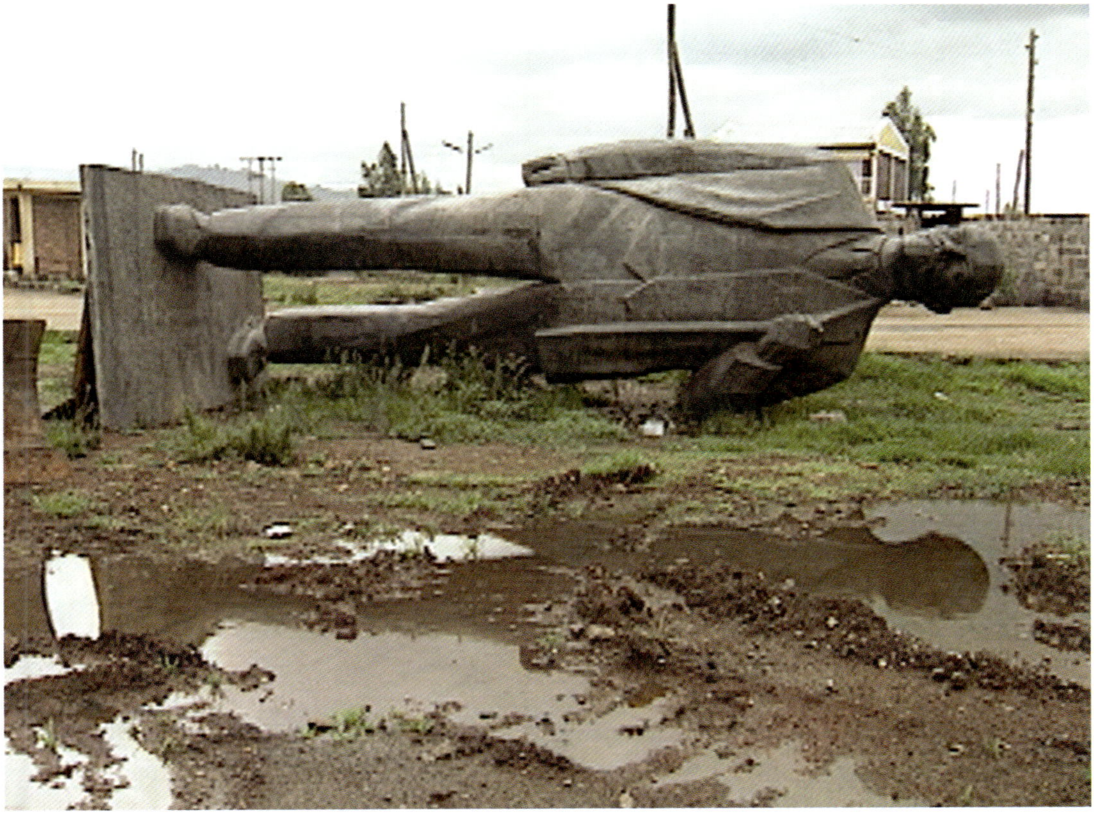

United States; that Russia was both backward and technically advanced at the same time; and that none of these things were true of Ethiopia in 1974, suffice it to mention serfdom and Nicolai Lobachevsky in one breath.[3]

Despite the relative poverty of the East European republics, Sekou Toure's Conakry and Mengistu's Addis Ababa could not have been but hardship posts for Marxist advisors from a moribund Second World that would soon line-up, hat-in-hand, alongside its disciples of yesteryear. Is this about the changing landscape of art? Absolutely. Particularly about the treacherous contours of the non-royal road to artistic integrity, continuity and freedom. The Ethiopian revolution had the audacity to produce an anthology of poetry that it entitled *The Rose Pen* – with a straight face! After such a title, to comment on the poems anthologised is to nit-pick.

The colossal statues of Marx, Engels and Lenin have been toppled by the populace, but Amharic, the language that was the primary beneficiary of Ethiopia's Marxist advances, still displays its numerous scars; it sounds like some sort of back slang, a ponderous Ethiopianese invented by bureaucrats with more aspiration than sense. The Amharic dictionary of socialist philosophy, compiled by native apparatchiks, manages to borrow not a single word from any of the eighty-some living Ethiopian languages. Instead, again and again, it makes a beeline for Ge'ez – a language dead these many centuries except to the theology of the Ethiopian Monophysite Church. Talk of contradictions African-style! Ge'ez failing, this dictionary, born of love of Ethiopia, resorts to the sister languages of Europe. Such is the power of self-misperception.

Whether dealing with the World Bank Group, the Museum of Modern Art, Marxist theory, postmodernism, or this or that artistic movement, the generative energies need to come from African psychic soil. The task is not so much one of intellectual acrobatics as one of refocusing one's senses on oneself, and then on one's small-scale community without forgetting that the larger world is, and always will be, out there and needs to be understood also.

DELUGE, 1997. Video still of footage from Ethiopian television showing a Menigistu parade.

It will be interesting to see what sort of spatial relations the organisers of the 2003 Venice Biennale will establish between the arts of Africa and those of the rest of the world. Interesting, but not of earth-shaking importance.

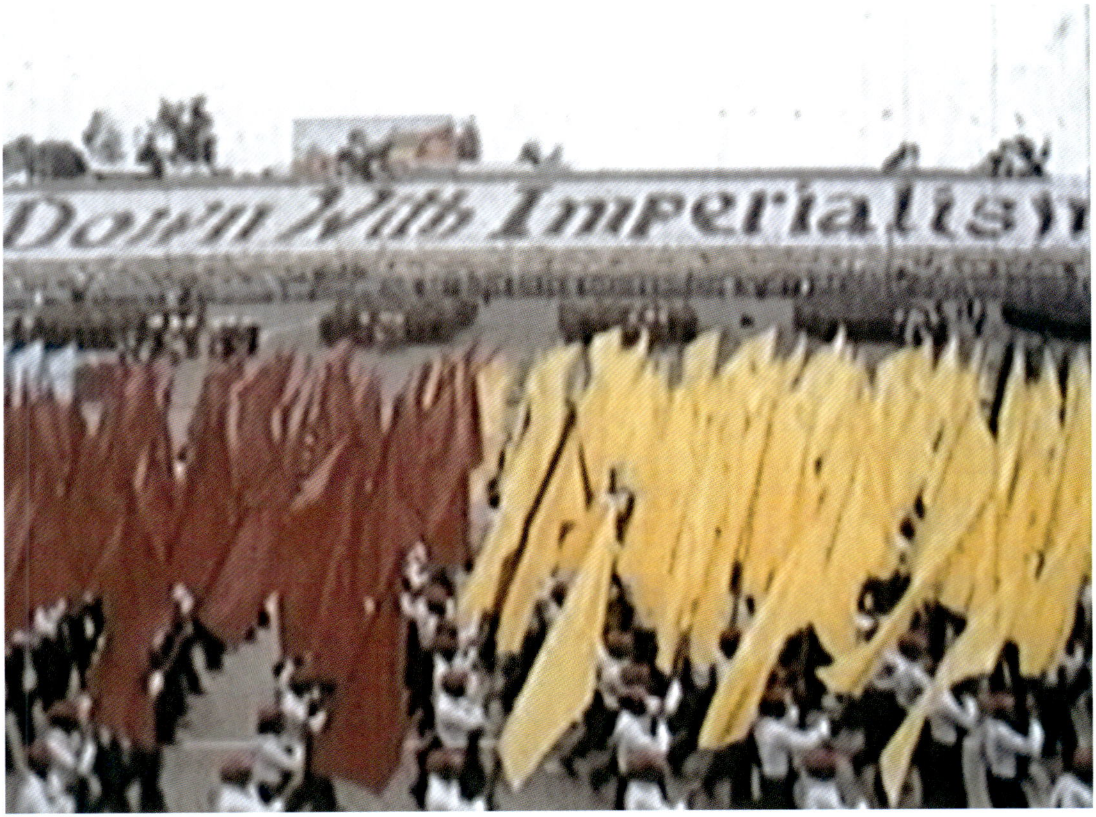

Emergent Forms: Sabah Naim Reconceptualises Movement

Yasmeen Siddiqui

Sabah Naim interrogates the possibilities of the gaze in this exhibition with her assemblages that are framed to relate two parts – an articulated photograph and a sculpture made from print media. Each piece suggests an entry to her evolving vocabulary of representations of city life. Signs are crafted with extrapolations from Cairo's street in order to posture the individual in their urban surroundings. The observations and ideas conveyed with dexterity and finesse in Naim's assemblages are elaborated on at a conceptual level in her first film that is also shown at this year's Venice Biennale.

For over two decades, art-historical discussion has rigorously engaged the concept of the gaze. Since the conversation began, the gaze has been subject to reconsideration vis-à-vis diversifying art audiences, art producers and art purveyors. Naim scrutinises an aspect of the gaze described by Norman Bryson:

> In so far as a manual or executive structure, moulded by the pressure of novel perceptual demands, and constantly falsified against the visual field, the schema is that which distorts reflection, that which can never produce representations containing 'true' information… the schema is an agent of anamorphosis, warping the visual field through a constant and internally consistent principal of deviation.[1]

The perceptual structure or grid, the schema, as expressed in the gaze Naim formulates, deconstructs outer realities and in the process of doing so purposefully disconnects from social formations. Naim transmits a reconfigured scenario revealing a gaze conveying the value system and hierarchy she uses to interpret movements.

Naim has been successfully negotiating the global art arena; she has entered it straddling a fault line, working at a time when artists appear to move around the globe, largely without apprehension or restriction. However, the majority of artists who participate on the international culture front arrive with a Western passport in hand, or a European language for communicating with key culture brokers. More often than

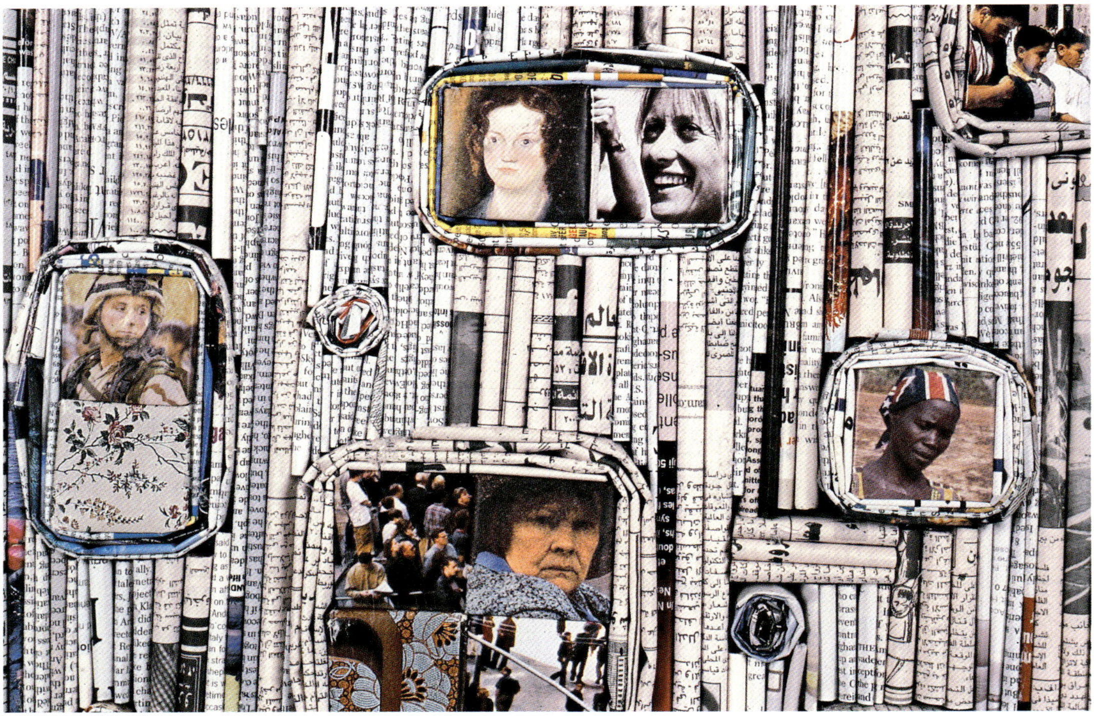

All images: *Untitled*, 2003. Mixed media.
Photographs: Muhammad Saif.

not, they also have independent financial support. However, artists such as Naim diverge from both this archetype of the trans-national artist and from possible expectations of what a Muslim woman contemporary artist might be. With conviction and clarity, Naim does not want to be discussed from the vantage point of feminist discourse.[2]

Reunion to Innovate the Gaze

Naim's photographic representations of the street's inhabitants and spaces had until now been exhibited as physically and conceptually distinct and separate from her wall-hanging sculptures looking at the political underpinnings of the media. Her painted and drawn upon photographs would be shown in the same space as her wall-hanging sculptures made of torn and reconstituted newspaper, but without a direct connection explicitly expressed. Relating the two art forms was the audience's prerogative rather than the artist's conception and creation. In this exhibition, Naim physically joins her articulated photographs and sculptures.

Presented with a new work that connects the two halves, the viewer is supplied a key. In both pieces, the decorative details – those added to the photographs and the patterns made of print media – reinforce the narrative. The painted and drawn details on the photographs are mirrored and magnified by the balls or massing spines made of newsprint, the two components juxtaposed to emphasise a decorative schema. The composition projects a gaze that, without hesitation, interrogates people's movement through the street and their relationships with those who share this space.

Alongside other Cairo-based artists (Hassan Khan, Heba Farid, Lara El Baladi, Moataz Nasr, Wael El Shawky for instance), Naim has been contemplating the organisation of the city and how public space is occupied and territorialised.[3] How does the passer-by negotiate their environment that forms and contorts in response and in reaction both to internalised social structures and modes of behaviour and to externalised physical obstacles and frameworks. For example, architect/artist

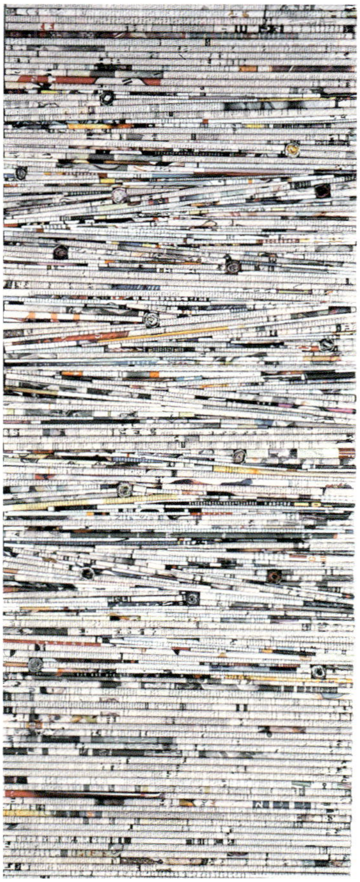

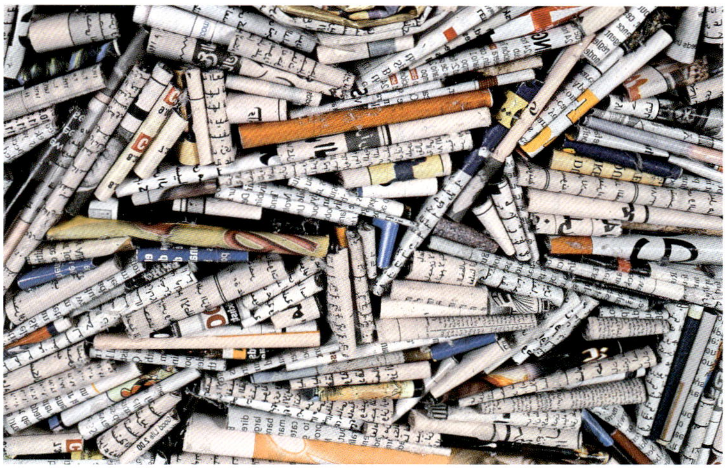

Tarek Naga built an installation, *Requiem* (2000), at the American University in Cairo that positions the viewer on a partially covered, wooden ramp that is in the process of warping and leads to a video loop of clippings from broadcast media. Drawing on French philosopher Henri Bergson, Naga's questions resonate in Naim's work that similarly interrogates the inherent instability and fragile equilibrium that permeate the behaviour of space. For Bergson, 'Form is essentially extended, inseparable as it is from the extensity of the becoming which has materialized in the course of its flow. Every form thus occupies space as it occupies time.'[14]

The process of building the assemblage begins with a photograph printed on a canvas. Naim renders the photograph, adding detailing with pen, ink, or paint. And then she sets the articulated photograph beside a panel of sculpted print media in one frame. Photographs are analysed and mined for material to extract and recompose according to Naim's intuitive reading of countless information bytes or perspectives captured in each image, rather than through an intellectual dissection of the scene. The gaze is formulated by Naim selecting and elaborating one or two stories from the plethora of interactions in the shot. To approach an understanding of these assemblages becoming two intimately connected halves – as images representing experiences, emotional connections and movement – demands individual attention.

Armed with a basic digital camera, Naim collects raw material. The details added to the photographs are extracted from elements revealed within the frame. For instance, a pattern on a skirt, a decorative architectural detail, or a section of graceful geometric tile work, is abstracted and the form is then drawn on to the image.

These articulations conjure a gaze that isolates characters in a scene, illuminating relationships between these individuals and qualitatively commenting on the characters and their occupation of space in the public sphere. The people in these candid, random photographs are anonymous. Different sorts of relationships appear: the familial bond of father and child walking a familiar path; an assortment of strangers waiting for

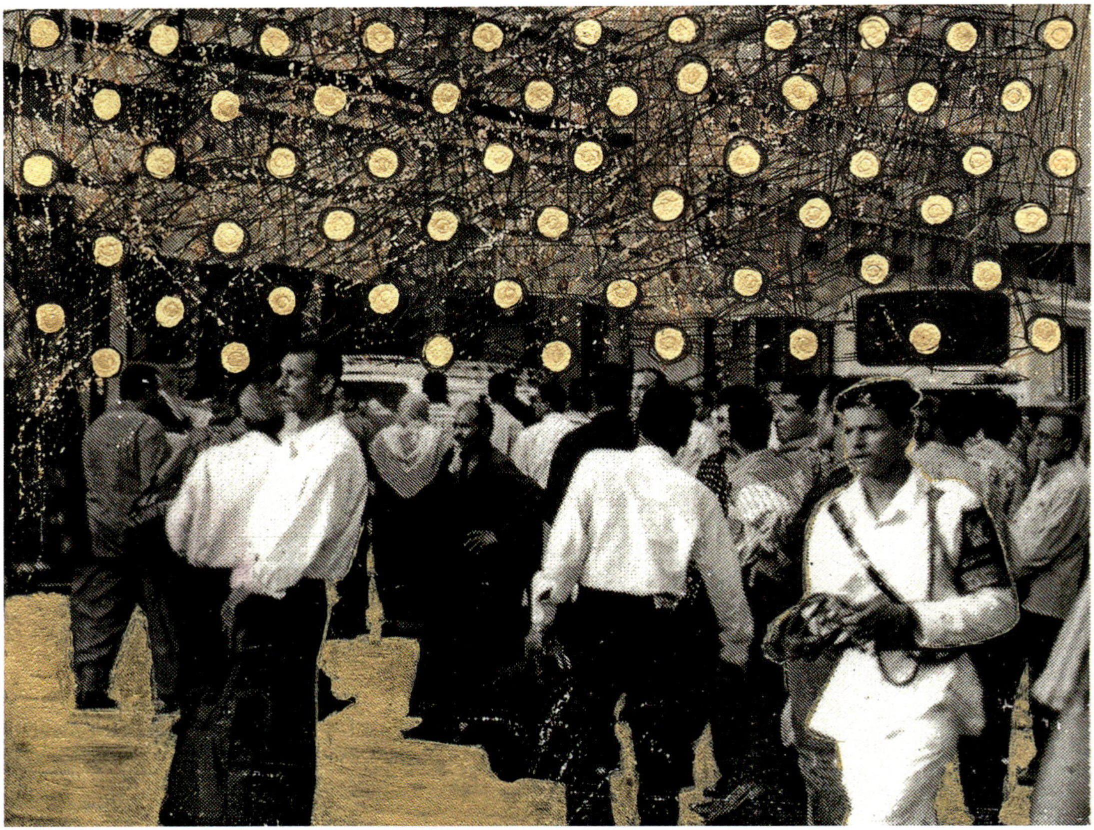

the same bus; or the displaced. Each frame reveals a scenario from the populated and lively, but also transient and abstract, shared street.

We can dissect her images, considering each space portrayed and its location. We can examine the spatial order, how structures are illuminated. And most critically we can consider how the represented space is experienced through her responses in the decorative details. Naim imbues the gaze with individuality and plays her chosen characters as part of a scene.

In each rendered piece, the narrative is coded. This process of modification distils, through colour and shapes and cuttings, Naim's perception. Every gesture and action is articulated by a set of rules afforded by the moment and extracted from the place from which the photograph originates. With its altered veneer, the finished image presents an enlivened gaze. Gold circles and flowers – reminiscent of the idealised four-petal version that children often draw – allude to innocence. Meanwhile, the harsh black slashes through the (usually male) passers-by speak of stripping the steadfast, erect and moving body from the scene. Although Naim resists a reading of her work through the filters of gender studies, in one piece it is difficult to ignore her aggressive response to the momentum exuded by a pack of men moving along the street. In contrast, parent/child pairings, women and people who do not overwhelm the frame – they are perhaps in transit, waiting for a friend or a bus – are articulated empathetically. Through each added detail, Naim permeates the street with her gaze by selecting figures to either embellish or negate.

Coupling two-dimensional photographs and three-dimensional assemblages so that they work in tandem suggests the potential influences of print media on society. Newspaper stands proliferate in Cairo, positioned at every major intersection, projecting opinions and information into the public domain. Naim claims her works assert a distinction between individual experience and the business of economics and politics conveyed by the press. The gaze standing alone, however, discloses a

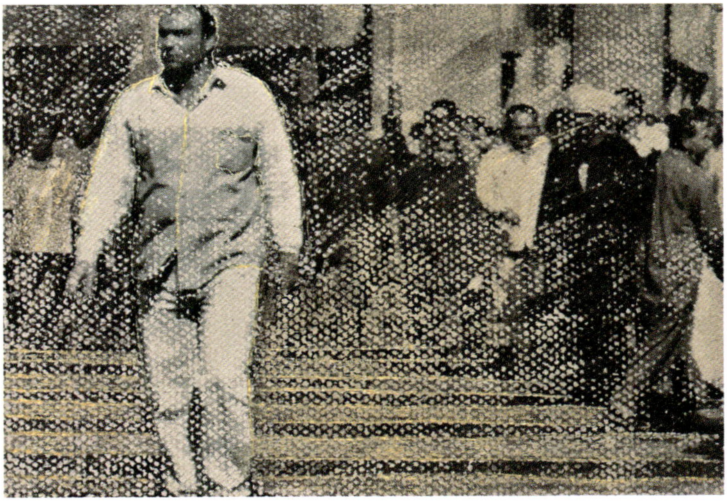

Left and right: *Untitled*, 2003. Mixed media. Photographs: Muhammad Saif.

more ambiguous divide between life and media. By mirroring representations of individuals in patterns made of print media, Naim expresses an intimate and informative relationship between the press and the people. Moreover, historically, newspapers and journals have provided women with a voice in the public sphere. Writing and publishing allowed women who, for social reasons, were prohibited from participating in public meetings to contribute to social and political movements.[5]

Contrasting the flatness of the photograph with the depth of the sculpture creates a dynamic gaze alluding to how print media's political and economic agendas might inform social behaviour as manifested in activity and movement. The eye glances back and forth resting for a moment on the singularity of a person and then moving to the matrix of layers of newsprint. The viewer is asked to question how the interloper – be it person or press – enters a physical or conceptual space and reconfigures that environment.

Represented in the sculptural half of the assemblage are the main characters taken from the photograph. This schematic device emphasises specific interactions and personalities. In one assemblage, sculpted segments from newspapers – arranged vertically and resembling the spines of books along a shelf – annunciate a series of black slashes drawn over a male pedestrian in the photograph. In another assemblage, portraits from the newspaper, framed in balls made from newsprint and set amidst a pattern of newspaper clippings, find their twin in the neighbouring photograph that leaves parallel faces undecorated, naked, exposed. Bi-directional, the gaze can potentially either gravitate from left to right – rendered photograph to sculpture – as viewers functioning in a European language might see, or from right to left – press to person – as Arabic readers might prefer.

Tearing segments from print media with the tenacity and politicism of Naim recalls a mid-twentieth century response to billboard consumerism in the form of *décollage*, which involved tearing from posters in public space. The movement went on to inspire the Situationist International, which questioned the relevance and agenda of

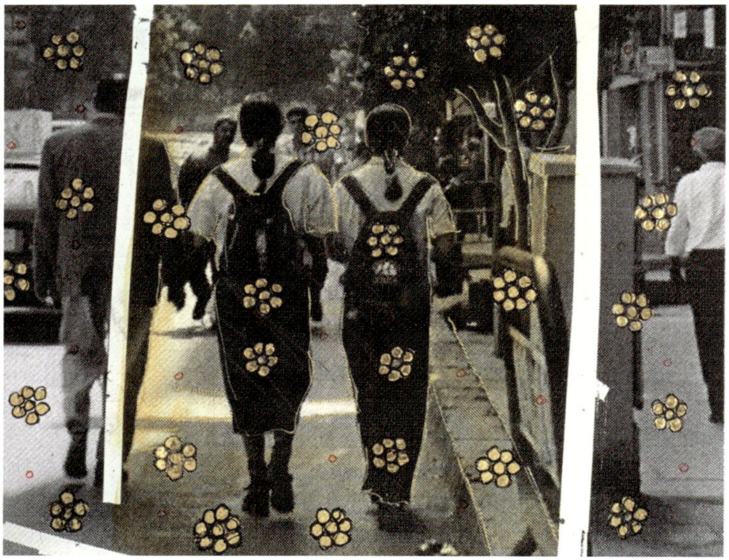

Left and right: *Untitled*, 2003. Mixed media. Photographs: Muhammad Saif.

advertising. Such sentiments are revived in our globalising world of tele-trading and rapid commercialisation.

As a medium for disseminating information newspapers print images of people associated with events or personalities. Naim's exhibited assemblages, however, challenge this assumption, as an array of the known and unknown appear alongside each other; one of the works includes the Brazilian super model Giselle, British actress Judi Dench, an African man and a soldier. By incorporating press images of people, some recognisable and others not, Naim questions the validity of print media as a disseminator of information. Why are some portraits associated with personalities and histories, while others are completely anonymous? Has Naim stripped personalities known to specific audiences and reduced them to faceless commentaries? Are the portraits of Judi Dench and Giselle nothing beyond archetypes to Naim?

Naim composes a gaze that calls into question the subject and its viewer. She examines how the media addresses the subject and what the subject means to its audience. Popular culture, militarism and random, foreign people are combined to formulate a gaze. Not all the included portraits engage every viewer. A strategic decision appears to have been made. Certain people, ideas and conventions are integrated to resonate with different audiences. Is Naim asking the viewer to reflect on who we know and understand and why? Or is she using this imagery simply as an aesthetic tool? What are an iconic face from a fashion magazine and an African face *à la National Geographic* doing in the same sculpture? She presents a puzzle that can be reassembled in different ways. According to what values and hierarchies does Naim assert and pattern the image? And does it strengthen or weaken her claim that the media is removed from living reality?

Move through Space and Time

Naim's line of questioning about what informs social behaviour and the impact individuals have on the formation of public

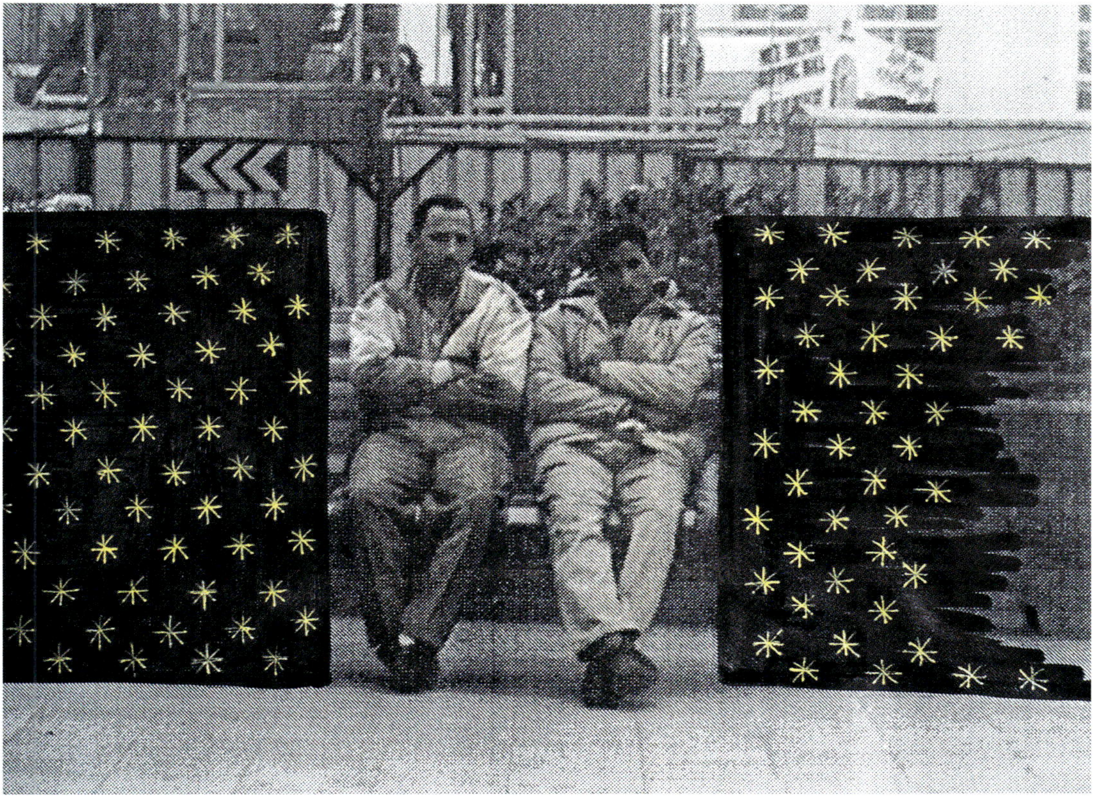

space culminates with her use of film. Employing the same technique of altering images using ink, pen, paint and also filters, Naim explores the frame that builds a film. In her bifurcated photograph and sculpture assemblages exhibited in a neighbouring space, Naim codifies personalities and movement and relationships. She touches on common concerns and hegemonic forces that inform our perception of the space we inhabit, how we should move through it and our impact upon it.

Entering the space where the film is projected, the interloper finds four potential surfaces and one is used to screen the film. Naim's fifteen-minute, black and white film is projected in an enclosed cube large enough to engulf the viewer.

Anthropologist, Pascal Augé, formulated an intriguing idea – 'any space whatsoever' – in his effort to elucidate the effects of modern urban planning on the human psyche and interpersonal relationships. This term describes an anonymous public space that functions as a film or theatrical set, as a point of transit between places of importance. You are in a square; you are there only because you are passing through en route home, or to the doctor's office, or work. In these spaces individuals become depersonalised. These places become homogenous, desingularising spaces.

Gilles Deleuze looks at the flipside of Augé's 'any space whatsoever' to explore how philosophers, artists and scientists, for example, attempt to create a sense of order and award value and meaning to 'anonymous' moments. In contrast to Augé, Deleuze – and in this vein also Naim – creates a condition for the emergence of uniqueness and singularity. The conventional, all-pervasive gallery space of the white cube serves a similar function; you enter to be taken to a conceptual space constructed by the artists and modified by the filter the viewer wears.[6]

Footage of a Cairo street during rush hour begins the art experiment that involves using pen and paint and filters to identify relationships and interactions. Paintings, drawings and decorative sketches are superimposed on to the images as a means of isolating individuals who enter the frame/set. Filters are used to highlight

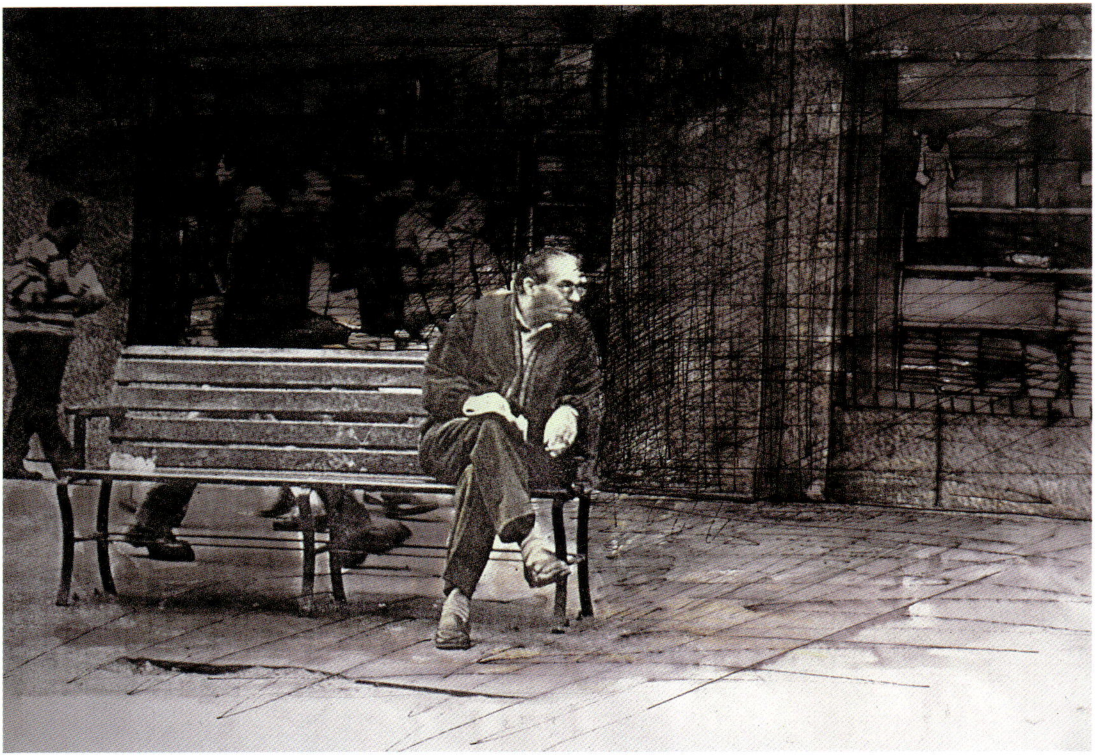

certain characters, bringing them to the forefront to usurp the frame from the street/set. The soundtrack remains faithful to the sounds of the street, altered only slightly to draw attention to an illuminated figure.

The candid and documentary-like quality of the footage, its rawness, implies authenticity and legitimacy as a snap shot of live, real time captured on film. Perhaps as a means of challenging this presumption, Naim highlights the false movement of film by deconstructing it into its frames. Each frame is articulated, altering the raw footage to convey a narrative. Isolating each frame with detailing, distinguishing it from the next frame that captures a moment 1/25 of a second later, Naim draws attention to the mechanism that reproduces an event as film does. When Naim deletes, illuminates, blurs and slashes bodies, the background, or buildings, she renders a wholly different meaning to the scene. Naim does not look to reveal the space in its essence but identifies specific narratives from the whole.

Breaking the moving image into its components, identifying movement as it is set in motion by the mechanical action of projecting frame by frame to affect a moving image points to the falseness of film as a record or document, especially broadcast media, and by implication print media.

Naim's Lexicon

What happens in and to public space? Physical structures form the set providing triggers and guides that direct movement and behaviour. People occupy space infusing the street with energies and also their physical presence. Larger, omnipresent, governmental and official forces enter the public sphere through the media. Naim codifies these forces in her assemblages and film to express how space is constructed and choreographed not only for sight, but also as visual markers and symbols that reference other sensations and relationships between bodies and objects. Naim interrogates the interrelatedness of people and place, the generative clash between figures and movement, building a visual vocabulary to describe the relationship between viewer and viewed.

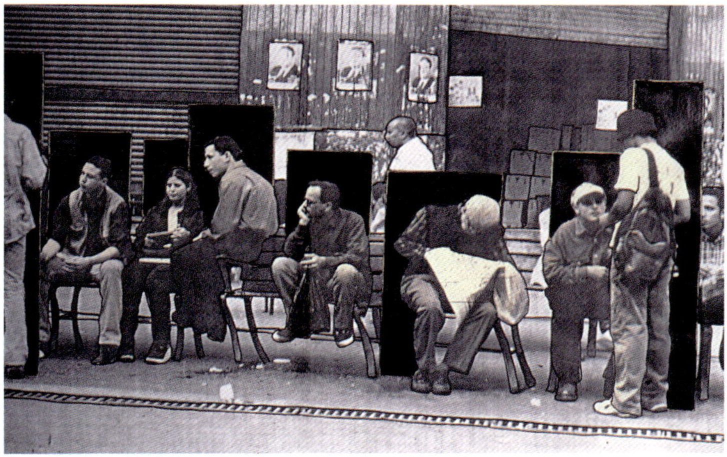

Left and above: *Untitled*, 2003. Mixed media. Photographs: Muhammad Saif.

Moataz Nasr, or the Evidence of Things Not Seen

Simon Njami

Moataz Nasr is Egyptian. In Senegal in 2002, at the Dakar Biennale, he discovered that he was also African. Of course he was aware of this before, but the physical experience of being in the darker side of the Sahara desert made him appreciate fully, for the first time, the indelible familiarity that exists between the different countries of the African continent. Regardless of – or perhaps because of – their history and regardless of their different influences and priorities shaped by different geopolitical and cultural climates, he could not help becoming aware that all those countries face the same questions. Any attempt to decipher the essence of Nasr's work has to make this realisation its starting point. An Africa suffering for lack of self-determination and for want of a dream. An Africa robbed of its dreams by the constraints of economic and political necessity. An Africa shackled by insoluble contradictions that prevent it from writing its own history.

Hence Nasr's Egypt is only a metaphor for a web of issues that reach far beyond the strictly local confines of his country. The work presented here is the product of fifty years of independence echoing questions posed throughout the continent, and beyond this, perhaps even echoing the basic questions posed by existentialist philosophers such as Edmund Husserl and Jean-Paul Sartre. What is freedom? What is initiative? How should we view ourselves within a context that is both specific and invasive? How should we view ourselves outside this context? And finally, who are we exactly when we say 'I'? Is this 'I' simply the echo of a history of which we are at once the inheritors and the destroyers? Does this 'I' represent a specific and unique entity, genuinely and intrinsically free to seek fulfilment? Or are we rather condemned to play our part in a collective story, the dénouement of which was predetermined way back in the mists of time? A story of which we can never become the author, as our deeds, our gestures and our most private thoughts have already been formulated for us? What does this 'I' represent, ultimately, if not an aborted dream? A useful dream, such as the illusion of pan-Africanism which never came to

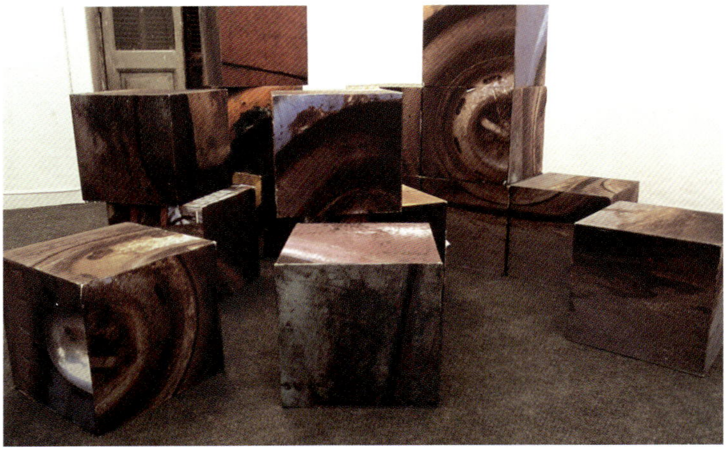

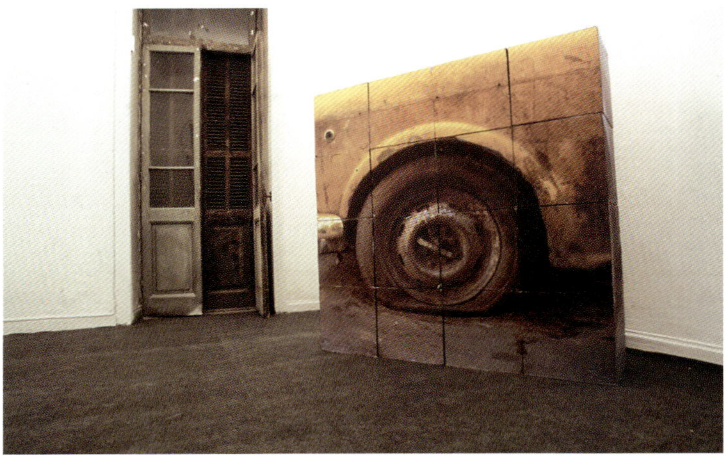

Fiat Nasr, 2002. Mixed media installation.

pass or the illusion of independence movements which happened to become nothing but failures and disappointments?

The answer is complex and presupposes an in-depth analysis of the postcolonial phenomenon that has helped to shape the essence of contemporary Africa. However, artistic creativity, providing a magnified reflection of the societies that have forged it, none the less offers us a few sketchy outlines of an answer. Born of historical upheavals, these artists carry the germ of the ideas that could enable us to decode a phenomenon that affects the entire planet. They are more or less the same age as the independent states of Africa. It opens up inexorably the path that leads to searching self-analysis, which in turn triggers the questioning of invalid assumptions. For unlike their Old World contemporaries, the children of this generation have every right to assume a familiarity with countries that they view as their equals.

Nasr is Egyptian, as we were saying, but by labelling him, we do not mean in any way to diminish the scope of his thinking or his aims. On the contrary, our view of the world is conditioned by what we are and by the unique experience that has made us thus. And if this experience may be transformed into something shared by humanity as a whole, it none the less keeps its specific social and historical context. This is echoed by the Ghanaian artist El Anatsui's observations on globalisation, or on universalism and its perverse effects: 'As for hybridity, the hybridisation of cultures, as of now, is to me more of a conjecture than a reality. I do not buy the idea of a universal culture. Every culture has its essence which, like the soul of man, you cannot change or infect easily.... Unless a culture has strength, it cannot contribute effectively to a universal, or multiversal, dispensation, and that, perhaps, is why it is dangerous for an artist easily to throw away his cultural heirloom and superficially take on an alien one.'[1] The question of identity – which clearly goes beyond the limits of nationality – is therefore central and fundamental to any movement towards freedom, because it is by knowing who we are and where we come from that we can share with the Other. And this very freedom is the identity claimed

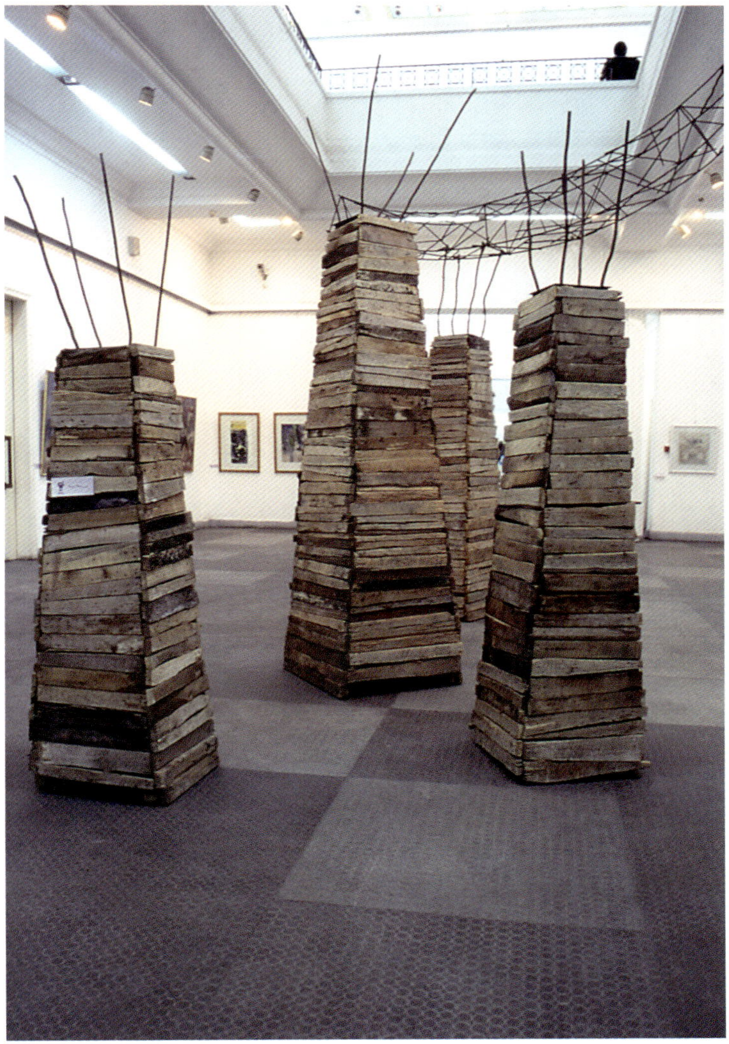

Modern Egyptian Obelisks, 1998.
Mixed media installation.

by Nasr. Multiple and singular. He will never leave his country, as he feels he has both rights and responsibilities there. He would not be who he is were it not for the legitimacy conferred on him by this mass of land. Abstract debates concerning the role of the artist – constantly rehashed over recent decades to take account of changing tastes and preoccupations – do not concern him.

Nasr is a true artist in that the fundamental question posed by his work has nothing to do with its usefulness, but rather forms part of the very essence of his personal experience: the air he breathes, his childhood memories, or – to use a word that is sometimes bandied about rather too easily – his 'roots'. It is this humanity that dictates his choices, not some popularist determination to democratise the act of artistic creation. The boundary between the private space of his studio and the public space in which the work is delivered up to the world is clear. The *agora*, the collective space of the museum or social meeting place, represents a discrete stage in the life of the work and one that is quite distinct from the act of creation. In Nasr's case, this does not suggest a return to the myth of the artist in his ivory tower, in splendid isolation from the world. Instead, the studio is the space to which the artist invites his street, his country, his continent and the world. The encounter that takes place there involves him, but as a protagonist in that world, in a necessary form of schizophrenia. An observer and commentator in the outside world, an anonymous constituent in the great mass of the people, once back in his state of solitude, he dissolves in the midst of those whom hitherto he had regarded as an alien body. In the silence of his studio he deconstructs the feelings and intuitions, the reflections and observations that he has brought back with him from the world outside. It is also within this privileged space that the osmotic process – transforming the self into the 'observed' – takes place. In this context, the word 'studio' should not be taken to mean the cloistered space occupied by artists in nineteenth-century Europe, however. Rather, it simply expresses the notion of a private space, reserved for the artist. It conveys that

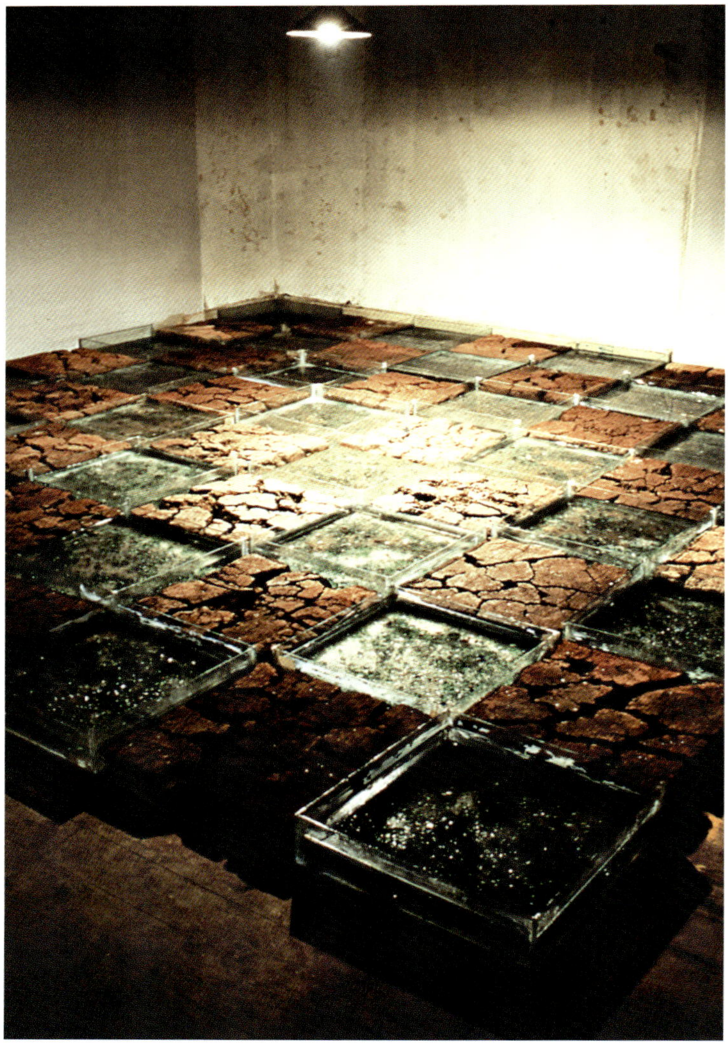

The Earth, 2000. Water and clay installation at Townhouse Gallery, Cairo.

ineffable moment when all the fragments of a complex tapestry suddenly come alive and arrange themselves around a specific framework. The notion of the studio or workshop should be experienced as a metaphor for a specific moment, a time of unique lucidity.

A conversation with Nasr – about rain or beauty, women or cigarettes – speaks volumes and is far more illuminating than any speech or lecture. He holds within him a suppressed anger and tension that only find full expression in his work. He has created his Egypt, a land at odds with the useful dream that has fed the struggle for freedom. He loves his people, but would like to love them more deeply, to help them to love themselves. For him, artistic commitment is not just an empty phrase. He has a part to play, like any other citizen, in his country's development. But this commitment should not be confused with the will to produce 'useful art', as championed by intellectuals such as Cheikh Anta Diop: a didactic form of education for the masses. The freedom that is implicit in all forms of creativity cannot be made subservient to the political aims of a Marxist-inspired philosophy, which itself obeys the revolutionary blueprint adopted by those who have fought for the independence of African countries and which envisaged the subjugation of the individual to the collective. This is a form of commitment concerned more with self-analysis; with the suggestion, through the feeling conjured by an image, of a sound or gesture; with sowing the seeds within the spectator of a reflection that is the only route to gaining awareness. Nasr's commitment corresponds to the quest contained in every artistic act, as defined by André Gide when he claimed that art is nothing but a political and social commitment.

Nasr's earlier works, many of which use video, also display this constant impulse to toy with the spectator's emotions and feelings. Video images are never used in isolation, but are invariably set within a precise architectural framework. In *One Ear of Dough, One Ear of Clay* (2001), the spectator is overwhelmed by a looming wall of ears which seem to both hear and see, a scary scenario which plunges us into a

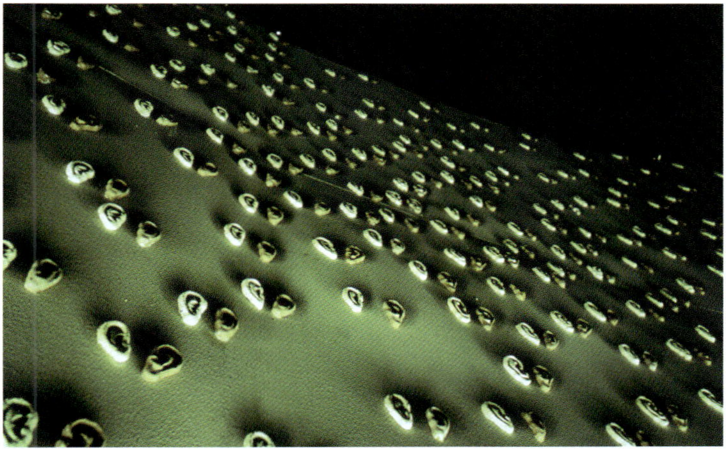

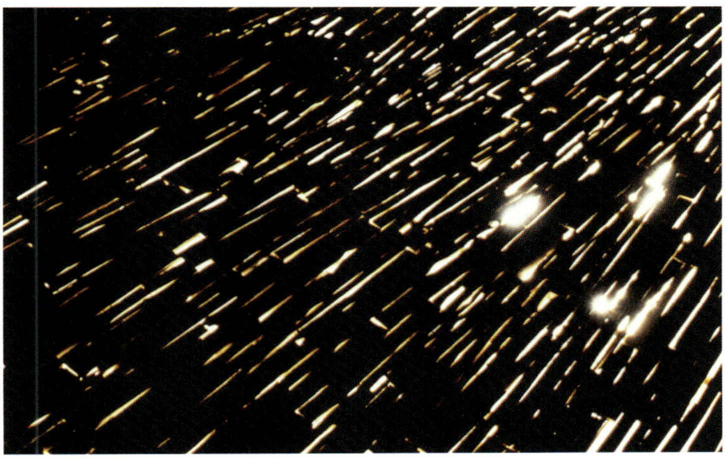

Above: *One Ear of Dough, One Ear of Clay*, 2001. Mixed media installation. Below: *The Sky*, 1999. Wood.

waking nightmare. The screen at the end of the wall acts as a counterpoint. The piece as a whole is an image of the totalitarian power of an omnipresent state and could easily be subtitled 'walls have ears'. In *Wheelchairs* (2001), we find ourselves in a sort of cinema auditorium, in which the audience – in the form of empty wheelchairs – gazes at the screen, evoking the metaphor of a sick society watching its life unfold before its very eyes. But rather than hammering his message home like a television evangelist, Nasr allows us our freedom. The forms are there to articulate those things that cannot be expressed. He leaves us free to see whatever we want to see in the wheelchairs according to our own individual conscience. In this way, a metaphor that has its origins in a commentary on Egyptian society proves equally valid in Paris, Dakar or New York. The finger is pointed at this state of impotent passivity to which we are all condemned at some time or other. We find this passivity again in a work such as *Water* (2002). Whereas in *Wheelchairs* we may act as both protagonists and spectators, in *Water* we are definitively condemned to watch and are denied any power to act. Like the waters of the Red Sea before they parted to let the Jewish people pass, the water that stretches out before the spectator seems to pose an insurmountable barrier. And we are forced to stand and watch, powerless to act, as a man appears to drown on a screen at the far side.

Powerlessness and frustration seem also to form the foundations of Moataz Nasr's latest project, *Tabla* (2003). The *tabla* is a small drum and, in African culture, the drum has traditionally been used to create not only sounds but also meanings, using a precise and established syntax to set up dialogues. Here, in a new play on the Hegelian paradox of master and slave, Nasr creates an opposition between the Drum and drums, the individual and the masses. Here again, social commentary is never far away. Returning to a scenario which he has used in other works and which sets up a dialogue between installation and video, he places some four hundred drums in front of a screen. Immediately, we are reminded of an orchestra and its conductor, which is

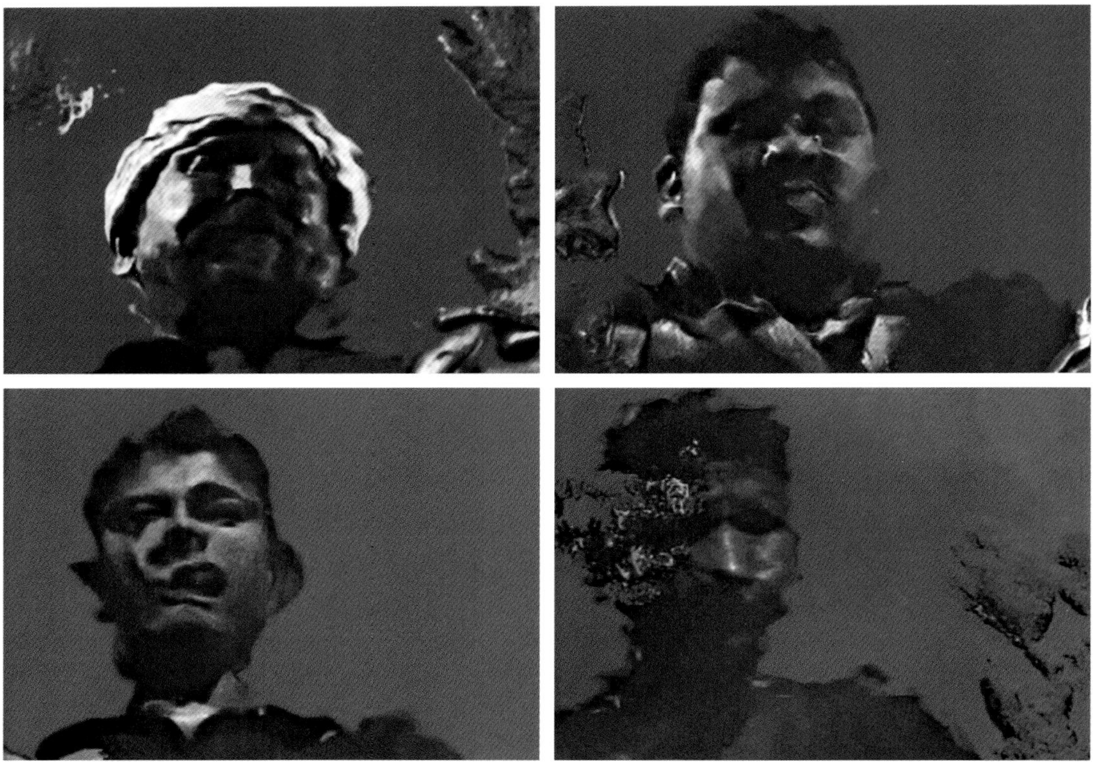

Water, 2002. Video stills.

further reinforced by the appearance on the screen of a musician whose face is hidden. We see only his hands, pounding the taut skin. The drum on the screen is elaborate, while those in the space in which the viewers stand are common or crude. Here Nasr brings the drama of power back to centre stage.

As I write these words, it is impossible not to project oneself beyond the national frontiers of Egypt. This work is not merely about the impossibility of dialogue between a particular leader and a particular people. The clamour of these drums, this cacophony orchestrated by the conductor according to his whim summons us back to the cacophony presently spreading before our eyes, from New York to Baghdad. What freedom and what choice do people have, save to follow their leaders' commands with blind obedience? While Nasr offers no definitive answer to these questions, he nevertheless allows us a glimpse of what James Baldwin described as 'the evidence of things not seen'.[2] The truth, if it exists, is more complex than it appears. But it requires that we should be constantly questioning, incessantly challenging the established order of things. Our voices, like those of these crude drums, are no less important than those of our leaders.

Moataz Nasr appears to have made it his mission to decode ideas that have been accepted with too much haste. He seeks to train the spotlight of his rigorous approach on the contradictions that we are expected to accept as theorems, on the aberrant courses of action that are sold to us as views of the future. He is not motivated by any political activism, nor by any messianic zeal to replace the old truths with new ones. Nasr seeks simply to safeguard for art the elements required for its own contradictions. For him, art and life are inseparable, as observed by Pierre Restany thirty years ago: 'Art is a phenomenon of language, and only that. Language, the expression of men's thoughts, is a living thing. There are times when the oscillating movements of art become locked or stuck, when art appears to have lost the internal factors necessary for its own counter-arguments, when it seems to be cut off from life.'[3]

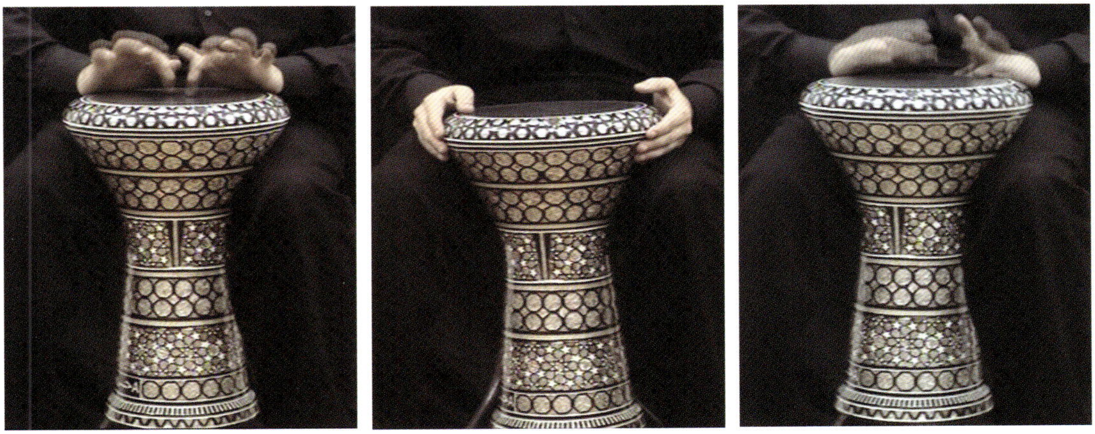

Tabla, 2003. Video stills.

So You Wanna Be...?

Niru Ratnam

I

I remember the first anti-globalisation march that took place in London. I'd heard that something was going to happen – I think I might even have briefly surfed the internet for information about it. Nevertheless I was too wrapped up in what I was doing and to be honest, the demonstration hardly figured in my consciousness. I left my gated loft-style apartment in Shoreditch to go down to Liverpool Street station. I was on my way to a meeting in a gallery in the West End, filled with the self-importance of a ligger who's made good. I was wearing a pair of slip-on Merrills, those three-quarter length trousers that were briefly fashionable on men that year, a v-neck vest top and a pair of wrap-around shades. When I got to the station, it was clear that I wasn't going anywhere. The place was filled with protestors, a variety of crusties, trancers, drum-bangers, students and skater-kids. I phoned up the gallery and told them that there was no way I could make the meeting. I considered my options – the demonstration looked not only fun, but as if something important was going on. Yet I was quite clearly clothed inappropriately – more for a fashionable bar than an anti-globalisation demo. But then again, the only person who seemed to notice that was me.

II

We live, more than ever before, conscious of the networks, narratives and discursive structures that, at best, surround us – but more often, attempt to place us and keep us in an allotted space. Such structures are often conceptualised as being like the internet, sprawling, without a centre and infinitely regressing into links and pathways. Networks of capital that position us as happy shoppers, narratives of information that assure us that it is our desires that they are satisfying. It is increasingly recognised that this myriad of endless loops are dangerous forms of power structures precisely because of their lack of centre. As Michael Hardt is so fond of saying, there are no Winter Palaces to storm anymore. There are no headquarters from which these networks of power emanate – just depersonalised power moving with stealth and rapidity, viral-like.

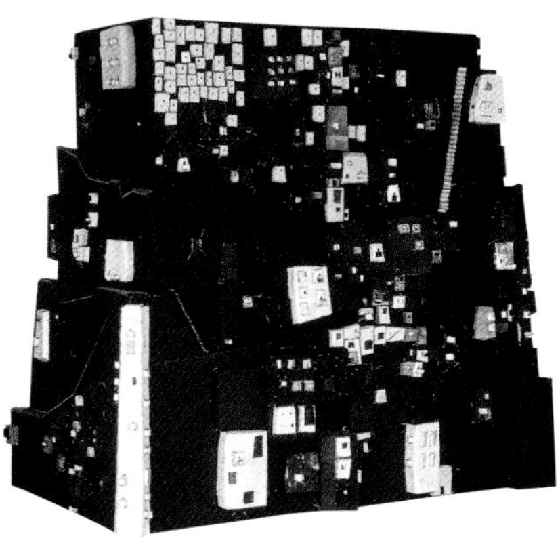

Untitled, 2001. Installation (detail), tarmac, galvanised wire, liquid tar, silver paint and wood, approx 2.95 x 4 x 1.75m.

But yet, we too form networks, work within structures, desire and gain pleasure from narratives. And perhaps, we'll revolt through them too. Although we are hailed, some element of agency remains; we choose to participate in certain networks and narratives in certain ways, to interact, to misunderstand, to allow ourselves to be momentarily placed, sutured into moments of productivity. To enter into doorways and rooms and territories that perhaps, on the face of things, we ought not to enter.

III

The doorway seems to have been drenched in tar – and there's some sort of script above it. Inside, there is noise. The sound of an orator, speaking seemingly urgently but in a language I do not understand – Arabic perhaps. There is also another insistent sound and this time I do recognise it – Cypress Hill's 'Superstar'. The walls have a number of concrete, silver and graphite windowpanes and balconies on them. They are lathered with a thick, viscous, oily, black, tarlike substance. Asphalt and liquid tar. *Sidi El Asphalt's Mulid* (2001). A saint's dance for oil whilst others wage war for it. Permanent war, perhaps the only way for capital to keep hold of a loosening grip. The balconies and the windowpanes are hung at all heights. They are also hung in adjoining rooms. They make the installation seem like an Egyptian alleyway or mini-townscape. A cabinet contains sweets – the thick, glutinous type alien to the boiled candy aisles offered by the grimy shops in the towns I grew up in. Fluorescent lights bathe this and one other of the adjoining two rooms of the installation in a bright, sickly glow. In the second room there is a deliberately badly executed mural with a deliberately amateurish figure of a camel on it. Its hump seems to contain craters, but on closer inspection they turn out to be speakers. There's no centre to any of this. In the first room, there is a film being projected. At first we see a belly dancer. Then she is replaced by a woman in a headscarf who swings her head and her body violently from side to side following the dervish in front of her. Others appear around her carrying out the same motion,

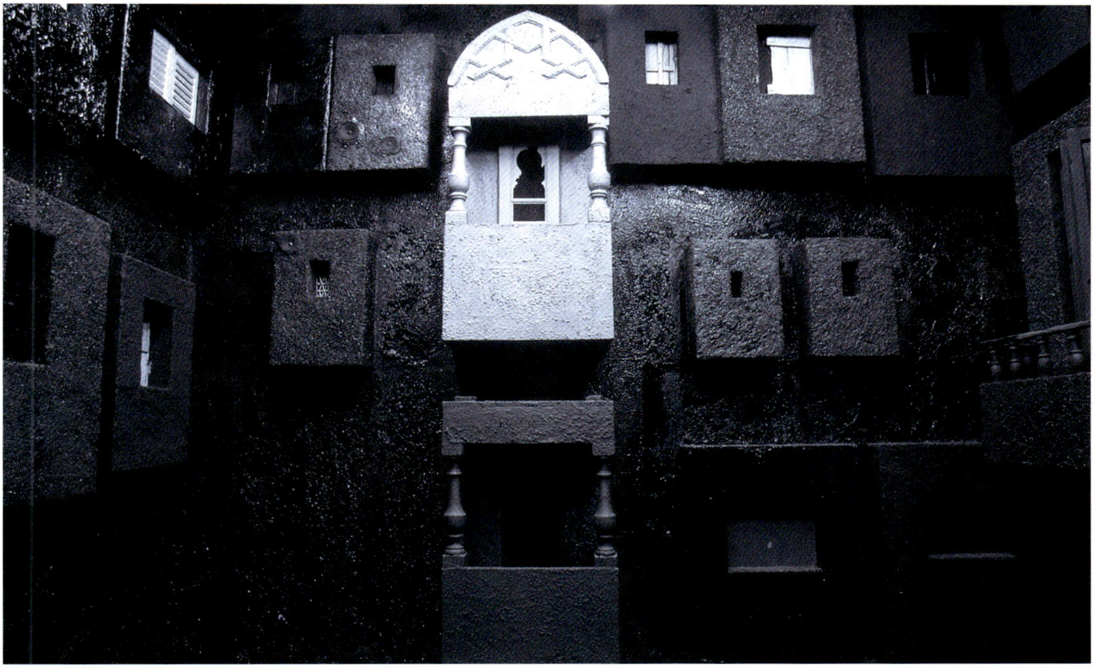

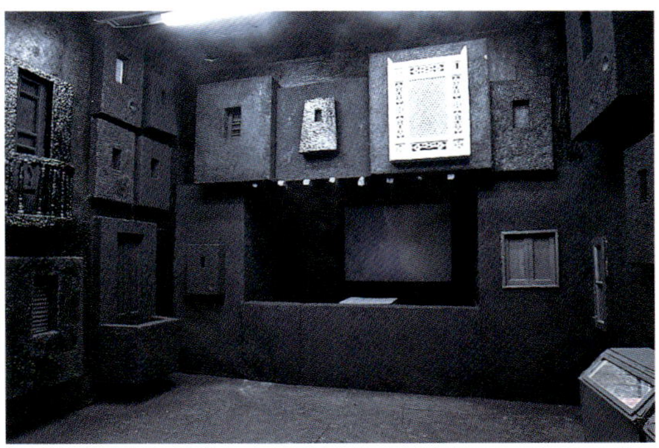

Above and right: *Sidi El Asphalt's Mulid*, 2001. Installation, asphalt, liquid tar, *gazairya* (traditional Egyptian sweets), silver paint, speakers, projector and mixed media, three rooms, each approx. 440 x 550 x 650cm.

dancing from side-to-side, the whole of their bodies locked into movement. They are following the dervish. They are following the urgent, almost hectoring tones of the orator. They are following Cypress Hill. So you wanna be a rock superstar?

IV

Wael Shawky, March 2001: 'The poetics of *Sidi El Asphalt's Mulid* are based upon political and social elements in contemporary Egyptian society, starting with the economic transformations of the 1970s leading through the waves of immigration to the Gulf in the 1980s and globalisation in the late 1990s up to the present moment.... The *mulid* [a festival to celebrate a birth] is a stereotypical image of Egyptian society that encompasses all its coexisting contradictions without allowing any of its poles to affect the other negatively or positively.'

V

Contradiction and transition. The nomad and the migrant are key figures for theorists of globalisation. They offer hope through their refusal of the positions allotted to them by capital. Wael Shawky explains, 'In its nomadic nature, the Bedouin community becomes a metaphor of sorts for globalisation; borders and space are broken and the tribal nature of nomads finds an equivalent in the idea of shared interests raised by the owners of capital – the driving force behind globalisation.'[1] Meanwhile, in London, the underclass of illegal immigrants keep the city going – doing the cleaning, cabbing, portering – all the jobs that the good citizens of this vibrant cosmopolitan city don't particularly want to do themselves. Not everyone's a cleaner – there are the pimps, hookers and hustlers. Beggars knocking on the windows of my convertible, reminding me of dim memories of Sri Lanka. Urchins and the disfigured, with plastic white cups for begging bowls. *Sidi El Asphalt's Mulid (Transitions)*, 2001, is a three-screen video projection with each screen viewed simultaneously. Some of the music is by

Sidi El Asphalt's Mulid (Transitions), 2001.
Three looped videos (unsynchronised),
5mins 20 secs, 6 mins 40 secs and
7 mins 50secs.

Gorillaz. I recognise it – I've got the CD above my stereo. The screen on the left keeps returning to images of the desert and the screen in the middle keeps returning to images of agriculture and pasture. On the other screen, some of the images are of a public religious festival – a *mulid*. As Shawky says, 'An essential part of the *mulid* is *zekr*… a Sufi religious ritual to reach a higher spiritual level or… a state of transition.' Transition and contradiction: the nomadic society is transforming to an agricultural society, the participants of the *mulid* are seeking a transition to a higher spiritual dimension. The band's been transformed into cartoon characters but I reckon I can still make out Damon Albarn's voice. Sufi magical squares appear on the screens. As Shawky notes, 'The interesting part is the way of translating a religious belief into a digital system of communication (you can not change any number or the matrix will lose its function).'

VI

There's no getting away from it. They look like they're dancing to Cypress Hill. Of course, they can't be, unless the dervish is into hip-hop or something. They look like they've been slowed down, edited to fit into the music and they do fit very well. A perfect, pop-video type fit. Can you get perfect fits between constituencies that know little and care to know little about the other? Is it just a piece of digital manipulation learnt in art school, culled from MTV? Or do they just, incongruously, fit for a moment? Or is the act of fitting them together the site of productivity and questioning?

VII

For Venice, Shawky proposes to do nothing less than recreate a popular public district. There will be buildings drenched in asphalt and liquid tar. The audience will be able to walk through narrow alleyways. Wael Shawky explains how, 'faith in the chemical content of the materials is the product of a long-entrenched religious culture, while the functionalism of building and construction comes out of a system based upon cultural pragmatism'.[2] There will be a series of images on screens and

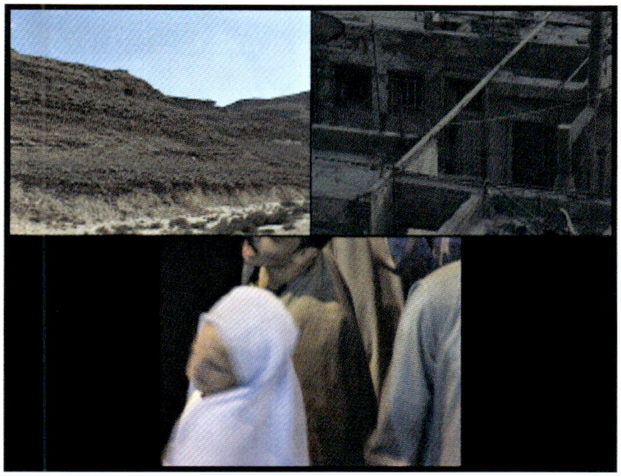
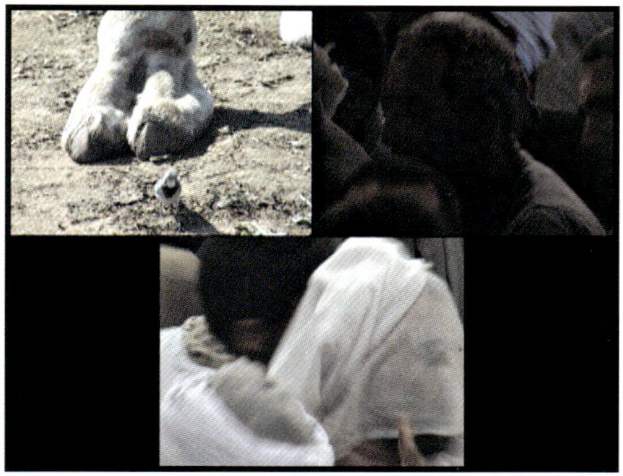
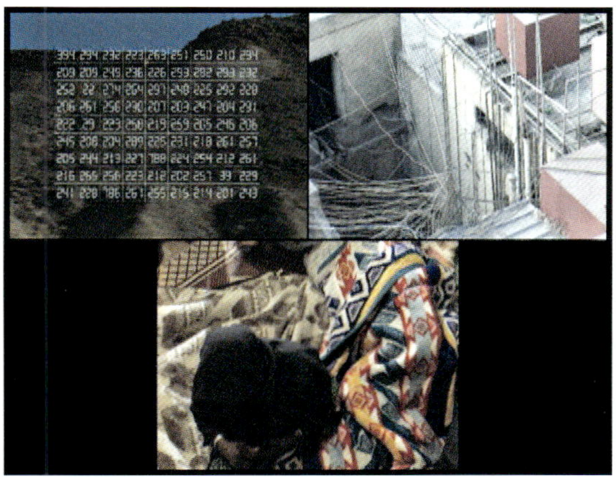
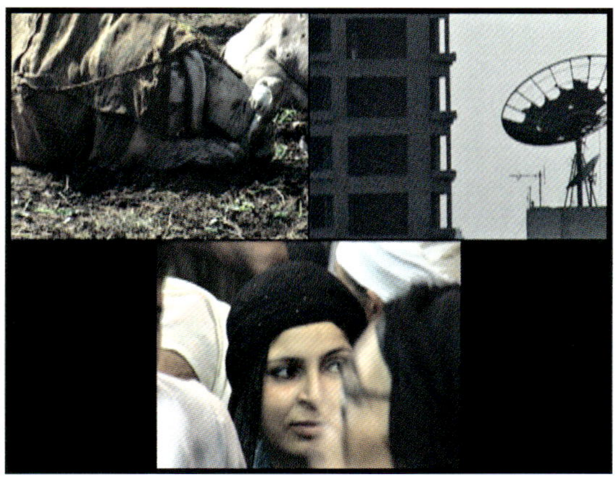

boards. ‘A series of images will randomly, but somehow in synchronisation, alternate through these screens’, says Shawky. I like the confidence in this statement – the belief that somehow these different images will randomly synchronise. There’s no explanation from Shawky as to how this will happen. They just *will*. Meanwhile, the soundtrack will combine harmony with discordance, with tracks occasionally overlapping, sometimes playing by themselves. Children speak in thickly inflected accents informing us about the runway they are constructing from tar: ‘It is evident from their tone that they do no fully comprehend the nature of their uttering.’ There are a number of different social orders within the piece: the children at work; the Bedouins constructing their houses and then covering them with liquid tar; a nomadic man leading a strange hybrid of a camel and a buffalo, passing in front of a number of different backdrops from Swiss mountain ranges to seascapes. These social orders alternately interweave, overlap, displace and ignore each other, somehow living within the same spaces but at a remove from each other – on occasion surprised, pleased, baffled and angered by each other’s presence. And this is the way we live today: theorists have rightly ditched the idea of the melting pot in favour of the indigestible and the incommensurable, but in so doing have been in danger of missing out on the startling congruities that crop up within differences. One of the oddest things about the anti-globalisation movement is the coming together of groups of people who really ought to hate each other, united in temporary alliances that oddly make sense. There might not be any Winter Palaces anymore, but opposition is also diffuse and decentred, swarming into the most surprising places. They’re dancing to the dervish and they’re dancing to Cypress Hill. Things randomly synchronise – *they just do*.

Text Credits & Notes
Artists' Biographies
Contributors' Biographies
Acknowledgements

Text Credits & Notes

The Revolution Stripped Bare
Gilane Tawadros

1 Gamal Abdel-Nasser, 'Need for Unity', see pp. 43–48.
2 Kwame Nkrumah, 'I Speak of Freedom', see pp. 49–52.
3 A. Laroui, *L'Histoire du Maghreb: un essai de synthèse*, Paris, 1970 (English trans. *The History of the Magreb*, Princeton, 1977). Cited in Albert Hourani, *A History of the Arab Peoples*, London: Faber and Faber, 1991, p. 394.
4 Frantz Fanon, 'On National Culture', *The Wretched of the Earth*, Harmondsworth: Penguin, 1990, 3rd edn, pp.187–88. First published in France as *Les Damnés de la terre* by François Maspéro éditeur, 1961.
5 Ibid, p. 199.
6 Nasser Rabbat, 'Hassan Fathy and the Identity Debate', see p. 202.
7 Hassan Fathy, 'Architecture for the Poor', see pp. 187–95.
8 Kobena Mercer, 'Frank Bowling's Map Paintings', see pp. 139–50.
9 Bheki Peterson, 'Clifford Charles and the Pleasures of Contemplative Insurgency', see pp. 151–58.
10 Ibid.
11 Mercer, op. cit.
12 Deepali Dewan, 'Tender Metaphor: The Art of Zarina Bhimji', see pp. 131–38.
13 Sarat Maharaj, 'Fatal Natalities: The Algebra of Diaspora and Difference after Apartheid', see pp. 79–90.
14 Elsabet Giorgis, 'Salem Mekuria', see pp. 219–25.
15 Kateb Yacine, *Afrique Action*, Tunis, 26 June 1961.
16 Kobena Mercer, 'Eros & Diaspora', in *Rotimi Fani-Kayode & Alex Hirst*, Paris and London: Revue Noire and Autograph, 1996, p. 108.
17 Rotimi Fani-Kayode, 'Traces of Ecstasy', see pp. 177–82.
18 Ibid.
19 Mark Sealy, 'A Note From Outside on Rotimi Fani-Kayode', see pp. 183–86.
20 Lisa Fischman, 'Untitled (A Way In)', see pp. 97–104.
21 Ibid.
22 Yasmeen Siddiqui, 'Emergent Forms: Sabah Naim Reconceptualises Movement', see pp. 233–42.
23 Sabah Naim, unpublished text, 2002.
24 Kader Attia and Jerome Sans, 'The Right Position', see pp. 105–18.
25 Ibid.
26 Wael Shawky writes: 'An essential part of the *mulid* is *zekr*… it is a Sufi religious ritual to reach a higher spiritual level or it is a state of transition.'
27 Niru Ratnam, 'So You Wanna Be…?', see pp. 251–57.
28 Wael Shawky, unpublished text, 2002.
29 Achille Mbembe, 'Provisional Notes on the Postcolony', see pp. 53–64.
30 Bheki Peterson, op. cit.
31 Moshekwa Langa, unpublished correspondence, 2003.
32 Okwui Enwezor, 'The Postcolonial Constellation', see pp. 65–78.
33 Kateb Yacine, *Le Poète comme un boxeur*, Paris: Editions du Seuil, 1994, p. 176. Translated by Barbara Mellor.

Maps of Emergency
Stuart Hall

1. Okwui Enwezor and Olu Oguibe, *Reading the Contemporary: African Art from Theory to the Marketplace*, London and Cambridge, Mass.: inIVA and MIT Press, 1999, p. 10.
2 As the introduction to the 1983 exhibition of Senegalese tapestries in New York, quoted by V.Y. Mudimbe (in 'Reprendre', *Reading The Contemporary*, op. cit. p.37), neatly put it.
3 Clifford Charles, in his personal description of the *Painting on Water* submission.
4 Ibid.
5 A Mercator projection (invented by Flemish cartographer Gerardus Mercator) is the standard Western projection of the globe, offering a very Eurocentric representation of it.
6 Irit Rogoff, *Terra Infirma*, London: Routledge, 2000, pp. 2–3.
7 Gilane Tawadros, 'Fault Lines: Contemporary African Art and Shifting Landscapes', press release, Institute of International Visual Arts, London, 2003, p. 1.
8 Ibid.
9 Edward Said, *Reflections On Exile and Other Essays*, Cambridge, Mass.: Harvard University Press, 2001, p 186. Also quoted by Christopher Bollas in Introduction to Edward Said, *Freud and the Non-European,* London: Verso and The Freud Museum, 2003, p. 8.
10 Edward Said, *Culture and Imperialism*, London: Vintage, 1994, p. 24.
11 Tawadros, op.cit., p. 1.
12 Eric Hobsbawm, *The Age Of Empire*, London: Wiedenfeld and Nicholson, 1987, p. 62.
13 The mandate was the 'cover' under which Britain intervened in East Africa and connived with handing over Palestine to the Zionist Commission and sold the Palestinian Arabs down the river.
14 H.A.L. Fisher, *A History of Europe,* Edward Arnold (ed.), vol. i, 1960, p 1275, quoted in Bernard Porter, *The Lion's Share*, London and New York: Longman, 1996, p. 255.
15 Said, *Culture and Imperialism*, op.cit. p. 263.
16 Partha Chatterjee, *Nationalist Thought and The Colonial World*, Minneapolis: University of Minnesota Press, 1993, p. 168.

17 See Nasser Rabbat's text on Hassan Fathy in this volume.
18 Partha Chatterjee, op.cit. p. 168.
19 Frantz Fanon, 'The Pitfalls of National Consciousness', in *The Wretched Of The Earth*, New York: Grove Press, copyright 1961, p. 121.
20 Fanon, op.cit., p. 124.
21 Fanon, op.cit., pp. 121ff and 139.
22 Stuart Hall, 'When Was The Post-Colonial?', in Iain Chambers and Lidia Curti, *The Post-Colonial Question.* London and New York: Routledge, 1996, pp. 248–49.
23 The ten largest MNCs have a total income larger than that of a hundred of the poorest countries.
24 The 2002 US Farm Bill recently subsidised the big American agri-corporations by $248.6 billion.
25 Wayne Ellwood, *New Internationalist,* no. 335, April 2003, p. 10.
26 Michael Hardt and Antonio Negri, *Empire,* Cambridge, Mass.: Harvard University Press, 2000.

Need for Unity
Gamal Abdel-Nasser

First published in Gamal Abdel-Nasser, *Egypt's Liberation: The Philosophy of the Revolution*, Cairo: General Organisation for Government Printing Offices, 1958, pp. 63–70.

I Speak of Freedom
Kwame Nkrumah

First published as the preface to Kwame Nkrumah, *I Speak of Freedom: A Statement of African Ideology*, London: William Heinemann Ltd, 1961, pp. xi–iv.

Provisional Notes on the Postcolony
Achille Mbembe

First published in *Africa*, no. 62 (1), 1992, pp. 3–37.

1 Cf. M. Bakhtin, *L'Oeuvre de Rabelais et la culture populaire du Moyen-Age et sous la Renaissance*, Paris: Gallimard, 1970.
2 See S. Labou Tansi, *La vie et demie*, Paris: Seuil, 1979, p. 41; Tansi, *Les Yeux du volcan*, Paris: Seuil, 1988; and Ibrahima Ly, *Toiles d'araignées*, Paris: l'Harmattan, 1982.
3 C. Castoriadis, *L'Institution imaginaire de la société*, Paris: Seuil, 1975, p. 475.
4 I use the notion of *cible* in the sense indicated by Foucault ('La gouvernementalité', in *Magazine littéraire*, no. 269, 1989).
5 Cf. J-F. Bayart, 'L'Enonciation du politique', *Revue Française de Science Politique*, no. 35, 1985, pp. 343–73.
6 See V. Azarya and N. Chazan, 'Disengagement from the State in Africa', in *Comparative Studies in Society and History*, no. 29 (1), 1987, pp. 106–31; J.L. Roitman, 'The Politics of Informal Markets in sub-Saharan Africa', in *Journal of Modern African Studies*, no. 28 (4), 1990, pp. 671–96; and J. Scott, *Weapons for the Weak*, New Haven: Yale University Press, 1985.
7 I use the term *commandement* in the way it was used to denote colonial authority. See R. Delavignette, *Freedom and Authority in French West Africa*, London: OUP, 1950, or, more generally, W.B. Cohen, *Rulers of Empire*, Stanford, CA: Hoover Institution Press, 1971.
8 Cf. *Nouvelle revue de psychoanalyse*, no. 2, 1970, particularly the contributions by J. Pouilon, A. Adler and P. Bonnafé, pp.131–94.
9 T.M. Callaghy, 'Culture and Politics in Zaire', unpublished, 1986.
10 M.G. Schatzberg, *The Dialectics of Oppression in Zaire*, Bloomington: Indiana University Press, 1988.
11 S. Berry, e.g., 'The Significance of Investment', paper presented at the 'Identity, Rationality and the Post-colonial Subject' conference, Columbia University, New York, 28 February 1991.
12 D. Parkin, 'The Creativity of Abuse', *Man* (n.s.), no. 15, 1980, p. 45. Cf. C. Toulabour, 'Jeu de mots, jeux de vialin', in *Politique Africaine*, no. 3, 1981, pp. 55–71; and Toulabour, *Togo sous Eyadéma*, Paris: Karthala, 1986, especially pp. 302–9.
13 R. Joseph, *Democracy and Prebendal Politics in Nigeria*, Cambridge: CUP, 1988.
14 See L. Maillart Guimera, *Ni dos ni ventre*, Paris: Société d'Ethnologie, 1981, and J-F. Bayart, *L'Etat en Afrique: La politique du ventre*, Paris: Fayard, 1989.
15 This is starkly evident in the colonial African novel, e.g., the classic F. Oyono, *Le Vieux Nègre et la médaille*, Paris, 1957.
16 See Schatzberg, *The Dialectics of Oppression in Zaire*, op. cit., and Schatzberg, 'Power, Language and Legitimacy in Africa', paper presented at the 'Identity, Rationality and the Post-colonial Subject' conference, Columbia University, New York, 28 February 1991.
17 See J.M. Ela, *Quand l'état pénètre en brousse*, Paris: Karthala, 1990, pp. 52–58.
18 See J.D. Gandalou's (*Dandies à Bacongo*, Paris: l'Harmattan, 1989) description of the *sapeurs* of Congo-Brazzaville.
19 On Kenya, see the headlines in the newspapers during the riots that followed the government's refusal to move towards a multi-party system, and note the way in which those who contested power were defined: 'Drug addicts are bent on breaking law', 'Chaos in Nairobi and Kisumu. Police battle with crowds', 'Police crack down on hooligans'....

20 I am borrowing an insight from the title of G. Bataille, *Death and Sensuality: A Study of Eroticism and the Taboo*, New York: Ballantine Books, 1962.
21 *Cameroon Tribune*, no. 4235, 5 October 1988.
22 Ibid., p.3.
23 Ibid.
24 See R. Joseph, *Le Mouvement Nationaliste au Cameroun*, Paris: Karthala, 1986; J-F. Bayart, *L'Etat au Cameroun*, Paris: Presses de la Fondation Nationale des Sciences Politiques, 1977; and P.F. Ngayap, *Cameroun. Qui gouverne*? Paris: l'Harmattan, 1984.
25 Here I adapt the title of the French translation – *Les Tyrannies de l'intimité* – of the conclusion of R. Sennet, *The Fall of Public Man*, New York: Knopf, 1977.
26 Cf. E. Goffman, *The Presentation of Self in Everyday Life*, New York: Doubleday, 1959, pp. 17 and 76.
27 J.B. Simgba, 'La communauté musulmane du Cameroun en fête', *Cameroon Tribune*, no. 4383, 8 May 1989, p. 7.
28 Understood here in the sense intended by Bayart, *L'Etat en Afrique*, op. cit.
29 See the comments of J. Omoruyi, 'Nigerian Funeral Programmes', in *Africa*, no. 58 (4), 1988, pp. 466–69.
29 See C. Vidal, 'Funérailles et conflit social en Côte d'Ivoire', in *Politique Africaine*, no. 24, 1987, and M. Gilbert, 'The Sudden Death of a Millionaire', in Africa, no. 58 (3), 1988, pp. 291–313.

The Postcolonial Constellation
Okwui Enwezor

1 Michel Foucault, *The History of Sexuality: The Uses of Pleasure*, New York: Pantheon, vol. 2, 1985, p. 10.
2 Édouard Glissant, *Poetics of Relation*, Ann Arbor: University of Michigan Press, 1996, p. 45.
3 Fernand Braudel's discussion of the structural transformation of the flow of capital and culture by distinct temporal manifestations, i.e., the paradigmatic and diagnostic attribute of historical events in relation to their duration. See Okwui Enwezor, 'The Black Box' in *Documenta11_Platform5: Exhibition Catalogue*, Stuttgart: Hatje Cantz, 2002, p. 44.
4 I have borrowed this term from the Brazilian artist Cildo Meireles's classic conceptualist work of the late 1960s titled *Insertions into Ideological Circuits*.
5 The Nobel economist Amartya Sen in an article 'Civilizational Imprisonments', *The New Republic*, 10 June 2002, pp. 28–33 gives the example of the cross-pollination of ideas between cultures which has continued unabated for two millennia. He distinctly argues the fact that 'what is often called "Western Science" draws on a world heritage. There is a chain of intellectual relations that links Western mathematics and science to a collection of distinctly non-Western practitioners.'
6 James Clifford, *The Predicament of Culture: Twentieth-Century, Ethnography, Literature, and Art*, Cambridge: Harvard University Press, 1988, p. 193.
7 For a thorough account and brilliant analysis of this issue, see Thelma Golden's ground-breaking exhibition catalogue *Black Male: Representations of Masculinity in Contemporary American Art*, New York: Whitney Museum/Abrams, 1994.
8 Wall label accompanying the presentation of the film extracts produced by the Tate Modern.
9 See Jurgen Habermas, *The Philosophical Discourse of Modernity*, Cambridge: Polity Press, 1987, for an extensive development of the discourse of modernity, modernisation, and the artistic and aesthetic corollary of modernism, particularly from the point of view of surrealism.
10 From an unpublished lecture and based on discussions with Carlos Basualdo.
11 See Samuel Huntington, *The Clash of Civilizations and the Remaking of World Order*, New York: Simon & Schuster, 1996.
12 See George Bush's speech before the US Congress in which he outlined a doctrine of stark distinction between states that belong to the moral universe of the civilised (sic) world and those others, especially Iran, Iraq and North Korea, who exist in the pool of darkness marred by evil intentions against a peaceful, civilised world.
13 This is in reference to Ronald Reagan's congressional address which gave us this classic characterisation of the Soviet Union, towards the end of the Cold War.
14 See Okwui Enwezor, 'The Black Box', op. cit.

Fatal Natalities
Sarat Maharaj

Thanks to Homi Bhabha for inviting me to explore some of these ideas in a contribution to the 'Re-inventing Britain' conference (March, 1997). These were developed further on my return to South Africa after twenty-five years to give a paper at the Johannesburg Biennale (October, 1997). The text was first published in *Photofile*, no. 57, October 1999, pp. 41–49.

1 Gilles Deleuze and Félix Guattari, *A Thousand Plateaus*, translation and foreword by Brian Massumi, London: Athlone Press, 1988, pp. 310–50. Also, Deleuze, *Negotiations 1972–1990*,

translated by M. Joughlin, New York: Columbia University Press, 1995, pp. 189 and 200.
2 Theodor W. Adorno to Walter Benjamin, 3 March 1936 in Ernst Bloch et al., *Aesthetics and Politics*, translated and edited by Rodney Taylor, London: NLB, 1977, p. 123.
3 Deleuze and Guattari, op. cit., p. 471.
4 Aimé Césaire, *Cahier d'un retour au pays natal. Return To My Native Land*, translated by John Berger and Anna Bostock, Harmondsworth: Penguin, 1969.
5 Theodor W. Adorno, *Negative Dialectics*, translated by E.B. Ashton, London: Routledge and Kegan Paul, 1973, p. 3.
6 Marcel Duchamp, *The Bride Stripped Bare By Her Bachelors, Even* which is made up of the *Large Glass* (1915–23) and handwritten notes written from 1912 onwards published as the *Green Box* (1934).
7 Henri Bergson, *Creative Evolution*, translated by Arthur Mitchell, London: Macmillan, 1954, pp. 287–384.
8 Theodor W. Adorno, *Against Epistemology*, translated by Willis Domingo, Oxford: Basil Blackwell, 1982, p. 46.
9 Marcel Duchamp, *Notes and Projects for the Large Glass* selected, ordered and introduced by Arturo Schwarz, translated by George H. Hamilton, Cleve Gray and Arturo Schwarz, London: Thames and Hudson, 1969, pp. 60–70, nn. 22–29.
10 Alighiero e Boetti, *Classifying the Thousand Longest Rivers in the World*, 1977.
11 Henri Bergson, op. cit., p. 10.
12 Boetti's Arte Povera/Neo-Futurist connections resonate with notions of 'lines of flight and measure' in Duchamp and the Futurists' own engagements with Bergsonism. For the latter, see Umberto Boccioni, 'The Plastic Foundations of Futurist Sculpture and Painting and Futurist Dynamism and French Painting' in *Lacerba*, Florence, 5 March 1913 and 1 August 1913, in Umbro Apollonio (ed.), *Futurist Manifestos*, London: Thames and Hudson, 1973, pp. 88 and 110. This is not unlike the Bergsonist/ Neo-Futurist echoes in Deleuze and Guattari's key concept of 'lines of flight and capture'.
13 Adorno, *Negative Dialectics*, p. 8.
14. Marcel Duchamp, *Notes and Projects for the Large Glass*, p. 138, n. 89.
15 Ibid, p. 150, nn. 96–97.
16 *A Thousand Plateaus* (1980) was written over seven years and billed as a sequel to *Anti-Oedipus*, London: Athlone Press, 1984, which was first published in 1972. The continuity of the project is signalled by their shared subtitle 'Capitalism and Schizophrenia'.
17 Deleuze and Guattari, *A Thousand Plateaus*, pp. 471–73, and Félix Guattari, *Chaosmosis: An Ethico-Aesthetic Paradigm*, translated by Paul Bains and Julian Pefanis, Sydney: Power Publications, 1995, p. 25.
18 Jay Naidoo, *Coolie Location*, London and Johannesburg: South African Writers and Taurus Publishers, 1990, pp. 116–17.
19 Marcel Duchamp, *Notes and Projects for the Large Glass*, p. 98, n. 60.
20 *The Debate on Zulu Origins* (a selection of papers on the Zulu Kingdom and early colonial Natal), Pietermaritzburg: Historical Studies Department, University of Natal, 23–24 October 1990, pp. 1–41.
21 Julian Cobbing, '"Shaka" a Latrine in which Whites Shat their Bad Memories and Alienation', in *The Debate on Zulu Origins,* p. 11. See also his 'The Mfecane as Alibi: Thoughts on Dithakong and Mbolompo', *Journal of African History*, 2, 1988, pp. 487–519.
22 Deleuze and Guattari, *A Thousand Plateaus*, op. cit., pp. 321–25.
23 Nelson Mandela, *The Star*, Johannesburg, 18 July 1991.
24 Heribert Adam and Kogila Moodley, *The Negotiated Revolution: Society and Politics in Post-Apartheid South Africa*, Johannesburg: Jonathan Ball, 1995, p. 74. Anthony Sampson observes with regard to representation and the Rainbow State. 'The existing executive came from every racial background. They include the Muslim Minister of Justice, Dullah Omar; the Minister of Water, Kader Asmal, ex-professor of law in Dublin who sounds Irish; the coloured Minister of Finance, Trevor Manuel, who looks white; the white deputy defence minister Ronnie Kasrils who sounds English.' Quoted in 'Men of the Renaissance', *The Guardian*, London, November 1997.
25 *The Star*, Johannesburg, 24 November, 1973, quoted in Noel C. Manganyi, *Alienation and The Body in a Racist Society: A Study of the Society that Invented Soweto*, New York: NOK Publishers, 1977, p. 7.
26 James Beresford, *The Guardian,* London, July 1995.
27 Thomas Hardy, *The Return of The Native,* Oxford: OUP, 1990, p. 276.

Issues Facing the African Arts
Landry-Wilfrid Miampika

First published in *Africultures. Postcolonialism: Inventory and Issues*, no. 28, May 2000. Reproduced Courtesy of www.africultures.com

Untitled (A Way In)
Lisa Fischman

An earlier version of this essay was published in conjunction with *Laylah Ali:*

Paintings On Paper, on view at Atlanta College of Art Gallery, Atlanta, Georgia, 10 October – 24 November 2002.

1. Jacob Lawrence quoted in Lowery Stokes Sims, 'The Structure of Narrative: Form and Content in Jacob Lawrence's Builders Paintings, 1946–1998', in Peter T. Nesbett and Michelle DuBois (eds), *Over the Line: The Art and Life of Jacob Lawrence*, Seattle: University of Washington Press, 2000, p. 203.
2. Rebecca Walker, 'Interview', in Jessica Morgan, Rebecca Walker and Suzanne Wise, *Laylah Ali*, Boston: ICA, 2001, p. 22.
3. Ibid, p. 23.
4. Laylah Ali, video interview, produced in conjunction with the exhibition *Laylah Ali: 2000 ICA Artist Prize*, Boston: Institute of Contemporary Art, 2001.
5. This point was inspired by a quote from comic artist Chris Ware, in Gene Kannenberg, Jr, 'The Comics of Chris Ware', in Robin Varnum and Christina T. Gibbons (eds), *The Language of Comics: Word and Image*, Jackson: University Press of Mississippi, 2001, pp. 178 and 180.
6. Laylah Ali, artist's statement.
7. A sense of generationality informs the recent exhibition *Freestyle* at the Studio Museum in Harlem, in which Ali participated, and which caused curator Thelma Golden to label a shift in identity politics among young African American artists as 'post-black'. See *Freestyle*, New York: The Studio Museum in Harlem, 2001.
8. Aaron Marcus, quoted in Kannenberg, op. cit., p. 197.

The Right Position
Jérôme Sans

Translated from the French by Barbara Mellor.

Through the *Mashrabiyya*
Ramon Tio Bellido

Translated from the French by Barbara Mellor.

The Poet as a Boxer
Kateb Yacine

Extracts from Kateb Yacine, *Le Poète comme un Boxeur: Entretiens 1958–1989*. Paris: Editions du Seuil, 1994. Translated from the French by Barbara Mellor.

Frank Bowling's Map Paintings
Kobena Mercer

1 John Tancock, *Frank Bowling*, New York: Center for Inter-American Relations, 1973.
2 Bryan Robertson, John Russell and Lord Snowdon, *Private View: The Lively World of British Art*, London: Thomas Nelson, 1965, and David Sylvester, *New Statesman*, October 1962.
3 Frank Bowling, 'is black art about colour?...', in Rhoda Goldstein (ed.), *Black Life and Culture*, New York: Thomas Crow II, 1971, p. 110.
4 John Hoyland and Tim Hilton (eds), *Hayward Annual*, London: Hayward Gallery, 1980, and Corinne Jennings (ed.), *The Search for Freedom: African American Abstract Painting, 1945–75*, New York: Kenkeleba House, 1991.
5 Ann Gibson, *Abstract Expressionism: Other Politics*, New Haven: Yale University Press, 1997; see also 'Two Worlds: African American Abstraction in New York at Mid-Century', in Jennings, op. cit.
6 Gibson, op. cit., p. 101.
7 James Clifford, 'Mixed Feelings', in Bruce Robbins and Pheng Cheah (eds), *Cosmopolitics: Thinking and Feeling Beyond the Nation*, Minneapolis: University of Minnesota, 1998.
8 Paul Gilroy, *The Black Atlantic: Modernity and Double Consciousness*, Cambridge: Harvard University Press, 1993; see also 'The Art of Darkness', in Gilroy, *Small Acts*, London: Serpents Tail, 1993.
9 Mel Gooding, '...through a door of space into memory and imagination', in Eddie Chambers (ed.), *Bowling on Through the Century* (exh. cat.), London: Arts Council Touring, 1996, p. 16.
10 Dennis de Caires, 'In Search of an El Dorado: The Paintings of Frank Bowling', in *Artscribe International*, no. 57, London, April/May 1986.
11 Jean Devisse and Michel Mollat (eds), *The Image of the Black in Western Art. Vol. II: From the Early Christian Era to the Age of Discovery*, Cambridge: Harvard University Press and Menil Foundation, 1979, p. 221.
12 Jean Seigel, 'Frank Bowling', in *Art International*, New York, May 1975, p. 23.
13 Frank Bowling, 'The Rupture: Ancestor Worship, Revival, Confusion, or Disguise', in *Arts Magazine*, New York, summer 1970.
14 Vivien Raynor, *New York Times*, 23 May 1986.
15 Eddie Chambers, *The Dub Factor* (exh. cat.), Ipswich: Christchurch Mansion, 1992, unpaginated.
16 James Snead, 'Repetition as a Figure of Black Culture', in Henry Louis Gates Jr (ed.), *Black Literature and Literary Theory*, New York: Methuen, 1984, p. 67.

Clifford Charles
Bheki Peterson

1 The view that South Africa is a unique and harmonious 'melting-pot' of diverse races and cultures.

2 See Walter Benjamin, *One Way Street and Other Writings*, trans. Edmund Jephcott and Kingsley Shorter, London: Verso, 1985, especially pp. 167–76 for a discussion of the 'porosity of the city'.

At Least One Person Was Killed
Prince Mbusi Dube

1 http://www.savewarchildren.org/exhibitHistory.html
2 http://www.gov.za
3 Thabo Mbeki, president of South Africa, State of the Nation address, 14 February 2003: http://www.anc.org.za/ancdocs/history/mbeki/2003/tm0214.html
4 Thabo Mbeki, statement on behalf of the National Congress, on the occasion of the adoption by the Constitutional Assembly of 'The Republic of South Africa Constitutional Bill 1996', Cape Town, 8 May 1996: http://www.anc.org.za/ancdocs/history/mbeki/1996/sp960508.html

Traces of Ecstacy
Rotimi Fani-Kayode

First published in Mark Sealy and Jean Loup Pivin (eds), *Rotimi Fani-Kayode & Alex Hirst: Photographs*, Paris and London: Editions Revue Noire and Autograph, 1996, pp. 5–10. Text reproduced courtesy of Autograph: The Association of Black Photographers, London, UK.

A Note From Outside
Mark Sealy

Extracts from *Rotimi Fani-Kayode 1955–1989: Communion*, London: Autograph, 1995.

Architecture for the Poor
Hassan Fathy

Extracts from Hassan Fathy, *Architecture for the Poor*, Chicago: The University of Chicago Press, 1973, pp. 1–26.

Hassan Fathy and the Identity Debate
Nasser Rabbat

1 The recent exhibition *Hassan Fathy, un architecte égyptien (1900–1989). La terre et la tradition* held at the Institut du Monde Arabe in Paris (4 December 2002 – 2 February 2003) offered a rare opportunity to view some of Fathy's early projects before his conversion to vernacular traditions.
2 There had been an earlier project in the USA, the Polk House in Aspen, Colorado, designed in 1972 but never built.
3 For this summary of Fathy's career, I consulted the following: Hassan Fathy, *al-'Imara al-Arabiyya al-hadariyya bi-al-Sharq al-Awsat*, Beirut: Jami'at Bayrut al-'Arabiyya, 1971; idem, *Architecture for the Poor*, Chicago: The University of Chicago Press, 1973; Nabil Faraj, *al-'Imara al-insaniyya lil-muhandis Hasan Fathi*, Cairo: Maktabat al-Anglo al-Misriyya, 1977; Jean-Pierre Cousin, 'Hassan Fathy', *L'architecture d'aujourd'hui* 195, February 1978, pp. 43–78; Hasan-Uddin Khan (ed.), *Hassan Fathy,* Singapore: Concept Media, 1985; James Steele, *The Hassan Fathy Collection: A Catalogue of Visual Documents at The Aga Khan Award for Architecture,* Geneva: The Aga Khan Trust for Culture, 1989; idem, *An Architecture for the People: The Complete Works of Hassan Fathy*, Cairo: The American University in Cairo Press, 1997.

The Global Village Revisited
Hamza Walker

First published in *Moshekwa Langa*, Chicago and Geneva: The Renaissance Society and Centre d'Art Contemporain, 2002, pp. 78–85.

1 Constant, 'New Babylon', in Libero Andreotti and Xavier Costa (eds), *Theory of the Dérive and Other Situationist Writings on the City*, Barcelona: Museu d'Art Contemporani de Barcelona, 1996, pp. 150–51.
2 Benjamin Buchloh, 'Structure, Sign, and Reference in the Work of David Lamelas', in *Neo-Avantgarde and Culture Industry: Essays on European and American Art from 1955 to 1975*, Cambridge, Mass.: MIT, 2000, p. 307.
3 Stuart Hall and Mark Sealy, *Different, A Historical Context: Contemporary Photographers and Black Identity*, London: Phaidon, 2001, p.53.
4 Matthew Tinkcom, *Working Like a Homosexual: Camp, Capital, Cinema,* Durham: Duke University Press, 2002, p. 15.
5 Susan Sontag, 'Notes on "Camp"', in *Against Interpretation*, New York: Anchor Books, 1986, p. 280.
6 Ibid.
7 Ibid, p. 283.
8 Kobena Mercer, 'Welcome to the Jungle: Identity and Diversity in Postmodern Politics', in Jonathan Rutherford (ed.), *Identity: Community, Culture, Difference,* London: Lawrence & Wishart, 1990, pp. 66–67.
9 Kobena Mercer, 'Iké Udé: A Dandy in the Naked City', in François Dion (ed.), *Subject to Representation: Essays on the Politics of Representation*, Ottawa: Gallery 101, 2000, pp. 34–35. The term 'hyperblack', cited in Mercer's essay, comes from Herman Gray,

Watching Race: Television and the Struggle for the Sign of Blackness, Minnesota: University of Minnesota Press, 1997.
10 Susan Sontag, 'Notes on "Camp"', op. cit., p. 290.
11 Ibid, p. 287
12 Michèle Bernstein, in *Theory of the Dérive and Other Situationists Writings on the City*, op. cit., p. 53
13 Unsigned tract, Unitary Urbanism at the End of the 1950s, Potlatch #20, in *Theory of the Dérive and Other Situationist Writings on the City*, op. cit., p. 84.
14 Constant, op. cit., p. 157.
15 Adrienne Rich, Atlas of the *Difficult World: Poems 1988–1991*, New York: Norton, 1991, p. 22.

Salem Mekuria
Elsabet Giorgis

1. Conversation with the artist, January 2003.
2. Messay Kebede, *Survival and Modernization, Ethiopia's Enigmatic Present: A Philosophical Discourse*, Lawrenceville: The Red Sea Press, 1999.
3. Ibid.

Fault Lines
Solomon Deressa

1 David Nettle and Suzanne Romaine, *Vanishing Voices*, New York: Oxford University Press, 2000.
2 Alfred Lord Tennyson's poem 'The Lotus-Eaters' was published in 1832.
3 Paradoxically, in the nineteenth and early twentieth centuries, Russia was simultaneously home to the great scientific achievements of the likes of Nicolai Lobachevsky and to the appalling barbarity of serfdom.

Emergent Forms
Yasmeen Siddiqui

1 Norman Bryson, *Vision and Painting: The Logic of the Gaze*, New Haven: Yale University Press, 1983, p. 134.
2 Insights from interviews by Jessica Winegar address reasons why contemporary women artists in Egypt have resisted being labelled according to their gender. Jessica Winegar, 'Representing Women. Women Representing Reflections on Art in Egypt', in *Civil Society: Democratization in the Arab World*, Ibn Khaldun Center for Development Studies, November 1999, vol. 8, issue 95.
3 Prita Sandy Meier, 'Territorial Struggles: Cairo and Contemporary Art', in *NKA*, spring 2003.
4 Henri Bergson, *Creative Evolution*, Lanham, MD: University Press of America, 1984 (1911).
5 Margot Badran, *Feminists, Islam and Nation: Gender and the Making of Modern Egypt*, Princeton: Princeton University Press, 1995, p. 61.
6 Gilles Deleuze, *Cinema 1: The Movement-Image*, Minneapolis: University of Minnesota, 1986–89, p. 109.

Moataz Nasr
Simon Njami

Translated from the French by Barbara Mellor.

1 El Anatsui, 'Conversation with Olu Oguibe', in *Third Text*, no. 23, summer 1993, p. 49.
2 James Baldwin, *The Evidence of Things Not Seen*, New York: Holt, Rinehart and Wilson, 1985.
3 Pierre Restany, *l'Avant-garde au XXe siècle*, Paris: Balland, 1969.

So You Wanna be...?
Niru Ratnam

1 Correspondence with artist, March 2003.
2 Ibid.

Artists' Biographies

Laylah Ali
Laylah Ali was born in 1968 in Buffalo, New York. Graduating from Williams College, Williamstown, Massachusetts in 1991, Ali went on to study under the Whitney Museum Independent Study Program in New York and Washington University in St Louis and also attended the Skowhegan School of Painting and Sculpture. Recent selected solo exhibitions include Indianapolis Museum of Art (2002); Albright Knox in Buffalo, NY (2002); Yerba Buena Center for the Arts, San Francisco (2001); the Institute of Contemporary Art, Boston (2001); MassMOCA, North Adams, Massachusetts (2000); Museum of Contemporary Art, Chicago (1999). Her work has also been included in group exhibitions, such as *Freestyle* (Studio Museum, Harlem, and Drawing Center, New York, 2001). In 2002, she completed an artist's book for Projects 75 at the Museum of Modern Art, New York. She is currently represented by 303 Gallery in New York City.

Kader Attia
Born in 1970 in Dugny, France, Kader Attia graduated from the Ecole Nationale des Arts Décoratifs in Paris in 1998. His recent solo shows include *Alter Ego* (Galerie Kamel Mennour, Paris, 2002), *Photostories* (Galerie Martine et Thibault de la Châtre, Paris, 2001); *Instants Urbains* (Galerie L'Oeil du Huit, Paris, 1997) and *Humanistes au Congo* (Centre Culturel Français de Brazzaville, Congo, 1996). His work has also been shown in a number of group exhibitions, among them, *Les Vertus sont des titres, les souffrances sont les droits* (FRAC, Poitou-Charentes, Angoulême, 2002) and *L'Etat des Choses: Part 1* (Kunstwerke Berlin, 2000–1). Attia now lives and works in Paris and has work in the collections of FNAC, Paris, and FRAC, Poitou-Charentes.

Zarina Bhimji
Zarina Bhimji studied at the Slade School of Fine Art and Goldsmiths' College, both in London. Her work has been shown extensively both in the UK and abroad and her solo shows include *Matrix* (Wadsworth Athenium Museum of Art, Hartford, Connecticut, 2003); *Art Now* (Tate Britain, London, 2003); Talwar Gallery, New York (2001); and *I Will Always Be Here* (Ikon Gallery, Birmingham, 1992). Her work has also been shown at Documenta XI (Kassel, Germany, 2002); *The Short Century* (Museum Villa Stuck, Munich, 2001), which toured to Berlin, Chicago and New York; and *No Place (Like Home)* (Walker Arts Center, Minneapolis, 1997). Bhimji is DAAD's artist-in-residence in Berlin in 2002–3 and received a Paul Hamlyn Foundation Award in 1999. Her work has been reviewed in a number of international publications, among them, *The Times*, *Artforum*, *The Guardian*, *The New York Times* and *Flash Art*.

Samta Benyahia
Born in Constantine, Algeria, Samta Benyahia now lives and works in Paris. She has been given a number of solo shows internationally at, among other places, Centre d'Art Passerelle, Brest, France (2003); Musée d'Art Roger Quilliot, Clermont-Ferrand, France (2003); Spacex Gallery, Exeter, UK (2001–2); La Corte Arte Contemporanea, Florence, Italy (2000); Art in General, New York (1996); and Centre Culturel Français (Algiers). Her work has appeared in a number of group exhibitions, including *Veil* (New Art Gallery, Walsall, UK, 2003); Biennale de Bamako (2003); *Harem Fantasies and the New Scheherazades* (El Centre de Cultura Contemporània de Barcelona, 2003); *Paris pour Escale* (Musée d'Art Moderne de la Ville de Paris, 2000–1) and the Havana Bienal (1994 and 1986).

Frank Bowling
One of the most important artists of his generation, Guyana-born Frank Bowling showed with the London Group (Tate Gallery, London, 1964) before going on to become their Vice-Chairman in 1965. He has had dozens of solo shows worldwide, including *Bowling Through the Decade* (University Art Gallery, Reading, 1989); Serpentine Gallery (London, 1986); *Frank Bowling Retrospective* (Polytechnic Art Gallery, Newcastle-upon-Tyne, 1978); and Whitney Museum of American Art (New York, 1971). The list of group shows is endless, but a selection of the most significant includes *Landscape as Metaphor* (Fitchburg Museum, MA, Newport Art Museum, RI, Farnsworth Museum, Rockland, ME, 1993); *A/Cross Currents: Synthesis in African American Abstract Painting* (Dakar Biennale, 1992); *The Search for Freedom* (Kenkeleba House, New York, 1991); and *The Other Story* (Hayward Gallery, London, 1989). His multiple honours include two Pollock Krasner Awards (1998 and 1992), two Guggenheim fellowships (1973 and 1967), the Grand Prize for Contemporary Art at the First World Festival of Negro Art (Dakar, 1966), and a Silver Medal from the Royal College of Art (London, 1962); and his work can be found in leading international art collections. Widely reviewed, Bowling's work is published in the monograph *Frank Bowling: Bowling on Through the Century* (1996).

Clifford Charles
Clifford Charles was the first black student to graduate with a BA in Fine Arts from the University of the Witwatersrand, during apartheid South Africa; he now lives and works in Johannesburg. He worked at the Dhlomo Theatre and was one of the artists who founded the Afrika Cultural Centre. For fifteen years, he has worked as an

'artist/activist' in unions, hospitals, youth groups and other social institutions. Charles has also designed numerous Protest Theatre productions. During the 1990s, he took part in a series of art exhibitions and was invited to speak internationally on his art. His work is held by the Johannesburg Art Gallery, the University of South Africa and numerous corporate collections; among the private collections holding his work is that of the First Lady Zanele Mbeki.

Pitso Chinzima
Born in Soweto, South Africa, Pitso Chinzima was taught and greatly influenced by the painter and sculptor Charles Sokhaya Nkosi as part of a fine arts programme called African Institute of Art in 1992. He has a BA in Fine Arts from the University of the Witwatersrand. Having worked as a lecturer, he is now Curator of Exhibitions at Johannesburg Art Gallery and a practising artist. His group exhibitions include Joubert Park Public Art Project (Johannesburg , 2001); *Babel Tower* (Civic Gallery, Johannesburg, 2000); *Art Dialogue* (Castle of Good Hope, Cape Town, 1999); and the 2nd Africus Johannesburg Biennale (Cape Town, 1997). He was nominated as a national representative for South Africa at the 25th São Paulo Bienal (Brazil, 2002). Having recently won the Johannesburg Art City competition, Chinzima is currently preparing for his first solo exhibition, *Night Vigil* (Sandton Civic Gallery, Johannesburg, 2003).

Rotimi Fani-Kayode
Born in Nigeria, Rotimi Fani-Kayode moved first to the UK and then to the US, where he received a BA from Georgetown University, Washington, D.C., and a MFA from Pratt Institute, Brooklyn, New York, before returning to London in 1983. He was a founding member and became the first Chair of Autograph: The Association of Black Photographers in 1987. Fani-Kayode died in 1989, aged just 34. He has had several solo exhibitions both in London and abroad, among them *Communions* (Impressions Gallery, York, and Chapter Arts, Cardiff, 1995), 198 Gallery, London (1990) and Black-Art Gallery, London (1991). Among the group shows to have included his work are *In Sight – African Photography 1940–1996* (Guggenheim, New York, 1996); *Significant Losses* (The Art Gallery, University of Maryland, 1994); Bamako Photo Festival (1994); Houston Photo Festival (1992); *Ecstatic Antibodies* (Battersea Arts Centre, London, 1990) and *Bodies of Experience* (Camerawork, London, 1989). His photographs are published in the monograph *Black Male/White Male* (London: Gay Men's Press, 1988) and *Rotimi-Fani Kayode & Alex Hirst* (Paris and London: Revue Noire & Autograph, 1996).

Hassan Fathy
The most renowned Egyptian architect of the twentieth century, Hassan Fathy was born in Alexandria in 1900 and worked on nearly two hundred major projects during his long career. While teaching at the Faculty of Fine Arts in Cairo, Fathy began work on the settlement at New Gourna (1946–53), which garnered international acclaim. He followed this assignment with a major project for Egypt's Ministry of Education. Later in his career, he entered into the international arena more fully, as an advocate of natural energy solutions for major community projects in the Middle East and researching the 'Cities of the Future' program in Africa. The Founding Director of the International Institute for Appropriate Technology (1976–80), his honours include the Chairman's Award from the Aga Khan Award for Architecture (1980) and the Gold Medal from the International Union of Architects (1984). Fathy's influential writings are published in *Architecture for the Poor: An Experiment in Rural Egypt* (Chicago: University of Chicago Press, 1973), a testament to his revolutionising architectural vision.

Veliswa Gwintsa
Veliswa Gwintsa is an artist and currently the curator of the Southern African Traditional Collection at the Johannesburg Art Gallery. In 2002, she curated *Amabal'engwe* (Durban), an exhibition of traditional southern African attires and *Biopel Ka Setso* (Johannesburg Art Gallery), an exhibition of traditional southern African material culture. Her artwork has been included in a number of exhibitions, both nationally and internationally, among them: *Show Me Home* (Johannesburg, 2003); *Cultural Week: Freedom Day Celebration* (Ethiopia, 1998); *Kulturaxe* (Slovakia, 1998); and 2nd Africus Johannesburg Biennale (Cape Town, 1997). Recently, she has had articles published in *Evocation of the Child* (Cape Town: Human and Rousseau, 2000) and *Grey Areas: Representation, Identity and Politics in Contemporary South African Art* (Johannesburg: Chalkam Hill Press, 1999) and the 2nd Africus Johannesburg Biennale catalogue (1997).

Moshekwa Langa
Born in South Africa, Moshekwa Langa graduated in 1993 and worked as a freelance television producer in 1996. He has presented his work at solo shows in a number of venues worldwide, among them, Galerie Bernier/Eliades, Athens, Greece (2000); the Renaissance Society, Chicago, and Centre d'Art Contemporain, Geneva, Switzerland (1999); and Rembrandt van Rijn Art Gallery, Johannesburg (1995). His group shows include *A Fiction of Authenticity*

(Museum of Contemporary Art, St Louis, 2003); *When Latitudes Become Forms* (Walker Arts Center, Minneapolis, 2003); *Looking Both Ways* (Museum of African Arts, New York, 2003), *Somewhere Better Than This Place* (Contemporary Arts Center, Cincinnati, 2003); *Africas: The Artist and the City* (Centro de Cultura Contemporània de Barcelona, 2001); *The Short Century* (Museum Villa Stuck, Munich, 2001, touring to Berlin, Chicago and New York); 2nd Johannesburg Biennale (1997); and *Die Anderen Modernen* (House of World Cultures, Berlin, 1997). He currently lives and works in Amsterdam and his work is published in *Moshekwa Langa* (Chicago and Geneva: Renaissance Society and Centre d'Art Contemporarain, 2002).

Salem Mekuria

Salem Mekuria is Associate Professor of Art, Wellesley College, Massachusetts, and an independent film producer, writer and director. Her film *'YE WONZ MAIBEL' (DELUGE)*, 1997 – a first person narrative exploring the momentous events which took place in Ethiopia between 1974 and 1991 – has won numerous awards. It has had a number of international screenings including at The House of Film Cultures (Berlin, Germany, 2001); the 6th New York African Film Festival (Lincoln Center, New York City, 1999); Zanzibar International Film Festival (2001); Vermont International Film Festival (1998); Amnesty International Film Festival (Amsterdam, 1998); the 2nd Johannesburg Biennale (South Africa, 1997); and the African Film Festival (Tokyo,1997). She is the recipient of numerous grants and awards including the New England Media Fellowship (2001); the Rockefeller Foundation's Intercultural Media Fellowship (1995); and a fellowship at the Bunting Institute of Radcliffe College, Harvard University (1990–92). Her other films are: *SIDET: Forced Exile* (1991), *AS I REMEMBER IT, A Portrait of Dorothy West* (1991) and *OUR PLACE IN THE SUN* (1988).

Sabah Naim

Sabah Naim was born and lives in Cairo, Egypt. She has a Master of Fine Art from the College of Art Education in Cairo and has exhibited her work both nationally and internationally. Naim has had solo shows at various venues in Cairo – Goethe Institute (2001), Gezira Arts Center (2000), Townhouse Gallery (1999 and 2000) and Cairo Atelier (1998) – and had her own exhibition as part of *Cairo Modern Art in Holland* (Circustheater, The Hague, 2001). Internationally, she has shown in a number of group exhibitions, including Lia Rumma Gallery (Naples and Milan, Italy, 2003); *Contemporary Egyptian Art* (which toured to Tunisia, Italy, Morocco and China, 2001–2); *Square and Circle* (Darag el Fan, Ashkal Alwan, Beirut, Lebanon, 2001); and the Biennale for Young Mediterranean Artists (Rome, Italy, 1999). Her work can be found in the Museum of Modern Egyptian Art and the Egyptian Ministry of Culture, as well as in private collections in Egypt, Italy, USA, Germany and Holland.

Moataz Nasr

Moataz Nasr was born in Alexandria, Egypt. He has had a number of recent solo exhibitions, among them, Franco Riccardo Arti Visivi (Naples, Italy, 2002): La Bodega Espace (Cairo, 2002); Townhouse Gallery (Cairo, 2001); and *Paintings* (Al Ahram House, London, 1999). His group shows include *disORIENTation* (House of World Cultures, Berlin, 2003); *EX-IN in Espacio C* (Camargo, Spain, 2003); *Espacios Mestizos* (Grand Canary Islands, 2003); *Videomarathon* (Chisinau, Moldova, 2002); *Ars Electronica* (Linz, Austria, 2002); *Dak'Art 2002* (Dakar Biennale, Senegal, 2002); *Intrinsecus/extrinsecus* (Studio Casoli, Milan, Italy, 2001); and *Cairo Modern Art Exhibition* (Denhag, Holland, 2001). Nasr was awarded the Ministry of Culture Prize at *Dak'Art 2002* and his work can be found in the collections of the Egyptian Ministry of Culture, the Egyptian Museum of Modern Art, the United Nations (ESCWA) in Beirut and the Egyptian Embassy in London.

Wael Shawky

Born in Alexandria, Egypt, Wael Shawky has a BA in Fine Art from Alexandria University and a MA in Fine Art from the University of Pennsylvania, where he was Assistant Professor in 2001–2. He was given a solo exhibition *Sidi El Asphalt Mulid* as part of the 2nd Al Nitaq Festival of Visual Arts (Townhouse Gallery, Cairo, 2001). His recent group shows include *Body and the Archive* (Artists' Space, New York, 2003); *video invitational* (f a projects, London, UK, 2003); *Close Up* (collaborative workshop and exhibition with Swedish and Egyptian artists, Townhouse Gallery, Cairo, 2002); *Square and Circle* (Darag el Fan, Ashkal Alwan, Beirut, Lebanon, 2001); and Rita Long International Art Symposium (Codema, Bayamo, Cuba, 2001). His awards include the Edna C. and Monroe Gutman Scholarship and Merit Award (University of Pennsylvania, 1999–2000) and the Grand Nile Prize (6th International Cairo Biennale, 1996). His most recent book is *Peripheral Insider* (Copenhagen: Museum Tusculanum Press, 2003).

Contributors' Biographies

Forum for African Arts
The purpose of the Forum is to promote contemporary African visual arts and culture, to help create a renaissance of artistic creativity by Africans, and to give them exposure on a global scale.

Solomon Deressa
Solomon Deressa was born in Western Ethiopia and grew up in Addis Ababa. He now lives some thirteen hundred miles west by northwest of the current axis of planetary power, in South Minneapolis. He taught humanities-type courses (critical thinking, writing, mythologies, the literatures of the mystical traditions, Native American Philosophies, etc.) for almost two decades in Minnesota's public universities and colleges until the mid-1990s when he switched to private consulting in communication. Those of his fellow Ethiopians who might have heard of him are likely to remember him as the one who writes poems in Amharic.

Deepali Dewan
Deepali Dewan is Associate Curator of South Asian Civilisations at the Royal Ontario Museum and Assistant Professor, Department of Fine Arts, University of Toronto. She has published extensively on contemporary art with a research focus on nineteenth- and twentieth-century visual culture in South Asia and the South Asia diaspora. Previously, Dr Dewan has worked at the Asia Society, New York, and the Walker Art Center, Minneapolis, and has taught at a number of colleges. She received a PhD from the University of Minnesota and has received fellowships from the American Institute for Indian Studies, the Social Science Research Council, the MacArthur Interdisciplinary Center for the Study of Global Change and the College Art Association.

Okwui Enwezor
Okwui Enwezor was the Artistic Director of Documenta XI (1998–2003) and served as the Artistic Director of the 2nd Johannesburg Biennale (1996–98). He is the founder and editor of *Nka: Journal of Contemporary African Art*, based at African Studies Center, Cornell University, Ithaca, New York. He was Adjunct Curator of contemporary art at the Art Institute of Chicago (1998–2001). He has curated numerous exhibitions and most recently organised *The Short Century: Independence and Liberation Movements in Africa, 1945–1998* (2001) and edited the accompanying volume. His books include: *Reading the Contemporary: African Art from Theory to the Marketplace* with Olu Oguibe (London and Cambridge, Mass.: inIVA and MIT Press, 1999); *Democracy Unrealized*, *Under Siege: Four African Cities*, *Creolite and Creolization* and *Experiments with Truth* with Sarat Maharaj, Carlos Basualdo, Mark Nash, Susanne Ghez, Ute Meta Bauer and Octavio Zaya (Stuttgart: Hatje Cantz Verlag, 2002). He is currently working on two exhibitions *Miraculous Weapons: Negritude, Modernism, and the African Unconscious* and *On Govermentality* and a forthcoming publication, *Archaeology of the Present: the Postcolonial Archive and the Photographic Discourse of African Modernity*. Enwezor is Visiting Professor at the Henry Clay Frick Department of History of Art and Architecture, University of Pittsburgh.

Lisa Fischman
Appointed Director of Atlanta College of Art Gallery in November 2000, Fischman was formerly Associate Curator of Contemporary Art/Education at UB Art Gallery (State University of New York at Buffalo). Previously a literary editor of *Your Flesh* magazine, Fischman has curated exhibitions by Laylah Ali, Mélik Ohanian, Buy-sellf, Juan Perdiguero, Joe Sacco, Judith Yourman, Sam Easterson, John Bankston and Tony Matelli, among others. In 2001, Fischman curated *Paradise in Search of a Future*, a two-part multi-site exhibition of solo projects on travel and tourism, which originated at the Center for Exploratory and Perceptual Art (CEPA Gallery), in Buffalo, New York. Fischman holds MA and PhD degrees in Art History and American Studies from the University of Minnesota.

Elsabet Giorgis
Elsabet Giorgis is a graduate in Museum Studies from New York University and has a Masters in Business Administration; until recently, she was Assistant Vice President for Mizuho Corporate Bank. She has written several articles on Ethiopian art and is both a consulting editor and contributing writer for *Nka: Journal of Contemporary African Art*. She also writes for the Institute of Ethiopian Studies at Addis Ababa University and has collaborated on the recent publication 'Trends of Contemporary African Art and the Place of Diaspora Ethiopian Artists', from the Sixth Annual Conference on the History of Ethiopian Art.

Stuart Hall
Emeritus Professor of Sociology at the Open University and Visiting Professor at Goldsmiths College, University of London, Stuart Hall is internationally regarded for his teachings on culture and society. He was the first editor of the *New Left Review* and was active in the peace movement and anti-racist work in the 1960s and 1970s. In 1964, he helped establish the

Centre for Cultural Studies at Birmingham University and went on to become its Director. He has lectured and published extensively worldwide; his books include *Different* (London: Phaidon, 2001); *Annotations 6: Modernity and Difference* (London: inIVA, 2001); *Stuart Hall: Critical Dialogues in Cultural Studies* (London: Routledge, 1996); *Questions of Cultural Identity and Resistance through Rituals: Youth Subculture in Post-War Britain* (London: Sage, 1996); *Modernity: An Introduction to Modern Societies* (Cambridge: Polity Press, 1995); and *The Hard Road to Renewal: Thatcherism and the Crisis of the Left* (London: Verso, 1988). He is Chairman of both inIVA (Institute of International Visual Arts) and Autograph: The Association of Black Photographers, both based in London.

Salah Hassan
Salah Hassan is the Chair of the Department of History of Art and Associate Professor of Africana Studies at Cornell University. He is editor of *Nka: Journal of Contemporary African Art* and consulting editor for *African Arts* and *Atlantica*. A regular contributor to art journals and edited anthologies, Hassan is author and editor of several books including *Unpacking Europe* (Rotterdam: NAi Publishers and Museum Boijmans van Beuningen, 2001), *Gendered Visions* (Trenton: Africa World Press, 1997) and co-editor of *The Muse of Modernity* (Trenton: Africa World Press, 1996). Hassan has curated *Unpacking Europe* (Museum Boijmans van Beuningen, Rotterdam, 2001); *Authentic/Ex-Centric* (49th Venice Biennale, 2001); *EV+A 2001 Expanded* (Limerick, Ireland); *<Insertions>* (Apex Art, New York, 2000); and *Modernit(ies) and Memor(ies)* (47th Venice Biennale, 1997).

Sarat Maharaj
Sarat Maharaj was born in Durban, South Africa. He was educated at one of the segregated universities of the apartheid system – the University of South Africa, Durban, for non-whites of Indian origin. He is now Research Professor at Goldsmiths College, University of London, and has recently been appointed Professor of Visual Art and Knowledge Systems, Lund University, Sweden (2003). He was Research Fellow at the Jan Van Eyck Akademie, Maastricht (1999–2001) and the first Rudolf Arnheim Professor at Humboldt University, Berlin (2001–2). A co-curator on the Documenta XI team (Kassel, 2002), he has lectured and published widely throughout the world on cultural translation and difference. He is an authority on the work of Richard Hamilton, Marcel Duchamp and James Joyce and his experimental writings include textiles art, sound work (Xeno-sonics) and visual theory constructions (Monkeydoodle).

Prince Massingham
Prince Massingham was born in Kliptown, South Africa. Since joining the Dhlomo Theatre Collective (the first theatre company in South Africa) in 1983 and being one of the first students to complete the Drama Diploma course at the Afrika Cultural Centre in 1986, he has taken part in numerous theatre productions and performed across South Africa. Between 1987 and the present he has run successful Theatre for Development workshops involving youth groups and organised theatre festivals. The early 1990s saw his directorial debut at the Afrika Cultural Centre, and he went on to write and direct a number of productions commissioned by UNICEF (1997–98), The Consumer Institute of South Africa (1999) and the Gauteng Consumer Affairs (2002). In 2000–1 he took part in a research programme dealing with arts and cultural groups in Gauteng, which resulted in two publications, *Lihlo la tsa Setso* (The Eye of Culture) and the special edition on arts and cultural groups in Gauteng.

Achille Mbembe
Achille Mbembe is a Senior Researcher at the Institute of Social and Economic Research, University of the Witwatersrand, Johannesburg, South Africa. He is the author of many books including *On the Postcolony* (Berkeley: University of California Press, 2001); *La naissance du maquis dans le Sud-Cameroun* (Paris: Karthala, 1996); and *Afriques indociles* (Paris: Karthala, 1988).

Prince Mbusi Dube
Prince Mbusi Dube is a printmaker, Education Officer and Curator at the Johannesburg Art Gallery and has worked in a range of outreach, exhibition and art curriculum development projects. He was selected as a National Curator for the South African representation in the 25th São Paulo Bienal in March 2002. His articles have been accepted for publication in two journals: *Langston Hughes Colloquy* (2003) and *Network 2000: In the Spirit of the Harlem Renaissance* (2003). He is currently working on a Dumile Feni retrospective exhibition which opens at the Johannesburg Art Gallery in October 2003 and tours South Africa in 2004.

Kobena Mercer
Currently Research Associate in the Department of Visual Culture and Media, Middlesex University, Kobena Mercer writes and teaches on the visual arts of the black diaspora. He is editor of *Black Film/British Cinema* (London: ICA, 1988),

author of *Welcome to the Jungle* (London: Routledge, 1994) and has contributed exhibition catalogue essays to *Black Male* (New York: Whitney Museum, 1994), *Pictura Britannica* (Sydney: Museum of Contemporary Art, 1997) and *Adrian Piper: A Retrospective* (University of Maryland: Fine Arts Gallery, 1999). Most recently his 'Romare Bearden: African American Modernism at Mid-Century' has been published in *Art History, Aesthetics, Visual Studies* (New Haven: Yale University Press and Clark Art Institute, 2002).

Landry-Wilfrid Miampika
Born in Congo, Landry-Wilfrid Miampika now lives in Spain, where he is Associate Professor of French Literature and Language at the University of Alcalà, Madrid, and Director of Ediciones Del Cobre, which publishes francophone literature. A literary critic and writer, he specialises in Comparative Literature and often lectures internationally. He has contributed to numerous magazines and publications and written the epilogues to both *Sexe et femmes en Afrique: domination masculine et condition féminine* (Paris: L'Harmattan, 1999) and the bilingual anthology *Voces africanas: Poesía de expresión francesa 1950–2000/Voix africaines: Poésies d'expression française 1950–2000* (Madrid: Editorial Verbum, 2000).

Adriano Mixinge
Adriano Mixinge was born in Luanda, Angola in 1968. He has a degree in history from the University of Havana and is currently preparing his PhD in contemporary art history at the Universidade Complutense in Madrid. He was head of the Department for Scientific Research at the Museu Nacional de Antropologia in Luanda. Commissioner for Angola at the first Johannesburg Biennale with *Entre a guerra e a paz*, he also curated the exhibition *Metáforas angolanas 1990–2001* in Paris and several other exhibitions with Angolan visual artists.

Gamal Abdel-Nasser
Gamal Abdel-Nasser was born in 1918. He was the first President of the Republic of Egypt, from 1954 to 1969. He founded The Free Officers, a military-based group, which would depose King Ahmad Fouad in 1953 and declare Egypt a republic. In 1956, his nationalisation of the Suez Canal was critical in the mobilisation of pan-Arabic, pan-African solidarity and resistance to imperialism. His institution of land reforms and economic development formulated a policy of Arabic socialism and, combined with his celebration of Arab national pride, was immensely popular throughout the Arab world. President Nasser died in Cairo in 1970.

Simon Njami
With PhDs in Law and Modern Literature, Simon Njami is the co-founder and Chief Editor of the contemporary African art magazine *Revue Noire*; a Visiting Professor in African Arts, Photography and Cinema at the University of San Diego; and an advisory board member of AFAA (Association Française d'Action Artistique). He has curated numerous exhibitions, among them the Fourth and Fifth Rencontres de la Photographie de Bamako in 2001 and 2003. He has also co-curated *Dak'Art*, the 2000 Dakar Biennale and in 2004 he will co-curate the São Paulo Bienal. Since 1990, he has contributed numerous essays to catalogues devoted to African art and his recent publications include *Blink* (London: Phaidon, 2001), *A Century of African Art* (Paris: Revue Noire, 2000) and *James Baldwin ou le devoir de violence* (Paris: Seghers, 1991).

Kwame Nkrumah
Kwame Nkrumah was born in 1909 and educated in Ghana, the United States and England. He led the Gold Coast to independence as Black Africa's first independent nation in 1957, renaming the country Ghana. He was pivotal in the anticolonialist movements of the 1940s and 1950s and was one of the organisers of the historic Fifth Pan-African Congress in Manchester in 1945. He convened and presided over the All-African People's Conference, 1958, as one of the most articulate and outspoken proponents of pan-Africanism. He was President of Ghana from 1960 to 1966 and author of numerous political works including *Toward Colonial Freedom* (1947); *I Speak of Freedom* (1961); *Africa Must Unite* (1963); and *Consciencism: Philosophy and Ideology for De-Colonization* (1964). Nkrumah was overthrown in a military coup d'état in 1965 and died in exile in Conakry in 1972.

Bhekizizwe Peterson
Bhekizizwe Peterson is Associate Professor in the Department of African Literature at the University of the Witwatersrand, South Africa. His works include *Monarchs, Missionaries and African Intellectuals: African Theatre and the Unmaking of Colonial Marginality* (University of the Witwatersrand Press, 2000) and two feature films, *Fools* (1997, Writer and Associate Producer) and *Zulu Love Letter* (forthcoming, Writer and Executive Producer).

Nasser Rabbat
Nasser Rabbat is the Aga Khan Professor of Islamic Architecture at the

Massachusetts Institute of Technology. His scholarly interests include the history and historiography of Islamic art, architecture and urbanism, and postcolonial criticism. Among his honours are: Chair of the Institut du Monde Arabe (IMA), Paris, 2003; American Research Center in Egypt (ARCE) Fellowship, 1999–2000 and 1988–89; and J. Paul Getty Postdoctoral Fellowship, 1993–94. His books include: *Thaqafat al Bina' wa Bina' al-Thaqafa: Buhuth wa Maqalat fi Naqd wa Tarikh al-'Imara. 1985–2000 (The Culture of Building and Building Culture: Essays and Articles on Criticism and History of Architecture. 1985–2000)* (Beirut: Riad Alrayyes Publisher, 2002) and *The Citadel of Cairo: A New Interpretation of Royal Mamluk Architecture* (Leiden: E. J. Brill, 1995).

Niru Ratnam

Niru Ratnam is Lecturer in Art History at the Open University. He is currently working on the course team producing *Art in the Twentieth Century*, a series of four books to be published by the Open University in conjunction with Yale University Press in 2003–4. He has written for a large number of publications including *The Face*, *i-D* and *The Observer*, as well as academic journals such as *New Left Review* and *Third Text*. He is on the editorial board of *Third Text* and *Visual Culture* and a trustee of the Whitechapel Gallery, London.

Jérôme Sans

Jérôme Sans has been Co-Director of the Palais de Tokyo in Paris since 1996 and is Adjunct Curator at the Institute of Visual Arts in Milwaukee, USA. He has curated and co-curated numerous international exhibitions, among them, *Tutto Casino* with Ludovico Pratesi (Villa Medici, Rome, 2002), *The Sky is the Limit* with Man Ray Hsu (Taipei Biennale, Taiwan, 2000) and the Danish Pavilion with Marianne Ockenholt (48th Venice Biennale, 1999, and Statens Museum for Kunst in Copenhagen, 2000). He has collaborated regularly with international art magazines, such as *Flash Art, ArtForum* and the *Journal of Contemporary Art*.

Mark Sealy

Having studied at Goldsmiths College and worked for both the national press and Network Photographers, Sealy became Director of Autograph: The Association of Black Photographers in 1991. Curator of several international photography exhibitions – including an audiovisual program for Rencontres d'Arles in 1993 and *Revealing Views* (Royal Festival Hall, London, 1998) – he has initiated retrospectives on the work of Gordon Parks and James Van Der Zee. Having edited works on Vanley Burke and Rotimi Fani-Kayode, Sealy most recently co-authored (with Stuart Hall) *Different* (London: Phaidon Press, 2001). A jury member for both the 1996 World Press Photography Competition and the 1997 Nikon-UNESCO awards, he was, until recently, a purchaser for the Arts Council of England's Art Collection.

Yasmeen Siddiqui

After completing her MA in Islamic Art and Architectural History at the University of Toronto in 1997, Yasmeen Siddiqui relocated to Cairo where she worked as an editor and writer until 2001. Currently living and working in Cambridge, Massachusetts, Siddiqui has contributed art reviews and essays to *The Brooklyn Rail*, *Nka: Journal of Contemporary African Art*, *Flash Art*, *The Cairo Times* and *Medina Magazine: Architecture, Interior Design and Fine Arts*.

Ramon Tio Bellido

Ramon Tio Bellido is Secretary General of AICA (International Association of Art Critics) and Chief Editor of *Ars Nova* magazine in Barcelona. After working for the Délégation aux Arts Plastiques from 1982 to 1990, he became Director of the Hôtel des Arts/Fondation Nationale des Arts, Paris (1990–93) and then Director of a Master's Program in Curatorial Studies, University of Rennes, Brittany (1994–2002). Curator of many exhibitions, his current show *Le XXème siècle dans l'art algérien* (2003) is touring to Marseilles and Paris.

Hamza Walker

Hamza Walker is Associate Curator at The Renaissance Society, Chicago. He has written for numerous publications and currently serves on the boards for LAMPO, a non-profit presenter of electronic music, and NOON, a journal of fiction.

Kateb Yacine

Born in 1929 in Constantine, Algeria, Kateb Yacine is one of the most respected writers in the Maghreb. While at school in France and at the age of 15, he was arrested and imprisoned during a Muslim demonstration against inequality in Sétif. Returning to Algeria in 1948, he joined the daily newspaper *Alger Républicain*, where he worked until 1951. His most famous novel *Nedjma* (Paris: Editions du Seuil, 1956) was published during Algeria's War of Independence against the French and is arguably one of the most important novels in the Francophone Maghrebi tradition. Yacine's other publications include *Le cercle des représailles* (Paris: Edition du Seuil, 1959); *Le Polygone étoilé* (Paris: Edition du Seuil, 1966); and *L'oeuvre en fragments* (Editions Sindbad, 1986). Yacine died in 1989.

Acknowledgements

The publishers would like to thank all the artists, lenders, writers and contributors; AFAA (Association Française d'Action Artistique), Paris; Aga Khan Trust for Culture, Geneva; American University, Cairo; Artsadmin, London; Autograph: Association of Black Photographers, London; British Council, London; Ford Foundation, New York; Salah Hassan, Kimerley S. Cornish and Eriberto Eulisse, Forum for African Arts; Mahita El Bacha Urieta and Bruce Haines, inIVA: Els van der Plas, Geerte Wachter and Malu Halasa, Prince Claus Fund; Francesco Bonami and the Venice Biennale 2003, in particular, Marina Bertaggia, Sarah Canarutto, Maria Luisa Frisa, Matteo Liguigli, Vera Mantengoli, Flavia Fossa Margutti and Renato Quaglia; Tom Postma Design; David Hawkins and Glenn Howard, Untitled; Manick Govinda; Uwe Kraus; Rachel Scott; Galerie François Barnoud, Lyon; Galerie Kamel Mennour, Paris; Goodman Gallery, Johannesburg; Mona Khazinder and the Institut du Monde Arabe, Paris; Mondriaan Foundation, Amsterdam; 303 Gallery, New York; and the Townhouse Gallery, Cairo.

Laylah Ali thanks 303 Gallery, Lisa Spellman and Simone Montemurno.

Kader Attia thanks Galerie Kamel Mennour.

Zarina Bhimji thanks Peter J. Mayers, Andrew Love, Sarat Maharaj, Manick Govinda, Arts Admin, Deepali Dewan, Okwui Enwezor, Late Jimmy Dean, Mahmood Mamdani, Gilane Tawadros and inIVA.

Samta Benyahia thanks Galerie François Barnoud for their financial contribution to the production of her work for *Fault Lines*. Thanks also to Houria Aïchi, Blue Silver, Ahmed Benyahia, Sylvie Couderc, Laurence Cyrot, Brigitte March, Christian Gattinoni and Pierre Giquel, Brigitte Zieger, Evelyne Jouanno, Estelle Pages and Hou Hanru. The work is dedicated to her brother Azzouz who was killed in 1997 by the barbarity that Kateb Yacine writes about; to Azzouz's children Hikmet and Nazim and their mother; and to the artist's mother, her brothers and her sisters, particularly to Ahmed who has always been by her side.

Moshekwa Langa thanks the Goodman Gallery, Johannesburg; Gallery Tanya Rumpff, Haarlem; Gallery Bernier-Eliades, Athens; Beam Systems, Amsterdam; Flo, Jason, John Sandra, Etzer, Martin and the members of the various houses of Potsdamer Str 159, Berlin; Henrike, Robin, Candice, Sabina, Paul, Clifford and all the people that worked with him on his project in various ways.

Salem Mekuria thanks the Long Bow Group, Geovision, Richard Bock, DVDLabs, BBI Engineering, Inc.

Moataz Nasr thanks Mr Mohamed Hassanen Heikal and the ABC Company, Egypt.

Wael Shawky thanks Ahmed Farag, Mahmoud Farag, Mohamed Farag, Sherif Saad, Henedak Abel Shafi, Ahmad Manawishi, Hesham Nazih, Mohamed Mortada, William Wells, Dina Ramadan, Lucy Till, Mahmoud Abdullah and Kareem Fanous.